UN IDEAS THAT CHANGED THE WORLD

UNITED NATIONS INTELLECTUAL HISTORY PROJECT

Ahead of the Curve? UN Ideas and Global Challenges
 Louis Emmerij, Richard Jolly, and Thomas G. Weiss

Unity and Diversity in Development Ideas: Perspectives from the UN Regional Commissions
 Edited by Yves Berthelot

Quantifying the World: UN Ideas and Statistics
 Michael Ward

The UN and Global Political Economy: Trade, Finance, and Development
 John Toye and Richard Toye

UN Contributions to Development Thinking and Practice
 Richard Jolly, Louis Emmerij, Dharam Ghai, and Frédéric Lapeyre

UN Voices: The Struggle for Development and Social Justice
 Thomas G. Weiss, Tatiana Carayannis, Louis Emmerij, and Richard Jolly

Women, Development, and the UN: A Sixty-Year Quest for Equality and Justice
 Devaki Jain

Human Security and the UN: A Critical History
 S. Neil MacFarlane and Yuen Foong Khong

Human Rights at the UN: The Political History of Universal Justice
 Roger Normand and Sarah Zaidi

Preventive Diplomacy at the UN
 Bertrand G. Ramcharan

The UN and Transnational Corporations: From Code of Conduct to Global Compact
 Tagi Sagafi-nejad, in collaboration with John H. Dunning

The UN and Development: From Aid to Cooperation
 Olav Stokke

UN Ideas That Changed the World

Richard Jolly, Louis Emmerij, and Thomas G. Weiss
Foreword by Kofi A. Annan

INDIANA UNIVERSITY PRESS
Bloomington and Indianapolis

This book is a publication of

Indiana University Press
601 North Morton Street
Bloomington, IN 47404-3797 USA

www.iupress.indiana.edu

Telephone orders	800-842-6796
Fax orders	812-855-7931
Orders by e-mail	iuporder@indiana.edu

∞ The paper used in this publication meets the minimum requirements of the American National Standard for Information Sciences—Permanence of Paper for Printed Library Materials, ANSI Z39.48-1992.

Manufactured in the United States of America
CIP and print line to come

LIBRARY OF CONGRESS CATALOGING-IN-PUBLICATION DATA

Jolly, Richard.
 UN ideas that changed the world / Richard Jolly, Louis Emmerij, and Thomas G. Weiss ; foreword by Kofi A. Annan.
     p.   cm.—(United Nations intellectual history project)
 Includes bibliographical references and index.
  ISBN 978-0-253-22118-6 (pbk. : alk. paper)—ISBN 978-0-253-35355-9 (cloth : alk. paper) 1. United Nations. 2. Human rights. 3. Economic development. 4. Economic development—Social aspects. 5. Economic development—Environmental aspects. 6. Conflict management. 7. Peacebuilding. I. Emmerij, Louis. II. Weiss, Thomas George. III. Title. IV. Title: United Nations ideas that changed the world.
 JZ4984.5.J66 2009
 341.23′1—dc22   2009011421

1 2 3 4 5 14 13 12 11 10 09

For Alison, Vera, and Priscilla

A map of the world that does not include Utopia is not worth looking at.

—Oscar Wilde, (1891)

Unless we aim for the seemingly unattainable, we risk settling for mediocrity.

—Sergio Vieira de Mello, 2007

Contents

Tables and Boxes

Foreword

Kofi A. Annan

It is a great pleasure for me to write a few words at the outset of this final volume in the United Nations Intellectual History Project Series, specifically to urge delegates and diplomats, pundits and politicians, staff members and scholars to read it closely.

From its inception in 1999, I encouraged support for the project from others, including financial support from several foundations. Now the project is in its concluding stage, having almost completed sixteen volumes as well as an oral history archive, I am even more delighted that the project's three directors asked me to write a few personal words to introduce this volume. Not all projects of the UN or about the UN manage to fulfill their initial hopes, let alone complete the original plan and throw in a couple of additional volumes to deal with gaps discovered along the way.

The United Nations Intellectual History Project has filled two critical gaps in documenting the UN's record over the last six and a half decades. First, its historical volumes have provided substantive accounts of the UN's work in major areas of economic and social thinking and action as well as in related areas where the more political boundaries of peace and development intersect—namely, human security, human rights, preventive diplomacy, and global governance. Many of the books deal with areas omitted or greatly underemphasized in other histories of the UN, such as the ideas, norms, and principles behind the UN's roles in statistics, economic development, or transnational corporations. This project has breathed new life into one of the UN's unique but often overlooked characteristics: the quality and diversity of its intellectual leadership and its values-based framework for dealing with the major challenges of our times.

Second, the project has interviewed seventy-nine persons, most of whom have worked much of their professional lives within the world body. This is a unique record of frank commentary about the past as well as of outspoken views on the UN's future. It has also cast interesting light on the background and motivation of people who have risen to senior levels within the organization

or in the multilateral diplomatic arena. These interviews are now available on a fully indexed CD-ROM and provide, like the printed volumes themselves, a unique and accessible resource for future scholarship about, analysis of, and operational efforts regarding the United Nations. One measure of the project's achievement is that in the last few years, in part stimulated by its interviews and publications, a number of UN organizations and a handful of governments also have embarked on their own institutional histories.

This final volume—which the authors unabashedly label "a grand synthesis"—makes some crucial points about the UN and its contributions to contemporary international society. These stories provide some good news and deserve to be better known and understood by all concerned with multilateral cooperation for at least three reasons. First, the UN's contributions to economic and social thinking, policymaking, and action have been more successful than generally realized. Second, the UN's work in the economic and social areas has often been outstanding—again of higher quality than often realized. The volume lists, for example, the nine winners of the Nobel Prize in Economics who have worked in or in close collaboration with the UN. This is in addition to the fourteen Nobel Prizes for Peace that have been awarded to the UN, to organizations within the UN system, or to key individuals who have contributed directly to its work. Third, many of the UN's contributions have been pioneering, or "Ahead of the Curve," as the title of the project's first volume put it. Sometimes these ideas have been accepted broadly and fairly quickly, such as goals to guide national and international development; in other cases, the UN has come up with what seemed at the time to be outlandish or controversial ideas or proposals—such as the need for concessional loans to poorer countries, special support for the least-developed countries, or debt relief—only to find that the ideas became mainstream after a decade or longer.

But the findings of the project are not all rosy, as the attentive reader discovers throughout this book. It also underlines key areas where the United Nations has failed or has been too slow or too timid in drawing attention to key problems or in putting forward proposals on which governments could act. These are listed in the chapter that presents a balance sheet of the UN's achievements. From the beginning, this project has had the ambition of being a "future-oriented history"—drawing lessons for the future and making some recommendations. These are set out in the final two chapters.

After my own ten years at the helm of the organization and some three decades before that in various positions and with different responsibilities throughout the UN system, I am ever more persuaded that the United Nations has a vital and inescapable role in the twenty-first century. The lessons since 1945, as set out in the United Nations Intellectual History Project Series, contain

many insights for our common future. I am grateful to Louis Emmerij, Richard Jolly, and Thomas G. Weiss for their unstinting efforts to document how UN ideas have been among the world organization's most important achievements. I am certain that this project will continue to inspire innovation and scholarship for many decades to come.

KOFI A. ANNAN
UNITED NATIONS SECRETARY-GENERAL, 1997–2006

Acknowledgments

It seems like yesterday that we were penning the acknowledgments for the first volume in this series, and now we are doing them for the final one. As the cliché goes, how time flies. The present volume represents another step in closing the gap in the historical record, this time by pulling together the lessons from the previous books commissioned by the United Nations Intellectual History Project (UNIHP) and adding some of our own thoughts. It is the final volume in this series but certainly not the final word.

We launched UNIHP in 1999 as an independent research effort based at the Ralph Bunche Institute for International Studies of The Graduate Center of The City University of New York. Here we would like to register our debt to numerous institutions and individuals who have made this journey both possible and productive.

We begin with those who financially supported this decade-long effort because we could not have done what we have without the understanding and generosity of these supporters. We are extremely appreciative for the generosity of the governments of the Netherlands, the United Kingdom, Sweden, Canada, Norway, Switzerland, Finland, and the Republic and Canton of Geneva; the Ford, Rockefeller, and MacArthur Foundations; the Carnegie Corporation of New York; the UN Foundation; and Ms. Alice Lobel of Paris. All this financial backing came with assurances of total intellectual independence—the sine qua non of such an endeavor. The final draft of this book, like the first one in our series, was completed while in residence in the comfortable surroundings of the Pocantico Conference Center in Tarrytown, New York, and we acknowledge support by the Rockefeller Brothers Fund for having made these stimulating and productive sojourns possible. We are also grateful to the Dag Hammarskjöld Foundation for having hosted us three times in order to discuss various drafts of books in our series, as well as to the United Nations Association-UK and to the Centre for International Governance Innovation for their assistance with volumes in the series. Details of this and other aspects of the project can be found on our Web site: www.unhistory.org.

In particular, we would like to single out several persons who got the fund-raising ball rolling and kept up the momentum. We are extremely grateful for the enthusiastic backing from the seventh UN Secretary-General, Kofi Annan, and other UN staff, who approached governments to help encourage their back-ing. Similarly, we are extremely appreciative to Vartan Gregorian, the president of the Carnegie Corporation of New York, who helped put together a coalition of willing U.S.-based foundations and to Gordon Conway and Lincoln Chen of the Rockefeller Foundation for having disbursed the first funds.

Our International Advisory Council is composed of eleven distinguished individuals whose guidance has been appreciable at various steps in this under-taking, and several of them contributed to both the written and oral parts of the project. A warm thanks is thus extended to Galal Amin, Margaret Joan Anstee, Lourdes Arizpe, Eveline Herfkens, Enrique Iglesias, András Inotai, Thandika Mkandawire, Gert Rosenthal, John G. Ruggie, Makoto Taniguchi, and Ramesh Thakur.

An earlier draft of this book was discussed in April 2008 at a special session organized by Finland's Ministry for Foreign Affairs, and we are grateful to Eija Limnell and Kirsti Lintonen for having made this possible. This occasion was an invaluable input into improving this final text. At that session, we received detailed comments from four of our authors—Devaki Jain, S. Neil MacFarlane, Bertrand G. Ramcharan, and Sarah Zaidi—as well as inputs from several Finn-ish colleagues, including Kai Sauer, Eeva-Liisa Myllymäki, Olli Ruohomäki, Ilkka Ristimäki, Tarja Väyrynen, and Raimo Väyrynen.

We also are delighted that these pages are graced with a foreword by former UN Secretary-General Kofi Annan. He was instrumental in encouraging the project and was a strong supporter, and we as project directors were continually inspired by his leadership. We are honored that the first and last book in the series have a foreword from this colleague and friend.

In this ten-year period, many staff members have been essential to the success of this project, and here we would like to single out a few for specific acknowledgement. On the research side, we begin with our colleague and friend Tatiana Carayannis, who was essential to the oral history and so much else for the first seven years of the project. Her camaraderie and common sense helped make possible this part of our work, and we are delighted to count her among our younger (*hélas*) colleagues. Ron Nerio helped finalize virtually all of the oral history transcripts and indices; he put up with various personality quirks and miserable handwriting to help produce what is a lasting historical resource. Sophie Theven and Diana Cassells provided essential background research for many of the interviews. And Yves Berthelot not only edited a book on regional

commissions but for five years headed our Geneva office, which was an essential resource for our efforts.

On the administrative side, we begin with Nancy Okada, who has helped to ensure the smooth running of a very complicated financial and administrative project with numerous moving parts; we literally could not have done this project without her. Teresa Booker and Elisa Athonvarangkul at the outset and Zeynep Turan more recently helped keep the ship moving and smiled when they should have screamed. Bree Zuckerman has been the project's Web master and also provided administrative assistance. The CUNY Graduate Center's past and previous presidents, Frances Degen Horowitz and William P. Kelly, have enthusiastically supported our efforts, and we are grateful to them for the congenial home provided for over a decade to us and various project personnel.

On the editorial side, Danielle Zach Kalbacher has helped shepherd numerous publications of the project in the last five years, and she once again applied her remarkable editorial skills to these pages. This book simply would not have been as readable or as sharp without her careful attention to content, logic, and presentation. Over the years, we have also benefited from the caring efforts of Indiana University Press's copyeditor, Kate Babbitt, who has improved immeasurably this and other final texts.

Finally, we wish to acknowledge the patience and support of our three spouses—Alison Jolly, Vera Emmerij, and Priscilla Read—who have humored us along. They are part in many ways of this history project, as they have been part of our past professional lives.

As we finalize these words in February 2009, the whole world is engulfed in recession and an economic and financial meltdown, yet coordinated international action plans have not even started. The risks and uncertainties make attempts to look forward even more hazardous than usual. Yet we have maintained the future orientation in this volume, and we are even more persuaded than we were at the beginning of the project that the world organization has a major role to play in responding to the present difficult and delicate situation. We have demonstrated in this volume how important and farseeing many past ideas and policy proposals of the UN have been. For all who are committed to the ideals of the United Nations, we hope that this volume provides an important source and encourages action to strengthen the role of the UN for the future.

RICHARD JOLLY
LOUIS EMMERIJ
THOMAS G. WEISS
New York

Abbreviations

CDP	Year of the Child Committee on Development Planning
CEDAW	Convention on the Elimination of All Forms of Discrimination against Women
CHR	Commission on Human Rights
CIEC	Conference on International Economic Cooperation
COMECON	Council for Mutual Economic Assistance
CRC	Convention on the Rights of the Child
CSW	Commission on the Status of Women
DAC	Development Assistance Committee of the OECD
DAWN	Development Alternatives with Women for a New Era
DEDAW	Declaration on the Elimination of Discrimination against Women
DESA	Department of Economic and Social Affairs
ECA	Economic Commission for Africa
ECAFE	Economic Commission for Asia and the Far East
ECE	Economic Commission for Europe
ECLAC	Economic Commission for Latin America and the Caribbean
ECOSOC	Economic and Social Council
ECWA	Economic Commission for West Asia
EPTA	Expanded Programme of Technical Assistance
ESCAP	Economic and Social Commission for Asia and the Pacific
FAO	Food and Agriculture Organization
FDI	foreign direct investment

G-77	Group of 77
GAD	gender and development
GATT	General Agreement on Tariffs and Trade
GDI	Gender-Related Development Index
GDP	gross domestic product
GEF	Global Environment Facility
GEM	Gender Empowerment Measure
GNI	gross national income
GNP	gross national product
HDI	Human Development Index
HIPC	heavily indebted poor country
HLP	High-level Panel on Threats, Challenges and Change
HPI	Human Poverty Index
HRC	Human Rights Council
ICC	International Criminal Court
ICF	International Carbon Fund
ICISS	International Commission on Intervention and State Sovereignty
IFAD	International Fund for Agricultural Development
ILO	International Labour Organization
IMF	International Monetary Fund
INSTRAW	UN International Research and Training Institute for the Advancement of Women
IPCC	Intergovernmental Panel on Climate Change
LDCs	least-developed countries
MDGs	Millennium Development Goals
MERCOSUR	Mercado Común del Sur; Southern Cone Common Market
NAACP	National Association for the Advancement of Colored People
NAFTA	North American Free Trade Agreement
NATO	North Atlantic Treaty Organization
NGOs	nongovernmental organizations

NIEO	New International Economic Order
NPT	the Non-Proliferation Treaty
ODA	official development assistance
OECD	Organisation for Economic Co-operation and Development
OEEC	Organisation for European Economic Co-operation
OHCHR	Office of the High Commissioner for Human Rights
OPEC	Organization of the Petroleum Exporting Countries
P-5	permanent five members of the Security Council (China, France, Russian Federation, the United Kingdom, the United States)
PRSPs	Poverty Reduction Strategy Papers
R2P	responsibility to protect
SCN	Standing Committee on Nutrition
SEEA	System of Environmental and Economic Accounts
SIPRI	Stockholm International Peace Research Institute
SNA	System of National Accounts
SSDS	System of Social and Demographic Statistics
SUNFED	Special United Nations Fund for Economic Development
TNCs	transnational corporations
UNCED	UN Conference on Environment and Development; Earth Summit
UNCHE	UN Conference on the Human Environment
UNCTAD	UN Conference on Trade and Development
UNCTC	UN Centre on Transnational Corporations
UNDAF	UN Development Assistance Framework
UNDP	UN Development Programme
UNEP	UN Environment Programme
UNESCO	UN Educational, Scientific and Cultural Organization
UNFPA	UN Fund for Population Activities
UNICEF	UN Children's Fund
UNIDO	UN Industrial Development Organization

UNIFEM	UN Development Fund for Women
UNIHP	UN Intellectual History Project
UNRISD	UN Research Institute for Social Development
UNSC	UN Statistical Commission
UNSO	UN Statistical Office
WFP	World Food Progamme
WHO	World Health Organization
WID	women in development
WIRs	World Investment Reports
WMDs	weapons of mass destruction
WMO	World Meteorological Organization
WTO	World Trade Organization

UN IDEAS THAT CHANGED THE WORLD

Introduction

• **Major Characteristics**
• **The Book**

Many view the United Nations as a rigid bureaucracy without sparkle, wit, or creativity. The general public—stimulated by the mass media—sees a traveling circus, a talk shop, and a paper-pushing enterprise. On and off there are tales of corruption. This is, we submit, a very uneven view of the world organization. How would we judge a story about Boeing or Airbus that only concentrates on its employees' globe-trotting, discussing the problems of the day, or sending e-mails to one another without mentioning the quality of its products, its results, and its plans for the future? In other words, a story of an enterprise is incomplete and misleading without a discussion of its goals and achievements, including its intellectual leadership.

Amazingly, such an intellectual history did not exist for the United Nations. Existing historical work mostly concentrated on the UN's political and security side, not its activities in economic and social development. Our original purpose was to complete the record. Ideas are at least as important for this area as for international peace and security. However, because of the interrelations between development, security, and human rights, this final volume more than occasionally embraces the political and security side, and several of our later volumes moved also in this direction—especially the ones on human security, preventive diplomacy, and global governance. But readers find a definite emphasis on economic and social ideas in both the series as a whole and in this volume.

International organizations live or die by the quality and relevance of the policy ideas that they put forward and support. And it is of the essence to emphasize them—the good, the bad, the ugly. This was well understood by the World Bank and the International Monetary Fund (IMF), which have invested heavily in documenting their histories, including the policy ideas that they have midwifed and pursued.[1]

In 1999, we decided to fill this gap—at least as best we could with available resources and within a decade—with the United Nations Intellectual History Project (UNIHP) as an independent endeavor. We benefited from the confidence and financial support of both governments and foundations that, like us, could not believe that this history had not yet been written.

This introduction provides the reader with the characteristics of the project as we see them, a flavor for some of the decisions that we made along the way, and a preview of the volume.

Major Characteristics

We structured UNIHP as a diptych, or a painting with two panels. The first consists of sixteen books, while the second panel offers one of these volumes, *UN Voices,* with excerpts from the oral histories as well as the complete transcripts. Each of these is sketched below along with other pertinent information.

Fifteen Volumes

As the titles of the fifteen books in the UNIHP series published by Indiana University Press make clear, we have opted for an approach by subject matter, asking what policy ideas the world organization has contributed over the sixty-five years of its existence. Eleven subjects were selected that each led to a book in the series. These publications provide most of the grist for our analytical mill in this synthetic effort to document *UN Ideas That Changed the World.* The authors and titles are listed at the back of this book. Three volumes in the series cut across topical lines. Our first book (by Emmerij, Jolly, and Weiss) was *Ahead of the Curve? UN Ideas and Global Challenges* (2001, also available in French, German, and Arabic), which is a synthesis *avant la lettre,* or our first effort to spell out the propositions that have guided this effort. The second book, edited by Yves Berthelot, *Unity and Diversity in Development Ideas: Perspectives from the UN Regional Commissions* (2004, selected chapters available in Russian and Spanish), is a combination of institutional and intellectual history. With contributions from Adebayo Adedeji, Yves Berthelot, Blandine Destremau, Paul Rayment, Gert Rosenthal, and Leelananda de Silva, it covers each of the UN's regional economic commissions and traces the policy ideas that emerged since their establishment. A third volume, by Weiss, Emmerij, and Jolly joined by Tatiana Carayannis, is *UN Voices: The Struggle for Development and Social Justice* (2005), which contains the most compelling extracts of the oral history component of the project. As such, it presents the main thoughts of the seventy-nine personalities whom we interviewed, who have played a role

in contributing to or carrying forward ideas within the UN and occasionally suppressing them! The complete interviews are available on a CD-ROM.[2] The current volume, *UN Ideas That Changed the World,* completes the series.

A related book, edited by Weiss and Sam Daws, *The Oxford Handbook on the United Nations* (2007), is a reference volume of the world organization containing contributions from almost fifty leading scholars and practitioners.[3] A consolidated index of topics treated in the volumes is available on the project Web site, www.unhistory.org.

A word is in order about our selection of topics and authors. There is no single way to organize research, and certainly not for such an ambitious project as this one. After numerous consultations and conversations with experts, including our own International Advisory Board, we took responsibility for commissioning volumes from the world-class authors who figure in our series. We were delighted to find qualified colleagues willing to take on topics about which they were extremely knowledgeable but still willing to do some archival digging and interviews that we required. All were given freedom and responsibility to organize their own digging, analyses, and presentations. For each volume, we ourselves along with an independent team of peer reviewers commented upon the accuracy and fairness in presenting the ideas and depicting where they came from, how they were developed and disseminated within the UN system, and what happened with them. The final texts are, needless to say, the responsibility of the people who authored them. Clearly had others been in the directorial driver's seat, there undoubtedly would have been different emphases and different authors; but we stand by our selections as a worthwhile contribution to debate. And we hope others will build upon our series and go well beyond these fledgling footsteps. Our intellectual history project is the first, not the last, installment in depicting the history of the UN's contributions to ideas.

Oral History

The second panel of the UNIHP diptych consists of oral history. We have already spoken of this project, listening to the voices of the personalities interviewed who have played a role in stimulating, and sometimes hindering, the identification and implementation of policy and ideas in the UN. Oral history is a tricky instrument and requires careful preparation and double-checking. Memory is unreliable and sometimes a person might consciously or unconsciously want to change or to hide certain events. An illustration of this can be found by comparing Stefan Zweig's *The World of Yesterday* with his *Diaries.*[4] The former is a book about his life written from memory in Brazil where he

had fled, after leaving most of his papers behind to escape the Nazis who had annexed his native Austria in 1938. The latter is a day-to-day account of many of the same events that he describes from memory in his book. The discrepancies are telling.

Our UN oral histories are anything but hagiography. Those interviewed (including the three of us) appear, warts and all. Every story is different; each voice is unique. The complete transcripts are separate documents to be remembered as such. The recorded conversations and corrected transcripts encapsulate a story within our story. The structure and subtlety of language in each person's interview, including his or her sense of irony and of imagery, provide a first-hand account of a personal and professional voyage through the intellectual history of the United Nations.

Outsiders—especially the next generation of students and scholars—rarely experience the UN at first hand but usually do so only through sound bites and editorials, Web sites and textbooks. The world organization thus seems more a collection of boring bureaucrats than a creative center of gravity for human and political interaction required for international problem solving.[5]

We have used the oral histories (and have selectively inserted excerpts here) to do what they do best, namely to give life, color, and imagination to the experiences of individuals and to extract the meanings that each attaches to them. These complement our research; they do not substitute for it. Whether it was the idealism of the early years of the UN, the anguish of the Cold War, or the initial euphoria and then the uncertainties of the post–Cold War era, our participants recall how their perceptions of events evolved, how tumultuous experiences forced themselves into public consciousness, and how they themselves changed their perspectives through knowledge, exposure, experience, and the passage of time. Oral history, with all its difficulties, gives fascinating insights, both about the person and about what makes the UN a creative organization.[6]

It is always too late to start oral history because there are many individuals who are no longer living to tell their story. In our case, in 1999 when we started, Mahbub ul Haq and Jan Tinbergen had recently passed away, as had many others who had played major roles in the UN's earlier years. Since we started, more than a sixth of the personalities whom we interviewed have died, including Victor Urquidi, Johan Kaufman, Bernard Chidzero, Celso Furtado, Hans Singer, I. G. Patel, Surendra Patel, Oscar Shachter, Mary Smieton, Kurt Waldheim, and Max Finger.

Who are the persons whose memories form our oral history? A little over half of them served directly in the international civil service. They come from thirty-five countries, covering all of the world's regions and most of the UN's major language groups. A third of those interviewed spent part or all of their

careers in academia and a quarter or so in government service in their own countries. A fifth are women, in part a reflection of the paucity of women in positions of influence in and around the UN until recently. Most of the interviewees have advanced degrees and about half studied economics, undoubtedly reflecting our focus on issues of economic and social development.

In terms of geographic distribution, a little over half trace their family origins from the industrialized North and nearly half from developing countries (Africa, Asia, the Middle East, and Latin America) in the global South. Ten percent come from the former eastern bloc, and forty percent from the West. Nearly one-quarter of them experienced the dislocation that comes from growing up as a refugee or in political exile. Many share strong recollections of their families' experiences during the Great Depression and World War II. Virtually all of them express powerfully the importance of international cooperation in improving the lot of the have-nots.

We repeat here what we wrote earlier about the selection of book topics and authors, namely that our choice of persons to interview inevitably involved subjectivity. We chose persons in senior positions who were able to reflect on several decades of experience, but this meant missing younger persons of the next generation. We concentrated on economic and social development and thus omitted many whose experiences were primarily in peacekeeping and humanitarian action. And we focused on the development and promotion of ideas, underplaying the contribution of many doers, not because they have not often generated important ideas but because their contributions are less frequently written down and accessible. Others would undoubtedly have selected some of the same but other persons as well. Again, we are pleased with the results and do not apologize for our selection. The voices resonating in our oral history are inevitably a small and very incomplete sample of those found in the United Nations. We can do little more than remind readers that there are thousands of others who contribute and have contributed to the international struggle for a better world and whose voices are consequential even if inaudible.

Other Considerations

Readers may be surprised to find that our history reveals not one United Nations but three. To pursue the metaphor of painting, the UN itself is best presented as a triptych. The first panel is the UN as an arena in which governments make decisions—in the Security Council, the General Assembly, the Economic and Social Council (ECOSOC), and many other bodies—about peace and security, economic and social development, human rights, labor, health, agricultural policies, and so on. The second panel consists of staff members in the

UN Secretariat and other organizations under the leadership of the Secretary-General and the heads of other components of the UN system. In terms of our intellectual history, ideas may come from within the Secretariat as well as from governments, but they may also come from another source. Here we find the third panel of nonstate or private voices with many timbres and at various decibel levels.

Article 71 of the UN Charter was a breakthrough in making room for nongovernmental organizations (NGOs). What we call the Third United Nations, however, is far broader. Although many organizations within the system have long benefited from this Third UN, only one formally incorporated it in its decision-making structure. The International Labour Organization (ILO) gathers governments, trade unions, and employers' associations in its Governing Body and General Conference. Many NGOs are admitted as observers elsewhere in the UN but are not yet part of the formal decision-making process, although they often have been active and energetic in pushing forward ideas and getting them taken seriously. Indeed, we have often found the Third UN to be the most important factor for explaining why ideas have been adopted or implemented. This growing factor is a topic to which we return in far more detail in chapter 2.

In the summer of 2005, for the UN's sixtieth anniversary, we published a monograph setting out the preliminary results of our project. *The Power of UN Ideas: Lessons from the First Sixty Years* was our initial effort to frame the current volume.[7] In that publication (still available on our Web site), we sought to pull together findings from across the series' already published volumes, but we also mixed in our own interpretation and experience.

We do the same in this volume and believe that there is value added. Indeed, after having spent the last decade of our careers collectively on this subject, we have a responsibility to put forth our own judgments and views. Reviewers of an earlier draft of this book urged us to do so, arguing that the experience with the project and a collective vantage point of two centuries justify running a few risks. We hope that the present publication does justice to the thoughts of our colleagues. Along with other readers, they will be the judges about this synthesis and our views on what the future intellectual history of the UN should be.

Just as independent investigations must be made of an organization's management and financial performance, organizations that are in the business of global action and policy advice must be subject to independent scrutiny with regard to the existence and soundness of their ideas. As mentioned, the World Bank has had two independent histories. The International Monetary Fund has an in-house historian, which obviously is different from producing an independent record and perspectives.

Although much has been written about the UN and a few specialized agencies have undertaken histories, no systematic intellectual history and evaluation have been made of the UN structure as a whole.[8] Nor, for that matter, have other organizations of the UN system taken on the task individually. This is a remarkable omission for an organization that gives policy advice on economic and social development issues, humanitarian aid, human rights, and human security. If, as we believe, the UN is the forerunner of a stronger and more coherent system of global governance for the twenty-first century, the lessons of its history are of critical importance for the future. However, in the wake of our initiative such efforts now gradually are under way. And so it should be.

An intellectual history should do at least four things. First, it should attempt to trace the ideas that an organization has identified, albeit recognizing that most ideas have many and distant origins. Second, it should examine the quality, validity, and the timing of these ideas. Third, it should identify missing ideas and why they are missing. And fourth, it should specify which areas in the future are in need of ideas and how the organization should change in order to ensure that the relevant ideas develop in good time are given a better chance of coming to fruition. We have tried to respond to these challenges but are acutely conscious of our failures and weaknesses in many areas. Despite our shortcomings, we do believe that we have made a contribution to correcting the historical record.

The Book

While none of us is shy, nonetheless we start by stating what should be obvious from the prose thus far, namely this is an extremely ambitious book in a relatively limited space. It should be clearly underlined that we have not written an institutional history of the United Nations and its component parts. This volume has three distinct parts. Part 1, "UNIHP at a Glance," consists of chapter 1, which provides an overview of the world organization's shifting emphases in ideas and actions since 1945, and chapter 2, which introduces the concept of the three United Nations and studies the impact of each. The latter identifies the four ways that ideas achieve impact, the major threads running throughout this book, and an explanation of why we think ideas matter. As indicated earlier, this and the third parts are more prescriptive than the second one.

Part 2 is titled "United Nations Ideas Changing the World." These nine chapters explore how crucial ideas have evolved over the UN's life, drawing on the evidence from one or more of our commissioned volumes. The chapter titles provide a sufficient flavor of their content, we hope, to whet the reader's appetite for this analytical synthesis of the findings from the project's volumes: chapter 3, "Human Rights for All: From Aspiration to Implementation"; chapter 4,

"Gender: From Eliminating Discrimination to Promoting Women's Rights and Empowerment"; chapter 5, "Development Goals: From National and Regional Policies to the MDGs"; chapter 6, "Fairer International Economic Relations: From Aid and Mutual Interests to Global Solidarity"; chapter 7, "Development Strategies: From National Planning to Governing the Market"; chapter 8, "Social Development: From Sectoral to Integrated Perspectives"; chapter 9, "Environmental Sustainability: From Environment and Development to Preserving the Planet"; chapter 10, "Peace and Security: From Preventing State Conflict to Protecting Individuals"; and chapter 11, "Human Development: From Separate Actions to an Integrated Approach." Many chapters also contain a box with the story or stories of individuals who have made a difference by their contributions to the First, the Second, or the Third UN—or sometimes all three.

Part 3 is titled "A Future for the UN and the Planet." From the outset of this project, we have promised our financial supporters, and ourselves, that we embarked on this adventure in order to learn lessons from the past for the future—to build upon the work of colleagues to help construct a more humane future. This critical part is the most personal and subjective in this volume. The first chapter in this part is titled "A Balance Sheet." Based on the preceding discussions of nine powerful categories of ideas, we explore in chapter 12 two counterfactual propositions—the world without the UN's ideas and the world with a more creative UN—as a means to defend our proposition that ideas and concepts are a main driving force in human progress and that they have been arguably the most important contribution of the United Nations. Readers will judge for themselves whether we have succeeded in the final two chapters, chapter 13, "Challenges Ahead," and chapter 14, "Strengthening Global Governance."

We have sought to make this volume as reader friendly as possible. We are aware that virtually no one—not even specialists and proponents of the United Nations and certainly not its enemies—is likely to read the sixteen volumes in our series. Here we go out on a limb and generalize to the maximum extent justifiable. We hope to generate debate, but we have not played up unnecessary provocations. We draw heavily on the detailed findings and data from the commissioned volumes in our series, updating the findings in some cases. We borrowed extensively from their findings with the goal of making their work available and read more widely. We hope that they will forgive our efforts at simplification.

The present volume is a synthesis of the series. Standing on the shoulders of the past, we peer into the future to determine what should be done for the UN to remain and become a more creative and productive intellectual actor with influence over the course of the twenty-first century.

PART 1
UNIHP at a Glance

We must make sure that [the UN's] work is fruitful, that it is a reality and not a sham, that it is a force for action and not merely a frothing of words, that it is a true temple of peace in which the shields of nations can some day be hung, and not merely a cockpit in the Tower of Babel.

—Sir Winston Churchill, 1946

1. Overview

- **Intellectual Contributions and Failures**
- **Shifting Preoccupations**
- **Intellectual Challenges Today and Tomorrow**

This chapter provides a brief overview of our interpretation of successful and failed ideas in the UN's history. There also is a short summary of future intellectual challenges. We do this to tease readers, presenting here a summary balance sheet that builds on the substantive and more analytical chapters in Part 2. For those who would like to fast forward, this is the meat of chapters 12, 13, and 14.

Intellectual Contributions and Failures

The balance sheet below enumerates credits and debits, intellectual contributions that were positive and timely or contributions that were untimely or did not come to fruition. They are presented in a largely chronological order that captures our judgment about impact. Obviously, others could justify different ranking.

On the credit side of the ledger, we would place the following items:

- Promoting human rights for all: A unique part of the UN from its beginning, this area of action has been broadened and deepened decade by decade. Initially its operational side focused on civil rights and on concerns for children and women and population, especially the expansion of access to education and health. Organizing conferences concerning priority areas of development in the 1970s and the 1990s, the UN raised awareness and mobilized action in countries around the world.
- Providing an international economic framework for national development policies: This was done as early as 1950 when several groups of UN-appointed experts—including W. Arthur Lewis, a later Nobel laureate in economics—tackled the issues of economic stability and growth within a global framework.

• Quantifying the world by providing a statistical framework to measure and compare progress in many economic and social areas: An early and remarkable illustration is the national accounts framework pioneered by the UN.

• Changing the debate about trade and development: Toward the end of the 1940s, the Prebisch-Singer thesis made its appearance, both at the UN in New York and the UN Economic Commission for Latin America (ECLA, later ECLAC when "the Caribbean" was added). It demonstrated that the long-term trend of the terms of trade was negative for developing countries. In other words, the latter could import less and less from industrial countries for the same unit of exports. Hans Singer was the first to publish on this issue, but Raúl Prebisch put it in a broader (global) framework by introducing the concept of center-periphery.

• Setting global goals: The UN system of organizations has set more than fifty specific, quantified, and time-targeted goals throughout its existence, of which the Millennium Development Goals (MDGs) are the most recent. Although received with skepticism in certain quarters, many objectives have been met or come close. A striking example is the eradication of smallpox within eleven years. Others range from the acceleration of economic growth over the 1960s to reductions of infant and child mortality in the 1980s and 1990s. A striking negative example is the unwillingness and failure of most industrial countries to meet the 0.7 percent aid target.

• Proposing development policies that combine economic growth with poverty reduction, productive employment creation, and better income distribution: This was particularly evident in the 1970s with the basic needs approach.

• Promoting the human development approach in the 1990s: This expansion beyond basic needs integrated economic and social development, human rights, and elements of human security and gave greater economic and philosophical depth to the human development concept.

• Bringing issues that combined concerns about the environment and development to global attention, most recently the threat of global warming, along with gender and population issues: Until well into the 1960s, these were virtually unknown except to specialists. The series of world conferences organized by the UN in the 1970s—sometimes harshly criticized as "gab fests"—put these issues squarely on government policy agendas. Combined with the series of global conferences and summits during the 1990s and in the new millennium, these issues as well as gender, population, and urbanization, among others, have received constant attention. Both public awareness and discourse around these issues have changed beyond recognition compared to the situation of three to four decades ago.

These credit items on the balance sheet emerged and were presented in different ways—sometimes as UN declarations or policy proposals, sometimes as programs for UN implementation, sometimes in technical reports analyzing weakness of the global economy that needed to be addressed. Common to all were new ways of thinking, new approaches, new ideas. Most of them were themes underlying the UN's work for long periods.

In Part 2 of the book we elaborate these credit items under the headings of the nine ideas where the UN has had a major impact, where it has "changed the world": human rights for all, gender equality, development goals, fairer international economic relations, development ideologies, social development, environmental sustainability; peace and human security; and human development. The subheadings of each of these chapters make clear that none of the ideas have been static and unchanging. Each has evolved over time and in relation to a changing world context. But in their different ways, each idea has made a major impact.

Our balance sheet contains the following debits, once again subjectively reflecting our grasp of realities and factors over the decades:

• Late reaction to the Washington consensus: Beginning in 1980 neoliberal economic and financial policies were introduced practically worldwide with mixed and in many ways negative results. The IMF and the World Bank made loans conditional upon the adoption of these policies. Hard-off developing countries resisted only meekly largely because of the debt crisis that started at the outset of the 1980s. The reaction of the UN was too little and too late. On the topic of debt relief, the UN—despite a handful of analyses, among others from the UN Conference on Trade and Development (UNCTAD)—was invisible for too long.

• Weak response to the special needs of the least-developed countries (LDCs): The UN organized three important conferences—in 1981, 1990, and 2001—to examine what could be done for these countries internationally and what they could do for themselves. But implementation lagged far behind the urgency of the problem. Most of these countries now find themselves even farther behind others in economic and social development, however measured.

• Too little done to introduce cultural aspects into the development equation: At a late stage, UNESCO tried to remedy this situation by producing a *World Culture Report* that made a valiant attempt to link culture and economic development. However, after two reports (1998 and 2000), the "series" was discontinued.

• Inadequate attention to international and national distribution of income and wealth: While they were at the center of UN attention during its first thirty years, these issues disappeared from the radar screen. Recently, they have resurfaced. The World Bank devoted its 2005 *World Development Report* to that issue while

the UN concentrated its 2005 *World Social Report* on "the inequality predicament."
Both reports, however, focus more on national than on international distribution
and redistribution issues.

• Tardy and weak reaction to HIV/AIDS: The World Health Organization
(WHO) initiated an early response, but this was aborted.

Our conclusion is that the balance sheet shows a small surplus. On the credit
side we find important pluses, but the debit side also weighs heavily. For the
world organization to remain viable, drastic changes in priorities and leadership are of the essence. The UN should recognize that ideas have been one of its
most important contributions and take steps to ensure that this side of its work
is strengthened for the future.

In making our calculation about the ledger, we have endeavored to weigh
the following considerations in qualifying an idea as "successful" or "failed."
An idea succeeds if it becomes generally accepted (often after a time lag) by
elite governmental circles as well as by civil society. The existence of financial
and institutional commitments also suggests that an idea has entered the mainstream and has policy traction. We also consider an idea successful if many
argue for its centrality even if it has not as yet received widespread acceptance
by political decision makers. It often takes time for visionary ideas to sink in.
Conversely, an idea fails when it remains marginal or simply receives no funding or has virtually no institutional manifestation. Again, the cutting edge of an
intellectual product may be dulled by the lack of receptivity, however accurate
and morally compelling the idea may be.

One of the more difficult variables to consider involves subjective analysis over time. Had one been trying in the early 1990s to judge the validity of
the impact of human rights ideas, for instance, by the extent to which they
were embedded institutionally through the position of a high commissioner for
human rights or an international criminal court (ideas that emerged in the late
1940s), the judgment would have been quite different later in the decade. In the
intervening years, the aspirations from half a century earlier took institutional
form in the creation of the Office of the High Commissioner for Human Rights
(OHCHR) and its concomitant enhanced funding and visibility.

Shifting Preoccupations

It is helpful to place the asset and debit sheet in a chronological context for what
we see as three distinct historical phases. Table 1.1 summarizes changing developments on a timeline of the shifting preoccupations inside and outside the
UN since 1945. Readers may wish to refer back to this table while reading other
parts of the volume. The following overview permits us to situate the world
organization's focus and roles and judge the minuses as well as pluses.

Table 1.1. Key Events over the UN's Lifetime

Decade	Global Landmarks	Main UN Events	Pioneering UN Documents
1945–1949	1945 World War II ends	1945 San Francisco conference, Trygve Lie elected first Secretary-General	1945 UN Charter
	1949 Truman's Four Point Speech	1945 Inaugural meetings of World Bank and IMF	1948 Universal Declaration of Human Rights and Genocide Convention
	1948–1952 Marshall Plan	1946 First General Assembly meets in London	1949 UN, National and International Measures for Full Employment
	1948–1949 Berlin Blockade	1945–1948 FAO, UNESCO, and WHO established	1949 UN, Relative Prices of Exports and Imports of Underdeveloped Countries
	1949 People's Republic of China proclaimed		
	1949 NATO and COMECON established		
	1950 World population at 2.5 billion		
1950–1959	1950–1953 Korean War	1949–1957 Long debates on whether to provide low-interest loans to developing countries resulting in creation of the Special Fund shortly after the World Bank creates the International Development Association	1950 ECLA, Economic Development of Latin America and its Principal Problems
	1955 Bandung conference launches Non-Aligned Movement	1953 Dag Hammarskjöld elected second Secretary-General	1951 UN, Measures for the Economic Development of Under-Developed Countries and Measures for International Economic Stability
	1957 Ghana's independence	1955 WHO launches malaria eradication program	
	1959 Inter-American Development Bank established (development banks for Africa and Asia follow in the 1960s)		
	1960 World population at 3 billion		

Table 1.1. (continued)

Decade	Global Landmarks	Main UN Events	Pioneering UN Documents
1960–1969	1960s Independence of thirty-two African countries	1960s First Development Decade	1961 UNESCO, Final Report of the Conference of African States on the Development of Education in Africa (analogous ones for other regions follow)
	1961 Berlin Wall erected	1961 Dag Hammarskjöld dies in plane crash; U Thant becomes interim Secretary-General	1962 UN, The United Nations Development Decade: Proposals for Action
	1962 Cuban Missile Crisis	1964 UNCTAD created	1964 UNCTAD publishes seven volumes of papers and proceedings from inaugural conference
	1964 Vietnam War intensifies	1965 Committee on Development Planning established within ECOSOC	1966 International Covenant on Civil and Political Rights
	1968–1969 Student unrest in Europe and Mexico pressures governments for domestic change	1965 WHO approves smallpox eradication plan	1966 International Covenant on Economic, Social and Cultural Rights
	1969 U.S. astronauts land on moon		1969 Commission on International Development, Partners in Development (also known as the Pearson report)
			1969 UNDP, A Study of the Capacity of the United Nations Development System
1970–1979	1971 Bretton Woods financial system abandoned	1970s Second UN Development Decade	1970–1976 ILO World Employment Programme: country reports on Colombia, Sri Lanka, Kenya, Philippines, and others.
	1971 People's Republic of China joins the UN	1971 Kurt Waldheim elected fourth Secretary-General	1972 UNRISD, Contents and Measurement of Socio-Economic Development
	1972 First commissioned report to the Club of Rome (Meadows et al., Limits to Growth)	1972 Conference on the Human Environment (Stockholm)	1974 World Bank/IDS, Redistribution with Growth
	1975 U.S. withdraws from Vietnam	1974 World Population Conference (Bucharest)	1976 ILO, Employment, Growth, and Basic Needs: A One-World Problem
	1973–1974 OPEC price hikes after Yom Kippur War	1974 World Food Conference (Rome)	1978 Declaration of Alma-Ata adopted at the International Conference on Primary Health Care affirms access to basic health services as a fundamental human right and sets a target of achieving health for all by 2000
	1976 Chairman Mao dies	1974 General Assembly Special Session on NIEO	
		1975 First world conference on women (Mexico City)	

	1977 First case of HIV/AIDS diagnosed in New York 1979–1980 Margaret Thatcher and Ronald Reagan elected 1974 World population at 4 billion	1976 UN Conference on Human Settlements (Vancouver) 1976 Tripartite ILO Conference on Employment, Income Distribution and Social Progress 1978 General Assembly Special Session on Disarmament and Development 1979 World Conference on Science and Technology and Development (Vienna)	1978 World Bank publishes first World Development Report
1980–1989	1980–1981 Worldwide economic recession 1981 Cancún conference marks end of so-called North-South dialogue that began in the mid-1970s 1982 Mexican debt default ushers in era of Bretton Woods policies of economic adjustment and the resulting lost decade of development 1984 Famine strikes twenty-six countries in Sub-Saharan Africa 1989 Berlin Wall falls 1987 World population at 5 billion	1980s Third UN Development Decade 1981 First UN Conference on Least Developed Countries (Paris) 1981 Javier Pérez de Cuéllar elected fifth Secretary-General 1984 Office for Emergency Operations in Africa established 1985 UNU-WIDER created 1986 World Bank establishes Structural Adjustment Facility for low-income countries 1988 World Meteorological Organization and UNEP establish the Intergovernmental Panel on Climate Change	1980 Independent Commission on International Development Issues, North-South: A Programme for Survival (also known as the Brandt report) 1980 UNRISD, The Quest for a Unified Approach to Development 1981 Lagos Plan of Action of the ECA and the Organization of African Unity challenged by the World Bank's Accelerated Development in Sub-Saharan Africa: An Agenda for Action, opening a decade or more of debate 1987 UNICEF, Adjustment with a Human Face 1987 World Commission on Environment and Development, Our Common Future (also known as the Brundtland report) 1989 ECA, African Alternative Framework to Structural Adjustment, Programs for Social Economic Recovery, and Transformation

Table 1.1. (continued)

Decade	Global Landmarks	Main UN Events	Pioneering UN Documents
1990–1999	Era of adjustment continues in most of Africa and Latin America	1990s Fourth UN Development Decade	1990 UNDP launches first Human Development Report
	1991 Soviet Union implodes	1990 World Summit for Children	1995 Commission on Global Governance, Our Global Neighbourhood
	1991 Former Yugoslavia implodes, leading to humanitarian crises	1991 Boutros Boutros-Ghali elected sixth Secretary-General	1996 UNESCO, Our Creative Diversity: Report of the World Commission on Culture and Development
	1994 Rwandan genocide	1992 Earth Summit (Rio de Janeiro)	
	1997–2000 Asian financial crisis	1993 World Conference on Human Rights (Vienna)	
	1999 World population at 6 billion	1994 International Conference on Population & Development (Cairo)	
		1995 Fourth World Conference on Women (Beijing)	
		1995 World Summit on Social Development (Copenhagen)	
		1996 Kofi Annan elected seventh Secretary-General	
2000–present	Global warming and climate change emerge as major issues	2000 Millennium Summit and Declaration, including adoption of MDGs	2000 Millennium Declaration
	China and India emerge as economic powers	2002 Conference on Finance and Development (Monterrey)	2001 Responsibility to Protect: Report of the International Commission on Intervention and State Sovereignty
	2003 Darfur war and killings	2007 Ban Ki-moon elected eighth Secretary-General	2005 Millennium Project Report, Investing in Development: A Practical Plan to Achieve the Millennium Development Goals
	2007–2008 Global credit crunch and economic downturns triggered by widespread exposure to U.S. sub-prime housing loans		2004 High-level Panel on Threats, Challenges and Change, A More Secure World: Our Shared Responsibility
			2005 UN, In Larger Freedom: Towards Development, Security and Human Rights for All
			2007 Intergovernmental Panel on Climate Change publishes its three-part Climate Change 2007 assessment and a synthesis report

The Early Years

The UN's attention to economic and social issues has shifted considerably over six and a half decades of its history. At the beginning, the major victorious powers—especially the United States, the Soviet Union, and the United Kingdom—were preoccupied with getting the new organization under way in a context of postwar recovery. With fifty-one member states present at the creation in San Francisco, there was a limited and often colonial perspective on issues relative to areas where the majority of the world's population lived. Attention to human rights became an important focus, with Eleanor Roosevelt chairing the commission that produced the Universal Declaration of Human Rights within three years. But the declaration was deliberately constructed to be an aspiration, to provide guidelines for national attention but not for international action. Moreover, the world body and most governments largely treated human rights and economic and social development as separate issues, pursued along parallel tracks—an approach that continued for the UN's first three or four decades.

The United States, which was strengthened rather than weakened by World War II, was in a position to take a more global view and to pursue initiatives within the organization in which it was by far the strongest power. This was not a decision motivated by liberal ideals but was rather a strategic calculation to continue the cooperative efforts that had been so necessary and successful in winning the war. A substantial literature developed, in fact, about the benefits of international institutions and the actions of hegemons (sometimes termed the "provision of public goods") including measures for stability.[1] This worldview quickly gave way to the confrontation of the Cold War, and the United Nations became polarized by this dominant global reality.

Indeed, the explosion of the first atomic bombs in August 1945 changed the equation completely, and military power once again became virtually the only lens through which international public policy was viewed. By the time the UN Charter went into effect in October, the glamour and glitter of the San Francisco consensus had already been supplanted by traditional power politics and balance-of-power and balance-of-terror calculations.

Nonetheless in January 1949, U.S. president Harry S. Truman made his historic Point 4 Speech, pledging "unfaltering support to the United Nations" and calling for a "bold new program for making the benefits of our scientific advances and industrial progress available for the improvement and growth of underdeveloped areas."[2] This followed the launch of the Marshall Plan in 1948, under which for four years 2 percent of U.S. national income was transferred each year to support European recovery—though, significantly, this was done outside the United Nations. It also followed the Berlin blockade that began in

June 1948. In 1949, COMECON, the Council for Mutual Economic Assistance between the Soviet Union and its satellite states, was set up, and soon thereafter the Soviet bloc's military equivalent, the Warsaw Pact, was put into place. The Cold War had already entered economic, social, and military relations, which were firmly solidified in April 1949 with the formation of the Western Alliance, the North Atlantic Treaty Organization (NATO).

The political structure of the world was also changing. In 1947, India and Pakistan became independent, and in 1949, the People's Republic of China was proclaimed. By 1957, Ghana had become independent, and prospects for rapid moves to independence by another thirty to forty African, Caribbean, and other colonies were on the horizon. The UN's economic and social preoccupations were shifting to development, the priority of newly independent states, but UN security efforts were seriously undermined as a result of East-West confrontation. Moreover, although the Economic Commission for Europe (ECE) was engaged in work on both Eastern and Western Europe and the Economic Commission for Asia and the Far East (ECAFE, which in 1974 became the Economic and Social Commission for Asia and the Pacific, ESCAP) was engaged in work on Japan, the creation of Organisation for Economic Co-operation and Development (OECD) in 1961 meant that the developed countries increasingly turned to their own organization rather than to the UN for analysis of regional problems.

It is essential to appreciate the importance of early development ideas produced within the UN, which can be distilled from three major publications published between 1949 and 1951. These were *National and International Measures for Full Employment* (1949), *Measures for the Economic Development of Under-Developed Countries* (1951), and *Measures for International Economic Stability* (1951).[3] Each of these reports was drafted by a team of prominent economists from different parts of the world with support from the UN Secretariat. The economists included some of the best. Among them were two who subsequently won Nobel Prizes in economics, W. Arthur Lewis and Theodore W. Schultz. Over the years, three Nobel prizewinners in economics have worked as UN staff members and six others have worked closely with the UN as consultants or advisers. (For these and other Nobel laureates, see the discussion in chapter 2 and box 2.1.)

These reports and their recommendations were ahead of their time, particularly in the international domain, by emphasizing international cooperation and solidarity rather than narrower perspectives of national interests. They sought to establish a new structural equilibrium in world trade within three to four years. They recommended that industrial countries take measures to encourage capital flows to developing countries to encourage rapid growth of production and real

incomes so that the world economy as a whole could attain a steady rate and pattern of growth. The reports sought to give priority to what were then called "underdeveloped countries"; they advocated increasing the rates of saving and investment and transferring labor from low-productivity rural areas to higher-productivity urban areas in these countries. They emphasized the need to lift the institutional constraints on economic development, such as the concentration of land ownership in a small number of hands and discrimination in banking systems and other factors that hindered the mobility of resources in and to these countries. They recommended attacking short-run fluctuations in the prices and terms of trade of primary products through negotiating international commodity agreements. They also asked the World Bank to substantially increase the flow of lending to developing countries in the event of recession.

Five years after its birth, the United Nations was thus ahead of the curve in thinking from a global perspective about approaches that would optimize the chances for a fairer distribution of the benefits of growth. What a difference it would have made to world development if this global approach had been pursued over two or three decades. Building on the positive experience of the Marshall Plan, for example, a massive and generous infusion of aid could have changed dramatically development prospects of postcolonial societies.

Hans Singer's work on the terms of trade is a second great idea and is the most important intellectual contribution he made while working for the United Nations.[4] In his oral history interview, he explains that talking to the unemployed in the United Kingdom during the 1930s had taught him to look at the world from the viewpoint of the underdog: "If you look at foreign trade from the point of view of the poor countries, exporters of primary products, what does it look like? It appears an unequal system that is weighted against them. That was the same way the unemployed in England looked at the unemployment insurance system."[5]

Singer, who died in early 2006 at the age of 95, worked under the general super-vision of Folke Hilgerdt, the director of the UN Statistical Office (UNSO), who provided a key link between UNSO's work and the statistical work of the former League of Nations on trade. Hilgerdt had been the principal author of the League of Nations publication *Industrialization and Foreign Trade,* which included an appendix on international trade from 1871 to 1938.[6] These data showed that during this time interval, the price index of primary products decreased significantly more than that of manufactured goods. Nothing was made of this in the summary of findings of the League of Nations report, but its statistics were available for Singer's research.

The Singer study showed that the terms of trade of underdeveloped countries had improved between 1938 and 1946–1948. However, he put this

improvement in a much longer historical perspective, showing that they had seriously deteriorated between 1876 and 1948.[7] This finding was contrary to classical theory. For certain fellow economists, this was already bad enough, but the political dynamite came from Singer's further conclusion that under-developed countries were contributing to a rising standard of living in indus-trial countries without receiving compensation. In his path-breaking 1950 ECLA report, Raúl Prebisch put these data in a wider policy perspective by developing the center-periphery framework.[8] Thus, what has become known as the Prebisch-Singer thesis about the secular decline in the terms of trade of developing countries was born, as well as ECLA's remedy in the form of a strat-egy for import-substitution industrialization, as set out in Prebisch's report. As mentioned, important early work on statistics and national accounting was another significant contribution of the UN.

During the 1960s, independence brought considerable economic and social progress to many developing countries. The UN declared the 1960s to be the Development Decade, proposed by U.S. president John F. Kennedy. This first of four such decades set a goal for accelerating the economic growth of develop-ing countries—which they exceeded on average while some fifty of them did so individually. The number of school enrollments and access to health services also expanded rapidly. Later in the decade, the WHO adopted the goal of the global eradication of smallpox, which was achieved in the 1970s. The United Nations also created new organizations—the World Food Progamme (WFP) in 1961, the UN Research Institute for Social Development (UNRISD) in 1963, the UN Conference on Trade and Development in 1964, and the UN Indus-trial Development Organization (UNIDO) in 1966. These added new ideas and themes to the UN's policy agenda.

The Middle Years

Yet all was not well. By the 1970s, it was clear that more fundamental changes were needed, both nationally and internationally, quite a few of which had been anticipated in the three UN reports produced around 1950. The UN responded by organizing a series of substantive discussions at conferences on key issues—on the environment, food and hunger, population, human settlements, employment, and science and technology. These included the UN Conference on the Human Environment (UNCHE, 1972), the UN World Population Con-ference (1974), the World Conference of the International Women's Year (1975), and the UN Conference on Human Settlements (HABITAT, 1976).

Internationally, the global economy was changing, reflecting shifts in eco-nomic power. The United States abandoned the fixed exchange rate for the dollar in 1971. Two years later, the Organization of the Petroleum Exporting

Countries (OPEC) shocked the world by increasing oil prices three to four times, transferring 2 percent of global income to OPEC from the oil-importing countries. OPEC increased oil prices again in 1979. Nonetheless, the efforts of developing countries to respond to such changes by creating a New International Economic Order (NIEO) fell on deaf ears. Instead, oil profits were recycled through the developed-country banking system and by the early 1980s, debt among the borrowing countries from the developing world had risen to very high levels.

At the same time, the 1970s were a creative time for the world organization. This was reflected in important work on development strategies, the informal sector, the environment, population, food, hunger, and gender.

The idea of a basic needs development strategy was born in the early part of the decade, growing out of dissatisfaction with the results of the core focus on economic growth in the 1960s.[9] Basic needs were defined in terms of food, housing, clothing, and such public services as education, health care, and transportation. Employment was both a means and an end, and the approach included participation in decision making. The first task was for a country to quantify basic needs requirements for a target year—for instance, twenty-five years in the future. In other words, what would national income twenty-five years ahead need to be in order to satisfy the basic needs of even the poorest 20 percent of the population? Having quantified gross domestic product (GDP) for the target year, one could then calculate the annual rate of economic growth required between the base and the target years.

Not surprisingly, in most cases the required rate of economic growth to meet basic need targets within the time frame was unrealistically high by historical standards—well over 8 percent per year over twenty-five years. East Asia and China have subsequently achieved such rates, but in the mid-1970s the East Asian miracle lay ahead. The only way to achieve the targets in full was to work at two levels: the rate of economic growth *and* income distribution. Indeed, if policy efforts had improved income distribution, the overall rate of required economic growth would not have been so high. It was shown in *Employment, Growth and Basic Needs,* a key publication of the ILO, that with "redistribution from growth"—that is, redistribution of future increases of income rather than redistribution of existing wealth—basic needs targets could be attained in most countries with an annual rate of growth of 6 percent, still high but within reach. By the end of the 1970s, it looked as though a more appropriate development strategy had been designed that effectively combined economic growth, income distribution, poverty reduction, productive employment, and meeting basic needs for the entire population.

An important addition to the debate on employment came with the concept of the informal sector, which became more widely known and eventually

accepted by economists after the report of the ILO Employment Mission to Kenya in 1972.[10] The popular view of informal sector activities was (and to some extent still is) that they are primarily those of petty traders, street hawkers, shoeshine boys, and other groups "underemployed" on the teaming streets of overcrowded cities. However, the evidence suggested that that the bulk of employment in the informal sector, far from being only marginally productive, is economically efficient and profit making, though small in scale and limited by simple technologies. Within the informal sector are found a variety of carpenters, masons, tailors, and other tradesmen as well as cooks and taxi drivers, workers who offer virtually the full range of basic skills needed to provide goods and services for large though often poor sections of the population. The concept subsequently was broadened to include many subcontracted activities of larger firms that use the informal sector to avoid the laws and other obligations that apply to larger firms.

The evidence suggests that since the 1970s employment has increased a good deal faster in the informal than in the formal sector. It is therefore impossible to judge how the employment problem has changed merely from the data on employment in the formal sector, which is what official statistics capture.[11] The informal sector has had a flourishing career, including in the financial arena with the award of the 2006 Nobel Prize for Peace to Muhammad Yunus, the founder of the Grameen Bank, who pioneered the provision of microcredit to millions of poor women in Bangladesh.

The UN elaborated other priorities during the 1970s. The global conferences on environment, food and hunger, population, women, human settlements, employment, and science and technology established these issues as critically important for national and international development. What was then the "Third World" or "South"—and is now called the "global South"—became a major force in flagging and then promoting alternatives. Sometimes in unison and sometimes with dissonant choruses, the pressure from developing countries became increasingly significant.

In particular, calls for the establishment of the New International Economic Order delineated a stark fault line between most developing and most developed countries. There were, of course, major differences of opinion about the NIEO among developing countries (with the least developed among them considerably less enthusiastic than their better-off brethren) as well as among those in the West (with the so-called like-minded countries, who were less hostile than the United States, the United Kingdom, and Germany).

That being said, for the most part developing countries, often working through the Group of 77 (or G-77, established as a caucus during preparations for the first UNCTAD), contended that a major source of their failures in the 1960s and the difficulties they faced was inequities in the operations of the international

economic system. They argued for a number of specific changes in the system, including a global fund to support a common framework for the management of commodity trade. In contrast to the idea of a NIEO, the other side (and the developed countries formed and clearly presented another side) emphasized the failures and weaknesses of developing countries and the opportunities that a global free market would bring. Immediately following the surge in oil prices in 1973–1974, both groups engaged in an acrimonious debate, as the economies of the developed countries were also suffering from the oil price increases.

However, this phase passed within two years or so, after which the position of developed countries hardened, to the point that these countries stated that it was simply not helpful to keep pressing for a NIEO. By the end of the 1970s, the issue of international economic restructuring from above was dead. A focus on changing the domestic policies and priorities of developing countries replaced the earlier felt need for international change. The policies advocated by developed countries and international financial institutions were premised on the belief that the state sector and regulation were constraints—even impediments—to growth.

The Last Twenty-Five Years

In the 1980s, as conservative governments were elected in the United Kingdom and the United States, a new economic and financial orthodoxy took over, emphasizing financial balance and low inflation over employment creation and income distribution. It took some time—and a lost decade or more—for international policymakers to realize once again that they should not be concerned solely with inflation, balance of payments, and GDP and that employment, individual incomes, income distribution, nutrition, food balances, and human empowerment were essential.

High levels of debt and world recession made the 1980s the years of structural adjustment, led by the Bretton Woods institutions and backed by increasing financial support from donor countries. UN institutions and economists were divided between those who weakly went along with tough-minded adjustment policies and those who argued for alternative policies to try to preserve the economic and social strategy priorities that had emerged from the debates of the 1970s but had been set aside. Though adjustment policies kept inflation at bay, the cost to poorer developing countries in terms of lost growth and severe setbacks to development and living standards were serious indeed. Only in the last few years has careful research begun to document the weaknesses of orthodox adjustment policies for poorer countries and their negative effects on growth.[12]

Around 1980 there was an international shift in focus and ideology that gave much greater weight to the Bretton Woods institutions than to the UN system.

This was partly caused by increasing problems of debt and recession and the weak reaction of the UN in the face of neoliberal economic and political orthodoxy.[13] The reason for the feeble reaction to the so-called Washington consensus was not just the force with which the neoliberal paradigm was put forward in major western countries but also genuine weaknesses in the economic performance of many developing countries and the Soviet-bloc countries in the 1970s.

During the 1980s, the UN played a role in articulating the need to re-balance economic, financial, and social policies. UNICEF published *Adjustment with a Human Face,* and the Economic Commission for Africa (ECA) argued for more attention to people and economic growth in the structural adjustment policies that were imposed on many countries.[14] These UN entities pointed out that inequality was increasing between and within countries.

In 1990, the first UN Development Programme (UNDP) annual Human Development Report was published, initially under the direction of Mahbub ul Haq. In cooperation with Amartya Sen and others, the human development approach responded to the same concerns as the idea of basic needs. But it was based on stronger theoretical foundations and broadened the development concept to include human rights and democracy. Human development includes employment creation, poverty reduction, human rights, inclusive democracy, cultural factors, and the role of the state.

The Millennium Development Goals are an indication of how important human concerns and a focus on people have become in UN thinking. These goals, which were adopted by the 147 heads of state and government present at the UN Millennium Summit in 2000, do not challenge earlier notions of the need for accelerated growth in developing countries, but they add a clear focus on meeting the needs of people, especially women, children, and the poor, especially in the poorest countries of the world. Nor do they call the distribution of income within countries into question, though the environment became a significant concern.

Human development thus emerged as a partially successful UN counteroffensive to the priorities of the Washington consensus. After the sharp neoliberal turn of the 1980s, UN development polices have again become more comprehensive. Development clearly is impoverished when human rights and human security are not guaranteed. Over the last six and a half decades, peace, development, human rights, and human security have come closer together, a remarkable conceptual advance that largely is a result of efforts within the UN system. The integration of these important facets of the human challenge may be the most significant intellectual achievement of the world organization. Human rights have now been integrated into a coherent philosophy of human development, providing a broader strategy for both economic development and human progress.

Moreover, UN peacekeeping—often called picturesquely "Chapter VI-and-

a-half" because it was not spelled out in the UN Charter but fell somewhere between peaceful resolution of disputes in Chapter VI and the enforcement authorized in Chapter VII—as well as other tools of conflict management received a new lease on life as the Cold War thawed. The UN's peace and security activities again moved into the forefront of international attention.

Conflict resolution has been accepted as an essential condition for development. In 1992, Secretary-General Boutros Boutros-Ghali issued *An Agenda for Peace,* which set out an international strategy for conflict prevention, peacemaking, peacebuilding, and peacekeeping.[15] These ideas were taken further in 2004, when the High-level Panel on Threats, Challenges and Change proposed that a commission on peacebuilding be created; this was done in 2006.[16] The jury is still out on how effectively the UN's Peacebuilding Commission will function, of course, but this attempt to ensure that countries do not relapse into war is worthwhile. Initial experiences in Sierra Leone and Burundi indicate that the commission serves a valuable purpose.

Spurred by several hard-hitting speeches from Secretary-General Kofi Annan, the UN also embarked on a series of debates exploring "humanitarian intervention" and the "responsibility to protect," a doctrine that argues that sometimes the welfare of human beings matters as much as state sovereignty. The future of development strategies consists of integrating economic and social development, human rights, and human security. The United Nations has contributed to this realization.

The broad lines of economic adjustment policies—with their emphasis on free trade, minimal state intervention, privatization, and fiscal conservatism—continued into the twenty-first century. But there have been at least four major modifications to earlier ideas and preoccupations. First, within the UN, the need to regenerate commitment to the broader elements of the development agenda led to another round of global conferences in the 1990s, this time adding children and human rights to earlier concerns with the environment, population, women, social development, urban settlements, and food security. In 1996, the developed countries in the OECD agreed that long-term goals were needed to shape international development policy. This opened the way for the Millennium Summit in 2000 and agreement on the Millennium Development Goals.

Second, although adjustment priorities are still in force at the IMF, much of the dogma of the Washington consensus has been weakening. There is increasing evidence of its failures in Africa and Latin America and from the preferences of countries in need of funds to turn to private sources of capital, where conditions are less onerous and negotiations can be concluded more quickly. More fundamentally, the global financial and economic crisis has laid bare the inadequacies of unfettered free-market policies, especially for the developed countries.

Third, there is growing awareness of alternative Asian development strategies,

which are highly visible in the successes of Korea, Taiwan, Singapore, Hong Kong, Malaysia, and China. India's path has been somewhat different from the others, but it too has achieved impressive growth since the early 1990s. All of these countries have achieved great economic success by following a different pattern from that of the Washington consensus model although they also have been severely hit by the global financial and economic crisis.

Fourth, and notwithstanding recent slowdowns, the surge of development over the last two or three decades in China and India has increasingly changed the balance of economic and political power within the global economy. The experience of these two giant countries, which together account for almost 40 percent of the world's population, has brought a shift in focus at the UN, which is closely watching these countries and the influence that they are having on economic and social trends in the global economy.

Omissions and Failures

The UN has undertaken many analyses on the external debt of developing countries and formulated many proposals for action. As early as 1964, UNCTAD identified the need for special attention to "the less developed among the developing countries." Four years later UNCTAD II passed resolution 24 (II) regarding the needs of these countries. In 1971, twenty-four countries were identified and placed on the original list of what became known as "the least-developed countries."[17] Today, the least-developed countries number fifty countries with a population of over 600 million, 10 percent of the world's population.

By the late 1970s, it was becoming clear that many of these countries were lagging seriously behind in development, however it was measured or defined. UNCTAD organized a first global conference on the least-developed countries in 1981. As these countries continued to fall behind, subsequent conferences were held in 1990 and 2001 that came up with specific ideas and targets, such as setting aside 0.15 percent of gross national product (GNP) in development aid to these countries. Though the UN has led the way in identifying many specific actions that could be taken to accelerate growth and development in these countries, international support has failed to materialize. Nor has the World Bank or the IMF formally recognized the category of least-developed country.

An attempt to address the debt relief needs of the least-developed countries emerged in the late 1980s. In its 1987 *Trade and Development Report,* UNCTAD analyzed the weaknesses of the international debt strategy that was pursued in the 1980s, emphasizing "the failure to conceive it within a broader strategy for accelerating growth in the world economy."[18] Notwithstanding this analysis and many proposals for action, it was another ten years before the governments of developed countries, working mainly through the World Bank, developed a

program for the heavily indebted poor countries (HIPC) and then it took several more years for them to determine that this version of the program was inadequate and introduce proposals to improve it. One must conclude that the HIPC program, even in its latest version, is too little too late, and in only a handful of countries does it seem to be succeeding. The UN may propose, but if governments of developed countries are unwilling to dispose, nothing much can happen. In fact, the principal reason for the delays was to buy time—for debtor countries to put new policies in place and for western banks to rebuild their "shattered balance sheets" to the point where they could afford to write off their bad sovereign debts.[19] The failures to respond to the clearly identified needs of the poorest countries should be judged, almost three decades after the first global conference, as one of the most serious omissions of action for development.

Another failure has been the late reaction to the HIV/AIDS crisis. Despite some promising beginnings in the WHO and elsewhere, intellectual and operational action fell dramatically short of the challenge until recently. It took more than a decade after the outbreak of the epidemic for a coordinated set of actions, led by UNAIDS, to be put in place. Today, with cumulative deaths exceeding 40 million, international action is still inadequate.

Intellectual Challenges Today and Tomorrow

In today's world of interdependence and increasing globalization and global economic crisis, numerous areas require new international thinking and research and the UN should be encouraged to do more creative work. Our priority list would include the following ten challenges to which the three United Nations (governments, staff members and secretariats, and nonstate actors) should turn their collective minds and energies. We return to these topics in Part 3:

• Long-run issues regarding the environment and the eco-sustainability of the planet need to be combined with national and global measures for recovery from economic and financial crisis

• Getting a better grasp of international migration and population—both the pull of economic opportunities and the push of armed conflict—and linked problems of urbanization and youth unemployment

• The perceived growing divide between the Islamic world and the West—indeed, between fundamentalists and ideologues of various stripes—with attention to the political, cultural, religious, and development dimensions of armed conflict, including the greed-motivating parallel economies

• New actions to overcome unequal global development, especially the fifty or so least-developed countries and more generally "the bottom billion"[20]

• Incorporating culture and human rights into development strategies

• Balancing regionalism with globalization
• Policies to harness the benefits and mitigate the downsides of the trend toward multipolarity and the rise of new economic giants
• Integrated approaches to human security that go beyond the traditional compass of territorial defense or military and security forces of countries
• Actions to promote and encourage a greater sense of human solidarity and commitments to human rights, democracy, and culture
• Measures to counteract the declining quality of education worldwide.

The challenges ahead for the world organization in the fields of economic and social development lie in such priorities and in strengthening the capacity to generate and disseminate ideas. Whatever one's views on the current state of the international civil service—the Second UN—the world organization clearly should strengthen its mechanisms to ensure creative thinking. Previous proposals for reform have totally neglected this vital dimension, and specific measures are required to strengthen this aspect of the UN's work in the future.

Based on our interpretation of the historical record, we would put forward the following three priorities:

• Recognizing that contributing to ideas, thinking, and analysis in all areas of international action ranks as one of the major parts of work at the UN. To this end, the UN needs to foster an environment that encourages and rewards creative thinking, analysis, and policy-focused research of high intellectual quality. This has implications for recruitment and promotion. The quality of staff members is essential, and no compromise must be made here. Moreover, providing more financial support for research, analysis, and policy exploration is a top priority. The terms on which such support is provided is especially important. It needs to be made available in adequate amounts and commitments need to be made for the longer term if the integrity and autonomy of UN organizations is to be enhanced.
• Strengthening the means for disseminating new ideas, analyses, and proposals is equally important. The UN's ability to reach large numbers of people with key reports is sometimes impressive. An outstandingly positive illustration of this has been the marketing of the Human Development Reports. At the same time, too many core reports languish on bookshelves or in filing cabinets. Discussion with governments should be held not only in intergovernmental settings but in capitals and among such diverse constituencies as NGOs, the business community, the media, and members of civil society.
• Rethinking and improving relations between the UN and the Bretton Woods institutions to encourage better interchange of ideas and experience and more balanced allocation of international resources between them is an important challenge.

Since 1980, the donor community has channeled increasing amounts of resources to and through the Bretton Woods institutions and increasingly followed their lead in terms of policy and action, both internationally and at the country level. This overwhelming focus on international financial institutions has often led to neglect of UN organizations. Our assessment of the record shows the many respects in which this has been counterproductive. The UN's contributions have been neglected in key areas where the Bretton Woods institutions were not active or, equally important, in areas where subsequent events have shown that earlier policies by the Washington-based financial institutions were wrong or too narrow. The need now is to achieve a better balance between the World Bank, the IMF, and the UN in policy leadership, funding, and support for national and international action. Stronger roles for the regional development banks and the regional commissions need to be made part of these reforms. It is good to note that new leadership and thinking in the international financial institutions goes in this direction.

Some important changes have recently begun to be put in place, many related to the adoption of the Millennium Development Goals in 2000 and the Poverty Reduction Strategy Papers (PRSPs) process at the country level. Under these, the Bretton Woods institutions, the donor community, and the UN, working under the leadership of UN resident coordinators, prepare PRSPs in conjunction with the national government and civil society organizations.[21]

We now are ready to spell out in the next chapter our analytical framework for ideas as followed throughout UNIHP's decade-long effort, but first we pause to listen to Nobel laureate Amartya Sen. "The UN is, of course, a practical body, and it is right that it would be mainly concerned with the urgent and the immediate," he told us. And then he concluded:

> Yet, it is also necessary not to be boorish in ignoring the ancestry of many of the ideas that the UN stands for and tries to promote. I think the UN has, taking the rough with the smooth, made good use of ideas, generally. But it varies a little between different parts of the UN system. As I have worked, over the decades, with different parts of the UN system, I have been impressed how some of them have been more explicit and more keenly aware of the sophisticated ideas that lie behind the day-to-day work and commitments of the UN. This can make a difference in giving intellectual depth to practical strategies.[22]

2. The Three UNs and Their Impact

- **Definitions, Dynamics, Methods**
- **Nature of Ideas**
- **Assessing the Impact of UN Ideas**
- **Conclusion**

Definitions, Dynamics, Methods

The United Nations has been active in the economic and social arena over the whole of its existence, taking on a wide range of contemporary problems. It has sometimes responded to issues too late, but at its best, it has tried to foresee them in order to forestall difficulties or disasters on the horizon. Because it is an international body, comprised of fifty-one member states at its birth and over 190 since 2000, formulating a UN view on problems and issues has inevitably involved great controversy. The greatest complexity involves the need to appreciate the different ways that events and problems appear in different parts of the world and especially how people in different countries are affected by them.

The complexities are increased because of the many different groups, perceptions, and forces active within the UN. In *Ahead of the Curve,* our first volume, we ended by asking, "What is the UN?" Is it an assortment of governments that disagree on most issues? Does it reach beyond to them to represent "We, the peoples"? Are there independent officials or are staff enslaved to repetition of national party lines? Is it a family of organizations, some close siblings and others estranged cousins—like the World Bank and the IMF?[1]

There were two parts to our answer at the time. The first part of our response was, "All of the above, and more." But in relation to ideas and policies—and much else of the UN's work—we recognized and applied the long-standing distinction introduced by Inis Claude in his classic textbook that there were two UNs: the arena for the world organization's member states and its staff members.[2] These first two United Nations hardly need elaboration, but now, having seen and analyzed much more, we recognize that there have been at most times and for most issues three distinct UNs in operation: the UN of governments,

the UN of staff members, and the UN of closely associated NGOs, experts, and consultants.

We define the "Third UN" as "comprising NGOs, academics, consultants, experts, independent commissions, and other groups of individuals who routinely engage with the First UN and the Second UN and thereby influence UN thinking, policies, priorities, and actions. The key characteristic for this third sphere is its independence from governments and UN secretariats."[3] Private consultants or university staff who are actively working on UN matters or have been commissioned by the UN would be part of the Third UN, as would legislators and members of Parliamentarians for Global Action or members of the UN Committee on Development Policy. We do not include the for-profit sector in the Third UN on the grounds that its primary focus is the bottom line. This is not to deny the importance of the Global Compact and similar schemes to encourage corporate social responsibility and private sector support for the world organization. We also recognize that where to draw the line encircling the Third UN at times involves difficult decisions—as with our decision to exclude the media, even members of that group that have long and steady commitments to the UN.

Deciding who is in or out of the Third UN is complicated for several reasons. While none of the three UNs is a monolith (and tensions within groups of states or among Secretariat officials and NGOs often are palpable), nonetheless the Third UN is the most varied. In addition, depending on the issues and the period in question, some NGOs may be closely involved with the UN on certain issues, such as debt relief or support for fair trade, but not with others, such as human rights or gender. For some debates, NGOs may be powerful in absolute numbers or influence or both, as for the environment, while in others their influence may be more marginal, as for disarmament. Or they may be involved at the time a particular topic emerges but lose interest over time. Hence, the boundaries of the Third UN must be defined in relation to the issue being considered and the moment. Moreover, over their careers, many individuals move between the UN and outside institutions such as governments, universities, or NGOs. This revolving door means that defining who is in and who is out depends on the time period under review. In short, membership in the Third UN is especially fluid, temporary, and contingent. Notwithstanding these qualifications, the Third UN plays and has played a significant role, especially in relation to the development or promotion of new ideas and in lobbying for them when the First and the Second UNs have been cautious, reluctant, or even hostile. This is clear in matters of human rights but also in other areas such as debt relief and challenging economic orthodoxies.

The UNIHP has adopted an eclectic, multidisciplinary approach that has made us aware of differences in how the mainstream disciplines perceive the

UN and how it operates. This also means that we may be subjected to harsh criticism by card-carrying members of a narrow disciplinary club—we have a sense that many of our colleagues who are economists or political scientists may think that we have lost our respective disciplinary marbles. Recognition of the Third UN is one such area in which we may be quite at odds with the mainstream—though perhaps the mainstream is catching up. Sociologists and anthropologists and many development economists and students of comparative politics have long recognized the importance of nonstate actors, as have a handful of UN organizations that includes the ILO, UNICEF, and the United Nations Development Fund for Women (UNIFEM).

During our own discussions about the Third UN, we have asked ourselves why it has taken so long for this part of the UN to be more generally recognized, especially among international relations specialists. One part of the answer is the long tradition among analysts, diplomats, and governments of approaching international relations essentially in terms of relationships between sovereign states. Such thinking goes back several centuries to conceptions of the state after the Peace of Westphalia in 1648, which are deep within the foundations of much teaching and analysis of the global system. We are reminded of the comment by John Maynard Keynes at the beginning of *The General Theory of Employment, Interest, and Money:* "The difficulty lies, not in the new ideas, but in escaping from the old ones, which ramify, for those brought up as most of us have been, into every corner of our minds."[4]

One particular category of the Third UN necessitates specific elaboration. These are the independent commissions, set up by the UN, governments, or some other party to explore alternative framings of a major issue. Prominent examples include the panel headed by former Canadian prime minister Lester Pearson that produced *Partners in Development,* a wide-ranging report that elaborated guidelines on aid and development policies for the 1970s. Later examples include *North-South: A Programme for Survival,* the so-called Brandt report (1980); *Our Common Future,* the so-called Brundtland report of the International Commission on Environment and Development (1987); *Our Global Neighbourhood,* the report of the Commission on Global Governance (1995); *The Responsibility to Protect,* the report of the International Commission on Intervention and State Sovereignty (2001); the deliberations of the Commission on Human Security in 2003; and the various reports of the early 2000s on UN reform.[5] All commissions should be counted as parts of the Third UN and have played an important role in developing ideas and feeding them into the UN system, usually at a high level.

UNIHP has identified eight distinct and ideational roles played collectively by the three UNs, sometimes in isolation and sometimes together or in parallel.

These roles are providing a forum for debate; generating ideas; giving ideas international legitimacy; promoting the adoption of such ideas for policy; implementing or testing ideas and policies at the country level; generating resources to pursue new policies; monitoring progress; and, let us admit, occasionally acting to bury ideas that seem inconvenient or excessively controversial. For those who like alliteration, these eight roles have been described as forum, fount, font, fanfare, framing, funding, following—and funeral.[6] The essential point is that the UN operates and achieves influence in many ways in its headquarters and at the country level. One must beware of being too reductionist. The three constituent parts of our analytical UN are anything but monoliths, and as each component is subject to variations and various power positions.

Usually all three UNs work in parallel and simultaneously to fulfill these roles, although usually not in unison. Indeed, there often are significant divergences in views among the most significant players within each of the three UNs—for instance, among major and minor powers among states (e.g., Russia and Luxembourg) or conservative and progressive ones (e.g., the United States and Finland), even if they are from the same region (e.g., Costa Rica and Venezuela). One secretariat of the UN system may have few partners but others may have many (e.g., UNCTAD and the World Intellectual Property Organization), and portions of the NGO universe may wish to collaborate with UN organizations whereas others are philosophically opposed (e.g., Oxfam and the International Committee of the Red Cross). Significantly, differences in the ways that various members of the three United Nations play their roles or in the tactics they pursue often provide an element of creative tension that leads to boldness and innovation, creating positions that governments alone might not otherwise adopt or might even avoid. Embarrassment, competition, and deference all play a role in stimulating reactions.

A few statistics may demonstrate the growing importance of the Third UN. At the founding conference in San Francisco in 1945, there were 1,500 NGO representatives and unofficial participants—mainly from the West and more particularly from the United States—compared with the 5,000 government delegates, media representatives, and other officials involved, including administrative and service staff. In 1992 at the Earth Summit in Rio, there were 17,000 nongovernmental participants from across the planet, and at the women's conference in Beijing three years later, there were 32,000, including 5,000 Chinese. UNICEF's World Summit for Children in 1990 stirred over 1 million people worldwide to join in candlelight vigils.[7] Apart from these special occasions, 2,870 NGOs are now officially registered with the UN and have "consultative status."

These numbers can be set alongside those of the Second UN. Today's professional and support staff in the UN proper total approximately 55,000, with

another 20,000 in the specialized agencies. These figures do not include about 15,000 in the Bretton Woods institutions and 100,000 temporarily employed in 2007 in peace operations. Naturally, these figures show enormous growth compared to the early days of the UN, when about 500 employees were employed in the first year (not including those in specialized agencies and the Bretton Woods institutions). The figures are also many times more than the total of 700 employed by the League of Nations at its peak.[8]

Relative to the wide-ranging mandates and activities of the 192 member states of the First UN, the employment of fewer than 100,000 regular staff in the Second UN across the globe is extraordinarily small by any reasonable standard in relationship to the contemporary needs and challenges of global governance. We have often argued that many of these people punch above their weight—as is suggested in box 2.1—but readers need to keep in mind that the United Nations proper employs fewer staff than the combined police and fire services of New York City and that the number of UN staff is fewer than the number of public employees of most medium cities around the world.

Box 2.1. UN Winners of the Nobel Prizes for Economics and Peace

A number of UN organizations and individuals who have worked for the UN as staff or delegates have received the Nobel Peace Prize for contributions to peace and world order. The Office of the UN High Commissioner for Refugees (UNHCR) was awarded the prize on two occasions. Less recognized, at least nine Nobel prize-winning economists have worked for the world organization, three as full-time international civil servants and the others as advisers or consultants.

Peace

• 1949: John Boyd Orr, first FAO director-general (1945–1948), for his work to eliminate world hunger

• 1950: Ralph Bunche, UN mediator in Palestine, for his mediation in the negotiations of the armistice between Israel and its four Arab neighbors

• 1954 and 1981: UNHCR, for its work with victims fleeing war

• 1957: Lester Pearson, president of the seventh session of the General Assembly, for his work in conflict prevention

• 1961: Dag Hammarskjöld, the second Secretary-General, for his efforts to create peace and goodwill among countries and peoples

• 1965: UNICEF, for its assistance to the children of the world

• 1968: René Cassin, vice-chairman of the UN Commission on Human Rights from its inception in 1946 until 1960, for his contribution to protecting human worth and rights

• 1969: The ILO, for its efforts to create social justice

• 1982: Alva Myrdal and Alfonzo Garcia Robles, for their work on disarmament negotiations in the UN

• 1988: UN Peacekeeping Forces, for their contribution in reducing tensions so that peace negotiations could begin

• 2001: The UN, jointly with Kofi Annan, the seventh Secretary-General, for their work for a better organized and more peaceful world

• 2007: The UN Intergovernmental Panel on Climate Change (jointly with Al Gore), for their efforts to build up and disseminate knowledge about human-made climate change and lay the foundations for measures to counteract it

• 2008: Martti Ahtissari, former UN under-secretary-general and peace negotiator, for his efforts to resolve international conflicts on several continents

Economic Sciences

• 1969: Jan Tinbergen, chair of the Committee for Development Planning, for his pioneering role in the development of economics into a science, contributions to development planning, and intensive research designed to assist the poor countries of the world

• 1973: Wassily Leontief, member of a UN expert group on disarmament and development, for his pioneering work on input-output systems and the application of this knowledge to important economic problems

• 1974: Gunnar Myrdal, executive secretary (1947–1956) of the UN's ECE, for his pioneering work on the theory of money and economic fluctuations and his analysis of the interdependence of social, economic, and institutional phenomena and extensive research into the problems of developing countries

• 1977: James Meade, staff member of ECE, for his work on international trade and capital movements

• 1979: W. Arthur Lewis, member of the 1950 UN Committee on Development Strategy and later deputy administrator of the UNDP, and Theodore W. Schultz, member of the 1950 UN committee, for their research on economic development that focused on the problems of developing countries

• 1980: Lawrence R. Klein, who pioneered the UN's LINK econometric model of the global economy, for his econometric models and his application of them to analysis of economic fluctuations and policies

• 1984: Richard Stone, chair of a committee of experts convened by the UN Statistical Office that elaborated the UN System of National Accounts (with James Meade), for his fundamental contributions to the development of systems of national accounts

• 1998: Amartya Sen, who wrote several publications for the ILO World Employment Programme in the 1970s and for the UNDP's Human Development Report in the 1990s (among many other UN involvements), for his contributions to welfare economics

Nature of Ideas

What do we mean by ideas? Let us elaborate briefly what we wrote at the out-set of the project. We define ideas as notions and beliefs held by individuals, NGOs, or governments that influence their attitudes and actions—in this case, toward economic and social development. The ideas mostly arise as the result of social interactions among individuals or groups within any of the three UNs or between them. Often the ideas take more definite shape over time, some-times as the result of research, often through debate or challenge, sometimes through efforts to turn ideas into policy.

Three types of ideas or beliefs—positive, normative, and causal—are worth distinguishing at the outset. Positive ideas or beliefs are those that rely on hard evidence, are open to challenge, and are verifiable, at least in principle. That DAC countries spent 0.33 percent of their gross national income (GNI) on development assistance in 2005 is an example of positivism. Normative ideas are beliefs about what the world *should* look like. That DAC countries ought to implement the UN target of spending 0.7 percent of their GNI on develop-ment assistance or that there should be a more equitable allocation of world resources are examples. Causal ideas, on the other hand, are more operational notions—often about what strategy will have what result or what tactics will achieve a desirable outcome. These ideas are often less verifiable and often have a normative element. At the UN, causal ideas often take an operational form—for instance, the calculation that over 0.5 percent of GNI will be needed as offi-cial development assistance (ODA) to support the Millennium Development Goals. Causal ideas can therefore be specific, but they usually are much less than full-blown theories.[9] For example, if we were to begin with the sweeping ethical proposition that the world should be more just, then the idea of a more equitable allocation of resources can be both a normative idea as well as a causal idea designed to improve international justice.

The recent research about the role of ideas that informs this project can be grouped into three broad categories. The first, institutionalism, is concerned with how organizations shape the policy preferences of their members. Exam-ples include Judith Goldstein's and Robert Keohane's analyses of foreign policy and Kathryn Sikkink's analysis of developmentalism in Latin America.[10] Ideas can be particularly important to the policymaking process during periods of upheaval. In thinking about the end of World War II, the Cold War, or post–September 11th challenges, for instance, ideas provide a conceptual road map that can be used to understand changing preferences and definitions of vital interests of state and nonstate actors alike. This approach helps us situate the dynamics at work among ideas, multilateral institutions, and national policies.

It also enables us to begin thinking about how the UN influences elite and popular images as well as how opinion-makers affect the world organization.

The second category focuses on the interactions of various groups, including, for example, Peter Haas's epistemic communities, Peter Hall's work on
analyzing the impact of Keynesian economists, and Ernst B. Haas's work on
knowledge and power as well as more recent work by Kathryn Sikkink on
transnational networks of activists.[11] This body of scholarly research examines
the role of intellectuals in creating ideas, the role of technical experts in diffus-
ing ideas and making them more concrete and scientifically grounded, and the
role of all sorts of people in influencing the positions adopted by a wide range
of actors, including and especially governments.

Networks of knowledgeable experts influence a broad spectrum of international politics through their ability to interact with policymakers irrespective
of location and national boundaries. Researchers working on HIV/AIDS or climate change can have an impact on policy by clarifying an issue so a decision
maker can explore which policy is in the interests of his or her administration.
Researchers also can help frame the debate on a particular issue, thus narrowing the acceptable range of bargaining positions in international negotiations.
They can introduce standards for action. These networks can help provide justifications for alternatives, and they often build national or international coalitions to support chosen policies and advocate for change. In many ways this
approach borrows from Thomas Kuhn's often-cited work on the nature of scientific revolutions.[12]

The third category that informs our work consists of the contributions
of so-called constructivists such as Alexander Wendt and John G. Ruggie.[13]
These analysts seek to determine the potential for individuals, governments,
and international institutions to be active agents for change rather than robots
whose behavior reflects the status quo. The critical approaches of those who are
influenced by the Italian school of Marxism, such as Robert Cox and his followers, are also pertinent.[14] These researchers view the work of all organizations
and their ideologies, including the United Nations, as heavily determined by
material conditions.

The UN system has spawned or nurtured a large number of ideas that have
both called into question the conventional wisdom and reinforced it. Indeed,
how to define what passes for "conventional" at a particular point in time in certain parts of the world is part of the puzzle that we have only begun to address.

As we argued at the outset, ideas and concepts have clearly been a driving force
in many areas of human progress, and they are arguably the most important legacy of the United Nations. They have set past, present, and future international
agendas for the economic and social arenas. Thus, the lack of attention to the
UN's role in generating or nurturing ideas is perplexing. As Oxford University

political economist Ngaire Woods summarized: "In short, ideas, whether eco-nomic or not, have been left out of analyses of international relations."[15] Many political scientists, especially analysts of international political economy and economic historians, are rediscovering the role of ideas in international poli-cymaking. We say *rediscovering* because the study of ideas, although relatively new in analyses of international politics and organizations, is the standard bill of fare for historians, philosophers, students of literature, and economists.

Five questions typically circulate around ideas, as we argued in *Ahead of the Curve*.[16] Which comes first, the idea or policy? Most approaches do not explain the sources of ideas, just their effects. They rarely explain how ideas emerge or change, with the exception of approaches that point to technological inno-vations. When analysts ignore where ideas come from and how they change, cause and effect are uncertain. Do ideas shape policy? Or does policy push existing ideas forward and perhaps even generate new ideas that may emerge in response to that policy or action? Do ideas serve, after the fact, as a convenient justification for a policy or a decision? Quentin Skinner raised these issues thirty years ago: "The social context, it is said, helps to cause the formation and change of ideas; but the ideas in turn help to cause the formation and change of the social context. Thus the historian ends up presenting himself with nothing better that the time-honored puzzle about the chicken and the egg."[17]

Are ideas mere products or do they have a life of their own? Our volumes have tried to trace the trajectory of ideas within the UN and examine how indi-vidual leadership, coalitions, and national and bureaucratic rivalries within the UN have generated, nurtured, distorted, and implemented particular ideas. At the same time, we have tried to discern how ideas, in and of themselves, have helped shape policy outcomes at the United Nations.

Should an idea be analyzed in light of the historical and social context within which it emerged and evolved, or can it be understood on its own, without ref-erence to context? We are partisans of the former school and thus assume that economic and social ideas at the UN cannot be properly understood when they are divorced from their historical and social context. The birth and survival of ideas in the UN—or their death and suppression—invariably reflect events and are contingent upon politics and the world economy.

At what point in its life or in which of its many possible incarnations should one begin to study an idea? We can only agree with Woods that "very few ideas are very new."[18] Frederick Cooper and Randall Packard point out that postwar modernization theory sought to transform individuals from "superstitious and status-oriented beings to rational and achievement-oriented beings."[19] But the idea of creating a new person is older than development theory. It could be traced back to the efforts of the earliest missionaries, the Enlightenment, Karl Marx, or, for that matter, to God with Adam's rib in the Garden of Eden.

A related issue concerns ownership. Observers are still arguing about whether Alexander Graham Bell deserves credit for inventing the telephone because so many others were toying with the same idea at about the same time. The difficulty of identifying which single individual or institution is responsible for the creation of an idea is manifest in the overlapping processes of multilateral affairs. An idea often evolves and ownership becomes more widely shared through group processes, which are particularly pertinent in multilateral institutions, where a multiplicity of geographic and other groupings is the only way of doing business and widespread ownership is indeed a goal of deliberations.[20] Hence, we have not undertaken the type of historical analysis pioneered by A. O. Lovejoy, who sought to trace an idea "through all the provinces of history in which it appears."[21] Rather, we have mostly picked up an idea at the time when it intersected with the United Nations. And even within the world organization's history, there are relevant antecedents that can only be treated cursorily.

Finally, it is necessary to not only assess the ideas themselves but also the influence of the carriers of ideas.[22] There is little consensus about which are more influential—in our case, whether the ideas or the key individuals in UN organizations or forums carried greater weight. This is particularly relevant for our treatment of experts and the Third UN. It can be argued that the more influential the members of an expert group or the greater their access to governmental policymakers, the greater the odds that their ideas will be adopted, irrespective of their inherent value. Ideas presuppose agents, and at the UN ideas cannot be divorced from agency, which is one reason we documented through oral histories the role of individuals in the evolution of international economic and social development.

In short, we have not sought to be philosophers or lawyers of ideas. We have not worried about the copyright for any particular idea, which is almost always futile. And thus, we have not dwelled on the precise origins of "UN ideas." For us, the important fact is that an idea exists and has entered into the arena of the United Nations. The project's bottom line has consisted of analyzing the evolution and impact of key ideas within the UN, especially how international economic and social concepts have been nurtured, refined, and applied under UN auspices.

Assessing the Impact of UN Ideas

From the beginning, the UN Intellectual History Project has examined how UN ideas affect actions and results in the real world—in other words, how and when they have made an impact and how and when they have fallen flat. As Lady Jackson, the late Barbara Ward, reminded us, "Ideas are the prime movers of history. Revolutions usually begin with ideas."[23]

We return to the propositions we put forward earlier. Ideas lead to action in many ways but never through a simple linear process that begins with the creation of a new idea and moves to dissemination of the idea to decisions by policymakers to implementation and on to impact and results. The process in most cases is very different, whether the idea is the discovery of new research findings about nutrition, the adoption of new thinking about international need for debt relief, or the growing awareness of the special problems of least-developed countries.

In our first volume, *Ahead of the Curve,* we identified four ways that ideas have impact. These are modified a bit here so we can focus more sharply on the processes by which ideas exert influence. Ideas:

- Change the ways that issues are perceived and the language used to describe them
- Frame agendas for action
- Alter the ways that key groups perceive their interests and thus alter the balance of forces pressing for action or resisting it
- Become embedded in an institution or institutions, which then adopt responsibility for carrying the idea forward and become a focus for accountability and monitoring

With respect to UN ideas, all four ways have usually been in operation, and our volumes have identified many examples where the UN has had an impact. The formulation of statistical norms and guidelines is one clear example. In *Quantifying the World,* Michael Ward traced the development in the early 1950s of the System of National Accounts (SNA), which provided the guidelines that even today enable and encourage countries around the world to calculate GNP and other core economic statistics on a standardized basis and, for better or worse, thus provide an economic snapshot of a country's economic performance. This has helped define agendas for economic policy and action in country after country, which in turn has created pressures to make better use of economic resources and calls from various quarters for more attention to social and other indicators. The SNA has been embedded in the work of the UN Statistical Commission (UNSC) and UNSO. Thus, in all four ways, the UN's early work on the SNA has maintained its impact for over fifty years. Ward concluded that "the creation of a universally acknowledged statistical system and of a general framework guiding the collection and compilation of data according to recognized standards, both internationally and nationally, has been one of the great and mostly unsung successes of the UN Organization."[24]

Another example is the UN's formulation and adoption of goals for development. Over almost half a century, the UN has debated, adopted, promoted,

supported, and monitored a succession of quantified and time-dated goals that have served as guidelines for economic and social development both nationally and internationally. In total, around fifty such goals have been adopted, the first being goals for expansion of education and acceleration of economic growth that were adopted at the beginning of the First Development Decade in the early 1960s. Later goals have covered reductions in child mortality, improvements in human welfare, moves toward sustainable and equitable development, and support for all of these efforts by the expansion of development assistance. The most recent are the MDGs for poverty reduction by the year 2015 that were adopted in 2000. They are probably the best known among all the goals, though they are in fact simply the most recent.

A review of performance shows that the goals have had considerable impact, probably more than most people realize. The idea of setting objectives is, of course, not new. But the idea of setting internationally agreed-upon targets as a means to foster economic and social development is a singular UN achievement. The results have generally been positive but mixed—far from full achievement but rarely total failures. A few, such as the goal in 1966 for the eradication of smallpox or the goal set in 1980 for a worldwide reduction of infant mortality rates and for increases in life expectancy, have recorded success—"complete achievement" in the case of smallpox eradication and "considerable achievement" in the other two.[25] Significant progress has been recorded for many other goals in many countries.

The most serious failures have been in Sub-Saharan Africa and the least-developed countries. The other weakest areas of performance have been, ironically, in levels of development aid among the developed countries. Except for Denmark, the Netherlands, Norway, and Sweden (and in the last few years, Luxembourg), developed countries have consistently failed to achieve the 0.7 target for concessional transfers to developing countries in general and have also fallen short of the specific targets for aid to the least-developed countries. The United States has never accepted that the target applies to it, though many of the U.S. population think that the government provides much more than this target level of aid. Actually, Washington is close to the bottom in terms of the percentage of GDP that OECD donors have devoted to foreign assistance.

Again we can assess the impact of UN ideas—in this case goal setting—by the four tests identified. Have the goals altered the ways development is perceived? Here the answer changes over time. The early goals for education, set at UNESCO meetings around the 1960s, were in part instances of preaching to the converted—countries newly independent or about to be independent that had already put demands for expanding access to education high on the political agenda. The UNESCO goals for rapid expansion at all levels did not so much shift perceptions of development as help give international legitimacy

to national ambitions that might otherwise have been treated (by the colonial powers) as unrealistic and even unjustified. The goals for economic expansion of the First Development Decade were certainly treated as overambitious when they were first set, even though, like the educational goals, in many countries they were exceeded.

But expectations about performance in the 1960s raised the stakes in later decades, and economic performance increasingly fell below the more ambitious economic targets. By the 1980s, UN economic goals were sidelined by the shift of economic power and influence to the Bretton Woods institutions, which introduced programs of structural adjustment and focused on economic and financial targets at the country level rather than on social outcomes. Given the disastrous declines in rates of economic growth and levels of economic performance that followed, it is impressive that considerable social progress was made in some areas of UN goals—in access to health care, clean water, and adequate sanitation and in reductions in rates of child mortality, for example—but not in others, such as access to education. These experiences, especially the failure of economic adjustment in the 1980s and early 1990s and the accusation that such policies were imposed from outside rather than adopted by the countries themselves, accounts in our view for the shift of developed countries and the Bretton Woods institutions in the late 1990s toward accepting outcome goals and the adoption of the MDGs in particular.

We have dealt with how UN goals have influenced the ways that development has been perceived and has influenced the national and international agenda for action. Goals have also served over the years as a focus for mobilizing interests, especially the interests of NGOs, and for generating pressures for action. This is clear with respect to the MDGs, but other goals have also served the same purpose: for instance, goals for expanding aid toward the 0.7 percent target, for debt forgiveness, and for priorities for women and children.

Nonetheless, it has become increasingly clear in reviewing the record that the generation and spread of ideas is not enough. Sometimes UN ideas have gained traction, but often they have spread with little effect. We have found a need to deepen our analysis from the ways ideas spread and are sustained to explore in more detail why some gain traction and others do not. Here we have drawn upon the work of Desmond McNeill. In the CANDID project, Morten Bøas and McNeill explored how ideas change and are changed as they move between international institutions. New ideas may spread, especially if they are gaining support from governments and the Third UN, but in doing so, the ideas are likely to be adapted and modified by the institutions into which they are moving so they fit existing priorities, programs of work, and paradigms. Students of bureaucracy will not be surprised at this. But as Bøas and McNeill show, the processes of adaptation, negation, and distortion of ideas to

make them fit existing agendas has often led to perceptions of change instead of bringing real transformation. The title of their research effort, "CANDID"—the Creation, Adoption, Negation and Distortion of Ideas in Development, summarizes the key elements of the process.[26]

We have also drawn on more recent work by McNeill to explore the factors that give some ideas clout while others largely remain on the sidelines.[27] We identify five such factors: the first four are international consensus and legitimacy; professional endorsement and interest; nongovernmental support; and financial backing. The fifth—and perhaps the most important for the longer run and certainly the most criticized in anti-UN circles—is the extent to which the UN organizations or institutions in which an idea is embedded take responsibility and initiatives for carrying the idea into action.

Robert Cox, who worked for the ILO for twenty-five years before moving to the academy to analyze international organizations, has suggested that the very existence of new institutions could challenge the rigidity of existing norms. "I guess the reason why new institutions are created," he states, "is that those people who feel that the new idea is important are doubtful that they are going to be able to put it into action through the existing institutions. It is the rigidity of existing institutions that leads to the idea that if you want to start something new, you have to create another institution." He went on to observe that "the hope of some people would be that by creating another institution, you can inject some part of that idea into the existing institutions—that they should play along with it. And they should be influenced by its existence and take account of it in their programs and work out collaborate relationships and so forth, which is sort of an ideal formula."[28]

In a number of ways, our overall approach resembles that of "regime" analysts like Stephen Krasner who explain the development of international cooperation and organizations as contributing to "principles, norms, rules, and decision-making procedures around which actor expectations converge in a given issue-area."[29] In short, international cooperation and stability are possible in an anarchic world—that is, without a world government.

When all five of our factors come together, ideas can gain clout. But in the UN, with its many members, this is rare indeed. Perhaps the main occasions were at the beginning, when the very idea of founding the organization gained consensus, stirred professional and nongovernmental interest, and received strong financial backing from the richest country in the world. At that juncture, the politics within deliberative bodies were less divisive. The Cold War was raging, but the West and (at the time) the supportive partners in Latin America were very much on the same page. Thereafter, the influx of newly independent states changed the dynamics, and the North-South divide rendered many ideas far more controversial.

The creation of the concept of GNP and the System of National Accounts described earlier is a case where Cold War divisions, though disruptive, were not enough to prevent or even slow action. The members of the Statistical Commission were mostly drawn from developed western countries, including all the directors.[30] The creative work drew heavily on some of the leading statisticians and economists of the time. Relatively little finance was required. Not surprisingly, the guidelines that the commission proposed matched the priorities of industrialized rather than developing countries and matched the priorities of market economies more easily than the nonmarket economies of the Soviet bloc, although UNSO published analyses on how comparisons could be made. Thus, backed by a level of international agreement that was tantamount to full consensus and professional and financial support, the proposed SNA moved ahead rapidly in most parts of the world. NGO support was not important at this stage.

Many other areas in which the UN has generated ideas have not had such backing, especially following the establishment of the Group of 77 in the lead-up to the first UNCTAD. This includes many and probably most of the UN ideas in the area of economic policy. Early UNCTAD work on trade policy, debt relief, and the formulation of targets for aid and the needs of the least-developed countries—work that extended over four decades or more—gained little clout, even though they were derived from careful and detailed analyses. The proposals eventually gained strong support from developing countries, although not at the outset because those not in the category not classified as least-developed often saw the categorization as a means to divide and conquer. The main developed countries distanced themselves from the issue. NGOs often provided support and have increasingly done so since the 1980s. But clout has been missing due to lack of support from two major quarters: financial backing from the main donor countries and (often) lack of support from mainstream professional economists.

The phenomenon of opposition to or weak support for UN ideas on economic and social policy from the mainstream of the economics profession requires more explanation. Many think of economics as the queen of the social sciences; economists are perceived as practitioners with robust theories that use ever-more-sophisticated econometric techniques to create evidence on which their ideas are based. Much of this reputation is justified. But on development matters—economic problems and policy issues from the perspective of developing countries—mainstream economics has mostly stuck to the tools and frames of neoliberal analysis. Outside this mainstream, there has been a significant and vocal professional minority, especially in developing countries and somewhat in Europe, sometimes economists working within structuralist

frames of economic analysis, sometimes social scientists working within other disciplines or multidisciplinary frames.

The Bretton Woods institutions mostly have worked within the mainstream, which many would attribute to the way the approaches and policy conclusions of mainstream economics largely match the interests of developed countries. The UN has mostly approached development issues from outside mainstream economics, in part reflecting the political priorities and broader interests of developing countries. Another important factor has been the great importance of non-economic professions in many organizations of the UN—the medical professions in the WHO, agriculturalists in the Food and Agriculture Organization (FAO), labor experts in the ILO, a diversity of educationalists and other scientists in UNESCO, and professionals of a wide variety of backgrounds and country experience in UNICEF, the WFP, and the UNDP. This diversity has meant that the UN has from the beginning approached development from much wider perspectives than the economists working for the Bretton Woods institutions.

Conclusion

The skills of all these different professions have challenged received wisdom and improved the results of international policy in the development arena. And sometimes, as with the UN's early economic work on the need for concessional finance for poorer countries and the proposals for a Special United Nations Fund for Economic Development (SUNFED), the world organization's work outside of the mainstream persuaded the more orthodox economists at the World Bank or the International Monetary Fund to think again after a few years. But on other occasions, as with the "adjustment with a human face" that UNICEF and the ECA called for in the 1980s, the Bretton Woods institutions have adopted the ideas only after fitting them within existing thinking, thus making far fewer changes to policies and practice than the UN had been calling for.[31]

Now to the nine ideas that have shaped the world.[32]

PART 2
United Nations Ideas Changing the World

Human history is not only a history of cruelty, but also of compassion, sacrifice, courage, kindness. What we choose to emphasize in this complex history will define our lives. If we can see only the worst, it destroys our capacity to do something. If we remember those times and places—and there are many—where people have behaved magnificently, this gives us the energy to act and at least the possibility of sending this spinning top of a world in a different direction.

—Howard Zinn, 1995

3. Human Rights for All
From Aspiration to Implementation

Although the Universal Declaration of 1948 is the brightest jewel in the crown of UN contributions to human rights, it was neither the first nor the only precious stone in an illustrious and gem-studded diadem. Bertrand Ramcharan states that in San Francisco in 1945 there was "a groundswell of sentiment that the 'new world order' should be built on a foundation of human rights."[1] Civil society organizations such as the World Jewish Congress, the Christian ecumenical movement, the American Law Institute, and leading academics—the Third UN—were all pressuring delegates and developing blueprints for an international bill of human rights.

Governments, especially the United States, the Soviet Union, the United Kingdom, and Latin American states, were supportive. In fact, the Dumbarton Oaks proposal, which was prepared by the big three in 1944, had stated that the new organization should promote respect for human rights and fundamental freedoms. All this was in sharp contrast to the League of Nations, which did not include any explicit reference to human rights in its founding covenant. The League was exclusively preoccupied with relationships between rather than within states.

In their UNIHP volume *Human Rights at the UN: The Political History of Universal Justice,* Roger Normand and Sarah Zaidi bring out the positives as well as the negatives of the extraordinary story.[2] They comment: "The speed with which human rights has penetrated every corner of the globe is astounding. Compared to human rights, no other system of universal values has spread so far so fast." In

his foreword to the volume, Richard Falk underlines the point: "Among the most improbable developments of the previous hundred years or so is the spectacular rise of human rights to a position of prominence in world politics. This rise cuts across the grain of both the structure of world order and the 'realist' outlook of most political leaders acting on behalf of sovereign states."[3]

At the same time, Normand and Zaidi also emphasize that the gap between values espoused and rights implemented remains large in every country, even though it has narrowed over the life of the United Nations. In spite of this progress, the absence of adequate mechanisms for implementing human rights remains most serious and contrasts sharply with the more powerful legal tools that exist to enforce international economic law. This asymmetry in enforcement capacity is particularly true since the emergence of the World Trade Organization (WTO) in 1995. Human rights in the world today serve "as both a source of universal values and an arena of ideological warfare."[4] Rhetoric is stronger than the machinery of implementation. This arrangement was by design, not chance. At the outset, Washington and London wished to avoid an activist system, and later when the United Kingdom decided that it could support limited types of intervention, Moscow joined Washington in ensuring that implementation was secondary. Race relations, colonial possessions, and gulags were all factors in this priority.

While not discounting the evidence throughout this chapter about the lack of compliance with lofty norms, nonetheless the importance of ideas shines through. For instance, former senior UN official and French ambassador Stéphane Hessel argues that changes in language are important even if they do not get translated immediately into action: "It is useful to have words, even if they are not followed by deeds. . . . There is a tendency . . . to say that it is better not to have words if you don't have deeds. . . . People who are not capable of having their words followed by deeds, should they therefore shut up?" Hessel goes on to answer his own question: "I would say the opposite. I would say that words carrying ideas have a long-lasting effect. If it had not been for people like Socrates or Hegel, we would not have the kind of view of the possible future of humanity that we do have. Therefore, it is good to have the Universal Declaration."[5]

Human Rights as Mobilization

In the early days of World War II, the Allies used references to human rights to mobilize support for the war effort. In 1939, Churchill proclaimed that the war was being fought "to establish, on impregnable rocks, the rights of the individual." In a speech to Congress in January 1941, Roosevelt announced his vision of security based on four freedoms—"freedom of speech and expression,

Box 3.1. Three Early Giants of Human Rights: Eleanor Roosevelt, René Cassin, John Humphrey

Though pressure from the Third UN has often forced the pace, strong leadership within the UN from the First and the Second UN has been critical for securing agreement, for providing professional guidance, and for drafting human rights documents with the highest professional skills and in ways that ensure strong legal and philosophical foundations.

Eleanor Roosevelt, widow of the four-time U.S. president and an impressive leader in her own right, chaired the negotiations of the Universal Declaration of Human Rights and took a most active role. Already known as an articulate advocate for human rights whose regular newspaper columns reached millions weekly, Mrs. Roosevelt used her skills to the fullest, albeit often to push for interpretations in line with U.S. policy rather than "as an independent champion of human rights."[1] But many have doubted whether the Universal Declaration would ever have been agreed upon without her forceful chairing, let alone with unanimity.

René Cassin, the foremost legal intellectual on the Commission on Human Rights, contributed much to the draft and discussions during 1947 and 1948. As a representative from France and a person of international stature, his experience derived from long experience and early work within the League of Nations. Cassin was a strong proponent for including measures of implementation of the Universal Declaration, a position opposed at the time by both Washington and Moscow on the grounds that such measures would imply interference in the domestic policies of countries. It took until 1993, almost fifty years, for an Office and a High Commissioner for Human Rights to be created at the World Conference on Human Rights in Vienna.

John P. Humphrey from Canada, the third key figure, is said to have produced the first draft of the Universal Declaration. He was director of the UN's Human Rights Division from 1946 to 1966, and during his career with the world organization he oversaw the implementation of sixty-seven international conventions and the constitutions of dozens of countries. He also was director of the International League of Human Rights and served as a member of Canada's Royal Commission on the Status of Women.

With the creation of the post of high commissioner for human rights in 1993, the opportunity was opened for outspoken leadership. To date, five high commissioners have held the post: José Ayala Lasso (Ecuador), Mary Robinson (Ireland), Sergio Vieira de Mello (Brazil), Louise Arbour (Canada), and Navanethem Pillay (South Africa).

1. Roger Normand and Sarah Zaidi, *Human Rights at the UN: The Political History of Universal Justice* (Bloomington: Indiana University Press, 2008), 148–150.

freedom of worship, freedom from want, and freedom from fear." Although human rights appeared in background documents to the Atlantic Charter of 1941, the first time human rights were mentioned formally was in the preamble of the Declaration of the United Nations in January 1942. The Allied Powers had used human rights ideas to mobilize support for the ideological war to defeat the evil enemy, but it was by no means their intention to make enforceable human rights part of the agenda of the new international organization. Nor did human rights figure at all prominently in the Dumbarton Oaks Charter, which produced only a vague reference to how the world organization should "facilitate solutions of international economic, social and humanitarian problems and promote respect for human rights and fundamental freedoms."[6]

This is where the Third UN played a major role, especially during the months between October 1944, when the Dumbarton Oaks meetings ended, and April 1945, when the San Francisco conference began. Civil society groups and individuals who had been agitating for human rights initially viewed the Dumbarton Oaks proposals as a fiasco and a betrayal and began to mobilize against the plans for the new international organization, expressing their opposition in conferences, media appeals, and direct lobbying. This stimulated a rapid response from the U.S. State Department in the form of a massive public relations campaign led by Archibald MacLeish and Adlai Stevenson to win support for the new world body and to avoid the debacle of nonratification by Congress that befell the League of Nations. It reached out to members of civil society and worked ever more closely with them, promising to develop strategies to better incorporate human rights into the emerging organization. As part of the effort to garner civil society support within the United States, the U.S. delegation to San Francisco also agreed to issue an open invitation for NGOs to attend the conference as observers. Roosevelt proposed that selected groups be invited and given semi-official status as consultants to the delegation, which led to forty-two such groups that provided 100 civil society consultants. Thus a precipitous downswing was turned into a sudden upswing of popular support, including high levels of professional support.[7]

Over 5,000 people attended the conference: 850 delegates, 2,600 members of the media, 1,000 conference staff, 300 security officers, and 120 translators. In addition, a vast unofficial presence blanketed the conference that included consultants and lobbyists who were mostly from the United States but included a few charismatic individuals from Asian and African colonies. This group formed the second largest contingent at the founding of the UN, around 1,500 persons. The forty-two civil society groups selected by the United States included only one, the National Association for the Advancement of Colored People (NAACP), that emphasized issues of racial inequality.[8]

The pressure from these groups helped ensure that the UN Charter included several provisions with dramatic human rights implications. These were to have long-term significance: the principle of self-determination for states; the principle of nondiscrimination on the grounds of race, sex, language, or religion among nations or peoples; the pursuit of international cooperation to promote human rights for all people; and universal respect for and observance of human rights and fundamental freedoms accompanied by obligations of member states to support measures to achieve these goals, as set out in articles 55 and 56 of the Charter. Article 68 called for the creation of a Commission on Human Rights (CHR) as an organ of ECOSOC. Once established, this commission was to consider the various proposals that had been submitted for an international bill of human rights.

However, the lofty words and sentiments about human rights had a catch. The major powers remained cautious and saw human rights mainly as aspirations. They wanted the UN to promote human rights but not actually to protect human beings. Enforcement was complicated when the human rights covenants were split into two separate agreements, one on civil and political rights and a second on social and economic rights. It was also easier to see how something like the right to assembly would be determined but far more difficult to think about the right to access to food. Moreover, measures of implementation—the third component of the vision of the proposed international bill of rights—was postponed *sine die*. Britain had its colonies, where most citizens had no vote and other rights were denied. The Soviet Union had its widespread repression. And in the United States, blacks still had no vote and segregation and racial discrimination were widespread. In San Francisco, seven white waitresses walked out of a hotel, refusing to serve black delegates, and black waiters refused to serve Indians traveling by train to San Francisco until whites had finished their meals.

Nonetheless, the extent to which human rights would grow as well as the link between promotion and implementation were underestimated. Eleanor Roosevelt correctly predicted that "a curious grapevine" would spread the ideas contained in the declaration far and wide.[9] The rest of the chapter examines that organic growth and the fertilizer applied by various parts of the three United Nations.

The Universal Declaration

The Commission on Human Rights met for the first time in early 1947 in a mood of excitement that soon gave way to more sober debate behind closed doors. The meetings of the commission were chaired by the highly venerated Eleanor Roosevelt, an elegant figure of world renown and widow of the former

American president. But Mrs. Roosevelt made it very clear in her leadership (and in her statement before the General Assembly in December 1948) that the declaration was not to be a treaty but a declaration of general principles of human rights and freedoms to serve as a common standard of achievement for all peoples of all countries. She was probably truer to Washington's position and to what was politically palatable in the United States than to her own true feelings. The risks and dangers of moving along the difficult road from rhetoric to implementation had been identified—and a roadblock had been erected; there would be a declaration rather than a legally binding treaty.

In addition to domestic concerns, the Cold War also played its part. The Soviet Union was in favor of economic and social rights but against civil and political rights. The United States was in favor of civil and political rights but against economic and social rights. This led, in the words of Normand and Zaidi, to the declaration becoming the central panel of a triptych. The other two panels were to be the International Covenant on Civil and Political Rights and the International Covenant on Economic, Social and Cultural Rights, on the one hand, and measures of implementation, on the other hand. It took eighteen years for the two covenants to be drafted and approved in 1966 and another decade for them to receive enough ratifications to come into force. The third panel of implementation remains unpainted even if numerous preliminary sketches have been made.

There were deep points of controversy all along the way, with different views among the primary groups of states: the western bloc, led by the United States and the United Kingdom; the communist countries, led by the Soviet Union; and Third World countries. The western position was that only "immediately realizable and justiciable rights—those rights capable of being adjudicated and enforced by domestic courts through traditional legal process" should be included. But Normand and Zaidi point out that the integrity of this position "was undermined by consistent Anglo-American efforts to deny enforcement measures and limit the jurisdiction even of civil and political rights in the colonial and federal contexts." The Soviet Union championed economic and social rights, minority rights, and the right of self-determination, but only through enhancing the government's authority in these areas. "On the issue of international supervision and enforcement, the Soviets were equally if not more intransigent than the Western powers." Third World countries "generally did not act as a monolithic group, although they tended to support the interdependence of all human rights and oppose the superpower alliance against meaningful implementation."[10]

Virendra Dayal, who served in several UN posts over three decades including as chef de cabinet for two Secretaries-General before heading up an Indian

human rights NGO, points to the evolution of human rights discourse as having implications for future ideamongers: "If you take, for instance, the ideas on human rights, there you can hardly say that the timing was perfect, and nor could you say that there was a great deal of packaging that was done. In fact, the ideas managed to survive in spite of the bad timing, and in spite of the third-rate packaging. They survived in spite of the Cold War and the apprehensions they caused among despotic regimes the world over." Why was this the case? "Because the ideas themselves were so remarkable, we have a body of normative law the likes of which the world has never seen before in respect of how human beings should be treated."[11]

Normative Striving

In spite of these controversies, the relatively slow progress with the covenants, and the lack of progress with regard to implementation measures, the record of human rights within the UN is "a story of striving."[12] And in many specific normative areas, progress was made. In 1948 alone, states approved the Convention on the Prevention and Punishment of the Crime of Genocide one day before doing the same for the Universal Declaration of Human Rights. Whatever the difficulties, we are now the inheritors of great normative human rights instruments that reflect striving within the UN system. Pride of place belongs to the Universal Declaration of Human Rights, the International Covenant on Civil and Political Rights, and the International Covenant on Economic, Social and Cultural Rights. But in addition, those early years eventually led to the conventions against racial discrimination, against torture, on the rights of the child, on the elimination of discrimination against women, and on the rights of migrant workers and their families. The covenants and the five conventions are widely ratified; the convention on the rights of the child is subscribed to by virtually all states. The convention on the rights of migrant workers and their families is the newest and thus the least ratified.

It is worth concentrating for a moment on the 1970s and 1980s, when dramatic progress took place as various Third UN groups unleashed their energies. The World Conference of the International Women's Year held in Mexico in 1975 was a major occasion. It was "tumultuous and ground-breaking" in bringing global attention to a multitude of issues concerning women and gender raised by the 8,000 or more people who attended the conference and the NGO parallel forum.[13] Though there were contentious divisions between developing countries that wanted to focus on economic and political equality in the context of the New International Economic Order and western states that argued that gender-based discrimination was the issue, the Mexico City gathering marked

a turning point for women's rights. The result was the Convention on the Elimi-nation of All Forms of Discrimination against Women (CEDAW), which the UN adopted in 1981.

In addition, states took several steps with long-term impact: 1975 was declared to be International Women's Year and 1976–1985 the UN Decade for Women; a fourteen-point list of goals to be achieved within five years was agreed upon; and, most important of all, delegates returned home inspired by the confer-ence and committed to mobilizing to make women's rights a reality, country by country. This was a powerful example of the Third UN mobilizing for action to implement human rights with a global momentum reinforced by later world women's conferences in Copenhagen and Nairobi and culminating in Beijing in 1995. At the time of writing, CEDAW has been ratified by 185 states. This story figures prominently in Devaki Jain's contribution to our series, *Women, Development, and the UN: A Sixty-Year Quest for Equality and Justice.*[14]

A second major example of the Third UN giving life to human rights came soon after, when nongovernmental organizations mobilized effectively for the rights of the child. In 1959, states adopted a ten-point Declaration on the Rights of the Child. Almost twenty years later, the Polish government sent the Com-mission on Human Rights a proposal to replace the declaration with a con-vention as one of the initiatives for celebrating 1979, the Year of the Child. In 1989, the General Assembly adopted the Convention on the Rights of the Child (CRC). In less than a year, the CRC received the forty endorsements necessary for the convention to come into force, and it quickly became the most ratified of all conventions. Today, 193 states, all but two countries (Somalia and the United States), have ratified the CRC. This impressive support is mitigated by reservations by one-third of the signatory states that have limited the scope of their obligations. Nonetheless, the speed and the scale of ratifications is a both a measure of support and an indication of the extent to which the Third UN, when mobilized, can achieve results.

The Declaration on the Right to Development

In sharp contrast to CEDAW and the Convention on the Rights of the Child, the Declaration on the Right to Development, adopted by the UN General Assembly in 1986, continues to be mired in controversy. It was first conceived in the 1970s, when developing countries were pushing for a NIEO. After sev-eral years of debate, the Commission on Human Rights created a fifteen-mem-ber working group, which met for five years and involved long and tortuous negotiations, making it one of the costliest undertakings of the commission at the time. In 1985, the working group presented its draft declaration, which the

General Assembly adopted with a vote of 146 to 1 (the United States being the sole vote against). Eight countries abstained (seven developed countries and Israel).[15]

The Declaration on the Right to Development introduced two new elements, each of which was highly controversial. First, in the eyes of supporters, it corrected the overly individualistic bias of the human rights tradition at the UN by introducing the idea of the collective rights of states to economic self-determination—what has become known as "third generation" rights to accompany the first (civil and political) and second (economic and social) generations of rights. The Universal Declaration had finessed this issue by stating in Article 28 that "everyone is entitled to a social and international order in which the rights and freedoms set forth in this Declaration can be fully realized." This referred to the rights of individuals, not states. In contrast, the Declaration on the Right to Development referred explicitly to the duties of states in Article 3:

> States have the duty to co-operate with each other in ensuring development and eliminating obstacles to development. States should realize their rights and fulfil their duties in such a manner as to promote a new international economic order on sovereign equality, interdependence, mutual interest and co-operation among all States, as well as to encourage the observance and realization of human rights.

Second, it established the idea of the collective rights of a group—a people or nation or an ethnic, linguistic, or geographical group—as long as it was possible to define an obligation and possible for a duty holder to fulfill them. The controversies did not simply die with the adoption of the Declaration on the Right to Development. A number of developed-country governments expressed strong reservations at the time of adoption, and the U.S. representative declared bluntly that "the view that States had the right to development was unacceptable."[16] Although opponents saw the right to development as a potentially revolutionary concept with many destructive implications, its defenders saw it as having done little more than synthesize strands of human rights with strands of development. Philip Alston, a distinguished expert on human rights, went so far as to describe the debates as empty, "little more than an exercise in shadow boxing."[17]

The High Commissioner for Human Rights

In the 1990s, member states took steps to strengthen implementation mechanisms for human rights. In 1993—forty-five years after the approval of the

Universal Declaration of Human Rights and twenty-five years after a review conference in Teheran—the World Conference on Human Rights was held in Vienna, the third in a series of high-level UN conferences in that decade. One hundred and seventy-one governments attended along with 2,000 NGO representatives, small in relation to the numbers attending earlier conferences on women's rights and the environment but important as a demonstration of growing public interest and commitment. The conference agreed upon some important follow-up mechanisms: the creation of a post for a high commissioner for human rights, the fusion of the Centre for Human Rights and the Commission on Human Rights, increased cooperation and further integration of objectives and goals between the Commission on the Status of Women and other UN bodies, and a five-year review of the implementation of the Vienna Declaration.

The creation of the Office of the High Commissioner for Human Rights was probably the most important action taken at a conference that veered between "Nightmare and Noble Dream."[18] The idea of a high commissioner for human rights (then with the title of attorney general) had been proposed as early as 1947 by René Cassin.[19] Various governments and various nongovernmental organizations had kept the proposal alive and submitted drafts over the following forty-six years, though never succeeding in getting the proposal accepted. In 1992, a large conference of human rights experts and activists meeting in Amsterdam agreed on the need for a new office headed by a high-level UN official to respond promptly and effectively to serious violations of human rights (including disappearances and political killings) and to become more generally a focal point for UN action on human rights. Amnesty International promoted the idea vigorously and made it the centerpiece of its proposals to the World Conference on Human Rights. At the eleventh hour the proposal for the creation of a high commissioner on human rights was adopted, though as a recommendation that the General Assembly should consider establishing the post at its next session.[20]

Even the next stage was far from easy. The General Assembly set up an informal working group as part of its Third Committee, which kept no records and allowed no press and, in the final stage, excluded NGOs from meetings. Such was the sensitivity of the topic among governments and the sharp differences over such issues as conditionality, fact-finding powers, and whether the high commissioner was to "recognize the importance of promoting a balanced and sustainable development for all people without conditions." Conditionality and fact-finding raised great suspicions among the developing countries, and the fact-finding clause was totally unacceptable to the West.

Nonetheless, agreement on the post of high commissioner was a remarkable

achievement. The post was to be filled by "a person of high moral standing and personal integrity" with "expertise in the field of human rights and the general knowledge and understanding of diverse cultures necessary for impartial, objective, non-selective and effective performance of the duties" of the post. Sean McBride, the founder of Amnesty International and at the time the secretary-general of the International Commission of Jurists, led the charge by NGOs that kept confronting the conservatism of governments.[21]

Equally important, the General Assembly reached agreement during its forty-eighth session on some key issues relating to the work by the high commissioner: the right to development was reaffirmed as universal and inalienable, fundamental to the rights of the human person. All human rights should be given the same emphasis. The recommendations of the Vienna Declaration should be implemented by governments and the UN "in cooperation with nongovernmental organizations." And finally, "The promotion and protection of all human rights is a legitimate concern of the international community."[22]

In short, an institution within the UN with high-level and visible leadership was established in 1993 to take a more active approach to implementing human rights. Certainly this creation gave a boost to the Commission on Human Rights, which began notably with the term in office of Mary Robinson (1997–2002), the second high commissioner and former president of Ireland. During the tenure of outspoken Canadian prosecutor Louise Arbour (2004–2008), the commission's budget expanded and its international presence grew. However, the sharp differences between countries on basic issues of human rights, especially between the major powers and some of the more radical developing countries, continue to limit the possibilities for action in many areas.

The Third UN was extremely active in advocating for more robust implementation mechanisms. One of its leading members, Philip Alston, explained that institutional independence from politics was necessary for human rights implementation. "Authentic human rights fact-finding and monitoring cannot be integrated into other activities. . . . The UN system should address the need to vest a central coordinating role in relation to all human rights matters in a single entity."[23] After the end of the Cold War, it became easier to move ahead with the establishment of the high commissioner post; it had often been the Soviet Union that actively obstructed progress on implementation mechanisms.

Ramcharan identifies a number of priorities: preventing and forestalling gross violations of human rights; taking a leading role in the formulation of strategies and programs to combat discrimination; encouraging human rights education in schools and universities in every country; and working with others to strengthen national protection systems. The last strategy includes supporting a peer review process and improving "the system of special procedures—both

rapporteurs and working groups working against torture, arbitrary executions, disappearances, arbitrary detention, violence against women and children, and other blots on civilization."[24]

However, the central issue of implementation remains, and the two schools of thought in the human rights arena are still at loggerheads. One claims that the rights of the state always prevail over those of the individual, who has no rights beyond those granted by the state. The other school holds that every individual has certain inalienable rights that ought to be recognized as sacrosanct, even by the state. In addition, most states, even those with robust legal systems, indulge in a game of double standards. For their own country they recognize certain rights but they do not recognize the rights of others—perhaps they recognize the political and civil rights of others but not economic, social, or cultural ones. For other countries, states may use a rights argument selectively, depending on the politics involved in the issue at hand. Countries also argue—in the press if not in their courts—that their national system of rights is more robust and better founded than that of the UN, so international systems of inspection or reporting often have little relevance to them. These countries tend to feel that monitoring of human rights applies only to other countries.

The Human Rights Council

At the UN World Summit in September 2005, these differences came to a head. Prodded by Secretary-General Kofi Annan, the World Summit agreed to set up a Human Rights Council to replace the much-criticized Commission on Human Rights. The commission's performance was often scandalous in the eyes of its harshest critics. Its fifty-three elected members in 2005 included Sudan when that government was pursuing slow-motion genocide in Darfur. Zimbabwe was a member while its government was bulldozing the houses of 700,000 suspected opposition supporters and rounding up journalists and other critics. That China and Cuba played prominent roles and that Libya is a former chair of the CHR added to the litany of embarrassments. The Secretary-General appointed a new element of the Third UN, the High-level Panel on Threats, Challenges and Change (HLP), whose final report recognized "eroding credibility and professionalism" and said that "States have sought membership of the Commission not to strengthen human rights but to protect themselves against criticism or to criticize others."[25] However, its recommendation was truly counterintuitive: it recommended universal membership instead of "only" one-quarter of the members of the United Nations.

In his only serious dissent from the HLP's recommendations, Secretary-General Kofi Annan went out on a limb and proposed that member states

"replace the Commission on Human Rights with a smaller standing Human Rights Council."[26] The inconsistency between a policy of augmenting the number of seats on the Security Council while reducing the number on the main human rights body was apparently considered unimportant by most diplomats. In September 2005, leaders argued about whether the proposed human rights council might one day become a principal organ, like the Security Council and ECOSOC, that could review the human rights of all members, not just those selected for special scrutiny. Views on the ultimate size still ranged from a more businesslike twenty to thirty to up to fifty, virtually the same size as the Commission on Human Rights.

World leaders at the 2005 World Summit were unable to agree on the details of a replacement, but at least those present did "resolve to create a Human Rights Council" as a subsidiary of the General Assembly, which would decide its "mandate, modalities, functions, size, composition, membership, working methods and procedures."[27] The proposal that members be chosen by a two-thirds vote of the General Assembly was eliminated as well as the possibility that it might someday be transformed into a principal organ. Protracted negotiations continued until March 2006, when the General Assembly finally abolished the old commission and determined the mandate and composition of the new Human Rights Council (HRC). The first members were elected by the General Assembly in May 2006, and the 47-member council convened in Geneva for the first time in mid-June.

Some were disgruntled because the HRC's mandate was mainly to promote human rights and it had no clear protection role. Others were displeased because the number of members of the new council had decreased, while others thought the body was still too large. There was criticism that membership was subject to only a simple majority vote instead of the more stringent two-thirds requirement.[28]

Although it probably is premature to evaluate the council, the preeminence of sovereignty over human rights is already clear. The fact that the United States chose not to be a candidate was seen as an ominous sign, as was the election of such other human rights "champions" as China, Russia, Egypt, Saudi Arabia, Pakistan, and Cuba. For the first session in June 2006, hopes were high but results proved disappointing. Although the HRC condemned Israel nine times, it condemned no other country. Both Kofi Annan and Ban Ki-moon questioned why the HRC could single out Israel but ignore Sudan, North Korea, and Myanmar. According to Nico Schrijver, "During its first year the Council faced more confrontations and polarization than even its discredited predecessor was used to experiencing during hot seasons."[29] Meanwhile, Bertrand Ramcharan provides an understatement, specifying that most human rights proponents are

"looking to a leadership and spearheading orientation for the new Council, as well as protection and coordination roles."[30]

Universal periodic review—a thorough scrutiny of all HRC member states during their three-year terms—was designed to be a key feature of the new institution. In April 2008 the procedure for conducting reviews was decided: each country will be reviewed only once every four years. As terms are for three years and states are ineligible for reelection after two consecutive terms, a government facing an embarrassing review could simply choose not to run for office. Furthermore, the involvement of government-appointed experts on review teams is still being discussed—probably the last way to ensure an independent and objective evaluation. Moreover, the culture for debates has changed, with neither governments nor NGOs naming countries specifically during official sessions. In short, the HRC seems more intent on not offending a country under review than on addressing human rights abuses.

Special rapporteurs, or independent experts, have been used over the years to highlight the precarious human rights situation in particular countries or cross-cutting themes in a number of states (for instance, on summary executions or indigenous peoples). But the June 2007 session of the HRC voted to terminate the mandates for the special rapporteurs for Cuba and Belarus as part of an attack on transparency and a defense of sovereign prerogatives. Human Rights Watch, for one, expressed grave concern about the selection process for the forty-one human rights experts or working groups focusing on particular themes, such as violence against women and arbitrary detention, and on specific countries, including Myanmar and Sudan. In the future, these experts will be appointed from a published roster of "qualified candidates," but the selection process includes a disquieting decision-making role for a committee appointed by the council's regional groups, another recipe for sovereignty rather than human rights considerations to be the top priority.[31]

This discussion of human rights demonstrates how firmly the sovereign equality of states and respect for domestic jurisdiction is entrenched. The central principles and main tenets from the Peace of Westphalia continue to impede effective international action to protect human rights. How else can we explain across-the-board foot-dragging even in the midst of mass murder and forced displacement in Darfur? Russia and China's lack of enthusiasm to have outsiders consider problems in Chechnya or Xinjiang is no less in evidence than the reluctance of the United States to have the death penalty or Guantanamo reviewed. As former U.S. ambassador Morton Abramowitz and Pulitzer prizewinner Samantha Power quip, "Major and minor powers alike are committed only to stop killing that harms their national interests."[32]

Nonetheless, governments also agreed in September 2005 to strengthen the

Office of the High Commissioner for Human Rights. It is staffed by professionals who have, among other tasks, been establishing human rights centers in troubled countries such as Cambodia, Guatemala, and Nepal and assisting special rapporteurs working on such thematic issues as torture. The summit document calls for doubling the budget of the high commissioner's office to permit recruitment of "highly competent staff."[33] The OHCHR's regular budget for 2006–2007 did indeed increase by 18.2 percent from the previous biennium budget, revealing movement toward fulfilling summit goals. In addition, voluntary contributions increased by $17 million.[34] The expansion of independent professionals to improve UN monitoring efforts seems likely to be a reality by 2010.

Making more room for independent voices—whether from nongovernmental organizations or the secretariat—and challenging human rights violators would fundamentally alter the way that states view their prerogatives within the United Nations. Another challenge is to build an international consensus behind policies that address the underlying cause of human rights deprivations and that defend basic rights whenever they are threatened—a substantial redefinition of the meaning of sovereignty. In terms of preventing future disasters, the redefinition of sovereignty should also include addressing many of the root causes of deprivation, a development task.

No human rights idea has moved faster in the international normative arena than what is now commonly referred to as the "responsibility to protect," the title of the 2001 report from the International Commission on Intervention and State Sovereignty.[35] The basic idea of this "R2P" doctrine is that human beings can count for more than the sacrosanct sovereignty enshrined in Charter Article 2(7) with its emphasis on noninterference in domestic affairs. As Kofi Annan graphically stated in 1998, "State frontiers should no longer be seen as a watertight protection for war criminals or mass murderers."[36] The topic of "humanitarian intervention" was controversial throughout the 1990s as fragile or failed states became the common bill of fare for UN operations. R2P is treated in depth in chapter 10, but it is mentioned here because if the Human Rights Council was doing its job and forestalling crises, there would be less need to intervene militarily to protect human beings whose governments are unwilling or unable to protect them.

International Judicial Pursuit

The 1998 Rome Statute establishing the International Criminal Court (ICC) entered into force on 1 July 2002 with the requisite sixty ratifications. In 2008, there are 105 states members of the ICC allied in permanent efforts to prosecute individuals for genocide, crimes against humanity, war crimes, and crimes of

aggression. Over forty other countries have signed but not ratified, but a number of important states (including China and India) have done neither. Moreover, the United States and Israel have both done what previously had been an unthinkable legal step: in 2002, they revoked their signatures.

How did this precedent-setting organization get off the ground? Answering this question is especially important because of the deep hostility from the globe's most powerful country.[37] Many find it puzzling, except on ideological grounds, to understand Washington's move away from being the traditional standard-bearer of human rights. Indeed, the United States originally led the charge in the 1948 General Assembly to establish such a permanent court following large-scale atrocities against civilians in World War II and the war crimes trials in Nuremberg and Tokyo. It was also an active participant in negotiations leading up to the drafting of the Rome Statute in 1998.

The idea was again championed in the wake of the end of the Cold War, and it received an additional push after the establishment of the ad hoc international criminal tribunals for the former Yugoslavia and for Rwanda.[38] The scale of atrocities in Europe and in Africa demonstrated the need for international justice in the 1990s, just as they had earlier. And the shortcomings in the ad hoc tribunals (including high costs and inadequate evidence) suggested additional reasons to create a permanent court that could also act as a deterrent for future thugs.

By the middle of the 1990s, governments across the North and the South as well as NGOs had formed coalitions to lobby for the creation of what would become the ICC.[39] This "like-minded group"—unusually in this case of the First and Third UNs—began with a modest hope, namely to bring together a kind of consensus at a preliminary diplomatic conference in Rome in July 1997. When the official UN Conference of Plenipotentiaries on the Establishment of an International Criminal Court—known informally as the Rome conference—convened a year later, the 60-country like-minded group was a formidable and persuasive coalition that joined forces with the 700 members of the NGO Coalition for the International Criminal Court. The momentum was such that in 1998 the Rome conference itself—which was negotiated under the auspices of the United Nations—moved toward a decision in spite of strong opposition from several members of the permanent five (P-5). Afterward, the signature and ratification process also moved on a fast track.

The need to set aside cookie-cutter country groupings as a way of understanding the First UN becomes clear when examining efforts to generate a Convention on Landmines and create the ICC—two tough cases regarding the high politics of international security. Progress on a long-standing idea—namely, the rule of law instead of the rule of the jungle in international affairs—resulted

specifically from ignoring the theatrical and automatic ideological divisions of North and South within the First United Nations and taking maximum advantage of the mobilization powers of the Third United Nations. While no two campaigns are identical, the efforts to agree on the Convention on Landmines were similar to the efforts to create the ICC in that both used two tactical advances: the agreement to move ahead without universal support and a broad-based working coalition of NGOs and states from both the North and the South. Rather than digging the chasm deeper and wider, like-minded partners found a way to build bridges. As Teresa Whitfield notes, a host of small and "ad hoc, informal, issue-specific mini-coalitions of states or intergovernmental organizations that become involved in and provide support for resolving conflicts and implementing peace agreements" have "become a critical element of an incipient system of post–Cold War global security governance."[40]

Conclusion

The contradictions and imbalances between public expectations of justice and the determination of states to protect their sovereignty, between powerful states seeking geopolitical hegemony and others seeking the protection of international law, and between rhetorical promotion and lack of effective protection are still very much with us. It is hard to argue that the dramatic advance in commitments on paper has been matched by more than marginal improvements in human rights conditions. Serious questions should be asked. For example, is the almost exclusive emphasis on political freedom and progress of western states an accurate reflection of most people's core values? Has not the failure to seek the social and economic justice that was promised in the Universal Declaration and other instruments been a substantial shortcoming? And what about American "exceptionalism"—the U.S. practice of standing outside the global legal consensus on issues such as the ICC, climate change, and other important problems, not to mention the questionable onslaught on international humanitarian law as part of the war on terror?

All these remain painful examples of the long struggle to establish an international system of human rights. Nonetheless, looking back, it is extraordinary how far the UN system has come since 1945. Looking forward, it is only too clear from many egregious failures of rights in the world today how far there is to go.

4. Gender

From Eliminating Discrimination to Promoting Women's Rights and Empowerment

- **Early Landmarks**
- **Global Conferences**
- **The Significance of CEDAW**
- **Gender and Human Development**
- **Conclusion**

From a contemporary vantage point, it seems extraordinary that there were just four women among the 160 signatories to the UN's founding document at San Francisco in 1945. Two other women were present at the conference but were not signatories. However, this handful of women established a sound foundation for the UN by making sure that women's issues were included. As Devaki Jain asserts in *Women, Development, and the UN: A Sixty-Year Quest for Equality and Justice*, "The simple act of inserting the word 'women' in the text made sure that the principle of equality between the sexes was part of the founding ideas of the organization."[1]

Subsequently, the UN's ideas, language, and activities have fundamentally altered the situation of women in country after country, especially through its promotion of human rights and the mobilizing influence of the four global women's conferences held in Mexico, Copenhagen, Nairobi, and Beijing between 1975 and 1995. These raised awareness, spread ideas, built confidence, and created alliances that changed gender politics and policy worldwide. In turn, the conferences—and the women participating in them—also changed the structure and attitudes of the UN, providing the mandates for CEDAW, UNIFEM, and INSTRAW (the UN International Research and Training Institute for the Advancement of Women). Equally significant, concerns for women's issues raised awareness of broader human concerns in the whole process of development.

These advances were the result of the vision and mobilizing efforts of women (and usually of some supportive men) in all three United Nations. The four women at the founding conference were members of government delegations—the First UN—though they were supported by a number of women in the

forty-two NGOs present—the Third UN. In the early years, several pioneering staff members—the Second UN—played key roles in focusing on the rights of women, especially in the Commission on the Status of Women (CSW). By the time of the four world conferences on women, NGOs had expanded enormously in numbers and influence (an estimated total of 32,000 participants were registered in Beijing from 189 governments and 2,000 NGOs), which added greatly to the energy and impact of these events. NGO members went back to their countries, both to report on what happened and to mobilize further national action. Thus, all three UNs have had an impact in changing attitudes about women within the UN and in bringing concerns for women and gender more squarely into policy and action in every region of the world.

More often than in most other areas of action, triangular alliances formed between women in each of the three UNs—women delegates to UN bodies, women working in the secretariat, and women working outside the UN. This alliance was visible in the first debate in the General Assembly, and it has continued in many other UN activities. Over the years, such alliances grew and became stronger. Jain reports that by 1980, "researchers, academics and activists from developing countries" had become "a communicating club, meeting frequently in various international forums, largely those convened by the specialized agencies," UN funds, and regional commissions.[2] Women's contributions have broadened definitions of poverty and deprivation, strengthened understanding of participation in decision making, and maintained an emphasis on issues of peace and reconciliation, often promoting a southern perspective. Less noticed is the fact that while developing countries strongly promoted collective or community rights, many Third World women insisted that it was important not to lose sight of individual rights.

Many of these advances for women built both on new thinking and on new initiatives for action in a process that was dynamic and interactive rather than simply linear. As Jain put it, "Women's ideation did not ride piggy back on the intellectual development of UN thought; their intellectual work constantly defined and redefined what equality meant for women and for those who are unequally placed." Women brought into development discourse the questioning mode: "Their quest for dignity and equal citizenship led almost to definition by negation, what is called in the Upanishads, *nethi nethi* . . . not this, not this."[3] Each advance, each achievement uncovered further goals and aspirations, just as climbing a mountain reveals a new peak on the horizon just as the first one is reached. Thus, the early goal of better welfare for women gave way to broader goals for women in development (WID), then to women and development, then to gender and development (GAD), then to mainstreaming and to the current realization that a combination of all of these is needed.

Early Landmarks

In the early years of the United Nations, women struggled to get a commission of their own. They succeeded in 1946 with the creation of the Commission on the Status of Women. But as Jain poses the underlying issue, one must ask whether women would have wanted their own space within the UN if they had been comfortable in the mainstream. These issue of whether to remain separate or integrate with the mainstream—"the common life which is the real life and not of the little separate lives which we live as individuals," as Virginia Woolf put it in *A Room of One's Own*—continues to haunt efforts to land UN values on the ground.[4]

Bodil Begtrup, the Danish delegate and advocate trained in wartime resistance who was the first chair of the CSW, was very clear in her desire to have a separate commission for women. To those who argued that women's problems should not be separated from those of men, she replied that at that stage of the battle (the early 1950s) such a contention was "purely unrealistic and academic." She pointed out that for the first time, women's issues could be studied on an international level and that it would be a tragedy to spoil the historic opportunity by "confusing the wish with the fact." And so the CSW came about, in spite of the hesitation among many member states about internationalizing the issue of women's equality. At the time of the League of Nations, for example, the United Kingdom argued that "the principle of the equality of the sexes is a matter for [each] state to determine under its domestic law according to its own circumstances and requirements."[5]

Nonetheless, the CSW was effective and influential, especially over the next three decades. While it was still a subcommission, it took the daring step of advocating that women be given full political suffrage worldwide—at a time when only thirty of the original fifty-one member states allowed women to vote. The very idea of men and women having equal rights was itself quite new on the world stage. Yet for the first time in an international treaty or instrument, the Universal Declaration of Human Rights in 1948 introduced this principle in unambiguous terms. And in 1952, responding to a call from the Sub-Commission on the Status of Women, the General Assembly adopted the Convention on Political Rights of Women "to implement the principle of equality of rights for men and women contained in the Charter of the United Nations."

Generating information on the situation of women worldwide was another important initiative of the early years. In 1947, the UN sent out a questionnaire on the legal status and treatment of women that gathered an unprecedented body of worldwide information. This was not only a statistical exercise but an analytical and intellectual one, documenting the broader dimensions of

discrimination and subjection and directing attention to the special needs of women and how they had to be accommodated.[6]

Even so, it was not until 1963 that the General Assembly asked the CSW and ECOSOC to prepare a comprehensive Declaration on the Elimination of Discrimination against Women (DEDAW). Devaki Jain describes this as "a defining point in the learning curve on women and equality in the UN."[7] It was the first time the UN had accepted the need to address discrimination from the perspective of women and to draft principles on which it would deal with such a problem. "DEDAW moved the idea of women's equality beyond the confines of a rigid legal construct by pointing out those extralegal barriers that were socially constructed and more resistant to change."[8]

The Economic Commission for Africa played a pioneering role in the 1960s. As Peg Snyder, the first director of UNIFEM recalls, the ECA had studied the role of women in community and urban development as early as 1960–1961. It also recognized the need to study population growth and the role of women in development, which was long before anyone else was discussing it.[9] In 1967, the ECA published *The Status and Role of Women in East Africa,* which documented the ways women so often shoulder most of the economic burden.[10] The ECA also published a database that predated by a decade other UN data-gathering about women and development. In 1975, it established the African Training and Research Centre for Women, the realization of efforts of many African women who had believed that such a research institute could provide solutions to their economic problems. The information the center gathered was distributed throughout the continent, creating a common knowledge base for women.[11]

In the 1960s, UNESCO also played a critical role, making clear the place of women in different situations and countries around the world and what was needed to open opportunities for their advancement. In 1968, UNESCO's director-general, René Maheu, maintained that "it is impossible to conceive of development, absurd to imagine the building of peace in minds and hearts, without the active cooperation of women."[12] UNESCO also published the early studies that quantified the discrimination girls suffered in basic education.

Ester Boserup, a Danish economist who had spent more than ten years working in the Economic Commission for Europe, changed knowledge and perceptions about women's work and roles in developing countries with her pathbreaking 1970 book *Women's Role in Economic Development.*[13] As Jain explains, "Her main contribution was her finding that with changes in technology associated with modernization and patterns of land use, the status of women was actually reduced on account of their marginalization in agricultural activities."[14] The main reason for this paradoxical conclusion was that development funding for agriculture ignored the subsistence farming that women typically engaged in. Her contribution was "extremely influential both on the design of development

cooperation and in promoting further research to reveal the vital role women played in the economies of the South." In light of her findings, donors began funding research on women as workers that Jain argues led to a new development definition called women in development.[15]

The development decades of the 1960s and 1970s set a frame for action, in principle for all governments and certainly for the organizations and funds of the UN. Although the First Development Decade made no mention of women, in 1962, a year after the decade was launched, the General Assembly instructed the CSW to prepare a report on the role of women in the social and economic development plans of member governments. Surprisingly, within the CSW, itself composed of government delegates, this was not welcomed with open arms. Some in the CSW held the opinion that the body should not give too much attention to economic development because it was not really a women's issue and it would detract from the commission's primary goal of securing women's equal rights. As Irene Tinker puts it, "They preferred to emphasize the human element in development and called for greater investment in women as human

---

Box 4.1. Women's Contributions and Leadership at the UN

Although scarcely visible on the UN's early agenda, women's and gender issues have become more central to international relations in general and to development thinking in particular.[1] The UN's four world conferences on women—in 1975 (in Mexico City), 1980 (in Copenhagen), 1985 (in Nairobi), and 1995 (in Beijing)—marked critical stages in elevating gender equality and women's rights on the global agenda.

Advances for women within the UN illustrate individual leadership and collective action, often combined. Such critical figures as Leticia Shahani, Lucille Mair, Nafis Sadik, and Gertrude Mongella led the way during global conferences. Women's leadership of six important UN agencies was another major step. Nafis Sadik, head of the UNFPA from 1987 to 2000, was the first woman to head a major UN agency; Sadako Ogata headed UNHCR from 1991 to 2000; Catherine Bertini headed the WFP from 1992 to 2002; Carol Bellamy headed UNICEF from 1995 to 2005; Mary Robinson was UN High Commissioner for Human Rights from 1997 to 2002; and Gro Harland Brundtland headed the WHO from 1998 to 2003. Louise Frechette was named the UN's first deputy secretary-general in 1998 and served until 2006. But behind the formalities have been many individuals like Bella Abzug and groups like DAWN that have strategized, organized, and advocated. This became clear in many of the project's oral history interviews.[2]

Leticia Shahani, a former UN assistant secretary-general from the Philippines who also served as secretary-general of the third global conference in 1985, noted with some irony the situation at the first UN conference on women: "Mexico was the host government, and . . . they couldn't allow a woman to chair. Yes, Mexico was the host government of the

resources."[16] However, by the Second Development Decade thinking at the UN had moved on, and the strategy called for the "full integration of women in the total development effort." It was apparently Gloria Scott of the UN Department of Economic and Social Affairs who took the initiative to insert this sentence.[17]

Global Conferences

The watershed for mobilization and worldwide action on women's issues at the UN was the first world conference on women held in Mexico City in 1975. This coincided with what the UN had earlier declared to be the International Women's Year, so there was much activity before the conference and a buildup of excited anticipation. Delegates to the conference came from more than 130 countries, 75 percent of whom were women. Even so, the Mexican hosts insisted that the conference would have to be chaired by a man.

The conference approved many resolutions that had long-term consequences and impact. Its World Plan of Action included crucial changes in data

first-ever World Conference on Women. But I guess that's how the world was then." She also explained some of the impact: Gender equity "went global," and agencies that once neglected gender issues were obliged to take them seriously. "That's one of the wonderful things that the UN can do—to put pressure on national governments to think and act on global issues which also affect domestic policies."

Singapore's Noeleen Heyzer, now the head of ESCAP after thirteen years at the helm of UNIFEM, explained the reasons for "mainstreaming" that emerged from the Fourth UN World Conference on Women in Beijing: "There was concern that women's perspectives basically can flow—in the words of Bella Abzug—into the 'polluted stream.' What you want is not to mainstream into the pollution; you want a clean stream. . . . People started talking about transformation, about structures of transformation. How do you transform development to be more empowering of women?"

Peg Snyder, who was on the ground at the creation of the ECA's center and went on to be UNIFEM's founding director, asserted: "I think that the global women's movement would be lost or at least much weaker without the UN. . . . I have more and more respect for leadership in that sense, of what a few strategically placed people can do by cooperating. . . . I think women captured the UN and made it their own vehicle for their movement to make sure that their movement was going to go ahead. In many ways, the UN was far ahead."

1. A lively account of the roles of many of the women cited here will be found in Devaki Jain, *Women, Development, and the UN: A Sixty-Year Quest for Equality and Justice* (Bloomington: Indiana University Press, 2006).

2. Quotations in Thomas G. Weiss, Tatiana Carayannis, Louis Emmerij, and Richard Jolly, *UN Voices: The Struggle for Development and Social Justice* (Bloomington: Indiana University Press, 2005) are as follows: Leticia Shahani 247, Noeleen Heyzer 256, and Peg Snyder 255.

collection and analysis to document the situation of women in different parts of the world. It triggered the creation of national institutions to deal with policy, research, and programs on WID. It agreed upon the creation of UNIFEM and INSTRAW. It also agreed that negotiations should be started to turn DEDAW into a convention, CEDAW. More important than all of these was the fact that women found one another and realized their common concerns. "The exposure strengthened their sense of identity as well as their . . . desire to engage with the UN. . . . Mexico-City provided more than a . . . Plan of Action; it was the jumping board for a new phase of the UN's partnership with the women's constituency."[18] For the first time, women had established a political identity and distinct visibility on the global stage.

The creation of UNIFEM in 1976 and INSTRAW in 1980 increased the UN's capacity to bring women's concerns to the international arena. However, UNIFEM gathered increasing momentum over the 1980s while INSTRAW struggled to make ends meet.[19]

The Mexico City conference was followed by one in Copenhagen in 1980 and a third in Nairobi in 1985. The ten-year interval between the Mexico City and Nairobi conferences was an important period during which "women's intellectual contributions on development increasingly became a major force, albeit slowly."[20] New thinking was supported by more information, the result of implementing the recommendations of the Mexico conference on data collection and establishing national machineries for research and policy on women's issues. The initial narrow approach that focused on women's status vis-à-vis men became enlarged to cover the broader implications of global economic, political, and social changes and their impact on women's lives in their entirety. Women from the developing world began to emphasize discrimination as stemming to a very large extent from mass poverty and general backwardness. They also began to emphasize the politics of North-South relations and to critique conventional ideas in development cooperation.

For a while, these different perceptions opened up divisions within the women's movement. Women from the South saw discrimination as closely related to inadequacies in the process of development. In contrast, women from the industrial countries tended to see discrimination only in the context of male dominance. At the midterm conference in Copenhagen in 1980, North American feminists were "surprised to discover that not everyone shared their view that patriarchy was the major cause of women's oppression."[21] In the North, equality with men was the issue. For women of the South, the issue involved much more.

While many criticize such gatherings as "talk shops," Mexican anthropologist Lourdes Arizpe provided a different view:

Even though it brings out resolution after resolution, so that you can paper the whole building with them, as I've heard it said, these resolutions place a mirror in front of governments and people. . . . I've seen it in many meetings, where the powerless Indian groups or women's groups have actually taken documents from . . . the United Nations, and presented these to the officials from their governments, and have forced their governments to be more accountable because there exists this document which has been signed and ratified by a majority of countries in the world, showing that this is the way that governments should behave, or corporations should behave, or men should behave.[22]

In a similar vein, Noeleen Heyzer, UNIFEM's third director and the first from a developing country, commented on the movement of ideas from the international to the national level. "The UN became the place where women could bring issues ignored at the national level into the international spotlight to be addressed by national governments." And she pointed out why that mattered: "When the ideas took a powerful form, they got recognized and accepted, because it spoke about women's lives. . . . With these international norms, women pressured for the revisions of national norms and policies based on international standards. We worked so hard to ensure that decision making in the courts and in the criminal justice system also changed because of new legal standards and norms. So ideas became action which changed people's lives."[23]

The Significance of CEDAW

Following the decisions at the world conference in Mexico, the second half of the 1970s saw the birth of the Convention on the Elimination of all Forms of Discrimination against Women, which significantly advanced the earlier declaration (DEDAW) that had been adopted in 1967. At least four points made CEDAW a pioneering instrument of human rights for women: it recognized the centrality of nondiscrimination to the equality of women; it included private acts in the definition of discrimination; it articulated prejudices, customary practices, and stereotyped roles for men and women as features to be eliminated; and it overturned the formal approach to equality and in its place established the norm of results or equality of outcomes—in other words, equality in real terms.

The "Women and Development" chapter of the ECA's 1979 Lagos Plan of Action contained "a detailed blueprint for women's economic empowerment, calling for education for women to prepare them for employment in business,

commerce, industry, and handicrafts and small-scale industries."[24] It called for full participation of women in all aspects of society. African women, at least in their interactions with the UN, were ahead of the rest of the world's women in terms of ideas and thinking during the 1960s and 1970s.

In spite of these advances, the 1980s brought major setbacks, especially in Sub-Saharan Africa and Latin America. Debt, recession, and ideological shifts to the right in the North brought fundamental changes. In 1980, a year after African governments adopted the Lagos Plan, the World Bank issued its own study, *Accelerated Development in Sub-Saharan Africa*. Backed by donor countries, this Bretton Woods approach became the dominant face in Africa and Latin America for at least the next decade, ushering in policies of structural adjustment.[25]

Yet, as has become clear in other volumes, the UN was increasingly marginalized from economic and social matters, though with some important exceptions. One was in matters of women and gender. As Jain notes, "National women's bureaus and UN focal points came into greater play as a result of the mandates of the 1985 Nairobi Forward-Looking Strategies," but "outside this corridor of power within the UN, things were falling apart."[26] Even as women fought to improve the understanding of women's location in their economies, inequality, poverty, and conflict were increasing in many countries, and women and children were often the hardest hit. *The World's Women 1970–1990: Trends and Statistics,* published in 1991, noted that structural adjustment programs, "disproportionately squeezed women out of public sector employment." Reductions in public spending for social initiatives, moreover, affected women the hardest.[27]

Notwithstanding these reverses, the 1985 Nairobi conference renewed momentum and energized the worldwide women's movement. It brought new understandings of the different links between women and development and ideas and practice in a number of ways. Whereas women from developing and developed countries had disagreed five years earlier at Copenhagen about which issues the worldwide women's movement should focus on, at Nairobi, women from North and South agreed that "political issues are women's issues and that the women's movement is a fundamentally political movement."[28] As Snyder recalls, "Moreover, western women had by then experienced the economic downturn, so they knew how it got in the way of advancement of women in their own countries."[29] Nairobi provided the women's movement the tools for advancing a comprehensive perspective on development issues.

In 1984, the organization Development Alternatives with Women for a New Era (DAWN) was born as part of the preparation for the Nairobi conference. DAWN broke new ground by "identifying regional crises as the peg on which to hang the analysis of women's situations: Africa's food crisis, Latin America's

debt, South Asia's poverty, and the militarization of the Pacific Islands. Poor women were not only totally engaged in the economies of these regions but were suffering from and responding creatively to these onslaughts." As Jain explains, the "new framework initiated a shift in development analysis characterized by the central location of poor women in development planning, the merging of 'women's issues' with macroeconomic structures and global crises, and the linkage of local organizing efforts with global themes and networks."[30] The structural roots of poverty lay not in insufficient economic growth but in "unequal access to resources, control over production, trade, finance, and money and across nations, genders, regions and classes."[31] The decade from Mexico to Nairobi was instrumental in making the 1995 Beijing conference pathbreaking. Jain argues that "the events of the period also foreshadowed the dramatic changes that were about to emerge, both in global governance and in people's responses to these changes."[32]

Structural adjustment increased inequality around the globe and revealed the fragility of gains made in human rights and development. The UN's responses to the growing crisis, such as its advocacy of microcredit for poor women entrepreneurs and later the Millennium Development Goals, were important but often failed to tackle the root causes of poverty and its attendant problems. Nonetheless, significant progress was made in several areas.[33]

Moreover, the 1980s stimulated debate about the idea of the "feminization of poverty." This was not a message that poverty had become feminized but rather that women had been pauperized. The point was made that poverty did not cause the subordination of women; indeed, a "poverty focus misses the range of interconnected gender issues across classes and socioeconomic strata."[34] Nor did the debate imply that poverty is unimportant. The important conclusion was that development would help women only if they participated fully in policymaking about it.

Gender and Human Development

The *Human Development Report 1995*, subtitled *Gender and Human Development,* was brought out by the UNDP as a contribution to the Beijing 1995 women's conference. It was bold and innovative, quantifying the value of the nonmonetized production by women (and men) in economic and household activities. Albeit a rough and approximate calculation, the report suggested that the unpaid and therefore uncounted contributions of men and women worldwide amounted to an addition to world production of about 70 percent of measured GDP, of which women provided more than half. The larger share of women's production in the total was hardly surprising, given that women work

longer hours than men in nearly every country of the world. But it was the first time such an estimate had been quantified on a global basis.[35]

The report also introduced two special indicators for measuring gendered inequality, the GDI (Gender-Related Development Index) and the GEM (Gender Empowerment Measure). Both are composite indicators—the former measures the average achievement of women compared to men in terms of the three basic dimensions of human development—living a long and healthy life, possessing useful knowledge, and having a decent standard of living. The GEM measures gender inequality in three measures of empowerment—political participation and decision making, economic participation and decision making, and power over economic resources. Noting the "fierce questioning" of the dominant development paradigm, the report argued that "investing in women's capabilities and empowering them to exercise their choices is the surest way to economic development."[36] It incorporated time-use data about women's work, pointing out that if the unpaid contributions by both men and women were recognized there would be far-reaching consequences for social and economic policy and for social norms and institutions. It also noted that no attempt should be made to offer a universal model of gender equality. Each society should debate the issues and tailor action in relation to the situation and the opportunities that are open for further advance.

The 1995 World Conference on Women in Beijing, the fourth in twenty years, was the culmination of a journey begun in 1975. It brought together all the elements of the diversity that was increasingly represented at the world venues, yet it represented the unity of women when they met "the Other," namely the state and unjust regimes, including economic ones, buttressed by traditions of patriarchy. Jain finds that Beijing "also was the end of a process. It had developed an agenda that could stay with the nations and movements for some time because it was so comprehensive. . . . There can be no real repeat of that performance."[37]

Since 1945, women have been a consistent and persistent voice in calling for peace and disarmament. Two of the early groups—the Women's International League for Peace and Freedom and the Inter-American Commission on Women, the former created during World War I and the latter in the decade that followed—were active in the peace movement. Two senior members of the Swedish government who had responsibilities for disarmament played leading roles in the UN's work on disarmament—Alva Myrdal and Inga Thorsson. In 1961, Women Strike for Peace protested the political and health effects of atmospheric nuclear testing, prompted by the discovery of strontium 90 in breast milk, a protest that contributed to the conclusion of the Partial Test Ban Treaty.[38] Many other examples could be cited.

The landmark achievement of recent times for women peace workers is resolution 1325, which legally requires member states to increase participation of women at all levels and stages of the peacemaking process. Unanimously passed by the Security Council in October 2000, the resolution came about through the efforts of UNIFEM and its director Noeleen Heyzer, who is currently the executive secretary of ESCAP. She used this resolution to illustrate the impact of ideas on government policy and pointed to women and the mechanisms to involve NGOs in helping brief the Security Council:

> We worked extremely hard to put the whole issue of women, peace, and security onto the Security Council agenda. The Security Council is an extreme case of a highly controlled arena and it is very difficult to put various issues on their agenda. To change the dialogue and to put in new issues that changes people's thinking is not easy. . . . We used what is called the Arria formula . . . to allow real consultation. . . . We brought women—the nongovernmental groups, and women themselves who were affected by conflict, to talk to the members of the Security Council to prepare for the Security Council resolution 1325 on women, peace, and security. UNIFEM's role was to get the space and to help women clarify their messages. We became the mediator of different worlds. It is not easy for different worlds to understand one another, I've learned. Therefore, we try to prepare the ground, help the women to crystallize their voice, make sure that their message is heard by members of the Security Council, and determine what the Security Council needs to hear before they can make certain kinds of decisions. . . . When that happened, a synergy took place. . . . Members of the Security Council after that said, "We will change our statement." Up to that time, they were not even willing to come up with a short resolution.[39]

For the first time, gender was included in the deliberations of the Security Council. With this resolution, the council moved from being a "gender-neutral" body to one that is committed to work for women's involvement at all levels of conflict prevention and peacekeeping.

Conclusion

From its beginning, the UN has played a critical part in defining the rights of women to equality. The world body has also played crucial roles in spreading awareness of how far the fulfillment of these rights lags behind commitments. At its best, the UN has also released the vision and energies of women, bringing them together from all parts of the globe for four world women's conferences:

in Mexico in 1975, Copenhagen in 1980, Nairobi in 1985, and Beijing in 1995. Jain summarizes the excitement and the shifts in focus: "The [international] women's movement has gone from its first intoxicating coalescence in the mid-1970s, through a period of learning to appreciate and value differences in the 1980s, to an explosion of new identities—as workers, as women, as thinkers, as activists. The growing pains of the movement . . . yielded valuable new insights about the valuation of women and their work and ways to use this knowledge to craft new models of development."[40]

Jain also brings out how these changes have accompanied a shift in thinking about development from North to South. She concludes that "the UN has often been a willing partner in the new intellectual exploration, incorporating women's knowledge and expertise into survey methodology, measurement tools, and policymaking." Advances in ideas and thinking have not been matched, however, by equally positive changes in the situation of women. Jain comments that "despite great leaps forward in theorizing about development that moved women from the periphery to the center and began to see them as the holders of solutions to global problems, the poverty of the world's women has increased and intensified. It seems time to take a step back and ask some larger questions about why this is so."[41]

Jain identifies several explanations. The first is "the failure to note, understand, and respect women's ideas and intellectual skills and outputs in the area of theoretical and analytical knowledge." While some of the values emerging from the understanding of poverty, inequality, discrimination, conflict resolution, deepening participation, and politics have been applied, implementation of these ideas have been mainly confined to women's and gender programs instead of being applied far more widely.[42]

This sidelining of women's intellectual contributions and leadership reflects a more general bias often embedded in traditional hierarchies. Jain puts it clearly and sharply: "turning away from giving recognition to women, their understanding of phenomena, their challenging of the basis of knowledge and their claim to be recognized, hinges on how women are valued, and hierarchies of values are embedded everywhere in the knowledge base. Unless that valuation of woman is . . . knocked down, the web of inequality in which women are caught may not quite tear."[43]

But this is not all. Jain points to a "restlessness within the women's movement" that led to a partial failure of the movement to reach the next stage of development. "Differences—of location, race, class, sexuality, and religion—have at times been emphasized at the expense of the commonalities . . . that can build strength to move forward."[44]

But coalitions bridging these differences are increasingly visible. The Third

UN has gained its power not just by professionals or experts working individually or by nongovernmental groups coming into the UN but also by these and other groups working and mobilizing together. Women's groups have been among these, but they are by no means the only coalitions or the only ones pressing for women's rights.

Nonetheless, women still need their own space. The "women's tent," as Jain calls it, is now a routine element of world gatherings, including the World Social Forum. The tent provides space "to share experiences, work through conflicts, build new strategies for change, create a solidarity based on their common experiences of being excluded. How women choose to use the space of their tent is the determining factor. Can they use it to expand their territory? Or will it become an isolated ghetto?" The women's tent is a symbol of the dilemma women have always faced, whether to enter the mainstream or remain apart.[45]

Jain's book ends with a rallying call:

> The women's movement needs to find new ways of moving forward, of gathering its capital of knowledge and experience and history and reshaping it into a new political force. It needs to build on its successful introduction of feminism as common currency—today "feminist analysis" is a term that is used just like political or economic analysis. . . . Women's increased visibility—an outcome of the spaces and opportunities for building opinion that UN conferences offered—has made it possible to insert women-oriented concerns and agendas into international discourse and practice. Many of the final documents of the various UN conferences during the period 1995 to 2000 have separate sections devoted to women, however inadequate and subject to critique they may be.[46]

However, there are important omissions with important implications for the UN's intellectual work. Jain notes that conference documents and declarations have not yet challenged the knowledge base from which they emerge; while the outcome documents include an acknowledgement "that women may not have the same concerns and interests as men," the rest of the document is likely to be permeated by a masculine worldview that is not challenged. Similarly, although feminist practices might define NGO forums, official conferences are still circumscribed by masculine forms of organization and government.[47]

The next generation of feminists will find a new path to equality. It is to be hoped that they will be able to cover the entire global governance landscape and place more emphasis on peace and security, on economic and social development, and on culture. Lourdes Arizpe suggests that people are no longer finding new meaning in development or in their lives "because the constitutive

aspects of culture have been completely left out of development models and out of contemporary politics."[48] Jain notes that caution is needed as culture is incorporated into women's agendas, however. Although she acknowledges the importance of the idea that culture "can revitalize a dominated, fragmented, poverty- and conflict-ridden South," she warns that many cultural traditions "have embargoes on many dimensions of women's concerns and freedom. It is here that culture clashes with women's access to the universality of human rights; often traditions and religious practices hurt and discriminate."[49]

However, Jain notes that such interpretations of culture and its implications can be resisted. Narrow perspectives need "to be overpowered by other interpretations of [culture] as sophisticated, open-ended, fluid understandings of self—a notable quality of women's use of identities." Kum-Kum Bhavnani and others have suggested a new paradigm for women and development called WCD: women, culture, and development.[50]

As Jain concludes, although the experience of the last six decades shows that "much can be accomplished when the synergy flows back and forth between the UN and the women's movement," the future shape of the women's movement with and within the UN is unclear. The political will to create change must be activated if women are to be brought fully into the mainstream with "equality in privileges, access to resources, and decision-making roles."[51] Progress has been made, no doubt, but more slowly than most women and many men would have liked. The balance between words and action is still uneven. Only the participation and support of all three UNs will enable the worldwide women's movement to change thinking at its core.

5. Development Goals

From National and Regional Policies to the MDGs

- **National Development Strategies**
- **National Development Theory and Practice**
- **Regional Perspectives on Economic and Social Development**
- **Conclusion**

After World War II and with the awakening of what were then called "underdeveloped countries," a new field of economics came into being. Development economics (or more broadly development studies) focused specifically on Africa, Asia, and Latin America—the Third World—to analyze needs and make proposals, as the Charter put it, "to promote social progress and better standards of life in larger freedom."

This new field has been under attack ever since it began. Mainstream economists maintained that no new specialization and no specific policies for developing counties were necessary. All these countries needed was to adopt the same policies as the already developed countries, the mainstream argument went. Actually this is what happened to a large extent in the 1980s. On the other hand, other economists and social scientists from developed and developing countries were of the opinion that development economics remained too close to mainstream economics and that home-grown policies had to be devised.

Pioneer development economists and sociologists argued that serious differences existed in the economic and social situations of underdeveloped as compared to industrialized countries. A few argued that cultural differences were key, but most felt that the differences were structural—as illustrated, among many examples, by huge poverty levels, low savings rates, scarcity of foreign exchange, weak industrial bases, widespread but hidden unemployment, and various forms of underemployment.

At the beginning, this new field was somewhat narrowly focused, although less so than is often described. Following the writing of Arthur Lewis, a major focus of the 1950s and 1960s was measures to boost national savings levels from

a low rate of 5 percent to a higher rate of 15 percent.[1] As we see in the next chapter, development economists saw aid as a critical measure to fill the gap between national savings and the investments required to jumpstart economic growth. They used simple economic analytical frameworks, like the Harrod-Domar model derived from Keynesian thinking, to calculate the levels of savings and investments needed to raise the annual rate of economic growth to 5 or 6 percent. These were deemed necessary to raise living standards faster than population growth.[2]

In subsequent years, more comprehensive and subtle approaches were formulated and moved closer to the mainstream, and here the UN also played an important role. This chapter explores the world organization's contributions by examining national development strategies, theory, and practice as well as how the UN viewed economic and social development through the prism of geographic regions.

National Development Strategies

For most of the UN's early decades, development thinking by and within the United Nations system was dominated by western ideas. This reflected the economic and political weight of developed countries in the world at the time. This remains true even with strategies that were originally conceived by thinkers and leaders from the global South and what formerly was known as the East (the socialist bloc).

The classicists and the other great names in development thinking were all from or were trained in Europe and the United States. After 1945, development thinking in the modern era saw a wider cast of characters that included a few figures from developing countries, but it remained a global concept that was not "deconstructed," to use Arturo Escobar's terminology.[3] The labor-surplus model, the "big push," balanced and unbalanced growth, "great spurt," and stages-of-economic-growth doctrines were all western ideas.

What is "western" about all this is that practically no account was taken of local thinking in and local theorists from developing countries. An important exception was Sir W. Arthur Lewis, though he rarely departed from his neoclassical upbringing.[4] Another important exception was Raúl Prebisch and others of the Latin American structuralist school that emerged in the late 1940s and 1950s within the UN's Economic Commission for Latin America. They saw development and underdevelopment as related processes occurring within a single dynamic economic system. Development is generated in some areas—the "center," which they defined as those countries whose economies were first penetrated by capitalist production techniques—and underdevelopment

is generated in others—the "periphery." Prebisch and his Latin American colleagues thus saw modern underdevelopment as a result of a process of structural change in the peripheral economies that occurs in conjunction with—is
conditioned by, but not caused unilaterally by—their relations with the center.[5]
So even here western influence was important, as it is in the writings of Samir
Amin, Fernando Henrique Cardoso, and others of the *dependencia* school.[6]

It is important to note the exceptions in Asia and East Asia. In 1918, Sun
Yat-Sen wrote the *International Economic Development of China,* arguing that
nationalism had to be mobilized to save the country from western political
domination. His three principles included nationalism, democracy, and "the
People's Livelihood."[7] In fact, after the establishment of the People's Republic in 1949, the Maoist strategy dominated Chinese doctrine until the mid-
1970s. Although today Mao's strategy is dismissed because of its excesses and
extremely high costs in terms of lives and human suffering, in some ways—
land reform, widespread literacy, public health, and disciplined administration,
for instance—it laid an important part of the foundations for China's subsequent dramatic economic advance. Less widely known in the postwar decades
were the impressive approaches to rural development, like the Saemaul Udong
movement of Korea. These and other experiences from East Asia rarely entered
the classrooms of western universities and thus generally were neglected in
mainstream thinking and teaching about development.

National contributions to development thinking in Africa were much gen-
tler. President Senghor of Senegal argued for Negritude, President Kenneth
Kaunda of Zambia for humanism, while President Julius Nyerere led the way in
Tanzania with Ujamaa. The latter gained qualified support from many donors
in the 1960s and 1970s but was abandoned with structural adjustment in the
early 1980s. Most of these ideas were treated more as political philosophies than
economic strategies, and thus western ideas and thinking remained dominant
in international development.

The resurgence of neoclassical economics since 1980 was of course totally
western bred, but so was the strategy of redistribution with growth and the
basic needs approach of the 1970s. Although the latter two were inspired by
and explicitly took into consideration the specific circumstances of developing
countries, they remained embedded in western concepts and thinking.

The events of the past few decades challenge much of the validity of these
western development theories, whether liberal or Marxist, neoclassical or post-
Keynesian. They did not and do not explain why so many countries were not
able to take off economically or are regressing to previous levels of economic
development. They also do not explain the "ennui" in the apparently successful countries. Examples are the economic stagnation and decline in Africa and

Box 5.1. The South Centre

For many years, commentators have noted that developing countries lacked a secretariat to help frame common Third World positions on matters for international negotiations. In short, the South had no equivalent to the OECD. Even the succession of high-level reports on development by international commissions, which began to appear with the Pearson Commission on International Development in 1969,[1] tended to be chaired, at least initially, by a person from the North (Lester Pearson, Willy Brandt, Olaf Palme, Gro Harlem Brundtland). At the Non-Aligned Summit Meeting held in Harare in September 1986, Malaysian prime minister Mahathir bin Mohamad announced the intention to create an august commission composed and staffed by persons from the Third World under the chairmanship of Mwalimu Julius Nyerere, former president of Tanzania.

The South Commission started its work in 1987. It consisted of personalities from the South such as Manmohan Singh, the present prime minister of India, who served as the first secretary-general, as well as others who figure prominently in UN history and these pages, including Gamani Corea, Aldo Ferrer, Celso Furtado, Enrique Iglesias, Devaki Jain, Shridath Ramphal, Marie-Angelique Savane, and Martin Khor.

In August 1990, Oxford University Press published *The Challenge to the South*, which came out in the final years of a decade that had devastated many economies of the global South.[2] The report made a strong case for self-reliant and people-centered development, mutual cooperation, and Third World solidarity in North-South negotiations.

Although the South Commission was not created at its initiative, the General Assembly in 1990 took note "with appreciation of the report" and invited "Governments and the organs and bodies of the United Nations system to submit their views on the conclusions and recommendations of the Report."

In 1995, the commission was transformed into the South Centre, with its secretariat based in Geneva. The South Centre issues policy papers, a newsletter, and a bulletin. Topics for study, generally in response to requests from the Group of 77 and the Non-Aligned Movement, have included foreign direct investment, reform of the United Nations, resource transfers and financial flows, the challenges presented by the WTO agenda, the implementation of Agenda 21, and science and technology. The South Centre also has studied various aspects of globalization as they affect the Third World.

The South Centre has undoubtedly produced a number of useful reports. But it is difficult to argue that it has served to produce the intellectual foundations for common Third World positions, let alone serve as an equivalent to the OECD. In spite of pleas from its founders, too little financing was made available from developing countries, in contrast to the OECD, which in 2008 had over 2,500 staff members and a budget of over $500 million.[3]

1. Commission on International Development, *Partners in Development* (New York: Praeger, 1969).
2. South Commission, *The Challenge to the South* (Oxford: Oxford University Press, 1990).
3. Statistics from the South Centre Web site, www.southcentre.org.

Latin America during the 1980s and 1990s; the imposition and the lack of success of structural adjustment programs, especially in Africa; and the rapid state-led industrialization of the East Asian countries, which cannot be explained by any rational criteria of the Washington consensus. All of those were not anticipated by either mainstream or more radical theories of development.

None of the theories—whether of the modernization, dependency, neoliberal, or Marxist variety—seems to be working in the sense that they have all resulted in errors, even if initial successes were secured. During the 1980s and 1990s, theorectical diversity was supplanted by a hegemonic neoliberal view of development based on "globalization" and "free markets" that effectively dismisses questions of ethnicity and culture and does not try to understand nationalism, fundamentalism, and terrorism.

The picture of progress and performance in the developing world is mixed and complex. Between 1950 and 1980, developing countries achieved considerable economic and social progress, more than was expected when the UN was founded. The UN exercised considerable influence on growth patterns until 1980. Since 1980, however, the Bretton Woods institutions—which did not support UN economic objectives but instead concentrated on narrower objectives—have predominated, and regional differences have been considerable. For the last three decades or so, East Asia has experienced a dramatic acceleration in economic growth to historically high levels; South Asia has followed more recently. Both of these regions have mostly followed strategies that depart from Washington consensus orthodoxies. In contrast, in Africa and Latin America, which were largely required to follow this orthodoxy as a condition for loans, there were marked economic slowdowns until the beginning of the twenty-first century.[8]

Goal-setting is one of the major UN contributions to national development of the last fifty years. The first goals were formulated in about 1960 in UNESCO regional conferences to expand education from 1960 to 1980. Soon after, U.S. president John F. Kennedy proposed the creation of a Development Decade in a speech to the General Assembly. This led to the UN goal that by the end of the 1960s, developing countries should have raised their economic growth rates to approach 5 percent per year and that developed countries should have increased their annual transfers of aid *and* foreign investment to 1 percent of their national income. Although these goals, when set, were dismissed as unrealistic, the goal for economic growth was in fact exceeded—developing country growth rates *averaged* 5.5 percent over the 1960s and the rates in fifty individual developing countries were above the target. Total transfers by 1970 reached 0.8 percent, four-fifths of the second target.

Over the years, the UN has set about fifty goals for economic and social

development. *UN Contributions to Development Thinking and Practice* undertook a goal-by-goal review of those with a quantified target and a specific date for achievement.[9] These goals covered faster economic growth, higher life expectancy, lower child and maternal mortality, better health and reduced disease, increased access to education, greater access to water and sanitation, reductions in hunger and malnutrition, moves to sustainable development, and support for all of these efforts by the expansion of aid.

The actual record of achievements has varied by goal and by period, usually far from full achievement but rarely total failure. On the whole, more successes have occurred than many people seem to realize. Progress on economic growth in developing countries was marginally better in the 1970s than in the 1960s—although after 1980, economic growth deteriorated for most of two decades, with the notable exceptions of China and several other East Asian countries and, after 1990, India and a few others. Performance on social goals has generally been considerably better than for economic goals, even in some cases with accelerated progress during the 1980s, what is often called the "lost decade" for economic development. For instance, the target that infant mortality rates should be reduced to 120 per thousand in the poorest countries by 2000 and to 50 per thousand in all others was achieved by 138 countries. Access to water and sanitation more than doubled over the 1980s. Progress in other areas like reducing malnutrition, iron deficiency, anemia, and vitamin A deficiency was considerable over the 1990s.

At least four conclusions can be drawn. First, although the record is mixed, achievements have on the whole been better than is commonly thought. Second, the most serious failures have been in Sub-Saharan Africa and in other least developed countries. Third, except for the Scandinavian countries and the Netherlands, donor countries have fallen far short of the targets for aid, both the 0.7 percent target for total aid as a percentage of GNI and subsequent ones for aid to the least-developed countries. Finally, the World Bank and the IMF never accepted UN goals over most of the period. In this respect, their commitments to MDGs represented an important change.

National Development Theory and Practice

There are two essential questions about development theory and practice. The first is whether the approach adopted up until now is comprehensive enough or still overwhelmingly dominated by narrow economic paradigms. The second relates to the problem of homogeneity—that is, how far development policies should be adapted and changed according to the structure or culture of a given region or country.

Both pose the question of whether there is one theory and one practice for the world with a little tinkering at the margins to take account of national and regional differences or whether there should be many theories and many practices in order to tailor development policies according to the structural and cultural cloth and habits of countries and regions.[10] So far the former approach has been adopted with mixed results. In the 1960s and 1970s, structural analysis provided an alternative to orthodoxy, with economists like Dudley Seers and Hollis Chenery using the structuralist frame. The structuralist paradigm emphasized the critical importance of the economic and social structure of each country for analyzing its development structure and for making policy. Seers and Chenery were leading proponents. Emphasizing the importance of the structure of a country's production, labor force, consumption, and external trade avoided the easy generalizations of neoclassical economics or the dogma of Marxist analysis. By the 1980s, with the resurgence of neoclassical analysis, structuralism mostly faded from the picture. But in the 1990s, evidence of the failures of neoclassical orthodoxy stirred innovative efforts to develop alternatives, albeit with broader frames and different foundations than before. Human development, building on the work of Amartya Sen, was one approach that was strongly promoted within the United Nations by the UNDP's annual *Human Development Report* (see chapter 11). Another was a more eclectic set of efforts to break free from the shackles of economics as a discipline by exploring alternative perspectives that go far beyond economics. We discuss this under two headings, broadening development theory and then parsing it nationally, locally, and culturally.

Broadening Development Theory and Practice

The UN has made important contributions in the attempt to move development theory and practice out of its narrow corner of economics. The United Nations Research Institute for Social Development made use of the so-called unified approach to development during the 1960s and 1970s. This was a reaction to the way economists and policymakers dealt with social issues as add-ons to economic policy rather than as integral parts of policy. Dissatisfaction with the marginalization of social and cultural dimensions of development in national and international policymaking led various UN agencies to support UNRISD's work on a "Unified Approach to Development Planning and Analysis," which emphasized distribution and services toward the poor, incorporating social factors into structural change, and technological research and innovation.[11]

In the mid-1970s, the ILO formulated the basic needs approach to develop-

ment theory and practice. The idea of "basic needs" originated in the psychology literature of the 1940s. The best-known publication in this connection was an article by Albert Maslow in the *Psychological Review* of March 1942 in which he distinguished five rungs on the needs ladder, starting with the very basic needs (for food, shelter, and clothing) and ending up with cultural needs.[12] The ILO concentrated on the first rungs of the ladder.

In the 1970s, work on basic needs took place in three different places almost simultaneously: in the Latin American Bariloche Project; in the Dag Hammarskjöld Foundation in Uppsala, Sweden; and in the ILO's World Employment Programme in Geneva.[13] The ILO defined basic needs in terms of food, housing, clothing, education, and public transport. The approach viewed employment as both a means and an end, and it included participation in decision making and human rights. This constituted a considerable broadening of development practice by explicitly including in the analysis employment, income distribution, participatory decision making, and human rights.[14]

The ILO's strategy for meeting basic needs on a global scale within a generation combined an acceleration of economic growth in poor countries with elements of distribution. Inspired by the ILO's work in Kenya, the World Bank and the Institute of Development Studies explored different combinations of "redistribution with growth" as macroeconomic approaches to development during the first half of the 1970s.[15] The most effective combination for rapid progress toward a reduction of poverty was by channeling an increasing proportion of additions to income to improve the production, assets, and skills of the working poor.

The work of UNRISD and the ILO were stepping-stones to a theory of human development that was elaborated by the UNDP in the 1990s under the leadership of Mahbub ul Haq in collaboration with Amartya Sen. And so the UN—mainly the Second and the Third UNs—over the 1970s and again since 1990 has been moving toward a global, universal concept of development within which physical and human capital accumulation and economic growth remain important but for which freedom, human rights, social objectives, and human security are becoming at least as crucial. In short, these UN efforts have instilled the idea that development should be conceived and planned as a multidimensional process that is political and social as well as economic.

Culture in Development, Nationally and Locally

There is a growing awareness of the importance of culture in the development process and of the cultural assumptions inherent in development theory and practice. One of the many paradoxes that have accompanied internationalization

and globalization is that local particularities are being stressed more than previously. Globalization seems to stimulate localization. Cultural pluralism becomes an integral characteristic of societies, and attention to ethnic identity is often a normal and healthy response to the homogenizing pressures of globalization. People seem to be turning to culture as a means of self-definition and mobilization.

UNESCO has addressed the role of culture in development because culture is an integral part of its title and terms of reference. In one of its important reports of the 1990s, it states that more cultural freedom leaves us free to meet one of the most basic needs, "the need to define our *own* basic needs."[16] But defining one's own basic needs is one thing; finding the way to meet them—and deciding which social and economic policies will make that possible—is another.

Examples of variations in development policies are commonplace. A key one is that of East Asia, where authorities have always maintained that globalization does not imply that a universal model or uniform set of rules—as, for instance, in the Washington consensus—should spread to all parts of the world. According to one Japanese authority, "We have to recognize that what can be called localization, or an identification with local cultural values, is proceeding along with globalization."[17] Most neoclassical economists tend to apply the same model unilaterally to all countries, neglecting historical, institutional, and cultural backgrounds. But there are critics of their neoclassical "universal model" who recognize the plurality of economic systems or cultures and emphasize the interaction among them. For them the key concept is diversity and interaction, not universality.

The need for a differentiated approach has long been obvious in view of the remarkable success of East Asia. This need is also felt because of the disquieting fact that in most countries that adopted the Washington consensus during the past twenty-five years or so, the distribution of income has worsened, poverty has increased, and employment trends have been very uneven. Economic growth during 1980–2000 was much lower in Latin America and even negative in Africa as compared to 1960–1980.[18] Causal linkages have not yet been well understood, but the association between the adoption of a uniform model and the accentuation of problems of inequality and poverty is a cause for serious concern. The distinguished Canadian development economist Gerry Helleiner judges the policies that were introduced during the 1980s as follows: "The legacy of the neoliberal thrust of the 1980s will be close to zero. They moved things back in the right direction but greatly overshot. It would have been wiser and less costly to move back in a more gradual fashion rather than in the really roughhouse manner in which they did."[19]

If one of the priorities of development is "to bring the millions of dispossessed and disadvantaged in from the margins of society and cultural policy in from the margins of governance," then adapting development models according to the needs, institutions, history, and culture of different societies is essential.[20] The margins of maneuver may not be huge, but they are wider than one might suspect. That much has become clear from the East Asian development experience. State approaches to national planning in Asia had considerable success. These combined national planning with active intervention in the economy such as banking support and selective market controls for particular industries as well as support for rural development and agriculture. In some countries, notably Malaysia, measures for shifting income distribution in favor of poorer groups were also a specific part of policy. The margins of maneuver relate to institutions, consumption habits, land rights, property rights in general, access to markets, distribution systems, and economic democracy. Growing internationalization and globalization may provoke diversity at least as much as they impose uniformity. A strong focus on a country's internal needs and structure combined with an outward-looking strategy for trade may be the best way to exploit the margins of maneuver.

Participation and empowerment are closely related to both cultural and economic rights and equality. Participation, a human right, is one of the key goals of cultural and economic policy because it opens up both the economy and culture to as many people as possible. It is often forgotten that East Asian countries could grow at the stupendous rates of 8 to 9 percent a year over such a long time only because there was full employment; virtually everybody participated actively in the economy. In other words, there was growth from below. One cannot expect countries to grow much beyond 3 to 4 percent until the bottom half of the population is participating and contributing productively. "The issue is not so much that of growth with distribution; growth with distribution can be achieved by a few cooks preparing a pie and distributing the pieces to a larger group through transfers," says Nancy Birdsall. "It is instead a matter of the poor becoming cooks too, and of more cooks preparing a bigger pie."[21] For the "poor" one can read immigrants, women, certain ethnic groups, the unemployed, and those employed but with low productivity.

On this theme of "one economics, many recipes," intriguing work has been done from the UN's early days, particularly by the world body's regional commissions. This has been elaborated in *Unity and Diversity in Development Ideas: Perspectives from the UN Regional Commissions*, the volume edited by Yves Berthelot, with chapters on the intellectual contributions of each of the five commissions. The next section explains their work.

Regional Perspectives on Economic and Social Development

The founders of the UN did not envisage the establishment of regional entities when they created the organization and its first specialized agencies. Even after the creation of the UN Economic Commission for Europe and the Economic Commission for Asia and the Far East (later ESCAP) in 1947, it took twenty-six years to establish the five regional commissions that compose the system.[22] The Economic Commission for Latin America (ECLA, later ECLAC) was created in 1948, the Economic Commission for Africa in 1958, and the Economic Commission for West Asia (ECWA) in 1973.

The early economic rationale for the regional commissions lay in the conviction that cooperation between countries of a region would be beneficial to all and could help prevent a repetition of the "beggar thy neighbor" policies of the 1930s. The institutional rationale was that wherever international cooperation and policy coordination are required, policies should be formulated at a level that internalizes the externalities or spillover effects of particular problems. The third rationale was that the benefits from cooperation with close neighbors are usually more immediately obvious than the benefits from global agreements.

Contributions by UN Regional Commissions

Both Gunnar Myrdal and P. S. Lokanathan (the first executive secretaries of the ECE and ECAFE, respectively) shared the view that cohesion and concerted action among member countries were mutually reinforcing and would facilitate reconstruction and development. They both had the idea that their member countries should be fully informed about their common problems and the negative impact that national approaches would have on their growth and welfare. With this in mind, they both decided to produce an annual survey of current economic conditions in their regions. ECLA, ECA, and ECWA followed suit. Written by secretariat teams and published under the sole responsibility of the respective executive secretaries, the annual surveys were forceful policy statements that showed a conviction that there were always solutions to apparently intractable problems. Before coming to policy conclusions and elaborating strategies, it was obviously necessary to have a reliable analysis of the region's economic and social situation. Therefore, the first invaluable achievement of the five secretariats was to collect statistical data. A preoccupation with detailed statistical and comparative analysis is a distinctive contribution of the regional commissions to the intellectual legacy of the UN.

Substantively, none of the regional commissions felt that the allocation of resources between sectors and states and consumers and investors could be left entirely to market forces. Each was convinced that government was the key actor in building up an economy that could meet the needs of the people. The instrument for guiding government action was planning. As noted in chapter 7, until the middle of the 1970s, this belief was not controversial. The regional commissions never advocated the sort of planning that characterized the centrally planned economies. Rather, they viewed plans as an instrument to clarify and prioritize goals and to secure cohesion between objectives and policy instruments. While the import substitution strategies, as recommended by Prebisch and ECLA in the 1950s, have been heavily frowned upon during the past two decades, they were followed by all presently developed countries, and often for a long time. As we make clear in the next chapter, no industrial country was able to develop without an initial period of protection.

The more creative policy ideas came from ECLA, the ECE, and the ECA, which even produced a counterstrategy to IMF and World Bank structural adjustment policies. The two other commissions were either more influenced by the received wisdom from Washington and Brussels or they were unable to do their own thinking outside of conventional boxes.

Regionalization and Globalization

The secretariats of the five regional commissions were convinced that regional cooperation was necessary not only for the maintenance of regional cohesion but also as a condition for development. From the end of the 1940s, regionalism had been seen primarily as a way to overcome the limits imposed by a purely nationalist approach to development. In the 1970s, it emerged also as a means for countries to have their views considered and taken into account in global debates. Many have doubts whether regionalism will continue to be relevant in the new century with the globalization of the world economy. The regional commissions had the opportunity to address the issue of regional cooperation in the documents that each prepared for UNCTAD X (2000) and that served as a reference in the debate organized by the UNCTAD secretary-general on that occasion.[23]

The least-expected conclusion of the debate, given the relentless publicity later accorded to the "global village" and global markets, was that the evolution of external trade within the regions of ECE, ECLAC, and ESCAP was toward closer integration between countries *within* these regions rather than toward a more global engagement. For the two other regions, ECA and ESCWA, the very low level of intraregional integration reflected their continuing dependence

on a few commodity exports. Obviously, regionalism is reinforced by development. However, it is uncertain whether increased regionalism necessarily undermines the multilateral trading system. ECLAC denied this proposition and forged the expression of "open regionalism," by which it meant opening to trade and economic integration with a region as a springboard for integrating later into the global economy.

Thus, a consensus seemed to emerge, at least within particular regions, that open regionalism not only does not undermine the trend toward globalization but actually helps to reinforce it. Under open regionalism, each region and subregion would establish rules and practices that maintain a minimum of fairness and equity in world trade and economic relations between countries in their region. In contrast, the commissions argued, the multilateral global trading system undermines itself by failing to bring fairness to international trade and financial relations.

This has been confirmed in recent years by the so-called Doha trade rounds in Cancún (2003), Hong Kong (2005), and Geneva (2008). This lack of fairness inherent in what is now called "globalization" has been one of the continuing concerns of the regional commissions. After the early denunciation of asymmetry in trade relations by ECLA in 1950, this became a leitmotiv of all regions. They denounced the asymmetry between those developing countries that, deliberately or under pressure, liberalized imports only to continue to face the same obstacles as always when they tried to export products to the markets of industrial countries. In the 1990s, the ECE criticized the obstacles to Eastern European exports of textiles, steel, aluminum, and equipment. As discussed in the next chapter, more recent WTO negotiations have made very little headway in making the global trade system more equitable and more balanced.

Before and after the financial crises of the 1980s and 1990s, the regional commissions warned against the dangers presented by the free movement of short-term capital. They argued that the constraints imposed on macroeconomic policies would undermine economic growth without securing the necessary national financial resources. These crises were not well handled by the international financial institutions. For instance, in Asia and Latin America, the IMF injected more liquidity only after countries had been most severely hit by the crisis and had been subjected to the fulfillment of conditions that delayed its actual provision when it was urgently needed.

The Continuing Importance of Regionalism

Globalization is currently both an alleged description of economic reality and a set of normative goals. As a description of the reality and trends since the 1980s,

it is exaggerated, since trade and financial flows have tended to be more important at the regional rather than global level. In its normative aspect, the globalization agenda turns out to be the traditional neoclassical, neoliberal agenda
updated for a world where geographic distance is alleged to have less significance for business activity. It was Henry Kissinger who highlighted the political dimensions of the debate over globalization versus regionalism when he
stated that "what is called globalization is really another name for the dominant
position and role of the United States."[24] Samir Amin clarified the point more
sharply: "I am not against globalization. I am against neoliberal globalization."[25]
Opposition to the neoliberal agenda may very well be one of the reasons why,
in the framework of the WTO negotiations, we see a growing importance of
regional coalitions that work to formulate their own proposals and counterpro-
posals aimed at correcting existing imbalances and asymmetries.

Regionalization or regionalism is here to stay. It remains an important instrument of international trade and a way to defend regional development interests
against premature exposure to the gales of globalization. This balancing act is
what "open regionalism" is all about. Rather than abolishing the regional commissions, as is sometimes proposed, they could be integrated into the regional
development banks. In this way the former would get financial and the latter
intellectual clout, a win-win situation. Such consolidated bodies would continue
to play an important and useful role in the realm of ideas, this time backed up
by financial means. They could creatively develop and help implement ideas that
respond to the needs of the countries in the region and beyond. They could
adopt global views or principles and advocate them in their respective regions.
The regional commissions, more so than the regional development banks, have
developed cultures and mindsets and accumulated experience that provide the
building blocks for a bottom-up process to improve development thinking and
practice. Backed by the capital of the regional banks, this can become a powerful
development instrument. The pieces should in our view be brought together, but
who will have the talent, the modesty, the courage, and the leadership skills to do
that? Myrdal or Prebisch could have done it, but even they would have found it
more difficult today to overcome the institutional complexity and bureaucratic
obstacles that such reorganization would involve.

Open Regionalism

ECLAC's work on open regionalism needs to be continued and intensified.[26]
Latin American governments are asked to experiment with the idea of using
economic integration as a springboard for integrating into the global economy. This was already the idea behind the Southern Cone Common Market

(MERCOSUR, or Mercado Común del Sur in Spanish), which promotes free trade and the fluid movement of goods, people, and currency. In this connection, it is significant that Latin America during the 1990s showed an increase in both interregional and extraregional trade, with the former outperforming the latter. ECLAC tried to reconcile unilateral trade liberalization with preferential trade arrangements and discussed how to convert subregional or regional arrangements into "building blocks" rather than "stumbling blocks" to a more open and transparent international trading system.

Regionalization during the 1990s began to go far beyond trade, backed up by increased intra–Latin American investment flows.[27] In parallel, the North American Free Trade Agreement (NAFTA) served as a magnet for foreign direct investment (FDI) from the United States. Thus, Mexico experienced an increase in flows from *North* America, averaging more than $6 billion annually between 1994 and the end of the decade, compared with around $2 billion in the preceding years. Labor migration to the United States from Latin America also grew significantly, along with workers' remittances to areas south of the Rio Grande. For a number of countries in the region, remittances had become a more important source of foreign exchange than foreign direct investment or even merchandise exports by the early years of the new century.

Perhaps the most dramatic change was the gradual shift during the 1990s from the traditional intraregional focus on integration (South-South) to a growing interest in interregional (North-South) agreements that link up commercially with industrialized countries in reciprocal free trade. However, this shift in policy is not shared by all Latin American countries; some prefer to consolidate regional integration before going North. But it is not a black-and-white picture. Brazil wants to put relatively more emphasis on regionalism. In a way, the Brazil group acts more like the East Asian countries, shifting gradually from import substitution to export promotion strategies instead of exposing themselves immediately to the onslaught of the global market—hence, "regionalism with a global twist."

ECLAC has contributed to a lively debate with a continuing skepticism regarding prevailing economic and financial orthodoxies. It was instrumental in redirecting policies toward a comprehensive strategy that combined sustained growth with financial stability and with due regard to greater equity and the consolidation of democratic institutions. ECLAC has consistently suggested that development does not occur spontaneously but is the result of a predetermined and well-reasoned strategy. The idea of an active state to move things along and to overcome structural impediments to growth became deeply embedded in its culture. As such, it has maintained a more balanced approach in the 1980s and 1990s than the adherents of the Washington consensus.[28]

It is this more balanced approach that must now be generalized and applied to the debate over "regionalization with a global twist" or "globalization with a regional twist."

Conclusion

During the 1960s and 1970s in the debate about national development strategies, initiatives and ideas came from the UN rather than from the Bretton Woods institutions. This situation was reversed in the 1980s, but in the late 1990s, the UN began to resume its more traditional and innovative role, although it generally still has much less influence than the World Bank and the IMF, which continued to receive strong donor support and the bulk of donor funds.

The relationship between state-led regionalism and private sector–driven globalization is embedded in both the UN and its regional commissions. The latter have documented that regionalism is thriving and can serve globalization well by preparing the countries of the region for the gales of competition that globalization implies. The regional commissions together with the regional development banks can produce a "globalization with a human face."

In our contemporary globalizing era, the edges of regions are blurred. But this reality may not be so new, as Karl Deutsch wrote: "For the political scientist the definition of a region is considerably more difficult than the definition of a rose was to Gertrude Stein. We cannot simply say, 'A region is a region is a region.'"[29] Nonetheless, it is clear that a substantial part of an economic and social "tailoring" should include insights from knowledgeable cloth-makers and seamstresses who are geographically proximate to those who will be wearing the clothes. That has been an important and continuing contribution of the UN system.

6. Fairer International Economic Relations

From Aid and Mutual Interests to Global Solidarity

• **Development Assistance**
• **International Trade**
• **Transnational Corporations and Foreign Direct Investment**
• **Globalization**
• **Conclusion**

The UN was far ahead of the curve around 1950 in conceiving a system of international economic relations that would serve all countries of the world well. It issued three major publications: *National and International Measures for Full Employment* (1949), *Measures for the Economic Development of Under-Developed Countries* (1951), and *Measures for International Economic Stability* (1951).[1] Each report was written by a small group of prominent economists from different parts of the world with support from the UN Secretariat—an early example of the Second and the Third United Nations working together. These publications and their recommendations were ahead of their time, particularly in the international domain. Among the recommendations at the international level, the most striking were the following:

• Establishing a new structural equilibrium in world trade as soon as possible
• Creating measures in industrial countries to encourage capital flows to developing countries in order to encourage their rapid growth of production and increase in real incomes
• Lifting the institutional constraints on economic development by diminishing through land reform the high concentration of land ownership, discrimination in banking systems, and other factors that hindered the mobility of resources
• Attacking short-run fluctuations in the prices and terms of trade of primary products through the negotiation of international commodity agreements
• Using the World Bank's potential for countercyclical action by securing a substantial increase in the flow of lending to developing countries in the event of a recession

• Introducing more flexible arrangements to the International Monetary Fund so it could respond more promptly in the event of a recession to overcome the temporary difficulties of member states

This was almost sixty years ago. The reports display a bold confidence. They use logical economic analysis to show how to tackle the issues of instability and growth in an international framework. At the time, the use of an international perspective was indeed pioneering and contrasted sharply with the narrow and nationalistic economic analysis of the 1930s. The reports also recognized how underdeveloped countries had an even greater stake in stability for their long-term development than industrial countries. Finally, they showed how action for the so-called underdeveloped countries could and should be combined with global action to avoid instability and recession.

However, the pioneering dimensions of international perspectives and proposals largely fell on deaf ears. Little action was taken in the light of these reports, in spite of the ways they identified specific international policy measures to make possible national action for countries in economic difficulties. The recommendations also ran into a brick wall at both the World Bank and the IMF. The tragedy of neglecting these recommendations was that no broader economic plan was put in place. Yet the powers of the time, mostly the United States with support from the United Kingdom and a handful of other developed countries, could have mobilized support for a broader international economic regime if they had had the vision or the wish to do so. In *The UN and Global Political Economy*, John Toye and Richard Toye carefully analyze the various reasons—ideological, economic, political—why what became described as an "extreme Keynesianism" of intervention in the international economy was not acceptable to the United States, neither to the government in Washington nor to the majority within the economics profession throughout the country.[2] The retreat from regulation and intervention in the international economy was reinforced by the needs of the United States as it rearmed for the Korean War. Ironically, U.S. spending removed any immediate danger of recession.

In the absence of early global action to foster balanced economic growth in developed and developing countries alike, the global failures of the 1970s and 1980s were predictable. Fluctuations in the international economy returned with a vengeance, following the breakdown of the Bretton Woods system in 1971 and the oil shocks of 1973–1974 and 1979. More than twenty years after the publication of the three UN reports, UNCTAD called for a common fund to support a range of commodity agreements, much as the report had recommended, as had John Maynard Keynes in the 1940s when he recommended such a strategy as the third leg of the Bretton Woods system. Without an international economic regime for balanced growth, the instabilities and higher oil

prices of the 1970s severely disrupted the world economy, even more so in the weaker and least-developed countries, setting up the debt overhang and debt crises of the 1980s.

Global approaches were sidelined. Many countries and experts ridiculed the Brandt report's intellectual attempt in 1980, and its idealistic vision remained a dead letter.[3] Instead, structural adjustment programs in each developing country became the norm and African and Latin American countries were forced to carry the full burden of adjustment themselves with far too little international support. The 1980s became the "lost decade" for economic growth—as, in many respects, did the 1990s as well—as growth rates in Latin America and Africa plummeted and per capita incomes declined. To illustrate the latter point, the per capita income of Latin America as a whole grew by 80 percent from 1960 to 1980. From 1980 to 2000, the growth in per capita income was a miserable 9 percent.[4] The contrasts for Sub-Saharan Africa covering the same two twenty-year periods are even more remarkable, 36 percent for the first and *minus* 15 percent for the second period.[5]

The need for structural adjustment is not really new, and in a world of open economies, governments of all stripes are obliged to adjust their policies. But there is no need in theory or practice for one-sided adjustment, let alone for the policies of World Bank and IMF that were implemented during the 1980s and much of the 1990s. More flexible countercyclical support in the form of foreign exchange and access to export markets, free from the risks of large commodity price fluctuations, as suggested in the UN reports almost sixty years ago, would have avoided many of the extremes of adjustment. Such measures are still needed.

The situation of the world economy and of the developing countries would certainly have been much better if the international (global) framework advocated by the UN in 1950 had been taken more seriously at the time or rediscovered and implemented two decades later. It follows that the UN and other international organizations have a most important piece of work ahead of them. We have entered the twenty-first century with a rapidly globalizing economy fueled by the private sector. This is engendering a highly skewed economic development in which a number of countries, including China and India, are doing very well but many others, especially poorer and weaker countries in Africa and Latin America, are falling behind.

Is it so difficult to come up with an international framework that ensures that no country is left behind? Throughout the UN's history, the dominant ways to help answer that question have been through development assistance through international trade and through foreign direct investment, mainly by transnational corporations (TNCs).

Development Assistance

In the 1950s, the UN introduced the novel idea of "development aid," as it was then called. Development aid started after World War II. Never in the history of international (economic) relations had the world seen *public* financial flows consciously moved from one country to another with the aim of assisting the receiving countries in their economic development. Of course, private financial flows had long been around, mainly in the form of FDI; an example is the private financing to construct railways in Latin America. But these were investments in search of profit. Official development assistance from developed to underdeveloped countries was unprecedented.

Obviously, new ideas rarely fall from the sky. In *The UN and Development: From Aid to Cooperation,* Olav Stokke identifies five traditions, or historical roots, underlying the postwar flows of aid:

• The humanitarian relief tradition, as in the long-standing Red Cross movements, dating back to the nineteenth century

• The solidarity tradition, arising especially from socialist and social democratic movements and from trade unions concerned to enhance the living standards and dignity of workers in all countries

• The missionary tradition, which already had established links with people in many developing countries

• The human rights tradition as an international pillar of humanism reinforced by the creation of the UN and the Universal Declaration of 1948

• The colonial tradition, which Stokke refers to as the "most powerful and systematic pre-aid influence on developments in the South by the North"[6]

The UN's launch into aid and technical assistance was triggered by President Harry S. Truman's 1949 Four Point Speech, given at his inauguration on 20 January 1949. Truman announced a program "for peace and freedom in four major courses of action." Point four reads as follows and is worth citing in its entirety:

> We must embark on a bold new program for making the benefits of our scientific advances and industrial progress available for the improvement and growth of underdeveloped areas.
>
> More than half the people of the world are living in conditions approaching misery. Their food is inadequate. They are victims of disease. Their economic life is primitive and stagnant. Their poverty is a handicap and a threat both to them and to more prosperous areas. For the first time in history,

humanity possesses the knowledge and the skill to relieve the suffering of these people.

The United States is pre-eminent among nations in the development of industrial and scientific techniques. The material resources which we can afford to use for the assistance of other peoples are limited. But our imponderable resources in technical knowledge are constantly growing and are inexhaustible. I believe that we should make available to peace-loving peoples the benefits of our store of technical knowledge in order to help them realize their aspirations for a better life. And, in cooperation with other nations, we should foster capital investments in areas needing development. Our aim should be to help the free peoples of the world, through their own efforts, to produce more food, more clothing, more materials for housing, and more mechanical power to lighten their burdens.

We invite other countries to pool their technological resources in this undertaking. Their contributions will be warmly welcomed. This should be a cooperative enterprise in which all nations work together through the United Nations and its specialized agencies wherever practicable. It must be a worldwide effort for the achievement of peace, plenty, and freedom.[7]

Members of the U.S. delegation came well prepared to the 1949 sessions of ECOSOC and other relevant gatherings within the UN system, determined to create a basis for a proper UN response to the president's challenge. They quickly took and retained an initiative in the process that led to the creation of the UN's Expanded Programme of Technical Assistance (EPTA).[8]

The economic rationale for introducing this novel idea was straightforward. Since underdeveloped countries did not produce sufficient savings, ODA was needed to reduce the savings-investment gap so that these countries could grow faster, thereby reducing the income gap between them and the industrialized countries. The original impulse, therefore, was one of international economic and financial solidarity in a world in which colonizers and colonized still existed side by side. However, World War II had profoundly shaken the pillars of the international system and the power and capitalist vision of the United States displaced the fading economic and colonial perspectives of Europe.

In the 1960s, another major initiative was the establishment of a development decade, the proposal of U.S. president John F. Kennedy to the General Assembly.[9] This quickly met with support from most other countries, both developed and developing, though not those from the Soviet bloc. Intellectually, the ideas came from outside the UN, specifically encouraged by Walt Rostow, who a year earlier had published his influential book *The Stages of Economic Growth* with its revealing sub-title, *A Non-Communist Manifesto*.[10] The goal of the development

Box 6.1. John Maynard Keynes and the Early Vision for Bretton Woods

The World Bank and the International Monetary Fund—the two economic institutions that grew from the conference at the resort in Bretton Woods, New Hampshire—were conceived during World War II. Their distinguished intellectual pedigree includes John Maynard Keynes, the most famous economist of his day, who had been asked to draw up ideas for a postwar international economic order to address the ills that he himself had so boldly and clearly identified as growing from the inadequacies and injustices of the Versailles settlement to World War I.[1]

In particular, his task was to mitigate the risks of repeating the economic setbacks and unemployment of the Great Depression of the 1930s. Within a few weeks, Keynes had written a brief but masterly paper setting out plans for an International Clearing Union. The core of Keynes's analysis was the recognition that all countries had a tendency to control their balance of payments by ensuring that their export earnings exceeded their imports (plus any net capital flows abroad). When every country tried to do the same thing, a deflationary spiral was created within the global economy. This was well illustrated by the Great Depression of the 1930s, when countries adopted beggar-thy-neighbor policies, cutting imports and trying to promote exports, thereby reducing global demand.

Keynes's solution was to create an international institution, together with incentives and rules of behavior for countries, under which imbalances would be kept to a minimum. Countries would be allowed to borrow internationally to meet imbalances that arose. Establishing the conditions for full employment in the major economic powers was a key objective. In several respects, the proposal envisaged an international central bank with powers and functions along the lines of the central banks in major industrial countries.

Negotiators at the resort in Bretton Woods, New Hampshire, made many compromises in 1944, but they agreed to set up the IMF and the World Bank. These institutions lacked many of the elements Keynes had envisaged, but they were still intended to provide international support for individual countries, including their pursuit of full employment policies, an objective that was built into the articles of association of both institutions.

In their operations, both institutions soon moved even farther from Keynes's original vision. After the collapse of the Bretton Woods agreement in 1971, the world economy entered a period of considerable instability, especially in the 1980s and afterward, an era of increasing debt problems that were especially acute for many developing countries. The IMF and the World Bank responded to these problems with structural adjustment policies, under which the burden of adjustment fell on individual countries, including the poorest. These policies often acted to multiply rather than diminish economic instabilities and human setbacks.

This was almost the opposite of Keynes's original vision.

1. John Maynard Keynes, *The Economic Consequences of Peace* (New York: Harcourt, Brace, 1919).

decade—which when it was introduced was seen as a one-off event but became the first of four decades—was that developing countries as a group and individually should accelerate their rates of economic growth to approach an average of 5 percent per annum by the end of the 1960s. Increases of international aid and private sector flows would support this acceleration, for which a total target of an estimated 1 percent of the GNP of industrial countries would be required. Once the broad goals were set, the UN played an important role in elaborating the other components of the decade, emphasizing to a degree often now forgotten that the program was one of "growth plus change," in which change referred to many elements of advancement linked to improving the social as well as the material conditions of people's lives. In sharp contrast to what was expected at the time, developing countries as a group exceeded the goal of 5 percent annual growth (as did fifty individual developing countries). In addition, international financial flows (public and private) reached 0.79 percent of the total GNP of individual countries.[11]

There were other important developments in the 1960s. These included the creation of the World Food Programme in 1961 and the establishment of UNCTAD in 1964. In addition, the Committee on Development Planning (CDP) was created in the mid-1960s at the initiative of Jan Tinbergen, who served as its first chair; it monitored progress during the First Development Decade and formulated proposals for the next development decade. The success of the decade, which was less apparent at the time than the statistics later showed, set the stage for a higher growth rate target for the Second Development Decade in the 1970s, for which the aid target of 0.7 percent of GNP of industrial countries was formally set. This target was specifically recommended in *Partners in Development,* the report of the Commission on International Development set up by Robert McNamara, the president of the World Bank, which was chaired by Lester Pearson, the former prime minister of Canada. Later endorsed by the General Assembly, it is arguably the most famous international statistical target ever set and never met.[12]

The 1970s marked the end of the golden age of the 1950s and 1960s, when the growth of both developed and developing countries was robust and fairly steady and unemployment in most developed countries was low. In contrast, for many developing countries, especially the least developed, the 1970s introduced decades of instability and economic setback. In 1971, the Bretton Woods system of fixed exchange rates collapsed. In 1973, oil prices surged, as they did again in 1979. The three- to four-fold increase in oil prices over 1973–1974 transferred about 2 percent of global income from the oil-importing countries to the oil exporters. This remarkable improvement in the fortunes of oil-exporting countries stirred hopes among developing countries more generally for fundamental

changes in the international economic system. However, negotiations for a New International Economic Order went nowhere and talk about it faded in the late 1970s. The idea was dead by the 1981 meeting of the Conference on International Economic Cooperation (CIEC) in Cancún.[13]

Worst of all, what appeared initially to be a ray of hope for the poorest countries—namely, that they could borrow some of the oil profits deposited into western banks at very low interest rates—proved disastrous. The surpluses that OPEC countries accumulated were indeed recycled to many of the poorer countries, but in the form of loans from western banks, initially at very low and sometimes negative real interest rates (the result of inflation reaching double-digit figures). Western bankers rushed to sign up developing countries to take these loans of "recycled petrodollars," supported by a chorus of support from the Bretton Woods institutions and others. UNCTAD warned of the risks of increasing debt, but to no avail.

The honeymoon of low or negative interest rates soon disappeared, however, with the arrival of the Thatcher-Reagan era in 1979–1980. Monetary policies tightened, interest rates soared, and the obligations of developing countries to service their debt became an unsupportable burden. Severe problems in Mexico precipitated a debt crisis in 1982, which had worldwide repercussions that lasted throughout the 1980s. As conditionalities for borrowing from the Bretton Woods institutions, many developing countries, indeed the majority of countries in Sub-Saharan Africa and Latin America, undertook programs of stabilization followed by a succession of very tough programs of structural adjustment. Although IMF lending is supposed to be temporary, over fifty countries have had spells of participation in IMF programs that have lasted ten years or more; eighteen such programs lasted for fifteen years or more.[14]

It took until 1989 before the developed world made any serious moves toward debt relief. In the words of Nigel Lawson, the UK's chancellor of the exchequer from 1983–1989, "The principal—though largely undeclared—objective of the Western world's debt strategy, ably co-ordinated by the IMF, was to buy time. ... Time was needed not only to enable the debtor countries to put sensible economic policies in place but also for the Western banks to rebuild their shattered balance sheets to the point where they could afford to write off their sovereign debts. For it was perfectly clear that the vast bulk of these debts would never come good—even though there was an understandable conspiracy of silence over admitting this unpalatable fact."[15]

The Washington consensus was too narrow, sometimes technically wrong, and essentially constructed around developed country interests and priorities. Debt relief programs were mostly too little too late and continued to be attached to conditionalities. Aid over the 1980s and 1990s was mostly given to reinforce

structural adjustment, and the Bretton Woods institutions coordinated much of the bilateral aid, largely pushing the United Nations out of the picture.

Over the years since 1950, ODA has evolved. Development assistance moved from one objective to another without having met the previous one. From reducing the savings-investment gap, the objectives of ODA within the UN moved to a wider agenda during the 1960s and 1970s: accelerating economic growth, supporting children, stimulating education, creating employment, and empowering women economically. After the economic collapse and conflict the end of the Cold War brought, aid was targeted to helping fragile states, supporting humanitarian action, reducing poverty, supporting human rights, and providing aid for trade, to mention just a few goals. Aid became a panacea, and in the end it met few if any of its many and shifting objectives.[16] The total volume of aid never reached the target of 0.7 percent of GNP set by the UN at the beginning of the Second Development Decade, although the Scandinavian countries and the Netherlands more than fulfilled this target. Nonetheless, ODA continues to be the one token of international economic solidarity in the world, most recently concentrated to a large extent on yet another objective, support for reaching the Millennium Development Goals.[17]

As we go to press, the United Nations has issued the latest data regarding the attainment of MDG 8, namely outside assistance for development. An inter-agency task force reported that ODA dropped 8.4 percent in 2007, hard on the heels of a 4.7 percent drop in 2006. The group pointed out that commitments to help the least-developed countries and Africa in particular had lagged substantially. The G-8 pledge at their Gleneagles meeting in 2005 to mobilize $25 billion for Africa rang particularly hollow, with just $4 billion actually delivered.[18] Clearly, changes in policy do not actuality make.

International Trade

Almost from the beginning, it became clear that major inconsistencies existed within international economic relations between aid and trade. Aid was intended to be a temporary measure to get developing countries on their feet and ready, among other things, to start exporting their own products and thus growing their own economies. But a lot has gone wrong. Not only has aid suffered from trying to meet too many objectives but inequities in international trade and negotiating trade arrangements have often taken away with one hand many times what aid was giving with the other. The West has preached free trade but has not practiced it. It practices protectionism, above all in agriculture. Even the least-developed countries were pressured to open their borders prematurely, making it next to impossible for them to build even a feeble

national industrial base. It is not surprising that radical critics argue that aid hides this reality behind gestures of generosity and in ways that in the 1980s and 1990s often helped bind developing countries to agreements that required them to open their economies to imports and investment from abroad.

As John Toye and Richard Toye observed in *The UN and Global Political Economy,* the world continues to be governed by a twin-track system. The UN, and more particularly UNCTAD when it comes to trade, provides a forum in which ideas, proposals, and policies are debated. In recent years, UNCTAD has started to act more and more as a think tank that formulates policy proposals for such issues as trade, commodities, debt, and transnational corporations. But when it comes to serious agreements and implementation, the debate shifts to institutions in which industrialized countries place their confidence. In matters of trade, finance, and development, industrialized countries prefer such bodies as the World Bank and the IMF, which have weighted voting systems, and the World Trade Organization, which, despite having a one-country, one-vote system, chooses to seek consensus rather than deciding matters by voting. We live with a global economic governance system in which discussion and implementation are the responsibility of different international organizations.[19]

Although not formally part of the UN, the WTO cannot be ignored in a discussion of the future of trade negotiations. In scope and ambition, it goes far beyond its predecessor, the General Agreement on Tariffs and Trade (GATT). The overall aim has broadened from nondiscrimination and the reduction of trade barriers to the adoption of policies that support open markets generally. New agreements cover trade in agricultural products, sanitary standards, textiles and clothing, technical barriers to trade, trade-related investment measures, trade in services, intellectual property rights, and the removal of various nontariff barriers. The WTO is potentially much more intrusive than GATT in national policies because it now makes rules across this substantial new agenda. Moreover, the WTO overrules national laws and requires countries to change existing domestic laws that conflict with the obligations of WTO membership. A new Trade Policy Review Mechanism obliges member countries to present regular public accounts of their compliance with these obligations. All this makes substantial incursions on what were matters of domestic governance before the Uruguay Round agreements came into force.

The latest illustration of the difficulties engendered by this attitude is the Doha Round, started in 2002. The WTO initiated this round after 9-11 with the explicit aim of making international trade regulations more development oriented. In 2008, the results are still lackluster. Due to unrelenting pressures by industrial countries—led by the United States and the European Union—the Doha negotiations have veered from their proclaimed objective of making development in poor countries a priority toward a "market access" direction in

which developing countries are pressured to open up their agricultural, indus-trial, and services sectors to imports and influence from industrial countries. A development-oriented outcome would have resulted in a significant reduction in domestic agricultural subsidies and tariffs in industrial countries while enabling developing countries to protect and promote the interests of their small farmers. It would also have allowed developing countries to promote industrial develop-ment while developed countries would have agreed to eliminate or significantly reduce their tariffs on imports of industrial goods and eliminate other nontariff barriers to imports. Similar priorities would apply to services.

At the WTO, developed countries have succeeded in marginalizing devel-opment issues. They have not been willing to reduce their domestic subsidies beyond current or already planned levels; their continued subsidies to agricul-ture are especially problematic. Developed countries want new modalities in services that would make it easier to pressure developing countries to liberalize their services sector, but developed countries are unwilling to make compro-mises in other sectors that have practical benefits for developing countries.

Industrialized countries have turned the negotiations into demands that developing countries open access to their markets in agriculture, industry, and services. As Indian commerce minister Kamal Nath pointed out in the June–July 2006 meetings of the WTO, this was supposed to be a development round, but the developed countries are trying to ignore development concerns and turn it into a "market access round."[20]

It is imperative that we re-balance the existing WTO rules and make the multilateral trading system more equitable. No agreement on the Doha Round is possible without a satisfactory outcome of the economic development problématique.

The Uruguay Round (started in 1986 and concluded in 1994) introduced new rules on the use of countervailing duties that permit a country to charge extra duties on imports if its domestic industry has been harmed by unfair export subsidies by another country. Most subsidies by a country to economic activi-ties that it considers vital can trigger countervailing action if they cause "mate-rial injury." Under the Tokyo Round rules, developing countries could decide not to participate in this subsidy code, but participation is now mandatory for all members of the World Trade Organization. The effect of this policy change outlaws the kinds of industrial subsidies that have been used by all developed countries historically, and by poor countries recently, to accelerate growth and development. There is some doubt among experts that the "Asian miracle" of the period 1965–1995 could recur under current WTO rules. The high growth of the so-called Asian tigers depended on selective departures from pure free-trade regimes, which are no longer possible under a strict application of WTO rules.

Existing inequalities of economic and political power between developed and developing countries justify a flexible interpretation of the rules. If there is to be any departure from free trade, it should favor the economically weak rather than the economically strong. There is a compelling case that the poorest developing countries should be given exceptional specific subsidies for the products of infant industries, with one proviso: such subsidies should be selective, temporary, and related to performance. That is the only way for developing countries to avoid repeating the errors of previous international trade policies.[21]

Here some historical perspective is essential. Today's developed countries succeeded in their development efforts after a period of protectionism. Alexander Hamilton, the first U.S. secretary of the treasury, understood this well and introduced protectionist measures against imports of British industrial goods.[22] The United States remained a highly protectionist country until World War II. For instance, the average tariff rate of the United States was 40 to 50 percent in 1875 and 48 percent in 1931.[23] Friedrich List, a German economist known for his theory of infant industries that argued that protection is necessary during the early stages of industrialization, generalized the Hamilton policy in his 1841 book *The National System of Political Economy* and introduced the term "kicking away the ladder" to describe eliminating these exceptional policies for latecomers to industrialization.[24] European countries all practiced protectionism historically and, as we have just seen, continue to do so now.[25] The economic success of East Asian nations has been attributed to their skillful combination of protection for their own growing industries and aggressive pursuit of exports abroad.

International economic solidarity has thus remained an elusive vision, in spite of ODA. Solidarity must mean more than charity. Good trade relations are based on relationships negotiated between well-informed trading partners on an equal basis. In contrast, many of today's relationships reflect asymmetries between the strong and the weak, the rich and the poor, creating a strong sense of injustice.

International economic and financial relations should be based on a different international system. Social justice cannot prevail in a world of nation-states where the laws of the jungle continue to prevail. With the hindsight of over thirty years, the ambitions of the G-77 to introduce important changes in the international economic status quo—encouraged by the success of the OPEC "coup" of 1973—are often ridiculed as naïve and based on wishful thinking. Such a judgment, based on the situation today, does not do justice to the NIEO initiative led by Algeria, Mexico, and other countries in the very different climate of the 1970s. We would be inclined to assert that an analogous initiative adapted to the situation of the twenty-first century would be very desirable in today's globalizing world. The NIEO can be seen as one of the first radical yet

coherent attempts to introduce a fairer system of global governance in order to realize a higher degree of international solidarity, reduce the important income differentials among countries, give developing countries more export opportunities in the markets of the industrial countries, discipline the power of transnational corporations, and establish the sovereignty of all countries over their natural resources—all things that are still necessary today.

The NIEO initiative failed for two principal reasons. First, failure was due to the negative reaction of the industrialized countries, except for some of the smaller ones. At the outset they were obliged to consider the alternative the NIEO presented because the OPEC increases in the price of oil temporarily shifted the balance of economic power. But as the first effects of the shock were absorbed, it was again politics as usual. Power returned to the West. And should one really be surprised? Has one ever seen a country giving away its international advantage voluntarily because of a long-term vision of the common good?

Second, the reason for the failure of the NIEO also lies with the developing countries grouped in the G-77. These countries had everything to gain from this initiative, but they had no clear, business-like vision of what they wanted or on what timetable. According to Gamani Corea, it was the UNCTAD secretariat that did the bulk of the work of putting together a package of demands without much guidance from the G-77.[26] The result was a long menu of dishes from which a good and balanced meal should have been selected. Instead, the G-77 kept ordering and ordering until they exhausted the entire menu and themselves. And the developed countries had no interest in the meal.

By the early 1980s the NIEO was dead. Margaret Thatcher and Ronald Reagan were in power, the Washington consensus loomed on the horizon, and the debt crisis was a fact. In fact, the industrialized countries came up with a new international order without calling it that. Their solution of structural adjustment policies was a euphemism for forcing liberalization of trade, privatization of state enterprises, and deregulation. This was imposed, not negotiated, and thus the rich countries did not have to make any concessions. Since 1980, international economic solidarity has basically been an empty slogan. Even the volume of development assistance decreased during the 1990s after the fall of the Berlin Wall did away with the competition from the communist bloc.

Transnational Corporations and Foreign Direct Investment

During the 1970s many actions of TNCs were controversial, and the United Nations decided to examine the behavior of these firms. This subject is dealt with in the UNIHP volume *The UN and Transnational Corporations: From Code of Conduct to Global Compact,* by Tagi Sagafi-nejad in collaboration with

John Dunning.[27] The UN decided to create both a Commission for and a Centre on Transnational Corporations (UNCTC) in 1974 upon the recommendation of the Group of Eminent Persons that had been appointed to study this issue. Sagafi-nejad and Dunning draw the rest of the UN system into their analysis, as the work of virtually all UN organizations impinges on TNCs.

Sotiris Mousouris, who helped establish the Centre on Transnational Corporations, has clearly stated the logic behind this effort of the UN: "The multinationals had become new powerful actors in the world stage but they were not fully responsible to any state. They had their own logic and goals, and the impact of their operations on their home or their host countries was not understood. They were challenging the authority of elected governments and could influence international relations. And the big question, of course, was what effect they had on development, on developing countries."[28]

The story is mainly one of cycles—from harmonious relationships between TNCs and society to antagonistic ones, with the UN trying to keep a scholarly detachment and mostly, but not always, succeeding. In the 1970s, TNCs came under serious attack because of actions of AT&T in Chile that led to the toppling and death of President Salvador Allende. This highly visible incident was accompanied by bribery scandals around the world that were revealed by a host of committees of the U.S. Congress. Although Washington subsequently became hostile to the UN's efforts, the world organization's role ironically was to a large extent inspired by the outcome of U.S. congressional committees and the hearings.

The main focus during the early years was on the elaboration of a code of conduct that would temper the revealed abuses of TNCs. That attempt was thorough and detailed, drawing on a well-informed and experienced panel of distinguished experts from around the world. But ultimately it was unsuccessful. In the 1980s, the climate around TNCs and FDI started to evolve. Developing countries actively sought investments from transnational corporations. This sometimes led to a "race to the bottom," with countries outbidding each other to offer the most favorable terms to corporations. The UNCTC, which was never as radical in its policy proposals as some of its member states, successfully guided the debate on the desirability and content of a code of conduct for transnational corporations. Many were surprised that the United States continued its critical stance toward the UNCTC when its own hearings had helped initiate activities during the 1970s. The United States was so opposed to the work of the UNCTC that it pressured Secretary-General Boutros Boutros-Ghali to dismiss the third executive director of the center in 1992, split the UNCTC, and transfer part of its work—mainly the FDI component—from New York to UNCTAD in Geneva.

In the meantime, other UN organizations proceeded with their activities

concerning TNCs. In 1977, the ILO adopted a Tripartite Declaration of Principles concerning Multinational Enterprises and Social Policy, a voluntary set of principles to "offer guidelines to [multinational enterprises], governments, and employers' and workers' organizations in such areas as employment, training, conditions of work and life, and industrial relations." Its stated aim is to "encourage the positive contribution which multinational enterprises can make to economic and social progress" while "minimizing their adverse impacts."[29] It passed because it was not binding and was couched in more conciliatory terms than successive drafts of the UN's Code of Conduct. As Sagafi-nejad documents, the WHO engaged in investigative research and launched a global campaign to publicize the adverse effects of tobacco use. It also aimed to develop global rules to curb advertising and sales, which culminated in the 2003 Framework Convention on Tobacco Control, which WHO members adopted at the fifty-sixth World Health Assembly. The WHO also exposed corruption in the marketing of breast-milk substitutes and various abuses in the pharmaceutical industry.

After the UNCTC moved to Geneva in 1993, its work was quiet, subdued, and mainly devoted to producing the World Investment Reports (WIRs), a series that started in 1991 and continues. The amount of data and information gathered over the years for the WIRs is useful and widely cited. However, it is surprising, to say the least, that over the past twenty years or so the UN has retreated from setting the intellectual agenda regarding TNCs and their role in the global economy, ecology, and polity. It has ignored the private sector for too long, and the Global Compact initiative by Kofi Annan, although welcome, is seen by many as too little and too late. The private sector should be seen as a source of ideas. It has research holdings of great importance. Yet there are also fears of domination by the increasingly consolidated TNCs that often operate beyond effective constraints in the globalizing economy.

Klaus Sahlgren, who was executive director of the UNCTC between 1975 and the mid-1980s, regretted the decision to move what had been the independent unit of the UN Secretariat in New York to Geneva within UNCTAD. The move, he said, failed "to keep a neutral, impartial image in the eyes of its clients, which were both West and South, and also business. Now to put it in UNCTAD, which had and still has, I believe, a public image of being the part of the UN which mainly interests itself in the problems of the developing countries, was a tactical mistake."[30]

Many other questions relate to the efficient and effective operations of transnational corporations: how to ensure the competition needed for market efficiency and what regulations are needed for safety relating to health, food, and other matters. The Global Compact is useful, but it fails in most of these matters. Given the history of the UNCTC, one must ask where such issues

can be debated and where decisions can be reached on the actions needed to create efficient and effective roles for the private sector in today's world. This has obvious connections with the issue of globalization and global governance.

Globalization

"Globalization has been with us since the dawn of history," Nayan Chanda reminds us. "But the notion of trying to govern the interconnections that it has produced is a more recent phenomenon."[31] Using the perspective of *longue durée* is useful because traders, preachers, adventurers, and warriors have continually linked communities and civilizations. At the same time, the intensity and ever-quickening rapidity of transboundary interactions in our era is unusual in that virtually no one and no place on earth has been completely untouched. And its scope continues to grow. In short, as Jan Aart Scholte tells us, "Obituaries for globalization are highly premature."[32]

Whatever one's position on how new or old the wine and the bottle, the world clearly is now in a globalized era whose tide is supposed to raise all boats. True enough, there have been several spectacular success stories. As early as the 1970s several smaller East Asian countries took off economically. After this, China and more recently India (whose combined populations constitute nearly 40 percent of the world's population) have been enjoying spectacular economic growth. Their acceleration has been strongly helped by their involvement in the global economy. Poverty in these two countries is diminishing (although a great many are still poor). The weight of China and India in the world population is such that global poverty figures also show a relative decline.[33]

Without in any way underestimating the performance of East and Southeast Asia and India, global economic statistics disguise the reality and lives of poverty of billions of people in other developing counties, not to mention for large numbers of citizens of China and India. As virtually every recent Human Development Report has documented, the income of the world's poor has remained low even when national economies have been strong. This also applies to the working and middle classes in the United States, whose purchasing power has remained stable or declined over the last twenty years. The rising tide of globalization has certainly lifted a number of boats, but it has left millions struggling in the water and has drowned many of the poorest. And the current global crisis has added at least 100 million persons to the numbers in poverty.

In other words, globalization is an uneven phenomenon. In some respects, it has been a step backward. Because of globalization, private enterprise, particularly transnational corporations, have found through international movement some of the freedoms that they had lost through national regulation in the

countries in which they are incorporated. So TNCs today can identify niches of least resistance in countries around the world, divide up their production activities and tax obligations, and change their headquarters to suit their corporate pocketbooks. In the same way, they have often escaped regulations relating to competition and labor laws. At the global level, there is no countervailing power and agreed-upon mechanisms of transparency and control.

As Sidney Dell, one of the UN's first and most eminent economists, said shortly before his death:

> There is no international agency that is dealing systematically with global questions of consistency and inconsistency. In matters of economic policy, the triumvirate of the IMF, the World Bank, and GATT/WTO as they function at present is not up to the task. There have been proposals to set up an Economic Security Council, to no avail so far. Thus the structural mechanism of global control has remained the same; that is unsatisfactory.[34]

If, therefore, there is to be more social justice in the world, less risk of terrorism, and less despair, the key is to create a system of global governance in order to make the globalizing world somewhat more civilized. Jan Tinbergen, who won the first Nobel Prize for Economics in 1969, has consistently and persistently called for this, identifying major components of national governments that were needed internationally, such as measures of taxation and redistribution and controls to ensure competition.[35] Robert McNamara, former president of the World Bank, also has come very close to arguing in favor of a world government.[36] As far as we know, he was the last well-known and respected personality to do so.

To repeat, it is in every country's interest for late developers to succeed in catching up because that is the only route to a world of less poverty and conflict. If their path is blocked "for legal reasons," the legitimacy of the present ideal of a liberal trade regime and economic order can only erode further, and when that happens world trading arrangements are bound to become more disorderly. The WTO and UNCTAD should come closer together and play complementary roles to create a world of economic equals. The same applies to the G-8 and the G-20.[37]

Good governance has become a much-used and much-abused term at both the national and international levels. At the international level an instrument or a set of instruments should be found to guide globalization that is driven by the private sector in a direction that will indeed lift all boats and that, therefore, will constitute a countervailing power to the might of TNCs and private enterprise.

Conclusion

Raúl Prebisch maintained that the attempt to elaborate a system of trade rules was backward looking. What the world needed instead was an agreed-upon set of policies to support the developing world. The creation of the WTO was a defeat for the viewpoint of Prebisch and others who argued passionately for different rules to privilege the less powerful. But it has been argued that WTO rules are in the interest of developing countries because they create a strong umbrella to shelter them from any arbitrary trade practices of large and powerful industrial countries. This argument must be qualified, however. We have argued that, for example, the Doha Round under the aegis of WTO rules has thus far been quite insufficient to regulate trade in a world of considerable economic inequality and that there is little likelihood that the poorest countries will derive anything close to what they require from the round should it resume.

Looking to the future, it is our contention that drastic policy changes should occur if the international economic and social situation is to become sustainable. Although progress is still slow, a breakthrough is possible. That such important changes can happen is now being illustrated by the pace of change in attitudes about the environment. Public opinion can change, even sharply and rapidly.

Such a breakthrough in the international economic and social field is not yet on the horizon and yet time seems to be running out. The ideals of justice and dignity cannot be realized by wishful thinking or by war and cries for democracy. What has the role of UN ideas been in getting us to the current situation? "In a funny way that isn't always clear and certainly does not have a uniform pattern, the ideas percolate through, and eventually influence outcomes," Canadian development specialist Gerry Helleiner argues. "The power of ideas is greater than the power of vested interests." He then quoted Lord Keynes as a wake-up call—"in the long run we are all dead"—as a prelude to his own bottom line: "But that doesn't alter the fact that ideas do move things as well as interests."[38]

Some historical perspective is useful here. In our first book in this series, we noted the need to think about a countervailing power to balance the might of the globalizing private sector. At the national level, this was achieved through the creation of the welfare state. But no such parallel exists for the planet. Global governance of NGOs or trade unions does not amount to a countervailing power to the might of private sector–driven globalization any more than it guarantees international peace and security in Darfur or Iraq. It may give

a push here and there and through the Global Compact or it may get some goodwill from some TNCs, but in no way do the current structures of global governance permit legislation in favor of global taxes, global redistribution of income, or consistency between aid and trade. In other words, the situation at the global level is not unlike the situation in the united Germany before Otto von Bismarck decided to introduce legislation for a less free but also less rapacious private sector.

Global governance is in reality an attempt to ensure some order and predictability for the globe in the absence of a world government. This reality is itself increasingly problematic in the face of the current global economic crisis and of such growing threats as climate change and weapons proliferation. We have much more to say about this in chapter 14.

7. Development Strategies

From National Planning to Governing the Market

- **Statistics and National Accounting**
- **The Rise and Decline of Planning and the Market's Revenge**
- **Conclusion**

Until well into the 1970s, the UN and the bulk of its member states believed that planning was indispensable for stimulating economic growth in an orderly and balanced manner. For instance, the United States expected developing countries to submit a national development plan when applying for development aid. The Harvard Development Advisory Service—as it was then known—sent highly qualified teams of experts to these countries in order to help them develop such plans. President Kennedy's Alliance for Progress for Latin America also was based on the elaboration of development plans.

This point needs to be emphasized because as of the 1980s, planning often became a four-letter word and developing countries were advised to rely on market forces alone and to forget the role of the state and of planning. Mainstream orthodoxy, led by the Bretton Woods institutions, alleged that society cannot be changed by human-made plans but only through market forces. Ironically, this was at variance with experience over the years that market forces alone could not take care of many social questions in an adequate and equitable manner, such as health care, education, and the environment. The role of the state and of planning had long been recognized as an essential part of effective government.

Adebayo Adedeji, a former Nigerian minister and for seventeen years executive secretary of the UN Economic Commission for Africa, showed how far the link between development assistance and planning could be pushed: "When Kennedy came to power, the administration announced an 80 million dollar allocation to Nigeria, provided the country had an acceptable development plan. A large team of Americans . . . came to Nigeria to join us in preparing the first post-independence national development plan, 1962 to 1968."[1]

It must be understood that until the end of the 1980s two very different

versions of national economic planning existed. The first is best illustrated by the former Soviet Union and its Gosplan. This extreme planning left no place whatsoever for the market. Everything was prescribed, from the number of boots to be produced to the number of passenger planes. The second version is the so-called indicative planning of which the French Commissariat au Plan was the prototype. Indicative planning left lots of room for market forces that were seen as essential for the flexibility of society and necessary to boost economic growth. At the same time, indicative planning tried to maneuver the market, set targets, and create incentives in order to stimulate investments and research in given sectors. In short, it attempted to "govern the market," the key feature of economic strategy identified with the highly successful East Asian countries.

UN development activities adopted the indicative planning approach. In 1963, a UN group of experts produced a report entitled *Planning for Economic Development*. The preface by Secretary-General U Thant stated that "the importance of national planning for economic development is almost universally recognized today. . . . Numerous developing countries as well as more advanced economies have employed planning as a tool for achieving their national economic goals."[2]

Indicative planning assumes a mixed economy in which the state would take initiatives for development to correct for what are called "market failures." In many developing countries, for example, market prices do not signal all the information required for optimal policymaking. Thus, according to proponents of indicative planning, it is not possible to leave the allocation of investments or other strategic decisions solely to market forces. The state would therefore have a vital role in setting development priorities, influencing the flow of resources toward them, monitoring progress, and stepping in with course corrections.

Both within and outside the UN, therefore, there was a widespread consensus in the early UN years about the need for planning. In 1958, Jan Tinbergen, a distinguished Dutch economist who in 1966 became the first chair of the UN Committee for Development Planning, published *The Design of Development*.[3] This publication drew on his experience in the Netherlands, where he had been the creator and first director of the Central Planning Bureau that still exists today. He also drew on his extensive experience as a UN expert in developing countries.

Even if ideas about the role of planning and market forces vary over time, good and reliable data is always needed. Though in the UN's early years, some economists spoke of "planning without facts,"[4] planning and economic policymaking always need reliable data to assess the present and the recent past and to provide the basis for economic, social, and demographic projections. The

UN from the beginning has played a key role in creating the statistical infra-structure for this type of information.

Statistics and National Accounting

In his book in the UNIHP series, *Quantifying the World,* Michael Ward under-lines the UN's contributions by noting that the "availability of worldwide data is a relatively modern phenomenon." He traces the role of the UN in provid-ing the statistical ideas and priorities about what ought to be measured and how countries could establish systems to collect, process, and publish statistical data on an internationally comparable basis. In all of this, the United Nations has had considerable success. Ward concludes: "The creation of a universally acknowledged statistical system and of a general framework guiding the col-lection and compilation of data according to recognized professional stan-dards, both internationally and nationally, has been one of the great and mostly unsung successes of the UN organization."[5]

Ward distinguishes three broad phases of UN statistical activity. The first was the original and formative period during the 1940s and 1950s. The second con-sisted of a longer period of innovation and organizational activity. The third and most recent phase, mostly since the 1990s, is characterized by maintenance of data systems and consolidation of methodology. These phases identified overlap at a number of points and "with the turn of the new millennium, the UN Statisti-cal Office has moved back to centre stage to begin forging new strategies."[6]

For the most part, the UN has been less an original source of new statistical thinking than an efficient innovator. It has played an important role in devel-oping, extending, and implementing in different parts of the world ideas that had been generated from various individuals and bodies outside the UN. Ideas clearly played an important part in the original setting up of the UN statistical service. They figured prominently in the discussions held to fashion the early international program of work. The early innovative role of the UN Statistical Office influenced the way the service operated for much of its life in promoting the development of national and international statistical systems.

By the 1970s, budgetary and resource constraints undermined UNSO's capacity to exercise oversight of the international statistical system. In some key data areas, it ceded ground (and thus UN authority) to other international bodies. Ward puts it starkly: Having given up "the crown jewels of statistical measurement and conceded control of statistical authority to institutions com-mitted to supporting the economic and financial agenda of Western orthodoxy," UNSO lost much of its claim to speak on behalf of the community of states, let alone for the poorest.[7] We explore this history more fully below.

Box 7.1. The Prebisch-Singer Thesis

The Prebisch-Singer thesis is the proposition that the terms of trade between primary products and manufactures have been subject to a long-run downward trend. The publication dates of the first two works that put forward the argument were nearly simultaneous. In May 1950, the English version of *The Economic Development of Latin America and Its Principal Problems,* by Raúl Prebisch—the executive secretary of the UN Economic Commission for Latin America—appeared under UN imprint.[1] In the same month, one of the first economists to be recruited into the UN, Hans Singer, who had already written an internal UN document on the issue in 1949, published an article on the consequences of foreign direct investment, "The Distribution of Gains between Investing and Borrowing Countries," in the *American Economic Review.*[2]

The significance of the thesis lay in its implication that barring major changes in the world economy, the gains from trade would continue to be distributed unequally between those who exported primary goods and those who exported mainly manufactures. In this way, inequalities of per capita income between these two types of countries would increase with the growth of trade instead of being reduced. This in the 1950s and 1960s was taken as an indicator of the need for both industrialization of and temporary tariff protection for developing countries.

In later years, Singer revisited this work, no longer seeing industrialization as "the great saviour" but putting more emphasis on relations between types of countries rather than types of commodities and on the distribution of technological power. He identified as critical factors the dominant role of research and development in developed countries and the structure of decision making in transnational corporations, both of which, he argued, continued to put poorer developing countries at a disadvantage.[3]

The Prebisch-Singer thesis contradicted a long tradition of contrary belief among economists. When Prebisch and Singer reversed the classical expectation of declining terms of trade for manufactures, their conclusions were immediately controversial, although they were later confirmed by many statistical studies in the 1980s and 1990s.

In their book in the UNIHP series, John Toye and Richard Toye conclude that the thesis should really be called the "Singer-Prebisch thesis" because Hans Singer was first in reaching the conclusions implied in the thesis.[4]

1. Raúl Prebisch, *The Economic Development of Latin America and Its Principal Problems* (New York: United Nations, 1950).
2. Hans Singer, "The Distribution of Gains between Investing and Borrowing Countries," *American Economic Review* 40, no. 2 (1950): 473–485.
3. D. John Shaw, *Sir Hans Singer: The Life and Work of a Development Economist* (Houndmills, Basingstoke, UK: Palgrave Macmillan, 2002), 58.
4. John Toye and Richard Toye, *The UN and Global Political Economy: Trade, Finance, and Development* (Bloomington: Indiana University Press, 2004), 111–116, 120–124, and 126–134.-

New Departures for Accounting Frameworks

The UN Statistical Office, which was formed in 1946, determined its main tasks to be standardizing statistical methods, developing common statistical measures, and coordinating data collection among countries and agencies.[8] Its first preoccupations were GNP, economic growth, and national accounts. In the years after World War II, full employment and stable economic growth were the high priority issues in North America and Europe. In contrast, hunger and poverty were the overriding concerns for the poorer countries. National accounts that focused on growth and employment, however, won the day, and they were developed into macrolevel statistical systems that focused on the principles of Keynesian economics. Western economic preoccupations trumped the concerns of poorer countries.

In hindsight, the early period must therefore be judged as an era of missed opportunity. It was a time when the UN failed to meet one of its first major challenges in establishing principles of measurement focused on the priorities of poorer countries and people and shirked its responsibility to develop systems that were responsive to different situations and alternative ideological viewpoints. Bringing a Keynesian perspective to economic statistics delivered benefits, but it also transformed the primary focus of data away from individuals toward an overriding focus on governments and government control of the economy, mainly through planning.

The priority UNSO attached to developing a system of national accounts thus drove the early UN agenda on statistics. All countries were encouraged to implement this system in order to provide each government with the essential standard tools to decide on macroeconomic policies. The System of National Accounts was first developed internationally by Richard Stone and James Meade at the Organisation for European Economic Co-operation (OEEC) in 1952 and was taken over, elaborated, and published a year later by the United Nations.[9] This pioneering work created an interrelated network of concepts and definitions that remain more or less unchanged to this day. Around the world, the core concepts of gross domestic product and gross national product and their associated macroeconomic components are universally recognized and understood.

Related concepts that have worked and are also now commonplace include the standardization of data concerning the national account system, trade and production statistics, and population and demographic statistics. To this should be added the significant early initiative the UN took in promoting gender distinction as an important data characteristic.[10] Other UNSO ideas, although

scientifically sound and conceptually innovative, never went very far. For example, in the 1960s, the System of Social and Demographic Statistics (SSDS) and the early formulation of social indicators were deemed inappropriate or conceptually inapplicable. Nor did UNSO pursue the collection and analysis of statistics on the distribution of income, consumption, and accumulation. In hindsight, it is unfortunate and somewhat surprising that the UN did not lead regarding these issues. So it was that during the 1960s and 1970s UNRISD, a small research institution of the UN, undertook the important work on measurement and social indicators that served as both a pioneering contribution in its own right and an important critique of conventional data-gathering by both social scientists and the United Nations. This work was a precursor to the Human Development Index of the 1990s.[11]

There are other areas of statistical importance where the leadership from UNSO has been less assertive and slow to take effect and thus the UN has yet to make its mark. Such topics include the measurement of poverty and different indicators of deprivation, human rights, security, inequality and wealth, and overall resource depletion. The lack of robust indicators of poverty and deprivation and the persistence of poverty are perhaps the most serious indictments of UNSO. Although it was initially set up to change the world through the creation of knowledge that would lead to policies to eradicate poverty, UNSO has settled over the years for the comfortable role of dealing with national economic conditions governed by a predetermined set of rules. But perhaps it is unfair to level criticism at the founders of the UN statistical system for failing to see that poverty and global inequality (rather than the reconstruction of postwar Europe) would become the most important economic and social challenges confronting the international system. The statistical challenge of the new millennium is for the UN to ensure that the necessary data is collected and made available so the global economy can be managed on a sustainable and equitable basis.

Integrating the New Priorities: From Demographic to Social and Environmental Accounting

The UN Population Division was created within the UN Secretariat in October 1946 to service the Population Commission that was set up at the same time. The division was charged with the primary task of estimating the size of the global population and quantifying its demographic composition and dynamic characteristics. There was more concern at the time about declining populations and birth rates in the industrialized world than anxiety about the enormous pressures of population expansion from the larger heavily populated areas of developing countries. (These were not yet called the "Third World"

and were still mostly under colonial administration.) The Population Division played a key role in setting up the UN Fund for Population Activities (UNFPA, later called the UN Population Fund). This fund was initially created in the Population Division in conjunction with conducting and financing the first world fertility survey.[12]

The issues of imbalance between population growth, income, and consumption levels and the world's resources are still among the most important global problems. Searching for solutions raises complex questions about the redistribution of income and world resources and about the environment, including climate change.

The Charter's edict for raising living standards eventually began to drive the work of social reporting that developed parallel to the UN's work on macroeconomic policies and statistics. But not until the mid-1960s did the UN support national, regional, and other international initiatives to compile social indicators on levels of living.

The first UN global report on women, *The World's Women: Trends and Statistics, 1991,* marked a watershed in the compilation of statistics relating to women. It gathered in one place, more or less for the first time, an extensive collection of statistics culled from various sources that related to the condition of women over the previous two decades.[13] It followed the latest best practice by emphasizing trends, not just snapshots from the latest data. It skillfully presented available data, even if it was partial or scattered, with a broad commentary, even when detailed statistics were missing or limited. A further breakthrough on women's statistics came with the publication of *The World's Women 1995,* which was prepared for the Fourth UN World Conference on Women in Beijing.[14] This document explicitly recognized that much of the official historical data on women did not adequately recognize their economic and social contributions in the internal economy and through household labor.

The incorrect and seriously misleading perception that work traditionally defined as "women's work"—that is, women's household labor—has zero value is still widely held. It is difficult to quantify the relative contributions of women and men in economic activities in which both are involved, such as livestock tending and harvesting. But that difficulty pales in comparison to attempts to put a value on women's domestic activities in the home. Not surprisingly, however, when the 1995 Human Development Report bravely attempted an estimate that included all nonmarket work of both women and men, the report concluded that "if women's unpaid work were properly valued, it is quite possible that women would emerge in most societies as the major breadwinners, or at least equal breadwinners, since they put in longer hours of work than men."[15]

A different but equally challenging set of issues arose in finding ways to incorporate environmental concerns into global statistics and national accounting. After the UN Conference on the Human Environment in Stockholm in 1972, which showed the need to link environment with development, planners and policymakers were ever more exercised to find ways to incorporate environmental concerns into development planning. Land had long been recognized as an important capital asset of a country, but with the new environmental awareness came recognition that overuse and pollution could turn land and other natural resources into "depreciating" or "wasting" assets.

Another strong influence at the time was the Club of Rome report *Limits to Growth,* which suggested that economic growth could not continue indefinitely because the supply of certain natural resources, notably oil, metals, and fertilizers, was finite.[16] In fact, the models on which the analysis was based were simplistic, and later research suggested that the real constraints to growth were the pollution of *renewable* resources like water, soil, air, and forests rather than physical limits to the supply of nonrenewables.

UNSO contributed to the technical debate on these matters in two ways. In 1984, it published *A Framework for the Development of Environmental Statistics,* which argued that environmental problems are the result of manmade activities and natural events in a sequence of action, impact, and reaction. This pioneering report was followed by other reports and manuals, including a comprehensive international effort to collect data on environmental indicators in 1999, which for the first time covered all countries except for OECD members.

Second, in 1993, UNSO developed the System of Environmental and Economic Accounts (SEEA) and published the *Handbook of National Accounting: Integrated Environmental and Economic Accounting.* This drew attention to the availability and maintenance of the different environmental services that natural assets provide, both to the community and to the economy sustaining that community. It showed how these elements could be incorporated into "satellite" accounts that could be linked to the main economic framework of national accounts.

Both of these developments have introduced and strengthened environmental data in national and global statistical systems. UNSO was the first to incorporate all elements of environmental degradation into a comprehensive national accounting framework linked to each country's economic and financial accounts and balance sheets. The approach challenged—and still challenges—commonly held notions about economic growth and the very meaning of conventional measures of GNP.

Moreover, there is growing recognition that an upper ceiling exists that is linked to the use of environmental resources. Environmental data and

accounting systems are essential to the analysis of such issues, all the more so as global warming brings changes in the global and regional patterns of temperature and other indicators of the world's environmental systems. Future efforts to reduce poverty and global inequality and to make development more sustainable will depend heavily on having reliable environmental data linked to economic performance.

The Implications of Globalization for Measurement

The accurate measurement of global phenomena is an area where UN coverage is deficient. There is a distinct difference between truly global concepts and world totals. World totals are simply straightforward additions and extrapolations from national measures. Such measures are international, but they do not necessarily represent the true nature of global phenomena. For example, because of international migration flows, the world population cannot be obtained by simply adding up national population totals.[17]

Globalization measures are being currently developed by the OECD and UNCTAD, but there is still a remarkable lack of truly global indicators. This is surprising as there is a considerable degree of political concern about how global development affects the fate of the planet and those who inhabit it. Most aggregate measures and indicators are still essentially international rather than global. The UN Secretariat has often, though not always, become more a passive recipient of data submitted and less an active interpreter and stimulus for data and interpretations that are not compiled or vetted by member states. While physical estimates of production exist, there are no robust measures of global output (especially by sector) and no official estimates of critical measures such as global inflation or global inequality and global resource depletion. Even estimates of the volume of trade in global merchandise are incomplete and demonstrate irreconcilable inconsistencies both in total and across countries.

It is curious that statistical estimates should be so incomplete for globalization, a topic of such obvious importance to contemporary well-being. Many smaller and weaker countries are worried about the way that private enterprise is extending its economic influence around the world. They fear that they may be unable to counteract intrusions by TNCs into important areas of domestic policy. Because national identity seems to be at stake, some countries believe that the UN should assume a more overarching international responsibility and authority for monitoring the activities of TNCs and analyzing their effects. This cannot be done without relevant knowledge and pertinent intelligence about the global ownership of the means of production.

The Rise and Decline of Planning and the Market's Revenge

During the 1960s, every branch of the United Nations became involved in collecting, evaluating, and disseminating the data essential for development planning and policy formulation. This statistical work was an important contribution to development thinking and practice.[18] Long-term planning and forecasting about key issues for economic and social development, such as population growth, food and educational needs, industrial production, and international trade, became key elements of and major contributions to the UN's First Development Decade.

Planning activities during the 1960s and 1970s in the UN as well as at the country level consisted mainly of making projections, forecasting how the future would look, and analyzing how a country or a region could best work its way toward that future. Important studies were undertaken on the major trends in world trade and trends in GDP and per capita income.[19] The Economic Projections and Programming Center of the UN published its first report in 1964.[20]

The regional economic commissions also became active in both methodological and empirical aspects of economic projections and planning. During the mid-1960s, the ECA made a series of projections running to 1975 about foreign aid, population, and national income for the entire region. ECAFE prepared a report on *Projections of Foreign Trade of the ECAFE Region up to 1980,* and ECLA made a systematic compilation of national accounts data in order to use them for the purpose of projections.[21] During the same time period, the United Nations Special Fund worked with the regional commissions to set up institutes of economic development and planning in Latin America (1962), Africa (1963), and Asia (1964).

Planning for economic and social development as advocated and practiced by the UN was very much of the indicative type. Until well into the 1970s, most countries accepted the necessity for this kind of planning as a major instrument for achieving rapid economic growth. In 1976, Michal Kalecki, the distinguished Polish economist, observed that "we are all 'planners' today, although very different in character."[22] But around 1980, a turning point arrived when the major powers and the Bretton Woods institutions emphasized market forces, privatization, and liberalization of trade. Planning was seen as the exact opposite of what suddenly became the new orthodoxy. In short, the pendulum swung from one extreme to the other.

However, turning points are often carefully prepared by active minorities who labor in the shadows until they can emerge in broad daylight. And so it was with a band of followers of neoclassical and neoliberal theory that became

the paradigm as of the 1980s. As early as the end of the 1960s, the criticism of import-substitution policies became more precise, technical, and empirical. Work was undertaken at the OECD Development Centre and the World Bank on the negative aspects of protectionism.[23] These studies pointed to a tendency for many developing countries to protect capital goods industries and pursue a strong anti-trade bias as the result of policies that sought to encourage heavy industrial development.

This early work was followed by other studies that strengthened the theoretical framework of the open-economy model and attacked strong state roles and the role of planning. One illustration is the pioneering work on the methodology of project appraisal and microlevel planning that Ian Little and James Mirrlees initially undertook for the OECD in 1968 and elaborated further in 1974. The project appraisal techniques they proposed used world prices as "shadow prices" to estimate what was argued to be the "true" costs and benefits of proposed investments. This builds a pro-trade bias in the appraisal methodology and therefore implicitly maps out a case for free trade and supply-side adjustment along neoclassical lines.[24]

An alternative view was presented by Amartya Sen and two fellow economists in a study undertaken for and published by UNIDO.[25] They distinguished between market considerations and social measures as ways to evaluate the success or failure of projects and whether or not lending institutions had gotten good value for their money. Their methodology identified what could be done through the market and what should be done with the helping hand of the state. Harvard economist Dani Rodrik has written extensively on this topic. He maintains that although there is "one economics," there are "many recipes" according to the country situation and the time in its economic history.[26]

Defenders of the neoclassical resurgence have argued that whereas neoclassical economics became more precise in its use of mathematics and application of econometrics, "development economics . . . has relied on large doses of casual empiricism, fairly unrigorous theorizing, and giving too much emphasis on the state."[27] But advocates of development economics offer important critiques of neoliberal orthodoxy as well. Frances Stewart, an early critic of free-market, neoclassical policies, concluded that "taking all these arguments together, there is no theoretical basis for concluding that an undistorted price system will lead to a higher level of welfare than one containing various government interventions."[28]

In the 1980s, the neoclassical and neoliberal approach had the upper hand. The arguments by economists such as Amartya Sen and Frances Stewart were largely brushed aside by what became the wisdom of the day. One of the more far-reaching effects has been the influence of Washington consensus policies on

the conditionality of structural adjustment lending by the World Bank and the regional development banks as well as on the conditions the IMF attached to its loans to developing countries.

Yet experience has shown that an unfettered market does not produce the growth neoliberal orthodoxy predicts. Robert Wade and other students of the East Asian experience have shown that governing the market is essential.[29] This approach has long been followed by Korea and the other East Asian countries that successfully followed a path to growth that contrasts markedly with the Washington consensus recipe. While there may have been too much emphasis on the role of the state during the 1960s and 1970s, the new orthodoxy went to the opposite extreme. Governing at the center, with a judicious mix of state and market action, is the answer.

Conclusion

Amartya Sen says that the world organization has been "at the center of it all" in terms of measuring development. But he added: "The UN was later on at the center of criticizing and challenging the ongoing reliance on the GDP. The critique came mainly through the *Human Development Reports* in particular and trying to replace the GDP by the Human Development Index."[30]

We elaborate in later chapters why and how the UN has been more than timid during and after a sudden transition from one extreme to the other, from planning to the emphasis on market forces. The remarkable point is that planning was done with very considerable success during World War II in both the United Kingdom and the United States. Planning is also routinely undertaken today by large firms, such as Walmart and Tesco.[31] If planning is the rational thing to do at the microlevel, why should it be so wrong at the macrolevel?

Apparently, each generation relearns the same lessons instead of standing on the shoulders of previous generations. Over the first three decades of the UN's history, most countries accepted that market forces cannot secure all policy objectives and that a helping hand from the state is crucial. That lesson was forgotten during the 1980s and the price was heavy: a lost decade or two in Latin America and Africa and the globalization of a world economy driven solely by market forces, punctuated by severe and costly crises. Now that the current global crisis affects developed as well as developing countries, perhaps the lessons may be learned, at least for the next decade.

8. Social Development

From Sectoral to Integrated Perspectives

- **Dramatic Population Growth**
- **Nutrition and Ending Hunger**
- **Food, Agriculture, and Nutrition**
- **Health**
- **Education**
- **Children**
- **Conclusion**

The social and human dimensions of development have been central to the United Nations from the beginning. We do not have a commissioned book on population, education, health, and children in the UNIHP series because these topics figure prominently in two of the volumes of the series.[1] The Universal Declaration of Human Rights spelled out "the right to education" and the need for education to be "directed to the full development of the human personality and to the strengthening of respect for human rights and fundamental freedoms. It shall promote understanding, tolerance and friendship among all nations, racial and religious groups." It also stated that "parents have a prior right to choose the kind of education that shall be given to their children."

More specific elements were included in the constitutions of the UN's specialized agencies. The WHO's constitution, for example, declared that "enjoyment of the highest attainable standard of health is one of the fundamental rights of every human being without distinction of race, religion, political, economic or social condition."[2]

The concept that these basic elements of life were rights shared by all humanity was one of the great and fundamental contributions of the UN and should be classed as one of its most important and influential ideas. Though the right to life had been recognized as part of the Declaration of the Rights of Man and Citizen at the end of the eighteenth century, the UN was the first to extend human rights to include health, nutrition, education, and the right to choose the number of one's children. The International Covenant on Economic, Social and Cultural Rights, which was adopted in 1966 and came into force in 1976, went a

long way in this direction. These early commitments were later elaborated, for example in the Convention on the Elimination of all Forms of Discrimination against Women, adopted in 1979, and in the Convention on the Rights of the Child, adopted in 1989.[3]

Skeptics might ask what recognition of these issues as human rights actually has brought to the pursuit of education, health, and the other human dimensions of development. Surely by their very definition issues of education and health had already been accepted as important matters of human concern. What more did acknowledging them as human rights contribute? There are at least six answers. First, by incorporating them as human rights, the UN gave them universal legitimacy, applicable to all persons on the planet. Second, recognizing them as rights internationally underlined the obligations of all states parties to ensure that they are fulfilled. Third, emphasizing rights directed particular attention and priority to meeting the needs of marginalized groups who are not yet enjoying them as opposed to improving the standards of education and health in general. Fourth, recognizing these things as rights made it possible for those deprived of these rights to use legal redress to demand them. Fifth, recognizing these human needs as rights asserted that meeting these needs is an end in itself, not merely a good investment that is instrumental to the fulfillment of other objectives. And finally, as stated in the Convention on the Rights of the Child, signature states committed themselves "to promote and encourage international co-operation" in which "particular account should be taken of the needs of developing countries."

The recognition of many of the human dimensions of development as rights did not mean that measures to implement them were fully incorporated in programs of action right away. There were many delays and failures in translating formal recognition into implementation.

This said, overall advance regarding social rights during the last six and a half decades has been extraordinary. Life expectancy in the world as a whole has increased by an average of twenty years since 1950, much more than in any comparable period of history. The increase has been most dramatic in developing countries. There has also been an enormous and unprecedented increase in the number and proportion of persons who are literate in developing countries, from about one-third in 1950 to well over three-quarters in 2000. The number of individuals educated to primary, secondary, and higher levels have also increased by multiples, in parallel with other human improvements as judged by a wide range of other indicators. The United Nations and its various agencies have played a significant and sometimes a leading role in these advances. This has been done typically by setting regional and international goals and guidelines, by mobilizing action, and by providing technical, financial, and other forms of practical support for translating the goals and guidelines into national

action, especially in poorer countries. However, success must not be overstated; and the quality of education and health care, for example, has slipped considerably in many countries, developed as well as developing, during the last two or three decades.[4]

Dramatic Population Growth

The number of people in the world grew more rapidly during the last six and a half decades than ever before. In 1945, world population was about 2.4 billion. By the end of 2007, it numbered 6.6 billion. Though the rate of increase has fallen considerably since the 1960s, in absolute terms the world's population continues to grow by sizeable increments. The UN's latest median projection is for the world's population to be around 9 billion in 2050. The highest projections forecast a total above 10 billion for 2050 while its lowest projections anticipate a total world population of 7.7 billion in that year.[5] There are reasons to wish that that the 2050 figure will be closer to the lower estimate than to the higher.[6]

Changes in the location and structure of world population have also been extraordinary:

- Today 80 percent of the world's population lives in developing countries. In 1900, it was 70 percent, and by 2050 it will be 90 percent. Today, 95 percent of the annual increase of world population, about 78 million, occurs in the developing world.
- In almost all parts of the world, people are living longer. Life expectancy has increased dramatically to reach 65 years today, compared to 45 years in 1950. By 2050, it is expected to be 76 years.
- The world's population is aging. Today one in ten of the world's population is 60 or older. By 2050, it is expected that it will more than double to two in nine. In developed countries at that time, one in three persons will be 60 or older.
- Fertility is falling. Couples in developing countries today have an average of three children. Thirty years ago they had six. More than half of all couples in developing countries today use contraception.
- Some 40 million people worldwide are living with HIV/AIDS, and 25 million have died from it since 1981. About 25 million of those with HIV/AIDS live in Africa, of whom almost 60 percent are women. Of the 7 million in urgent need of retroviral drugs, only about 2 million receive them. In Sub-Saharan Africa there are 12 million HIV/AIDS orphans.
- Most of the world's population now lives in urban areas. In 2006, for the first time, more people around the globe lived in cities than in rural areas.
- The number of migrants who have moved to another country is 125

million today, compared to 75 million in 1965, still a tiny fraction of total world population.[7]

From the beginning, the United Nations has treated the analysis of and projections of the world's population as one of its clear responsibilities. Surprisingly, however, population growth was not treated as a major policy issue for the first two decades of the UN's existence. Three reasons seem to account for this neglect: uncertainty over the figures; a preoccupation with declining population in developed countries; and, most important, the controversial nature of population policy and debates about it.[8] All three reasons reflected the caution of governments, the First UN, that was expressed in many bodies. Except for India, where a series of censuses since 1881 had created awareness of and concern about population growth, little was known about the demographic situation in most regions of the developing world. Thus, population and rates of population growth were seen as issues for study, not issues to cause general alarm or require urgent action.

In spite of this slow beginning, over its lifetime the UN has given increasing attention to population policy, moving from caution and reticence to advocacy and action on a global scale. In the 1950s and 1960s, evidence emerged that the world's population was increasing at about 2 percent per year, double the rate earlier assumed. This was largely the result of work by individuals in the Second and Third UNs, including some distinguished demographers in both camps.

In 1966, ESCAP organized a meeting on family planning in Asia, and in 1974 the UN organized the first World Conference on Population in Bucharest. By then, seventeen Asian countries had developed population policies and most Asian countries had family planning programs. The Bucharest conference encouraged all countries to prepare population policies and integrate them into social and economic plans and establish a high-level unit to deal with these issues. By 1983, 70 percent of the countries that had attended the 1974 conference had done so.

Debates about population issues have always stirred strong feelings among all three parts of the UN. In the 1970s, the governments of many developing countries strongly emphasized fertility control. At the time, this was encouraged and supported by the UN and many donors, including the United States. Later the emphasis on fertility control became highly controversial. National family planning policy in India and especially the one-child family policy in China meant that strong U.S. support in the 1970s shifted to strong opposition in the 1980s.

These debates notwithstanding, in the world of ideas, the UN from the beginning stressed the "right of persons to determine in a free, informed and

responsible manner, the number and spacing of their children."[9] Moreover, the UN has always stressed the close links between population and development, emphasizing that "the basis for an effective solution of population problems is, above all, socio-economic transformation."[10]

At the second World Conference on Population and Development (Cairo, 1994), the right to choose was widely publicized, strongly promoted, and firmly established. The declaration and plan of action of the conference also contained strong commitments to women's empowerment and gender equality; improvement in maternal and reproductive health, especially safe motherhood; and actions to reduce child mortality. More than before, the focus and operational emphasis for policymakers shifted to empowerment of women, reproductive health, and the reduction of child mortality.

In spite of this leadership, notably by members of the second UN in UNFPA and the WHO, members of the First and the Third UNs remained and remain sharply divided over issues of population policy. Most Catholic and Islamic leaders strongly oppose contraception and other "artificial" methods of avoiding or spacing births, and a number of governments echo these views. Much of the agenda for empowering women is also opposed because it threatens the traditional beliefs and practices of patriarchy. At the same time, some neo-Malthusians argue strongly for much stronger birth control policies and for rapid and direct actions to reduce fertility. Those who adopt this stance argue that rather than relying on women's right to choose as a method of reducing fertility, women's empowerment in all areas is essential. They feel that true economic and social development cannot happen without empowerment of women.

Will this be enough to deal with population problems over the next few decades? World fertility rates have fallen to 2.7 in the early twenty-first century, compared to 4.5 in the early 1970s. Fertility rates are now below replacement level in some sixty countries of the world that contain almost half the world's population. These include the developed countries, countries in transition, China, and other better-off developing countries. It is in the poorer and least-developed countries, especially in Sub-Saharan Africa, where fertility rates are still high, though in every case, the rate is well below that of thirty years earlier.[11]

Even with these reductions in fertility rates, the ever-growing base means that world population will continue to increase. This is true for three main reasons. First, there will be continuing population growth in countries where fertility rates are still above replacement level. Second, there is a "population momentum," meaning that even in countries with low fertility rates, population will continue to grow for a generation or two because of the disproportionate share of the population of childbearing age. And third, medical and economic advances are likely to extend life expectancy.

As part of this global demographic transition, the world population is ageing, including in developing countries. This will result, among other effects, in increasing dependency ratios, greater pension burdens, and challenges to health and long-term care systems. The United Nations has already begun to study these issues and has recently offered publications on ageing populations; this focus will need to continue.[12]

Nutrition and Ending Hunger

The idea of eradicating hunger on a global scale emerged at the conference in Québec in October 1945 that launched the Food and Agriculture Organization. In a visionary speech, John Boyd Orr set out this hope and, on the strength of it, he later claimed, was elected as the FAO's first director-general. Immediately, the organization set to work to prepare a world food plan that would be overseen by a world food board. This received almost universal support; only two countries opposed the idea, the United Kingdom and the United States. But these two countries had the controlling voice, so the idea was dropped, and Boyd Orr abruptly resigned. He received the Nobel Prize for Peace in 1949 and was elevated to the peerage the same year, a somewhat British way to deal with awkward idealists who act before their time has come.

The idea of international action to improve world nutrition and end hunger had been set out a decade or two earlier by the League of Nations. In the midst of the worldwide recession of the 1930s, Australia's prime minister, Stanley Bruce, challenged the conventional wisdom that declining commodity prices should be countered by cutting production. Bruce proposed that the League of Nations explore what might be done to mobilize cooperation for a world food plan based on expanding food production to meet human needs. The resulting report, *The Relation of Nutrition to Health, Agriculture and Economic Policy,* published in 1937, became a best seller.[13]

Almost forty years later, the vision of eradicating hunger in the world was set out again at the World Food Conference in 1974. U.S. secretary of state Henry Kissinger raised the issue because he was concerned about the instability and unpredictability of world food stocks and the overall food situation. He was also preoccupied with the possibility that food would be used as a strategic weapon just as oil had been. In a much-quoted statement, Kissinger proposed that "Within a decade, no child will go to bed hungry; no family will fear for its next day's bread."[14] As a result of the 1974 conference, the International Fund for Agricultural Development (IFAD) and the World Food Council were created. They joined the FAO and the WFP as the institutional manifestations of the UN's normative commitment to ending hunger.

This forecast of hope took no account of the setbacks of recession and structural adjustment in the 1980s, nor was it much remembered when the economic imbalances and pressures of debt arose. Some did remember. Julius Nyerere, president of Tanzania, asked in the 1980s: "Must we starve our children to pay our debts?" But his appeal mostly fell on deaf ears.

The third occasion for a big push for ending hunger came in 1996, when the FAO convened the World Food Summit, at which 186 countries participated. This time around, the goal agreed upon was more modest: to halve the number of people "living in food insecurity" by the year 2015. Four years later, the Millennium Summit incorporated the goal of halving the number in hunger as one of the MDGs, along with the establishment of the Food Insecurity and Vulnerability and Mapping Systems at the FAO to track progress toward that goal.

The fourth occurrence came in 2008, at the time this account was being finalized. World food prices had soared to record levels earlier in the year, especially the prices of food grains, and most commentators, including the FAO, predicted that high price levels would continue. The impact of price increases of 25–50 percent or more on poor households, which often spend 70–80 percent of their income on food, was severe, and there were food riots in twenty-four countries. A World Food Summit was held in Rome in June 2008 and commitments were made to increase emergency aid as well as longer-term pledges to scale up investments in agricultural growth, new technologies, and small-scale agricultural producers. The MDG for halving the numbers in poverty and hunger by 2015 was reaffirmed at the 2008 summit, but the vision, enthusiasm, and bold thinking of earlier years was sadly missing. Subsequently, food prices fell with the onset of recession, but for many in poverty, this was to substitute one cause of difficulty for another, even more serious one.

Food, Agriculture, and Nutrition

Technical assistance has been a major component of the FAO's activities over most of its life. The FAO's work has also involved preparing major surveys of the world's food situation; by 1999, it had published six such surveys. More recently, the focus has shifted to food security, defined by the World Food Summit in 1996 as existing "when all people, at all times, have physical and economic access to sufficient, safe and nutritious food to meet their dietary needs and food preferences for an active and healthy life."[15] Food security and the right to adequate food both emphasize the right of individuals or households to have access to income or food-producing resources. Food aid and aid for agriculture and rural development have also been an important part of the UN's work, mostly provided by the WFP and IFAD.

Nutrition has been a focus for UN ideas and action from the beginning. It is fundamental to building and maintaining the capabilities that are at the root of human development. Mothers need good nutrition to give birth and care for (and breastfeed) young children; children need good nutrition for physical growth and mental development; adult men and women need food and good nutrition to work and maintain health and vigor. Good nutrition is a key element for healthy life as people age.

While this may seem obvious, many myths and misunderstandings exist about nutrition and malnutrition. It is too readily assumed that malnutrition is the result of insufficient food intake. In fact, malnutrition of young children in developing countries is more usually the result of diarrhea and other sicknesses that are the consequence of lack of breastfeeding for the very young, bad sanitation and dirty water, poor hygiene, and lack of shelter and inadequate care. Malnutrition among older children and adults is also likely to be the result of these insufficiencies, though inadequacies in diet quality as well as quantity are also crucial factors.

The "hidden hungers" of iron deficiency (which affects 4 or 5 billion of the world's population) and deficiencies of iodine or vitamin A (which affect 1 to 2 billion) do lasting damage, especially among young children. Indeed, recent research shows that malnutrition in the womb and for the first two years of life has long-term consequences, some of which are not revealed until the person reaches sixty or more and suffers higher rates of heart disease, diabetes, and cancer. Long before that, malnutrition plays a huge and largely unappreciated role in the global burden of disease. Malnutrition also reduces mental capacity and accounts for over half of all child mortality.[16]

Much of this understanding is the result of research and careful review of evidence over recent decades. No one body of the UN is responsible for all of nutrition matters; nutrition issues apply to many sectors of the organization. The WHO and FAO have long been engaged, respectively in the health and agricultural dimensions. The World Bank and IFAD have been involved with investment in agriculture and rural development, and the WFP and the UN High Commissioner for Refugees have been involved with support and food supplements, especially in emergency situations. From their earliest years, UNICEF and the UNDP have operated nutrition programs and have learned much from this experience. Altogether, some twenty-four funds and organizations of the UN are involved in nutrition matters. Before one voices the criticism that this diversity might divide the attention of the UN, let it be underlined that these funds and organizations have long been brought together in the UN Standing Committee on Nutrition (SCN), which since 1977 has served as a global forum for sharing research and operational experience.[17] Unusually for

UN committees, but like the Intergovernmental Panel on Climate Change, the SCN also includes research scientists and government representatives; it thus includes persons from all three UNs.

Early child nutrition is one of the areas marked by impressive advances in the last quarter-century. In 1980, over 170 million children under five were underweight (the most basic indicator of malnutrition), some 38 percent of the age group. By 2005, this number had fallen to almost 125 million, under 23 percent of the age group.[18]

Progress in reducing malnutrition has been remarkable for at least three reasons. First, the improvements have been steady, substantive, and widespread, encompassing many parts of Asia, Latin America, the Middle East, North Africa, and Oceania; this positive development has taken place in nine subregions of the world. Indeed, the only areas that have not improved are situated in Sub-Saharan Africa. Second, nutritional improvements have taken place over years that have included periods of great economic difficulty, often of stagnation or decline. Third, the evidence for the nutritional status of young children is more reliable than it used to be for the estimates for undernourishment and malnutrition of adults. Progress is mostly calculated using sample survey data or direct evidence, not indirect estimates. This does not mean that there are no errors or biases, but professionals agree that the data is more reliable than previously.

Improvement of statistics on under-five nutrition is one of the supportive elements of nutritional advance in recent decades. In 1975, only a handful of countries had data on the nutritional status of their population. At present, and often as a result of help from the UN, some eighty or ninety countries have such data, mostly covering several points of time, which makes it possible to show trends in nutritional status.

In addition, we now have information on other dimensions of nutritional improvement. From 1980, data exists by region for wasting and stunting, and the trend shows impressive improvements. The proportion of stunted children has fallen in India and other countries of South-Central Asia from over 60 percent to barely 33 percent; in East Asia from over 50 to some 10 percent. In China and the rest of Southeast Asia, the proportions have also fallen considerably.[19]

But there is one widespread and important setback to all this improvement. Obesity, fat intake, and the prevalence of overweight children has risen in all regions of the world, including Sub-Saharan Africa. The levels are still far less than those of underweight and stunting, but this trend is the opposite of what is needed for good health and nutrition.

Health

Over the years, the WHO, often with other UN partners, has led the way in conceptualizing and promoting health as a human right and research, statistics, and epidemiological analyses on a global basis. It has also spearheaded global action to reduce and eradicate communicable diseases and increase access to primary health care.

Health in the WHO's perspective has increasingly meant health in mind and body, mental as well as physical health. Both are critical for an individual's cognitive and emotional and physical capacity, the elements that make it possible for an individual to enjoy a full life in his or her community. This broad conceptualization of health is necessary for a full life.

The Universal Declaration of Human Rights did not cover the right to health as such, which would have been unrealistic, but it did include "the enjoyment of the highest attainable standard of health." In subsequent years, notably at and after the WHO/UNICEF International Conference on Primary Health Care in Alma Ata in 1978, the world organization's strategy has focused on achieving "Health for All," to which was initially added the target date of "by 2000."

Operational activities to reduce and eradicate communicable disease initially focused on malaria and smallpox. The UN's first policy decision on malaria was taken in 1955 when the WHO launched its Global Malaria Eradication Campaign. In spite of enormous efforts in the 1950s and some remarkable initial gains, malaria eradication failed. Eradication programs were never integrated into national health services, the mosquitoes developed resistance to insecticides, and the malarial parasites developed resistance to the chemotherapy used to treat malaria.

The goal was subsequently modified from eradication to control, using diverse techniques adapted to the specifics of each environment. But notwithstanding some progress in the 1970s and 1980s, the malarial situation subsequently worsened. At the turn of the century, there were 300 to 500 million new clinical cases of malaria each year, with 1.5 to 2.7 million people dying of the disease each year. Ninety percent of the deaths occur in Sub-Saharan Africa.[20]

In contrast, smallpox eradication was one of the early and great successes of the United Nations, though not until after years of heated and tortuous debate in the World Health Assembly (the forum that governs the WHO) and two decades of struggle and pioneering action. The WHO's first director-general made an unsuccessful attempt to persuade the World Health Assembly to undertake a program of smallpox eradication in 1953. Five years later, a Soviet delegate persuaded the WHO to accept responsibility for a global program, but member states approved a budget with only minimal funds. One reason, in

addition to the WHO's preoccupations with the malaria eradication program, was that many governments were skeptical about the feasibility of smallpox eradication, especially in Africa. Only in 1967 was there agreement on an intensified and coordinated program; this led to an unprecedented range of efforts on a worldwide scale. At first, mass vaccination campaigns were launched in thirty countries where smallpox was endemic. These gave way, in the 1970s, to a "surveillance containment strategy," under which "flying squad" teams were rapidly dispatched to vaccinate all contacts whenever and wherever a possible case was discovered. By 1975, the number of countries where the disease could still be found had fallen to three: India, Bangladesh, and Ethiopia. The last case of smallpox was reported in Somalia in 1977, carried by nomads from Ethiopia. The WHO formally declared the disease extinct in 1980 after an interval to check that there had been no resurgence.

The costs and benefits of smallpox eradication, though often quoted, are worth summarizing again because they impressively demonstrate the remarkable benefits of coordinated international programs. The total cost of achieving smallpox eradication was officially estimated to be about $300 million at the time, one-third of which came from international sources and two-thirds from the afflicted countries. In terms of benefits, the world now saves at least $2 billion each year by avoiding the need to purchase smallpox vaccine, support vaccine administration, or apply international health regulations and related costs.

The dramatic eradication of smallpox was not the only UN success of mass action. Between 1950 and 1965, 46 million patients in forty-nine countries were successfully treated with penicillin against yaws, a tropical disease that affects the skin and bones. Yaws is no longer a significant problem in most of the world. The global threat of plague has also declined in the last four decades, largely due to the use of antibiotics, insecticides, and other control measures.

Two other efforts of global eradication are under way: the eradication of polio and guinea worm. Though eradication has not yet been realized, major advances have been achieved. The WHO launched a global campaign to eradicate polio in 1988, when the disease was endemic in 125 countries and paralyzed 1,000 children a day. UNICEF, Rotary International, and the Centers for Disease Control and Prevention joined the campaign, making it the largest internationally coordinated public health project in human history. By 2006, only four countries remained where the endemic transmission of wild polio had not yet been interrupted: Nigeria, India, Pakistan, and Afghanistan. The number of cases had fallen to under 2,000 a year.

Over the last two decades, the WHO and UNICEF, in conjunction with the Carter Center (another example of multiple UNs acting together), have led efforts that have reduced the number of cases of guinea worm by 99 percent, from 3.5 million cases in around twenty countries of Asia and Africa in

1986 to fewer than 10,000 cases in five countries of Africa in 2008—an impressive accomplishment.[21] The first target date for full eradication was set as 1995; the present target date is 2009. Such slippage illustrates the difficulty of the challenge.

The UN's concern with development has always been multidisciplinary, and it has been influenced by the perspectives and approaches of many professionals of different disciplines. Nonetheless, the WHO for its first forty years was by its own admission too neglectful of the socioeconomic dimensions of health. The WHO's organizational culture has been dominated by scientists, doctors, and medical experts.[22] The 1998 *World Health Report* noted that "up to 1978, the biomedical model of health systems predominated and the health sector was confused with the medical sector."[23] Change came with the adoption of the Primary Health Care initiative in 1978, a joint initiative of the WHO and UNICEF that envisioned "an acceptable level of health for the people of the world by the year 2000."[24] Primary Health Care drew on the thinking and experience of both organizations. Launched in Alma Ata, it was recognized from the beginning that the initiative would require multisectoral action, community involvement, and appropriate technology.

Three years after UNICEF and the WHO launched Primary Health Care, the World Health Assembly and the UN General Assembly adopted the Global Strategy of Health for All by the Year 2000. The goal of ensuring health for all was a fundamentally new approach to health care.[25] The underlying principles included universal access to care and coverage on the basis of need, commitment to health equity as part of development oriented to social justice, community participation in defining and implementing health agendas, and intersectoral approaches to health care.

UN preoccupations with health contrast sharply with those of the Bretton Woods institutions. Not until 1979 did the World Bank create a health department and decide to fund stand-alone health projects in addition to health components in other projects.[26] As World Bank historians comment, "The full embrace of health and education as productive investments was germinating under cover of the basic needs proposal of the late 1970s, but its official recognition came at the close of the McNamara period, most publicly in the 1980 *World Development Report*." They comment revealingly that "pure welfare spending, or income transfer with no convincingly 'productive' outcome was generally frowned upon" at the Bank, although isolated investment projects in education and health were launched as both academics and policymakers became more interested in the economics of education and health.[27]

Over the years, the WHO has established itself as one of the most professional of the UN's specialized agencies. It conducts a wide range of epidemiological analysis and research, it oversees a system of statistical definition for a

wide range of data, and it collects data, publishes statistical findings, and analyzes the data it collects. This is not the place to summarize the elements of such a broad-ranging piece of modern international organization except to comment that the world would face many risks to health without this global system. As two analysts have commented, because we are "united by contagion," global health governance is growing.[28]

Education

The UN has made four fundamental contributions to ideas in education: it has declared that education is a human right; it has set goals for the expansion of access to education and improvements in the quality of education; it has done education planning and monitoring; and it has provided support for education, especially in poorer countries. The Universal Declaration of Human Rights not only stated that education was the right of everyone but elaborated some closely related points: "education shall be free, at least in the elementary and fundamental stages," "elementary education shall be compulsory," technical and professional education shall be made "generally available," and higher education shall be "equally accessible to all on the basis of merit."

In 1948, it was estimated that more than 40 percent of the people in Latin America were illiterate, more than 60 percent in Asia, and more than 80 percent in Africa. Such deficiencies underline the bold and visionary nature of these early declarations.[29] It is difficult to imagine statements of similar boldness being made today.

Implementation has, in fact, been extraordinary. Over the sixty years since the Universal Declaration of Human Rights, primary school enrollments in developing countries have grown about two and a half times, from 235 million to 600 million. Enrollments in Africa have increased almost eightfold, in South Asia six times, in the Arab region three and a half times, and in Latin America and the Caribbean nearly three times. This far exceeds rates of expansion over any comparable period in industrialized countries.[30]

Nevertheless, the right of everyone to education is still far from being achieved. Worldwide, it was estimated that over 70 million children of primary school age were out of school in 2005; almost seven out of ten are boys.[31] In that year, 70 percent of school-age children were enrolled in school in Sub-Saharan Africa, 90 percent in South Asia, 95 percent in North Africa, 86 percent in the Middle East, 97 percent in Latin America and the Caribbean, and 94 percent in Southeast Asia. In recent years, enrollments of girls have grown faster than of boys, though primary school attendance rates are still lower for girls than for boys, as are primary school completion rates and secondary school entrance and enrollment ratios.

Setting time-bound quantitative global goals has been an important contribution of the UN. UNESCO was the first UN organization to do this in relation to economic and social advances. It organized a series of regional conferences between 1959 and 1961 to plan for the expansion of access to education. Each conference took stock of the educational situation, explored recent trends, and set regional education goals for 1980. These included the achievement of free primary education by 1980 as well as an ambitious expansion of secondary education, technical training, and higher education. Common to all the conferences was a focus on the long-term goals for 1980 and a more immediate short-term plan that typically focused on the first five years after each conference.

What progress was made? By comparison with all earlier experience, the expansion of access to education in the 1960s and 1970s was rapid, although education for all was achieved only in East Asia and Oceania. In Southern Asia and Sub-Saharan Africa, expansion was also fast but not sufficient to deliver education for all, notably because school-age populations were growing more rapidly than was at first realized.

All this took place before the World Bank started lending on a larger scale for primary education, part of the important changes brought about by its president, Robert McNamara. As the World Bank history explains, these changes began in 1968 with a cautiously worded report by Edward Mason that argued for a gradual broadening of secondary vocational and technical education that would then spread to increases in primary and university education. He presented his argument entirely in terms of productivity with "no reference to equity, poverty or non-economic educational objectives."[32] The Mason argument was a result of the growing interest in the economics of education, which viewed education as an investment in human beings. Even in 1970, after the World Bank Board had considered the new policy proposals, it limited its action to experimental and demonstration projects rather than embarking on the expanded engagement with primary education that Mason has proposed. As earlier, the board made no reference to equity or poverty.[33] Once again, the UN had led the way.

Over the 1980s, the increase in national debt, declines in export earnings, and adoption of adjustment programs that included cutbacks in spending for health and education, often under heavy pressure from the IMF and World Bank, meant that primary schooling in most African countries declined both in quality and quantity. Enrollment ratios fell. Primary schools typically struggled on with few if any books and with teachers who were paid sporadically, if at all. Compared with the vision of two decades earlier, the national and international neglect of the rights of all children to education in the 1980s and 1990s was a tragedy and a disgrace.

In hindsight, the 1950s and 1960s can in fact be seen as pioneering times for ideas, research, and policymaking in matters relating to education and what

today is often called human resource development. Economists and planners launched new initiatives to calculate the benefits of education and research on the sources of growth and began to shift ideas about capital investment from physical to human capital. In the early 1960s, UNESCO published a massive bibliography of the burgeoning list of books, articles, and research papers on the economics of education.[34]

However, there are many ironies and contradictions in the early years of global education history. Neither UNESCO nor other UN organizations directly contributed much to the new economic thinking about education. In fact, UNESCO had only a single economist on its staff who followed the work on the economics of education undertaken elsewhere (mostly in universities and research institutes). This work focused heavily on the costs and benefits of education. Calculating rates of return to education was the predominant methodology of the field at this time. Though more than a thousand books and articles were published on the economics of education in the 1960s, the extent to which these arguments contributed to policymaking on education in the Third World or even to the rapid rise of enrollments is debatable. In most developing countries, especially newly independent ones, the expansion of education was the result of an inescapable political imperative. Most political leaders sought expansion of education at primary, secondary, and postsecondary levels, and bilateral donors largely agreed with these goals. The World Bank, the main international institution that might have been expected to be influenced by the potential payoff from investing in education, was still hesitant about providing financing for education on a large scale.

In fact, it was the Organisation for Economic Co-operation and Development that first developed a systematic methodology for education and manpower planning, the "Mediterranean Regional Project." The OECD did a number of country studies in the Mediterranean region and in a number of nonmember developing countries, including Argentina and Peru, thanks to a large grant from the Ford Foundation. The country studies followed a pragmatic methodology to analyze education and training situations, mostly at secondary and higher education levels. In addition, with the assistance of Jan Tinbergen, the OECD developed a methodology for quantitative planning models to assess educational requirements for economic development.[35] Thus, economic planning applied to education arose within the institution created to coordinate economic policy among the developed countries, not within the UN.

Children

The UN Intellectual History Project has focused on ideas, not on institutions; institutions appear in the volumes of the series only when they have made

intellectual contributions. Here obviously UNICEF should be mentioned. UNICEF's contribution from the beginning has been its unique and creative focus on children and its fresh and often unconventional ideas about what is needed for their full and sustained development. Although UNICEF is primarily an operational agency working in over 100 countries, its pioneering and multidisciplinary mandate and its decentralized field operations, from which it could learn and share ideas, have meant that it has also made intellectual contributions to international thinking.

A first major contribution emerged in 1964 from a conference in Bellagio that explored how concerns for children could better be integrated with development planning instead of simply being included as an implicit part of planning for health, education, and other social sectors. Distinguished members of the Third UN were invited, including Jan Tinbergen, V. K. R. V. Rao, and Alfred Sauvy, as well as Hans Singer and Dick Heyward from the Second UN.

A major conclusion of the conference was that UNICEF should help develop a country program for children in every member state. This approach involved three components. The first was a professional, multidisciplinary situation analysis of all the major problems affecting children in a country. The second involved an analysis of what the country needed to do to respond to these needs of children. And the third was an analysis of how best UNICEF could use its limited resources in that country to catalytically assist the government and other groups to embark on the broader programs required.

By the 1980s, UNICEF's program approach was well established, but other urgent problems were arising due to the economic orthodoxy that held sway. Debt and economic setbacks were affecting many developing countries, especially those in Latin America, the Caribbean, and Sub-Saharan Africa, and adjustment policies were the order of the day. UNICEF responded in two ways. One was through the development of *Adjustment with a Human Face,* which articulated a program of advocacy to make the case to the IMF and World Bank that the nutritional status, health, and education of children should be protected in the process of adjustment. How could one believe, UNICEF argued, that the economy of a country was being strengthened if its children, the human capital of the future, were being weakened by cutbacks in expenditures on nutrition and education?

Second, UNICEF argued that times of economic difficulty required not the abandonment of actions for children but concentrated attention on high-priority actions pursued in cost-effective ways. Several such measures, including the expansion of immunization, the encouragement of breastfeeding, and the promotion of oral rehydration to tackle diarrhea, the biggest cause of child mortality, were identified, along with complementary actions such as birth spacing, education of females, and food supplementation. In a program of social mobilization,

UNICEF enlisted governments and civil society to generate nationwide action and public support for these activities in more than 100 developing countries. The "heart" and "brains" of UNICEF was Jim Grant, a visionary leader on a global scale. As executive director from 1980 to 1995, he launched these activities as a worldwide Child Survival and Development Revolution initiative (see box 8.1).[36]

The result was that in the 1980s, in spite of economic setbacks and often a decline in per capita incomes, child mortality fell rapidly, often faster than in previous decades. By 1990, the number of under-five children who died each year had been reduced to 12 million from almost 15 million in 1980, in spite of an increase in the number of children born and in spite of the severe economic setbacks of the decade. By 2007, the number of under-five deaths had fallen below 10 million.

Over the 1990s, the idea of a rights-based approach to development took hold. The Convention on the Rights of the Child had been formulated in the 1980s, at first led mostly by visionaries from UNICEF's national committees with the support of various governments (the Third and First UNs).[37] As the

Box 8.1. Jim Grant: Mobilizing the UN for Action

Jim Grant, UNICEF's executive director from 1980 to 1995, showed how the international standing, financial resources, and leadership of a UN organization could be used to catalyze practical action around the world that was focused on achieving basic goals. UNICEF had from its early days been a field organization, directing attention to the needs of children and providing practical support for health, education, water, and other vital services. Over 80 percent of the organization's staff lived full time in developing countries, many outside capital cities. Grant's leadership showed how a UN organization could be raised to a new level of focus, commitment, and impact.

In the early 1980s, almost 15 million children under five were dying each year, overwhelmingly in developing countries and mostly from readily preventable causes, like measles, whooping cough, polio, and other communicable diseases for which vaccines were available. Diarrhea was another big killer for which oral rehydration therapy (ORT) was an effective remedy, if only mothers and other family members knew what to do.

Grant launched the Child Survival and Development Revolution initiative in 1982 to mobilize action country by country, with the goal of achieving 80 percent coverage of immunization against the six main killers by 1990. Starting in Colombia, Burkina Faso, and Turkey, the initiative spread to more than 100 countries with UNICEF field offices. Working with WHO and other specialized agencies, UNICEF led the charge for a campaign to accelerate national action.

Mobilization of civil society members was a key element. Using the media to spread

efforts gathered momentum, all three UNs started working together. By 1989, the CRC was formally agreed to, and by 1990, in an unprecedented few months, the necessary forty ratifications had been received and the CRC came into operation. Today, the Convention on the Rights of the Child is the most ratified of all human rights conventions.

After rapid ratification, the issue arose as to what part UNICEF should play in working with countries to implement the convention. After further debate and analysis, it became clear that the essence of a rights-based approach to development lay in three components: ensuring that the rights of the child became a reality for all children in each country and in the world; using the CRC as a guideline for how the services to achieve these rights would be delivered; and recognizing that state signatories had responsibilities for the global delivery of these rights, especially in education and health for children in poorer countries.

The significance of the CRC and the UN experience promoting it shows the evolution of UN ideas and action from emphasizing advance within a sector (e.g., education or health) to a rights-based approach. The other element is the

knowledge and awareness of the importance of immunization and ORT, UNICEF worked with NGOs, churches, mosques, Rotarians, and other local groups in country after country, energizing the health and school systems and moving toward the goal, often pioneering new approaches on the way. By 1986, sixteen countries had reached the 80 percent goal; by 1988, the total was thirty-four and by 1990, it was sixty-four. Most other countries had greatly increased coverage, even if the goal had not been fully reached.

In short, when the data was in, the visionary goal had largely been achieved as a global average. More important, child deaths had fallen to about 12 million by 1990. Today, child deaths are below 10 million each year—still too high but a remarkable improvement from 1950 figures, when 24 million children were dying each year at a time when the child population was well under half the present level. Reducing child mortality has also helped reduce fertility and population growth rates.

Jim Grant demonstrated the value of leadership of the Second UN, the importance of goals, and the need for system-wide focused support for follow-up national action. In 1990, with the help of heads of state from six countries, UNICEF organized the first World Summit for Children, which seventy-one heads of state attended. This was a culmination of the actions for children in the 1980s and a springboard for launching a new set of goals for children in the 1990s. These goals were later broadened into other areas and laid the basis for the Millennium Development Goals adopted in 2000.

Sources: Maggie Black, *Children First: The Story of UNICEF, Past and Present* (Oxford: Oxford University Press, 1996); and Richard Jolly, ed., *Jim Grant: UNICEF Visionary* (Florence: UNICEF, 2001).

intellectual evolution away from advances in individual sectors to an integrated view of human development across sectors.

Conclusion

Concern for all people in all countries has been part of the UN's mandate and mission from the outset, an obligation grounded in human rights and the needs of development. This concern stimulated calls for action and for the UN to lead in the areas of education, health, nutrition, and ending hunger, as well as, from the 1970s, for policies designed to slow population growth and improve the situation of women, including policies to improve maternal health. From the earliest days, the UN has focused on children with programs of support for children in emergency situations and, beginning in the 1950s, more general support for policies to reduce child mortality and improve child health. The UN also incorporated concerns for children in economic and social development. In contrast to the emphasis on education as an investment that has long dominated much economic analysis, the UN has always emphasized a broader understanding of the role of education in promoting understanding, tolerance, and friendship among all nations and all racial and religious groups.

In the basics of education, health and nutrition, the human situation in all regions and almost all countries of the world is today measurably better than when the UN was founded, not only for children but also for women and men. Through its funds and specialized agencies, the UN has encouraged and supported these advances, providing technical advice, help with planning, and financial support; setting goals; mobilizing social support; monitoring progress; and setting these national actions in a regional and global context. In some countries, such as Korea, Malaysia, Barbados, and Mauritius, the advances are such that countries that were once classed as poor and underdeveloped have achieved levels of basic education, health, and nutrition comparable to those in many developed countries. This shows what can be done. But the fact that so far this is the situation in only some developing countries is a stark reminder of how far individual countries and member states collectively have to go to realize the UN's early vision.

9. Environmental Sustainability

From Environment and Development to Preserving the Planet

- Searching for Sustainability and Global Resource Management
- Environment and Development
- Climate Change
- The Kyoto Protocol: Moving beyond Bali
- Other Continuing Challenges
- Conclusion

Changes in global awareness, thinking, and concern about the environment have been truly fundamental over the UN's life, probably exceeding even changing ideas about human rights. As with human rights, the UN has often taken the lead internationally in ways that have challenged and changed conventional thinking. The landmarks of these changes include:

- 1962: The UN Declaration on Permanent Sovereignty over Natural Resources detailed the rights of countries to freely manage natural resources for the benefit of the population and national economic development
- 1972: The UN Conference on the Human Environment in Stockholm pioneered the idea that environmental and development ideas must be approached together
- 1982: The UN Convention of the Law of the Sea gave rise to extended resource rights for coastal states, protection of the marine environment, and an international deep-seabed regime based on the nascent principle of the common heritage of humankind
- 1987: The World Commission on Environment and Development report *Our Common Future* introduced the concept of sustainable development that would meet "the needs of the present without compromising the ability of future generations to meet their own needs"
- 1988: Creation of the UN Intergovernmental Panel on Climate Change, which has provided the lead for the growing international consensus on the global problems presented by climate change

• 1992: The UN Conference on Environment and Development (UNCED), known also as the Earth Summit, took stock of progress since the Stockholm conference, linked environmental protection to poverty eradication, and emphasized priorities for the least-developed and environmentally most vulnerable countries

• 2007: The fourth assessment report of the Intergovernmental Panel on Climate Change found that evidence for global warming and climate change is unequivocal and that humans are responsible for this change, largely because of increases in carbon emissions

From each of these landmarks, ideas have evolved as part of a much broader process of rethinking in many countries and regions. This process has typically included contributions from the three United Nations. In the area of environment, perhaps more than in other areas, sympathetic governments, especially Scandinavian countries, took the lead. Sweden and the others from that region have often provided the initial motivation and financial support, backed up by evidence from leading scientists and well-organized NGOs. The World Conservation Union, Greenpeace, the World Wildlife Fund, Friends of the Earth, Conservation International, and the Sierra Club are leading examples of concerned NGOs in the Third UN.

Searching for Sustainability and Global Resource Management

UN ideas have made essential contributions to elements of new thinking about creating sustainability on the planet in three broad areas: resource management, the environment, and population. In *Development without Destruction: The UN and Global Resource Management,* Nico Schrijver identifies three major ways that new thinking in these ideas has had an impact.[1] First, the UN has been instrumental in generating widespread interest in the management of natural resources by taking account of economic, social, and environmental aspects of such management. Second, new concepts of resource management have been introduced, such as resource sovereignty, the global commons, sustainable use of natural resources, and sustainable development. Third, the UN has created a major push to put population and environmental problems high on national agendas through the world conferences of the 1970s and 1990s.

More generally, sustainable development has become a leading theme in national and international political debate, beginning in 1987 when the World Commission on Environment and Development issued its report, *Our Common Future.*[2] This commission was established by Secretary-General Javier Pérez de Cuéllar and was headed by Gro Harlem Brundtland, three-time Norwegian prime minister and later WHO director-general.

Box 9.1. The Intergovernmental Panel on Climate Change

The World Meteorological Organization and the United Nations Environment Programme established the UN Intergovernmental Panel on Climate Change in 1988, with remarkable results. Between 1988 and 2008, the panel issued four assessment reports.[1] Each report has presented a comprehensive assessment of the existing stock of knowledge on all aspects of climate change. The panel has also produced special reports on more specific issues.

As part of the latest and fourth assessment report, three volumes representing the contributions of several working groups were released. An important synthesis report that brought together the major findings of the earlier three volumes was published in November 2007, which incorporated advances in scientific knowledge related to climate change. This has had a major impact on public opinion and awareness among world leaders.

The major achievement of the panel is that it has established a consensus among its scientific members from governments and countries around the world, who number more than 1,000, that the evidence for global warming and climate change is now unequivocal. More important, the IPCC consensus is that the human influence on this change is now well established scientifically. In the absence of drastic mitigation of emissions of greenhouse gases, temperature increases by the end of the twenty-first century are projected to be between 2 and 4 percent.

Rajendra Kumar Pachauri, who was elected chair of the IPCC in 2002, shared the Nobel Prize for Peace in 2007 on behalf of the IPCC with former U.S. vice-president Al Gore, who released the documentary film *An Inconvenient Truth* about the effects of global warming in 2006.

1. IPCC, *Climate Change: The IPCC 1990 and 1992 Assessments* (Geneva: IPCC, 1992); IPCC, *Climate Change 1995: IPCC Second Assessment* (Geneva: IPCC, 1995); IPCC, *Climate Change 2001: Synthesis Report*, ed. R. T. Watson and Core Writing Team (Cambridge: Cambridge University Press, 2001); IPCC, *Climate Change 2007: Synthesis Report*, ed. Core Writing Team, Rajendra K. Pachauri, and Randy Reisinger (Geneva: IPCC, 2008).

A key document in the early debate about global resource management was the 1962 UN Declaration on Permanent Sovereignty over Natural Resources, also referred to as the "economic pendant" to the decolonization declaration. This and subsequent resolutions detailed the rights of countries, including the right to freely manage natural resources for the benefit of the population and national economic development. The next step was to extend sovereignty over marine resources as well. This resulted in a thorough revision of the traditional law of the sea.

The Third UN Conference on the Law of the Sea (1973–1982) gave rise to the

exclusive sovereign rights of coastal states over an extended continental shelf and a 200-nautical-mile Exclusive Economic Zone. It also introduced an international deep-seabed regime based on the principle of the common heritage of humankind rather than awarding rights of ownership to the country or company claiming first discovery. Nico Schrijver's UNIHP volume demonstrates that the new international resource regime of the law of the sea has proven irreversible, albeit with major loopholes. For instance, its efforts to provide coastal developing countries with protection against distant fishing fleets and mining companies have met with only limited success.

Environment and Development

Over the years, concepts of resource management have totally changed, shifting fundamentally from ensuring national rights to encompass a much wider range of environmental problems that have an impact upon countries and regions far beyond national borders. These were rarely mentioned until the 1970s, although in 1969 Secretary-General U Thant alerted the General Assembly to the problems of the human environment in words far ahead of their time: "For the first time in the history of mankind, there is arising a crisis of worldwide proportion involving developed and developing countries—the crisis of the human environment."[3]

In 1972 the UN organized in Stockholm the Conference on the Human Environment, the first of the global conferences of the 1970s. It was a pathbreaking event, politically and conceptually. Although the Sierra Club had been founded in 1892 and Rachel Carson had written her polemic, *Silent Spring*, in 1962, the UN's spotlight on the global deterioration of the natural environment was a quantum leap forward. Despite growing awareness of increasing pollution and environmental damage in the industrial countries and rising fears that scarcities of raw materials would, in the words of the first report to the Club of Rome, set limits to growth, plans for the UN conference initially met with massive criticism from several industrial countries and strong skepticism from developing countries.[4]

Maurice Strong, a Canadian entrepreneur and visionary who later championed issues about the environment and development in a number of UN assignments, was appointed secretary-general of the conference. In preparation for the conference, he gathered a group of experts from both North and South at Founex (near Geneva) to explore the issues.

The group in Founex, a clear example of the Third UN in action, focused on bridging the great differences between the environmental priorities of developed countries and the development priorities of developing countries.

Common ground in this conflict was found by shifting the emphasis from the environment alone to the need for a new strategy that combined priorities for the environment and development, both nationally and internationally. These were included a year later in the Stockholm conference declaration, which called for the elimination of mass poverty and the creation of a decent and human environment. As Ignacy Sachs, who was there, told us, "The Stockholm conference emphasized the idea that development and environment management are complementary. To those who claimed that to protect the environment it was necessary to stop growth, the conference replied that there was an alternative, namely to change the pattern of growth and the use of its benefits."[5] Some environmental problems would inevitably arise as a consequence of industrialization, but they should and could be minimized through appropriate policies, the declaration claimed. This was a major advance in thinking and political agreement, one of the UN's fundamental contributions to the topic.

The outcome of the Stockholm conference was a comprehensive program that integrated the economic, social, and political dimensions of environmental issues. To carry the ideas forward, the conference agreed to establish a new body, the UN Environment Programme (UNEP).

Twenty years later, the UN Secretary-General established the World Commission on Environment and Development (also known as the Brundtland Commission) to explore a more integrated approach to this issue—a further example of turning to the Third UN for ideas and guidance. Building on an earlier notion of sustainable use of natural resources, the commission's report defined sustainable development as "development which meets the needs of the present without compromising the ability of future generations to meet their own needs."[6] In 1987, the General Assembly welcomed the report, and in 1989 it decided to convene a further UN Conference on Environment and Development, in view of what General Assembly resolution 44/228 called "the continuing deterioration of the state of the environment and the serious degradation of the global life-support systems that could result in an ecological catastrophe."[7]

The resulting 1992 Earth Summit in Rio de Janeiro was the largest summit yet held to that time with 172 governments represented, including more than 100 heads of state. The conference reviewed progress and produced the Rio Declaration on Environment and Development as well as the program of action Agenda 21. It also opened up for signature the United Nations Framework Convention on Climate Change. Ten years later, in 2002, the UN held the World Summit on Sustainable Development in Johannesburg. Its mandate was to take stock of the implementation of the measures agreed to in Rio.

Over that decade, major shifts in global thinking had taken place and a better understanding of the nature of environmental problems had developed.

By 1992, the emphasis had shifted from absolute scarcity of certain nonrenewable resources—as some viewed the environmental problem in the 1970s—to the pollution or destruction of renewable resources, especially water and air, soil and forests. But the focus soon shifted again. As more evidence of climate change emerged, global warming became one of the most recognized and most serious environmental problems. Until the 1990s, the problem of the environment had been defined as how to survive in a global fishbowl. In 1997, the UN conference in Kyoto introduced the problem of what to do when the fishbowl is put into a microwave.

Many practical initiatives have followed from these conferences, and progress has been considerable, including the adoption of the UN Convention on the Law of the Sea and the Convention on Prevention of Marine Pollution by Dumping, and the Vienna Convention for the Protection of the Ozone Layer (1985).[8] The 1992 Rio conference led to further conventions on climate change, biodiversity, and desertification. It also agreed to create the Global Environment Facility (GEF) to provide funding and technical assistance to help developing countries meet their convention obligations regarding preserving biodiversity, protecting forests, and improving soils. In 1997, with increasing evidence of global warming, the Kyoto Protocol was adopted at the third session of the Conference of the Parties to the UN Framework Convention on Climate Change to strengthen the provisions of the climate change convention. The protocol, which entered into force in 2005, set binding targets to reduce greenhouse gas emissions in thirty-seven industrialized countries and the European Community.

Nonetheless, because of the hostility of certain major powers (especially the United States and Russia) and the lack of restrictions on the high levels of pollution developing countries generated (especially China and India), the ability of the Kyoto Protocol to adequately respond to these urgent and substantial environmental problems has been severely limited. The series of decisions reached at the UN Climate Change Conference held in Indonesia in December 2007 known as the Bali roadmap is designed to remedy this in the post-Kyoto period (after 2012).

Nonetheless, global understandings and perceptions of environmental issues have changed remarkably and rapidly over the last thirty years. At the UNCHE in Stockholm in 1972 and for the next twenty years or so, environmental matters were mainly related to questions concerning scarcity, pollution, desertification, deforestation, sustainability, and the relation between environment and underdevelopment. Gradually the issues of the survival of the planet and sustainability that have arisen from problems like climate change have been given more and more attention.

In our first publication, we gave considerable attention to trends in thinking since 1972.[9] Now we turn to the debate about climate change, which has major implications for global resource management.

Climate Change

The transformation of awareness and understanding of climate change and the recognition that it is to a large extent a human-made phenomenon is one of the most dramatic changes in ideas and perceptions of the last two or three decades.[10] Though many scientists have contributed to this understanding (although a small and decreasing minority still raise doubts about the validity of these ideas), the UN's Intergovernmental Panel on Climate Change has provided much of the scientific authority for these findings and given them global legitimacy and outreach.[11] The IPCC, which has more than 1,000 members drawn from scientists in countries round the world, has reviewed the data, analyzed its implications, made projections, and created a global consensus about the seriousness of the issues and the urgent need for action. It released its most recent findings and predictions in *Climate Change 2007: Synthesis Report.*[12]

It is now confirmed that human influences on global warming have been five times greater than those caused by solar variations. During the twentieth century, the average temperature increase globally was close to one degree Celsius and the average rise in sea level was more than 15 centimeters. These changes were accompanied by an increase in the frequency and intensity of extreme precipitation events, floods, and draughts. If no decisive action is taken, the temperature could increase between 2 and 4 degrees Celsius during this century. The impact of climate change is severe and is increasing over time. It will have the most severe consequences in the poorer regions of the world, all the more so if nothing is done. Here are several examples of what might happen:

• New data confirm that losses from the ice sheets have substantially contributed to the increase in sea level over the period 1993–2003. There is evidence that climate change will bring more intense tropical storms as warming oceans generate cyclones like the devastating one that hit Myanmar in May 2008.

• By 2020, agricultural yields in some countries could be reduced by up to 50 percent. In subtropical and tropical regions, a temperature increase of 1.5 to 2.5 Celsius could lead to a decline in productivity of crops such as maize and wheat. Climate change is already affecting rainfall, and drought-affected areas in Sub-Saharan Africa could increase by 60 to 90 million hectares.

• In Asia, mega-deltas such as Kolkata, Dhaka, Irrawaddy, and Shanghai are at

risk of coastal flooding, as are other cities in the world that are located in coastal areas.

• An important proportion of plant and animal species will be at risk of extinction if increases in global annual temperatures exceed 1.5 to 2.5 degrees Celsius.

• It is estimated that by 2080, an additional 1.8 billion people could be living in a water-scarce environment. Changes in runoff patterns and glacial melt will add to ecological stress, compromising flows of water for irrigation and human settlements in various parts of Asia and Latin America. By 2080, global climate change could increase the number of persons affected by malnutrition by 600 million.

• Rich countries are already taking action to prepare public health systems to deal with future climate shocks, such as the 2003 European heat wave. However, the greatest health impacts will be felt in developing countries, both because of high levels of poverty and because of the limited capacity of public health systems to respond.

• Around half of the world's coral reef systems have already suffered bleaching as a result of warming seas. The collapse of corals would be a catastrophic event for human development in several countries. Beyond their value for nutrition of the poor, coral reefs generate income and exports and, in some regions, support the tourist industry.

In 2007, *The Economics of Climate Change: The Stern Review,* a major report released by the UK government, built on the IPCC's findings to draw up an agenda for action.[13] The report put forward a major set of economic proposals that were backed up by the key conclusion that the cost of strong and urgent action on climate change will be less than the cost of inaction and the destructive impact of climate change under business as usual. Nicolas Stern, head of the UK Government Economic Service, argued that there is no longer a justification for believing that the scientific understanding of climate change is flawed or that the remaining areas of uncertainty imply that current knowledge is insufficient for taking action.

Under a business-as-usual scenario, the level of greenhouse gases could more than triple by the end of the century. This implies a 50 percent or greater risk that global average temperature change during the following decades will exceed 5 degrees Celsius. Stern contended that a temperature increase of that magnitude would dramatically change the physical and human geography of the world.

A few skeptics still believe that the human influence on climate change is vastly exaggerated. For that minority, Stern has the following piece of advice:

The economics of climate change are fundamentally about the economics of risk. If you act on climate change and invest in bringing forward new

technologies, and it turns out to be the biggest hoax ever perpetrated on mankind, as a US senator has described, you will still have acquired a lot of new technologies that are probably quite useful. If, on the other hand, you do nothing you may quickly end up with a lot of irreversible and severe damage. . . . Given the scale of the outcomes that are likely under a no-action scenario, maintaining this view must be regarded as reckless.[14]

The *Stern Review* estimates that the cost of action would amount to 1 percent of GDP, which is barely a quarter of the level of global military expenditures and less than the military spending of over 110 countries in 2005.[15] Although large in absolute terms, this amount is a small fraction of the world's national income and is small compared to the annual economic growth it would make possible. It also seems a modest expenditure to forestall the worst—an insurance policy of sorts.[16]

The UNDP Human Development Report for 2007/2008, *Fighting Climate Change: Human Solidarity in a Divided World*, emphasized the human consequences of climate change and argued for placing "ecological imperatives at the heart of economics." The reports state that the process should begin in developed countries but move to "a binding international agreement to cut greenhouse gas emissions over a long time horizon but with stringent near-term and medium-term targets."[17] The major developing countries must be a party to such an agreement and its commitments; China surpassed the United States in 2008 as the world's biggest producer of greenhouse gases, and India is also gaining in this race toward a dubious distinction.

These three reports—the IPCC's *Climate Change 2007: Synthesis Report*, the *Stern Review*, and the UNDP Human Development Report of 2007/2008, all of which were issued in 2006 and 2007—issued a call to urgent action. Each emphasized that it was not too late to forestall catastrophic climate change. Together, they outline specific recommendations for international cooperation and multilateralism to effectively address climate change and avert significant negative consequences for human development today and for future generations. However, action will have to be faster, much more comprehensive, and much more serious than previous UN debates and commitments.

The Kyoto Protocol: Moving beyond Bali

The Kyoto Protocol is annexed to the international UN Framework Convention on Climate Change with the main objective of reducing greenhouse gases that cause climate change and strengthening sink capacity, the capacity of the planet's ecosystem to absorb greenhouse gases and other carbon emissions. The evidence that climate change results from human actions, mainly the ever-

increasing amount of carbon emissions, has become much stronger over the last two decades. This finding was in no small measure due to the work of the Intergovernmental Panel on Climate Change, which produced a series of compelling reports by the hundreds of scientists who are members of the panel.

The Kyoto Protocol was limited and heavily flawed from the very beginning, reflecting the politics of reaching any agreement other than equitable burden-sharing. Huge emitters such as the United States, China, and India have not signed the pact because they do not see it as in their best interests. The objective of the protocol, namely the reduction of average global temperature, is not yet within sight. Indeed, twenty-three of the twenty-four warmest years since record-keeping began in 1850 have occurred since 1980. Sea levels have risen by an average of 3.1 millimeters per year over the period 1993 to 2003, a rate of increase that is almost twice the historic average. The incidence of major floods, the number of wildfires, average wind speeds, and the frequency of cyclones have all risen in the past two decades. Emissions of greenhouse gases continue to rise. In the face of these facts, a global consensus has now emerged on the need to curb carbon emissions. However, there is as yet no consensus on how to share the burden of such a policy among countries.

Among the various approaches that have been proposed, one is the creation of an International Carbon Fund (ICF).[18] The ICF would begin by setting a target in terms of the amount of emissions reduction necessary to keep the concentration of carbon below an agreed-upon ceiling, say 450 parts per million.[19] The target would be global but delivery would need to be national and local. Once the target is set, the fund would allocate quotas—a proportion of the target for which each participating country would be responsible. Although the target and the allocations would be centralized decisions, the ICF will not tell individual countries how to meet their national goals. This would be left to the market, including elements of choice that reflect national culture, and would produce many different solutions. Finally, the ICF would establish a system to monitor and verify action on reductions and provide loans or grants to the poorest countries to fund clean low-carbon development. The ICF would also create a trading exchange designed to ensure that emissions are reduced in the most cost-effective way. The currency would be carbon reduction units.

The UN Climate Change Conference in Bali in late 2007 focused on setting up a framework after 2012 when the present phase of the Kyoto Protocol comes to an end. Major elements of such a framework would include establishing an agreed-upon threshold at which dangerous climate change would begin, say at 2 degrees Celsius above preindustrial levels; agreeing to reduce greenhouse gas emissions by 50 percent of 1990 levels by 2050; implementing

targets for developed countries under the current Kyoto Protocol commitment period (until 2012); and cutting greenhouse gas emissions by at least 80 percent by 2050 and 30 percent by 2020. Finally, major emitters in developing countries would need to work to cut emissions by 20 percent by 2050. These cuts would start in 2020 and would be supported through international cooperation in the areas of finance and transfer of low-carbon technology.

The UN Climate Change Conference in Bali once again put the spotlight on the limits of ideas in the face of power. After the deadline for an agreement had been reached, 187 states present (including China and the United States) unexpectedly resumed talks on the global effort to rescue the planet from climate change. This culminated in the so-called Bali roadmap—a two-year negotiation process to guide the establishment of a new treaty by 2009 to replace the Kyoto Protocol, which expires in 2012. While countries agreed to green technology transfer, funding for poorer countries, and cuts in greenhouse gas emissions, no clear goals or timetables were set. At the close of the conference, newspaper articles with such titles as "We've Been Suckered Again by the US. So Far the Bali Deal Is Worse Than Kyoto" and "Answer to Hot Air Was in Fact a Chilling Blunder" accurately captured the outcome.[20]

Deep concessions were made so that the United States would sign on, yet Washington still had "serious concerns" about the inadequacy of responsibilities assigned to developing countries.[21] Russia, Canada, and Japan also objected to some of the agreement's key aspects. Meanwhile the G-77 and some NGOs were disappointed at the lackluster final text. Indeed, the ambassador of Grenada described the outcome as "so watered-down" that "there was no need for 12,000 people to gather . . . in Bali. We could have done that by email."[22]

Pessimism about this outcome, however, should be tempered by the changes in scientific and public reactions to climate change and global warming that have already taken place in only a few years. The importance of actions by individuals, groups, and committees, mostly the Third UN, should not be underestimated. Prominent individuals like Al Gore hammered away doggedly for decades about the need to face the problem of climate change. He faced indifference, cynicism, and even ridicule before the breakthrough of his movie, *An Inconvenient Truth*, and the recognition provided by the Nobel Prize for Peace in 2007. In short, people and groups of people can make a difference. Woodrow Wilson stated to the press in 1915, "Opinion ultimately governs the world."[23] Opinion today may be distorted by spin, but we are persuaded that in the long term it will win out. With respect to climate change and global warming, the main issue is whether the change in public opinion, already so visible, will bring political action in time.

The world is only at the beginning of the process of understanding the wider

consequences of economic expansion on a global scale in a planet of finite resources. It lags far behind in the task of mobilizing the national and international commitments required to take action to deal with the consequences before they prove overwhelming. This race for survival is one of the highest priorities for global governance in the years ahead.

Other Continuing Challenges

Although the "new" problems of climate change and global warming now garner considerable attention, the "old" environmental problems—some of which have direct links with the "new" problems—are still with us and often are getting worse. This is the case with acid rain, air pollution, overpopulation, rainforest destruction, and desertification.

Another example is related to the rapid expansion of car use in countries such as China and India and other developing and emerging countries. This is further stimulated by the production of inexpensive cars—India is now producing cars that sell for $2,500. The implications for air pollution and carbon dioxide emissions of such looming consumption by new members of the middle class entail huge negative environmental costs. What type of intellectual framework might help? "'Deep ecology': the sense of the interdependence of humanity with nature, and the constraints on the survival within nature . . . is maybe where it could come from," said former ILO staffer and later distinguished political scientist Robert Cox. "Out of that could come the kind of alternative thinking that would affect the way we organize society, the economy, and even politics."[24]

In spite of declining birth rates, population will continue to increase over the coming decades. As nations develop, the combination of a growing population and increasing incomes will create additional pressures on the environment in many ways. Mobilizing action to tackle global warming should be combined with continuing efforts to improve national and international resource management if the challenge of sustainable development is to be politically acceptable and sensitive to human needs.

Conclusion

Global resource management, which was introduced in the UN in the 1960s, is still the broad concept within which environmental and global warming problems should be situated. The need to tackle specific issues globally is growing. In the face of climate change and other elements of the environmental equation, nothing short of a planetary perspective is feasible, and this reality

is increasingly accepted. It is a tribute to UN pioneers that such an idea was promoted fifty years before it was popularly accepted.

The history of the concept of sustainability demonstrates how ideas can catalyze political and institutional forces. Once this occurs, the prospects are altered for forming new coalitions that tip the balance in favor of modest and sometimes more dramatic policy changes to address global problems. As former senior UN official Jan Pronk summarizes: "A new coalition [emerges], with the help of different groups, which in the past were antagonizing each other."[25]

The UN had and continues to have an important role in influencing trends in natural resource management and innovations. This was the case when the concept of resource sovereignty was introduced, for which rights and duties were twin elements. Nations have a sovereign right to national resources but they also have a sovereign duty to use these resources for national economic development and the well-being of the entire population, to grant foreign investors fair treatment, and to conserve the environment.[26] The latter element evolved into the concept of sustainable development, of which curbing climate change has become a major component.

The notion of the "common concern of humankind" emerged as a compromise position in response to apprehensions states expressed about UN ambitions to internationalize resource management and the environmental regime. This concept underlies the conventions on climate change, biological diversity, and anti-desertification. It failed to create all the conditions necessary to create an international regime, yet it still conveyed the global scope of the problem at hand and took some account of the rights of future generations.

Political debates in a variety of UN forums have resulted in new concepts for resource management, such as resource sovereignty (on land and in the sea), the global commons, and sustainable development. They are all sensitive and controversial issues. Functional rather than territorial arrangements have been negotiated that facilitate the sharing of the world's resources through cooperative regimes designed to combat climate change, preserve biological diversity, and promote sustainable fisheries and forestry. As Nico Schrijver concludes, "These are considerable achievements but . . . current concepts are incomplete and existing institutions insufficiently equipped to curb the alarming rates of resource degradation and to provide . . . regimes aimed at an integrated ecosystem approach for sustainable development."[27] Correcting these deficiencies is one of the biggest challenges for the UN in the years ahead; the future and well-being of people worldwide depends on it.

The stakes are large. We close this chapter with the words from Barbara Ward, who wrote with remarkable foresight twenty-five years ago in *Progress for a Small Planet*:

Precisely those areas where immensity and distance have seemed to reign—climates, oceans, atmosphere—are beginning to be seen as profoundly interdependent systems in which the cumulative behaviour of the inhabitants of the planet, the various activities of each seemingly separate community, can become the common destiny of all. . . . If we can learn from the growing . . . risk in our present practices to determine that the next phase of development shall respect and sustain and even enhance the environment, we can look to a human future. . . .

The only fundamentally unresolved problem . . . is whether the rich and fortunate are imaginative enough and the resentful and underprivileged poor patient enough to begin to establish a true foundation of better sharing, fuller cooperation, and joint planetary work. . . . In short, no problem is insoluble in the creation of a balanced and conserving planet save humanity itself. Can it reach in time the vision of joint survival? Can its inescapable physical interdependence—the chief new insight of our century—induce that vision? We do not know. We have the duty to hope.[28]

10. Peace and Security

From Preventing State Conflict to Protecting Individuals

- **Replacing Conflict with the Rule of Law**
- **Preventive Diplomacy**
- **Disarmament and Development**
- **Peacekeeping**
- **The Responsibility to Protect**
- **Human Security**
- **Conclusion**

Four fundamental ideas have traditionally driven UN responses to the challenges of war and armed conflict: replacing war and conflict with the rule of law and negotiations; using preventive diplomacy by the Secretary-General and others to forestall conflicts; linking measures of disarmament to development in order to diminish the structural causes of war and conflict; and interposing international buffers and observer forces to keep the peace when belligerents consent to their presence. Early in the twenty-first century, an innovative fifth idea entered the mainstream at the United Nations, the responsibility to protect (R2P) individuals when their own governments are manifestly unwilling or unable to do so. Together, these five constitute elements of a sixth idea—human security—that shifts calculations away from the exclusive concern with the military security of states toward the safety and empowerment of individuals.

After more than six decades that have been punctuated by at least 150 national or regional conflicts and wars that have caused at least 20 million deaths, one could easily conclude that the UN's efforts in the areas of peace and human security have failed. Set against the record of the half-century before the world organization was created, however, the change has been remarkably positive. The death toll of the two world wars of the twentieth century was 70 to 90 million.[1] As Eric Hobsbawm points out, the "total wars" that involved all major powers and took place on a world scale in the twentieth century were more deadly and destructive than any previous wars; the losses literally are incalculable.[2] Robert J. Rummel's scholarly career has been spent counting how many people have been killed in the wars, pogroms, genocides, and mass murder.

His estimate for the twentieth century is 217 million.[3] And of course this figure does not include the many more individuals who have lived diminished lives as refugees, internally displaced persons, detainees, widows or widowers, orphans, and paupers as the result of war.[4] Yet terrible as the armed conflicts since 1945 have been, in terms of the number of people affected, the UN has made important contributions to peace and human security.

Moreover, the death statistics indicate only part of the UN's record of conflict management. The changes in norms and ideas have been substantial. As we mentioned at the outset, the United Nations Intellectual History Project has emphasized assessing the historical record regarding economic and social development. But as we proceeded, it became clear that development, human rights, and human security should be seen and treated as part of a broader and more interactive whole. The powerful ideas of human security and preventive diplomacy that blossomed toward the end of the 1990s thus became central to our book series.

ILO head Juan Somavía was once Chile's permanent representative in New York and before that headed NGOs. Thus, he has a vantage point informed by his experience in all three United Nations. He emphasizes that the UN has played "a very fundamental role as a legitimizer of ideas that are nascent, of things that are out there. . . . The moment the UN begins discussing an issue, and it becomes part of programs, and institutional debate . . . it legitimizes something that otherwise could be perceived of as marginal in society."[5] This chapter endeavors to introduce many ideas that grew from the Charter's clarion call "to save succeeding generations from the scourge of war."

Replacing Conflict with the Rule of Law

With the UN Charter came a sea change in international attitudes about war, from both a legal and operational perspective. Powerful countries could no longer engage in aggression without challenge from the international community, nor could they engage in military operations without seeking some form of international legitimacy as justification. The 2003 U.S.-led war in Iraq continues even while these words are being written, but Secretary-General Kofi Annan has stated that the war was illegal—somewhat tardily, to be sure. Before the war began, many members of the public in the United States, the United Kingdom, and others elsewhere marched in opposition, calling for the United States to take the issues that precipitated the conflict to the Security Council. Like those opposed to the invasion and occupation in the first place, critics came to understand the importance of Charter principles that outlawed the use of military force unless authorized by the Security Council or used in genuine self-defense. Neither of these conditions obtained for the U.S.-led coalition that invaded Iraq.

In earlier times, appeals to patriotism and national interests usually trumped concerns for justice, but the Charter and debates in the Security Council, however inadequate they are and however they are influenced by narrow calculations of national interests, have set out a frame of law to which parties often appeal for justification. Moreover, these appeals are made to a Security Council that includes representatives of some of the smallest and weakest countries. In addition, the world's media can use these standards to judge the legality of decisions to go to war.

While economic and military power still dominate geopolitics and the issues underlying most conflicts and while the Security Council's composition and procedures are contested (the five victorious powers in 1945 are still permanent members with veto power), the legal context in which countries go to war and make peace has undergone a fundamental change from what existed before the birth of the UN. The imprimatur of the Security Council imparts a legitimacy that cannot be replicated by unilateral decisions or even decisions from a multinational coalition and regional organizations.

In addition, the last six and a half decades provide several positive examples of how attitudes toward war and conquest have changed profoundly. The ending of many centuries of Franco-German military conflict is perhaps the most dramatic, although there are other examples in Europe and smaller examples in Latin America, as for example between Chile and Argentina. The ending of military control of colonies is another. It is important not to overstate these successes, but it is equally wrong not to recognize the changes. In *Parliament of Man,* Paul Kennedy, the distinguished Yale University historian, summarized the momentous transformation in the post-1945 landscape:

> Despite mankind's dreadful deeds and follies over the past centuries, we have advanced. It is worth recalling, for example, that about four hundred years ago Swedish, Danish, Italian and French soldiers (among many others) hacked and burned their way all over Europe; during the past fifty years they have instead been sending peacekeeping contingents everywhere from the Congo to the Middle East.[6]

Preventive Diplomacy

One of the clearest and most innovative ideas of the Second UN initially came from Ralph Bunche in the early 1950s, though it was developed further and more formally by Secretary-General Dag Hammarskjöld a few years later. That concept is preventive diplomacy. Bertrand Ramcharan's volume in this series tells the remarkable story of the unfolding of this idea at the UN. The concept of preventive diplomacy emerged in response to a diversity of worldwide

challenges and combined intelligent foresight, careful and well-informed analysis, and bold initiative. The record is far from perfect, as one would expect, but Ramcharan identifies many cases where preventive diplomacy has succeeded. The fact that the former Finnish president won the Nobel Peace Prize in 2008 for his efforts in UN mediation in crises ranging from Namibia to Kosovo is the most recent illustration of preventive diplomacy's capacities.

Anything that falls in the category of "prevention" poses especially difficult analytical questions. It is very difficult to find what worked and why and far easier to point to what failed. Perhaps more important, it is harder still to point to successful prevention, since nothing happens. Politicians like to take credit but the dog that does not bark is hard to take credit for. Moreover, it is easier to mobilize political support for a crisis than to do so beforehand.

Box 10.1. U Thant and the Cuban Missile Crisis

The Cuban Missile Crisis was undoubtedly one of the most dangerous moments in human history, when the world came closest to nuclear war during the "thirteen days" from 16 to 28 October 1962.

On 15 October, a U.S. reconnaissance aircraft discovered that the Soviet Union was secretly installing missile bases in Cuba. U.S. president John F. Kennedy announced on 22 October that he had ordered a naval quarantine around Cuba that would become operational two days later. On 25 October, American and Soviet naval vessels came into close proximity; a USSR submarine captain was authorized, as we now know, to use nuclear weapons. On 27 October, a Soviet commander shot down an American plane that was flying over Cuba.

In a little-known series of events, U Thant contributed to defusing the crisis. In an address to the Security Council on 24 October, the interim Secretary-General (he had been given a three-year term when Dag Hammarskjöld died in the Congo a year earlier) underlined the dramatic human stakes and called for urgent negotiations between the parties. He informed the council that he had sent urgent appeals to President Kennedy and Soviet chairman Nikita Khrushchev for a moratorium of two to three weeks—the Soviet Union would voluntarily suspend all arms shipments to Cuba and the United States would voluntarily suspend the quarantine and agree to stop searching ships bound for Cuba. He also appealed to Cuba's president, Fidel Castro, to suspend the construction of major military facilities and installations on the island during the period of negotiation. U Thant made an open-ended offer of his good offices to facilitate these negotiations.[1]

On 25 October, Khrushchev wrote to the Secretary-General accepting his proposal. The same day Kennedy communicated his appreciation for U Thant's message but also his conviction that the key to a solution lay in the removal of the weapons from Cuba. Soviet vessels continued on their way to the quarantined waters.

That very day, U Thant made an urgent appeal to the two leaders. A confrontation

Secretaries-General normally stay behind the scenes and engage in what Dag Hammarskjöld recommended should be standard operating procedure, "quiet diplomacy."[7] While states like to take credit, they also like to have a scapegoat, a role often assigned the United Nations ("the UN failed to do X, Y, or Z"). But the UN can rarely take credit for victories in preventive diplomacy.

A notable example of the payoff that comes from the UN's impartiality was U Thant's role in defusing the Cuban missile crisis by shuttling messages and mediating (see box 10.1). But each of the Secretaries-General can point to some successes, from Trygve Lie to Ban Ki-moon. While visible photo opportunities enter media accounts—for instance Javier Pérez de Cuéllar and Alvaro de Soto in Central America in 1992 after successful negotiations to end El Salvador's decade-long war—instances that do not make headlines are also of

between Soviet and U.S. vessels would destroy the possibility of negotiations. He requested Khrushchev to instruct any Soviet ships already sailing toward Cuba to stay away from the interception area for a limited time. He also asked Kennedy to instruct U.S. vessels in the Caribbean to do everything possible to avoid direct confrontation with Soviet ships. He told both sides that if he received the assurance he sought, he would inform the other side of that assurance.

Kennedy immediately accepted the proposal, contingent upon acceptance by Moscow. Khrushchev also accepted the moratorium. He informed U Thant that he had ordered Soviet vessels bound for Cuba to stay out of the interception area temporarily. On 26 October, U Thant sent a message to Prime Minister Fidel Castro informing him of the encouraging responses and asking that construction of major military installations in Cuba, especially those designed to launch medium- and intermediate-range ballistic missiles, be suspended. Castro sent a forceful response complaining about the United States but extending an invitation for U Thant to visit Cuba for direct discussions.

After the American and Soviet acceptances of U Thant's appeal, and using the time that his efforts had gained them, Kennedy and Khrushchev had their own exchange and agreed on the formula that eventually ended the missile crisis. U Thant traveled to Cuba on 30–31 October for conversations with Cuban leaders that allowed them to let off steam.

In his letter of 28 October to the Soviet premier, Kennedy wrote: "The distinguished efforts of Acting Secretary-General U Thant have greatly facilitated both our tasks." American and Soviet negotiators later sent a joint letter to U Thant: "On behalf of the Government of the United States of America and the Soviet Union, we desire to express to you our appreciation for your efforts in assisting our Governments to avert the serious threat to peace which arose in the Caribbean area."[2]

1. Bertrand G. Ramcharan, *Preventive Diplomacy at the UN* (Bloomington: Indiana University Press, 2008), 106.

2. Ramcharan, *Preventive Diplomacy at the UN*, 83; Avalon Project, "The Cuban Missile Crisis: Editorial Note," available at http://avalon.law.yale.edu/20th_century/msc_cuba263.asp.

consequence. Indeed, some recent work by the Human Security Report Project headed by UN staffer Andrew Mack points to the increased presence of multilateral cooperation, especially the UN's mediation and peace operations, as being at least partially responsible for the decline of many indicators of death and violence in the last decade.[8] However, although increased multilateral cooperation is inversely correlated with indicators of death and violence, it does not necessarily follow that increased multilateral cooperation caused the decline in death and violence.

Members of the Second United Nations have taken many preventive diplomacy initiatives, either the Secretary-General himself or one of his special representatives. Occasionally, members of the First UN, notably the president of the Security Council or other diplomats from its member states, have also taken multilateral rather than bilateral initiatives. For example, Canada's foreign minister (and later prime minister) Lester Pearson is usually credited along with Hammarskjöld for the invention of peacekeeping.

The creative roles all the Secretaries-General have played emerges from Ramcharan's account, especially the role of Dag Hammarskjöld, who put down the "markers on the practice of preventive diplomacy" that are still very much in use today. The Secretary-General's engagement should not be automatic. He (to date, all incumbents have been males) should decide if and when his involvement might bear fruit or not; and he is the one who decides when and where to send his representatives on special missions or post them for a longer time in particular field situations. Ramcharan points to the utility of such troubleshooting. While sometimes an idealistic stretch, the concept of preventive diplomacy is also expanding to addressing root causes of armed conflict, including economic and social causes. To use terms that are currently fashionable, Hammarskjöld "had an operational and structural approach to preventive diplomacy."[9]

Hammarskjöld's ideas fired the imagination of diplomats, scholars, statesmen, and believers in the UN. After his tragic plane crash in the Congo in 1961, other Secretaries-General continued his legacy. Pérez de Cuéllar and Boutros-Ghali both helped this process, the former elaborating the need for a global watch in *Perspectives for the 1990s* and the latter stressing the need for economic and social equity in *An Agenda for Peace*.[10] Kofi Annan added the challenge of comprehensive preventive strategies, adding the concept of "two sovereignties" and emphasizing the concept of "the responsibility to protect" that the International Commission on Intervention and State Sovereignty put forward (see below). Over the years, the concept of preventive diplomacy has evolved; Annan eventually spoke of a "culture of prevention."[11]

Another step forward was the work of the Third UN in the form of the Carnegie Commission on Preventing Deadly Conflict, which was stimulated by the tragedy and abject failure of prevention in Rwanda. The commission's 1997

report led to a vast expansion of research and advocacy.[12] As a follow-up to this report, the International Crisis Group, a highly successful and visible member of the Third UN, was created in 1998 in Brussels to keep crises before decision makers by performing independent research and analysis of the type that would be politically risky for the Second UN.

Ramcharan identifies the continuing role of preventive diplomacy. Addressing the structural causes of violence requires action—reducing poverty, moderating regional or ethnic inequalities, and empowering women, in particular. The early warning process also needs to be strengthened. Although the Secretary-General will continue to have the major role, he requires strong backing from the Security Council and the General Assembly. The Secretary-General should encourage action by other institutions within the UN system and elsewhere. "The idea of preventive diplomacy is one of the great UN ideas," Ramcharan tells us, "that will be around for as long as the world organization exists, for behind it is a simple faith that whatever might be done to head off crises or conflicts should be considered."[13]

Disarmament and Development

As Thomas Weiss and Ramesh Thakur point out in their volume in our series on the unfinished journey toward meaningful global governance, major powers, especially those that possess nuclear weapons and other weapons of mass destruction (WMDs), have always preferred to keep serious discussion about arms in the bilateral arena. As the members of the club with nuclear capabilities have expanded to include India, Pakistan, North Korea, and undoubtedly Israel, these countries have tried as well to keep UN deliberations at arm's length. In spite of the rhetoric of nonproliferation, the current Non-Proliferation Treaty (NPT) regime is under stress and perhaps at the breaking point. While thirteen treaties have been negotiated under UN auspices, nuclear states exhibit a strong preference to keep prerogatives to themselves and to use the United Nations to help prevent states that do not have WMDs from acquiring them.[14]

Linking disarmament with development has been another UN contribution to ideas. The results are modest, to be sure. However, compared to the relative neglect elsewhere, the UN has over its history displayed a sustained preoccupation with the topic. The link between development and disarmament is a contemporary extension of the "guns and butter" argument that only the UN seems to address. In contrast, the Bretton Woods institutions neglected disarmament for their first four decades of existence, after which the issue gradually became part of their analysis of the effectiveness of public spending programs. Even after the end of the Cold War, arms reduction remained controversial and politically charged.[15]

All three of the UNs have taken the lead on disarmament issues at various times. In 1955, France was one of the first governments to introduce proposals linking disarmament with development; it proposed that all participating states agree to reduce their military spending by a certain percentage that would increase year by year. All nations would follow a common definition of military spending according to this plan, and reductions would be monitored. The resources released would be paid into an international fund, 25 percent of which would be allocated to development, the rest used by the government whose defense expenditures were reduced.

Other proposals followed, notably by the Soviet Union in 1956 and Brazil in 1964. In 1973, the General Assembly adopted a resolution calling for a 10 percent one-time reduction in military budgets by the five permanent members of the Security Council. The General Assembly encouraged other states to do the same, noting that 10 percent of the sum saved would be allocated to development. In 1978, several more proposals were made linking disarmament with development, including proposals by Senegal and France.

Over the years, work by staff members of the Second UN has explored similar themes. The action proposals for the First Development Decade included references to the potential contribution from disarmament to development. This included the calculation that an acceleration of economic growth in developing countries from 3.5 to 5 percent per year could result if no more than 10 percent of the savings from halving military spending was reallocated to development.[16] Such was the scale of military spending during the Cold War. Military spending has taken other forms since the Cold War ended. To put things in perspective, the record-breaking $5 billion the UN spent on peace operations in 2008 represents less than half of 1 percent of world military spending and a conservative estimate for one month of U.S. expenditures for the war in Iraq and Afghanistan; the true cost of what the United States spends on "the war on terror" may be as high as $12.5 billion per month.[17] World military expenditure in 2007 amounted to over $1.3 trillion.[18]

The most creative and comprehensive of the UN reports on disarmament and development was the so-called Thorsson report of 1982. This was produced by a group chaired by Inga Thorsson, then minister for disarmament of Sweden. The report drew on a background paper by Wassily Leontief, the Nobel prizewinner in economics in 1973, that made technical calculations and projections on the relationships between disarmament and development. The Thorsson report brought together disarmament, development, and security. It analyzed the strongly negative relationship between arms spending and economic growth in developing countries and criticized many of the earlier UN studies that had been done by the Secretariat for being too timid in emphasizing the evidence because of the obvious sensitivities in the First UN. The Thorsson

report's strong conclusion was that "the world can either continue to pursue the arms race with characteristic vigor or move consciously and with deliberate speed toward a more stable and balanced social and economic development. It cannot do both."[19]

The study was presented in 1982, seven years before the fall of the Berlin Wall. Although it was considered wildly optimistic and visionary at the time, the report's disarmament scenario and its projections to the year 2000 in fact provided a fairly accurate approximation of the arms situation in that year. However, the benefits of disarmament in the 1990s emerged in a different way from those the report projected. The assumption over the decades had been that reductions in military spending would free up resources that could then be used for other purposes and that an important proportion would go to development of the South. The reductions in arms spending by a quarter or more from 1989 to 1996 in the United States and in many other countries were put to a different use and therefore had a different effect. As argued independently by Lawrence Klein and Joseph Stiglitz, U.S. reductions in arms spending led to major reductions in the deficit.[20] This in turn reduced interest rates in the United States and elsewhere and contributed to the long boom in the world's largest economy. The spillover effects on the rest of the world spread the benefits and stimulated growth elsewhere.

In other words, the peace dividend came not as increased expenditure from freed-up resources but rather from higher growth stimulated in many countries around the world. This clearly is not the peace dividend that was envisioned by the Thorsson team and other proponents of slashing military expenditures. Instead of furthering development in the poorest countries, economic growth was stimulated in the rich countries and benefits trickled down to the poor countries, although not to all and certainly not to the least developed among them. Furthermore, the potential benefits to countries with the lowest incomes have often been offset by the obligation to follow the structural adjustment policies championed by the Bretton Woods institutions and by the disruptive effects of local wars facilitated by the trade in small arms.

Even before the beginning of the wars in Iraq and Afghanistan, military expenditures were on the rise again in the major powers and in a number of developing countries, though by no means in the majority of them. The authoritative Stockholm International Peace Research Institute (SIPRI) has estimated that world military expenditures have reached about 2.5 percent of world GNP, an increase of 45 percent in real terms since 1998—the low point of post–Cold War military expenditures. China and India have also increased their military spending and arms exports, and Russia and Eastern Europe have recorded the highest growth in military spending since 1998. In 2007, the United States was at the highest level since World War II and accounted for 45 percent of

world military expenditures. The next highest military spenders in 2007 were the United Kingdom, China, France, and Japan, each of which spent about 4 to 5 percent of the world total. Germany, Russia, Saudi Arabia, and Italy each accounted for approximately 3 percent of the world total. Although military spending in the poorer developing countries forms only a small proportion of the world total, the high and rising prices of oil and other fossil fuels and raw materials have added to the drain of military expenditures in a number of these countries, where increasing government revenues have been channeled directly into funding military programs.[21]

Peacekeeping

The Charter's framers ensured that the effective mobilization of military power under international control to enforce international decisions against aggressors would distinguish the United Nations from the League of Nations.[22] The onset of the Cold War made this impossible on a systematic basis because one or more of the P-5 vetoed UN efforts. A new means of maintaining peace was necessary, one that would permit the world organization to act within carefully defined limits when the major powers agreed or at least acquiesced.

It is a commonplace to point out that peacekeeping is not specifically mentioned in the Charter but became the organization's primary function in the domain of peace and security during the Cold War. The use of troop contingents for this purpose is widely recognized as having begun during the 1956 crisis in Suez. Contemporary accounts credit Lester B. Pearson with proposing to the General Assembly that Secretary-General Hammarskjöld organize an "international police force that would step in until a political settlement could be reached."[23] Hammarskjöld, Ralph Bunche, and Brian Urquhart helped put flesh on the bones of Pearson's proposal.

Close to 500,000 military, police, and civilian personnel—distinguished from national soldiers by their trademark powder-blue helmets and berets—served in UN peacekeeping forces during the Cold War, and 700 lost their lives in UN service during this period. Alfred Nobel hardly intended to honor soldiers when he created the peace prize that bears his name, but in December 1988 UN peacekeepers received the prestigious award.

The lack of any specific reference to peacekeeping in the Charter led Hammarskjöld to coin the phrase "Chapter six and a half," which referred to stretching the original meaning of Chapter VI. Certainly peacekeeping "can rightly be called the invention of the United Nations," as Secretary-General Boutros Boutros-Ghali claimed in *An Agenda for Peace*.[24] Despite the lack of consensus and the multiplicity of sources,[25] former UN under-secretary-general Marrack Goulding provided a sensible definition of peacekeeping: "United Nations

field operations in which international personnel, civilian and/or military, are deployed with the consent of the parties and under United Nations command to help control and resolve actual or potential international conflicts or internal conflicts which have a clear international dimension."[26]

From 1948 to 1988, peacekeepers typically served two functions: observing the peace (that is, monitoring and reporting on whether cease-fires were being maintained) and keeping the peace (that is, providing an interpositional buffer between belligerents and establishing zones of disengagement). The forces were normally composed of troops from small or nonaligned states; permanent members of the Security Council and other major powers made troop contributions only under exceptional circumstances. These lightly armed neutral troops were symbolically deployed between belligerents who had agreed to stop fighting; they rarely used force and then only in self-defense and as a last resort. Rather than being based on any military prowess, the influence of UN peacekeepers in this period was the result of the cooperation of belligerents mixed with the moral weight of the international community of states.[27]

From 1948 to 1978, the United Nations deployed thirteen peacekeeping operations. In the ten years after 1978, however, no new operations materialized, even as a rash of regional conflicts involving the superpowers or their proxies sprang up around the globe.[28] The increased tensions between East and West spelled the temporary end of new UN deployments after the Reagan administration assumed power in 1981. Elected on a platform of anticommunism, the rebuilding of the national defense system, and fiscal conservatism, the administration was determined to roll back Soviet gains in the Third World. Washington scorned the world organization and cast it aside as a bastion of pro-communism and Third World nationalism. The new administration tarred the UN's peacekeeping operations with the same brush. Central America, the Horn of Africa, much of Southern Africa, and parts of Asia became battlegrounds for the superpowers or their proxies. This situation changed only with the Mikhail Gorbachev regime in the Soviet Union and the advent of glasnost and perestroika, which led to a renaissance in UN conflict management in general and peacekeeping in particular.

The post–Cold War era led to a vast expansion of UN peace operations. While growth slowed somewhat in 2007, the United Nations still deployed over 100,000 persons in peace operations in that year—about 82,000 uniformed personnel (troops, observers, police) plus another 20,000 civilian staff—at a cost of $5 billion.[29] Approved operations that are not yet on the ground could increase those numbers still more dramatically in 2008.

In spite of problems in execution, the evolution of the idea of lightly armed peacekeeping soldiers toward the more robust forces imagined in the UN Charter certainly qualifies as one of the world organization's success stories. The

report of a panel chaired by UN troubleshooter and former ambassador Lakhdar Brahimi said that the UN needed to learn to say no rather than agree to impossible mandates without sufficient resources. The panel went on to say that international civil servants at the UN, who are politically neutral officials, should provide sound advice based on a thorough assessment of options. This advice should be independent of what might be politically popular or might fit the preconceptions of decision makers and should be free of fear of consequences.[30] In short, Brahimi urged the Second UN to tell the members of the First UN in the Security Council what they should hear, not what they want to hear.

Another innovation grew from the host of civil wars in fragile and failed states in the tumultuous 1990s: the use of military force for the purpose of protecting civilians caught in the crosshairs of violence. The need to find a way to justify respecting this humanitarian impulse led to another expansion of the UN's role. We now turn to the bold thinking that laid the basis for that expansion.

The Responsibility to Protect

Perhaps the most dramatic innovation of the UN in the last few years is the idea of the responsibility to protect.[31] No idea has moved faster in the international arena of norms than what is now commonly referred to as "R2P." Indeed, *The Responsibility to Protect* is the title of the 2001 report of the International Commission on Intervention and State Sovereignty (ICISS), an impressive example of the Third UN in action.[32] The basic idea behind the R2P doctrine is that human beings can count for more than the sacrosanct sovereignty enshrined in Charter Article 2(7), which emphasizes noninterference in domestic affairs. The ICISS grew directly from the inability of the Security Council to act in two particular instances: the mass murders in Rwanda in 1994 and the Kosovo disaster in 1999. The former resulted in action that was too little and too late to halt 800,000 deaths in a matter of weeks, and the latter, in the view of many, in too much action too soon when NATO began its "humanitarian bombing" without Security Council approval.

Over the years, a blurring of domestic and international jurisdictions has taken place. This became more evident with the UN's willingness to override sovereignty by using military force to save threatened populations in the 1990s. The rationale came from Frances Deng's concept of "sovereignty as responsibility" to help internally displaced persons and Secretary-General Kofi Annan's pleas for "two sovereignties."[33] As a result, the four characteristics of a sovereign state—territory, authority, population, independence—spelled out in the 1934 Montevideo Convention on the Rights and Duties of States have been complemented by another characteristic: an obligation (or at least a modicum of obligation) to respect human rights. State sovereignty seems less sacrosanct today

than in 1945, although the speeches by states in UN gatherings take advantage of the last bastion of sovereignty.

The ICISS, which was financed and facilitated by the government of Canada and was chaired by Gareth Evans and Mohamed Sahnoun, was the Third UN in action. The commissioners pushed the envelope in three ways. First, the report's opening sentences insisted that sovereignty also encompassed a state's responsibility to protect populations within its borders, a topic that political philosophers had debated since the Westphalian system began. Committed advocates of human rights and robust intervention now see state authority as the foundation of enduring peace and reconciliation and recommend fortifying failed or fragile states. This realization does not reflect nostalgia for any national security state of the past but is a realistic appraisal of a new bottom line. It is not UN human rights monitors or NGOs (as important as these members of the Second and Third UNs may be) but rather reconstituted and responsible states of the First UN that will guarantee the protection of human rights.

Second, the ICISS moved thinking away from the rights of outsiders to intervene toward a framing that spotlights those suffering from war and violence. Abandoning the vocabulary of the French Doctors Movement—*le droit d'ingérence,* or the right to intervene—shifted the fulcrum away from the rights of interveners toward the rights of affected populations and the responsibilities (if not the legal obligations) of outsiders to come to the rescue. The new perspective thus prioritized the rights of those suffering from starvation or systematic rape and the duty of states and international institutions to respond. Rather than looking for a legalistic trigger to authorize states to intervene, R2P specified that it is shameful to do nothing when conscience-shocking events cry out for action.

Third, the commission developed a three-part framework for the responsibility to protect that included the responsibility to prevent and the responsibility to rebuild before and after the responsibility to react in the eye of a storm. It is essential to do everything possible to avoid military intervention—prevention—and to commit to work to mend societies should the use of military force be required.

The work of the commission was helped by the fact that Secretary-General Annan, the only UN insider to have held the world organization's top job, had an excellent grasp of the politics of norm-setting. In his oral history interview, he explained the utility to the UN of outside intellectual energies:

> There are certain issues that are better done outside and there are certain issues that can only be done inside. . . . But take a look at the intervention issue. I couldn't have done it inside. It would have been very divisive. And the member states were very uncomfortable because, as an organization,

sovereignty is our bedrock and bible—here is someone coming with ideas which are almost challenging it. So I had to sow the seed and let them digest it but take the study outside and then bring in the results for them to look at it. I find that when you are dealing with issues where the member states are divided and have very strong views, and very strong regional views, if you do the work inside, the discussions become so acrimonious that however good a document is, sometimes you have problems. . . . But if you bring it from outside . . . they accept it.[34]

The concept of the responsibility to protect gained traction at the largest-ever gathering of world leaders in September 2005 in New York. The overall treatment of R2P illustrates how consensus-building can sometimes take place around even the most controversial issues and with opposition from the strangest of bedfellows—in this case, the United States and the Non-Aligned Movement.[35] The final text of the World Summit Outcome Document of 2005 reaffirmed the primary roles of states to protect their own citizens and encouraged international assistance so weak states could exercise this responsibility. At the same time, it also made clear that international intervention is needed when countries fail to shield their citizens from or, more likely, actively sponsor genocide and other mass-atrocity crimes.

The NAM undoubtedly will continue to reiterate publicly its rejection of the so-called right of humanitarian intervention and the United States will likely continue its refusal to be committed to military action by others. But the bottom line is clear: when a state is incapable of safeguarding or unwilling to safeguard its own citizens and peaceful means fail, the resort to outside intervention, including military force (preferably with Security Council approval), remains a possibility. Again, normative advance does not necessarily mean action, as the 300,000 dead and 3 million displaced in Darfur demonstrate. But a norm is emerging with considerable state practice behind it that articulates the collective international responsibility to protect human beings whose governments refuse to do so or are actually the cause of murder and ethnic cleansing.

Shortcomings abound. Some are concerned about the danger that the R2P idea will actually cause some genocidal violence that otherwise might not occur by creating a moral hazard that stimulates reaction to government repression by a population that misguidedly thinks that the international community of states will come to their rescue.[36] And, of course, the political will to support the new idea remains problematic unless there are geopolitical as well as humanitarian reasons to do so. According to the R2P report of the ICISS, the threshold for military intervention is high—it includes not just substantial human rights abuses but also such mass atrocities as genocide, war crimes, crimes against humanity, and ethnic cleansing.[37]

However, that military force used with international approval for human protection remains a policy option at all represents a significant new middle ground in international relations. We should not expect instant results when such momentous normative change threatens the very foundations of the Westphalian order and indeed of the United Nations. However, both the First and Second UNs have been central to the emerging norm that sovereignty does not imply a license to kill; and the most recent normative push came from the Third UN in the form of the International Commission on Intervention and State Sovereignty.

Human Security

The sixth major contribution of the UN in the area of peace and security is its development of the concept of human security, perhaps the most radical shift in thinking on peace and the avoidance of conflict since the UN was founded. The issue emerged as such an important one that we felt compelled to commission Neil MacFarlane and Yuen Foong Khong to write an additional volume in this series, *Human Security and the UN: A Critical History*.[38]

The notion of human security was first presented in the *Human Development Report 1994*: "The concept of security has for too long been interpreted narrowly: as security of territory from external aggression, or as protection of national interests in foreign policy or as global security from the threat of a nuclear holocaust. It has been related more to nation-states than to people."[39] This report argued for the need for new thinking—for a concept of human security focused on the protection of people from a variety of threats to their life and dignity.

The new expanded concept includes threats to economic security as well as threats to food security, health, the environment, and communities. The report outlined key features of this expanded concept of human security: it is people-centered, universal, interdependent, and easier to ensure through early prevention than through later intervention. In the report's words: "Human security can be said to have two main aspects. It means, first, safety from such chronic threats as hunger, disease, and repression. And second, it means protection from sudden and hurtful disruptions in the pattern of daily life."[40]

The concept was in large measure the intellectual creation of Mahbub ul Haq and the UNDP's Human Development Report team, an example of the Second UN operating with admirable openness and intellectual independence.[41] Oscar Arias, the Nobel laureate and twice president of Costa Rica, also played an important role. He gave credibility to the idea in part because he came from a country that had abolished its army nearly fifty years earlier and had thus proven the feasibility of introducing fresh nonmilitary approaches. Human

security also reflected the new possibilities and priorities that emerged with the end of the Cold War, which had produced a decrease in East-West tensions but a rapid proliferation of small arms and increasing divisions based on ethnicity and identity in a growing number of civil wars. People were being targeted for removal, torture, rape, and/or death because of who they were rather than what they did. All these factors encouraged the development of a people-focused concept of security.

The conflict dynamics of the post–Cold War period contrasted sharply with earlier types of conflict. From the seventeenth to the mid-twentieth centuries, conflict between states had been the main focus of war. This in turn had contributed strongly to crystallizing the ideas of national or state security. But with the end of the Cold War in the late 1980s, the changing context was favorable in some quarters of all three UNs to move from preoccupation with the security of the state toward a refocusing on the security needs and aspirations of human beings.

The new ideas of human security were not without controversy, some of which remains. Nor was there—or is there—an agreed-upon and uniform definition. In spite of this, within a decade, the human security concept became central to the review of security issues within the UN and within the reports of several UN-related commissions: the International Commission on Intervention and State Sovereignty, the Commission on Human Security, and the High-level Panel on Threats, Challenges and Change. All were examples of the Third UN seizing a new idea and carrying it forward.

Moreover, some states such as Canada, Japan, Norway, and Switzerland rapidly and publicly embraced the concept. The importance of ideas can be gleaned by seeing the importance of human security considerations in overseas development assistance and investments by these countries and others. Their decisions about resource allocations in bilateral aid programs as well as the priorities in international financial institutions and in the UN system emphasize the focus of human security on individuals rather than states.

However, many other states do not accept the concept. Still others actively resist replacing or supplementing state security with human security in a way that defines "security" as including other notions than military expenditures. They perceive such a redefinition as a challenge to state prerogatives. The United States, Russia, and China appear to fall into this category, as do many countries in the global South.

Views are changing, and something of a middle way may be emerging. Many states and international organizations accept that the security claims of individuals deserve higher priority and are not necessarily subordinate to those of states.

Definitions of Human Security and Evolution of Concepts

A focus on the human being defines the referent object of security away from the state and toward the individual person. But as MacFarlane and Khong emphasize, ambiguities remain about what exactly is being secured. There are a number of alternative conceptions. One is the protection of rights grounded in treaties and other instruments of international law. A second is "freedom from fear," the protection of people from threats of violence. A third engages the much broader notion of sustainable human development, where human security involves economic, food, health, environmental, personal, community, and political security. The first two echo but go beyond the laws of war, articulated, for instance, in the Lieber manual for the Union Army in the U.S. civil war, the Hague conferences at the turn of the century, and the International Committee of the Red Cross's 1949 Geneva Conventions and the 1977 Additional Protocols.[42] Though MacFarlane and Khong applaud re-balancing the state and the individual as referents of security, they judge as ill advised the move to extend the domain of what counts as security beyond protection from violence.

While acknowledging the seminal and constructive role of the UNDP in focusing the concept of security on people and in highlighting nontraditional threats, one influential analysis subsidized by a favorable government (Canada) suggested that the UN approach to the concept "made it unwieldy as a policy instrument." It took issue with the original emphasis in the 1994 Human Development Report on threats associated with underdevelopment and suggested that this led the UNDP to ignore "the continuing human insecurity resulting from violent conflict."[43] It argued for a narrower interpretation of human security, one that focused on the protection of human beings from violence.

This narrower approach was initially followed within the United Nations. In September 1999, Secretary-General Kofi Annan delivered a report to the Security Council in which he outlined dimensions of threats to human security, concentrating on armed attacks against civilians, forced displacement, the intermingling of combatants and civilians in refugee camps, the denial of humanitarian assistance and access, targeting of humanitarian and peacekeeping personnel, the widespread availability of small arms and anti-personnel land mines, and the humanitarian impact of sanctions.[44] As he told us during his oral history interview: "One has to be able to define it more narrowly than is being done presently for it to be meaningful and helpful to policymakers."[45]

In July 2000, the Security Council called upon ECOSOC to take a more active role in preventing the structural causes of conflict and urged that these

efforts be integrated more effectively into development assistance strategies. In response, Annan reiterated his commitment to moving the UN from a "culture of reaction to a culture of prevention."[46] He emphasized the importance of dealing with the structural causes of conflict, including economic factors, arguing that structural conflict prevention is in essence sustainable development. His recommendations included the need to address the socioeconomic root causes of armed conflicts and the need for UN development cooperation to focus on decreasing structural risk factors that fuel violent conflict such as inequity, inequality, and insecurity. In brief, the Secretary-General argued for a strategy that would achieve both "freedom from want" and "freedom from fear."

Through its resolution 1265, the Security Council expressed its willingness in 1999 to respond to situations of armed conflict in which civilians are targeted or humanitarian assistance to civilians is being deliberately obstructed. But several questions remained unanswered. What was the threshold for action and how was international society to respond? Under which conditions was humanitarian intervention justified?

These questions became the main subject of the ICISS report discussed above. The commission's report, released in 2001, clearly stated that when states could not or would not protect their citizens in the face of avoidable catastrophe, the responsibility to protect shifted to the broader society of states.

This seemed to leave a dispute between the "development first" and the "security first" camps in the human security community. However, the two propositions are not mutually exclusive, and further consideration of human development produced a merging of the two discourses. The reports of the 2003 Commission on Human Security[47] and the 2004 Secretary-General's High-level Panel on Threats, Challenges and Change both emphasize that the well-being of humans and the capacity of communities and individuals to protect their economic welfare are key considerations in the broader account of human security. This, of course, reflected the 1994 Human Development Report and a recognition that had been articulated earlier in the 1980 Brandt report.[48] Economic threats to human beings can be just as fatal as physical threats from violence. Juan Somavía questions "why it seems to be more urgent for the United Nations to act when someone is killed by a bullet than when someone dies of malnutrition."[49]

One may argue about the advantages and disadvantages of broadening the concept or whether it has been diluted too much. It is unquestionable that the concept of human security has encouraged a much deeper and more detailed consideration of individual economic well-being as an aspect of promoting the security of individuals. But a joint publication by the World Bank and the Human Security Project notes that "these two approaches to human security [narrow and broad] are both people-centered and are complementary rather

than contradictory. But because the 'broad' concept includes everything from poverty to genocide, it has so far proved too all-embracing to be helpful in policy development."[50] Some perspective is provided by Margaret Anstee, the first woman to rise to the rank of under-secretary general: "Security embraces the whole question of the basic welfare of human beings. Nobody can be considered to have security if they don't have enough to eat, or they don't have access to basic needs." Looking back on her experience on the front lines of war-torn Angola, she noted ruefully: "I didn't have time to make definitions. I was dealing with the problems of security all the time. Human security in Angola was at about the lowest ebb that you can possibly imagine by any possible definition. It still is. When people are under fire, or not getting enough to eat, or not having the real basics of life, you just don't define it. You deal with it. . . . It was easier for me to define human security when I was in Vienna than it was when I was in Angola."[51]

Broad or Narrow?

MacFarlane and Khong argue for a conception of human security that retains human beings as the center but confines what constitutes security threats to conscious threats against physical integrity that are planned and perpetrated by states, individuals, or groups that aim to do harm to people. This perspective enables human security to make inroads into mainstream security discourse even if it distresses those who cast their analytical nets more widely. MacFarlane and Khong have company in their effort to maintain a narrower focus. "Much of the literature on the broad concept of human security is simply an exercise in re-labeling phenomena that already have perfectly good names: hunger, disease, environmental degradation," writes Andrew Mack. "There has been little serious argument that seeks to demonstrate why 'broadening' the concept of security to embrace a large menu of mostly unrelated problems and social ills is either analytically or practically useful."[52]

Conceiving of human security threats as organized violence applies the brakes to the broadening of the concept advocated in the *Human Development Report 1994*, the Commission on Human Security's report *Human Security Now*, and the report of the Secretary-General's High-level Panel on Threats, Challenges and Change. At the same time, adopting the criterion of organized violence has two advantages: it is more manageable and it builds bridges to mainstream thinking on security issues. Protecting the individual from violence is analogous to protecting the state from military attack. By retaining the individual as the referent but by omitting threats that would normally fail the "organize to harm" test, the definition of the authors of these reports is exempt from the criticism that by covering everything, all meaning is lost.

But does bringing together issues involve more than merely renaming other problems as issues of human security? The High-level Panel argued that it does. "Today, more than ever before, threats are inter-related and a threat to one is a threat to all. The mutual vulnerability of weak and strong has never been clearer. Development . . . is the indispensable foundation for a collective security system that takes prevention seriously." The report elaborates: "Development and security are inextricably linked. A more secure world is only possible if poor countries are given the chance to develop. Extreme poverty and infectious diseases threaten many people directly, but they also provide a fertile breeding ground for other threats, including civil conflict. Even people in rich countries will be more secure if their Governments help poor countries to defeat poverty and disease by meeting the Millennium Development Goals."[53]

The approach thus appears to be more than simply renaming. It recognizes the interrelated actions required to deal with these multiple causes, prevent them from arising, and control them when they do. It also emphasizes issues of budgetary allocation and trade-offs: military spending to achieve security compared to spending on nonmilitary actions, such as expenditures so police can control urban crime or spending on public health measures to control disease. Space is inadequate here to summarize and assess the evidence for interconnectedness. But unless one wishes to argue that there is no connection, the case for taking account of the interactions and consequences seems overwhelming. At the same time, sequencing and priority setting are also essential, and proponents of broader notions of human security are obliged to go beyond recommendations to do everything at once, which is not only politically naïve but irresponsible in policy terms. The specifics and trade-offs of meeting human security goals can and should be properly analyzed at country level.

A further question is whether human security is likely to achieve coequal status with (if not replace) the dominant military and state-centric approach to security. With military spending having risen to the highest levels of spending (in real terms) since World War II, skeptics may comment that this seems unlikely. But human security in the *Human Development Report* was presented as a concept applicable to all countries, not just to superpowers. The concept also is normative; its values embrace the view that the security of people should be rated higher than the security of states—and indeed, the values question whether what states often present as necessary to the security of their citizens is more likely a disguise for the ambitions of their rulers and the interests of their military or of arms producers and traders.

The complexity of the causes of terrorism raises similar issues, though more sharply in the present global context. The causes are indeed complex, diverse, and difficult to analyze, as are the responses required to control and diminish

the risks, both nationally and internationally. But can one seriously suggest that the interacting causes should not be explored, analyzed, and attacked—either in the UN or outside—simply because they are highly complex? Indeed, the UN has a special role in all this precisely because the causes and perspectives on the issues are international and multicultural and differ so sharply between regions and countries.

The idea that the concept of human security may encourage military responses to whatever security problems are identified—an argument put forward by MacFarlane and Khong as a possibility—is a risk that should be explored. It is true that the Bush administration has relied heavily on military solutions, internationally and nationally, even though initially after 9/11, some analyses examined the links between human security, human rights, and human development in an attempt to identify the economic and social root causes of terrorism.[54] Some analysts already point to the risks of "securitization" or "militarization" of the global development and humanitarian agenda. But others have sharply criticized this possibility for reasons of human security. Indeed, many close to the UN and elsewhere would argue that military approaches could be counterproductive and should give way to broader nonmilitary solutions. For instance, when French foreign minister Bernard Kouchner suggested that R2P be invoked in relationship to the foot-dragging by Burmese generals after Cyclone Nargis in May 2008, many Association of Southeast Asian Nations (ASEAN) countries were concerned that the "shot over the bow" would be counterproductive in getting the regime to agree to provide better access for humanitarians. The fact that diplomacy led to modestly better access to Burma and that no use of the military occurred may prove this contention, but it may also be that Kouchner's threats made negotiation possible by both ASEAN and senior UN officials.

The *Human Development Report 1994* presented human security as part of its proposals for reducing military spending and shifting some of this spending to nonmilitary investments directed to the prevention and control of threats to human security. In that report, Oscar Arias set out detailed proposals for a global demilitarization fund.[55] Such a fund would have provided resources and incentives for disarming and demobilizing armed forces, for reintegrating military personnel into society through retraining programs, for promoting arms control and the shrinking of arms production facilities, and for encouraging education of civil society members and their participation in fully democratic political life. A number of these activities have, in fact, been funded in limited ways, often by aid donors, although a global disarmament fund as such has not been agreed upon. The state remains the principal provider of security in most countries, however defined.

Conclusion

Do previous discussions in this chapter suggest that we are raising excessive hopes about the UN's capacity to follow through on ideas with implementation? Without doubt, the UN has a mixed record of responding to security crises and challenges, but not more than in other sectors of its activities. Indeed, in the areas of preventive diplomacy and peacekeeping, the record shows that the United Nations has numerous positive achievements to its credit. Moreover, the Charter is constructed so that interventions for peace and security occur only when the dominant powers want to see action—and inaction occurs when they do not. Thus, the capacity of the UN Secretariat (the Second UN) to follow through is independently important but generally not as important as the wishes and support of the major powers (the most critical part of the First UN).

One of the lessons emerging from UNIHP is that the UN's record in matters of economic and social development has generally been more positive than many believe. There is room for initiative in health and education and other matters of development policy that simply does not exist for the Second UN as it works on peace and security matters around the edges of the very public goldfish bowls of the Security Council and the General Assembly. This lesson is likely to continue with respect to human security, for which the margin for maneuver is greater for the Second UN and the Third UN than it is in the high politics of international peace and security.

In many areas of human security, centralized decision making is not required. There is no need to take all issues to the Security Council, where veto power and national interest are inevitably on display. Decision making outside the council and the General Assembly is often better and less contentious than within it. Decisions in the WHO or in the UNDP, UNICEF, the UNFPA, or the WFP have generally been more technical and less politicized than in the Security Council or General Assembly. There is no reason to think that recognizing issues as part of an agenda for strengthening human security should change these traditions.

We do not want to close this discussion without giving an indication of progress made during the last 100 years, progress achieved principally since the end of World War II. Toward the end of their volume on human security, MacFarlane and Khong make a comparison between the situation at the beginning and the end of the twentieth century:

> In 1900, there was no significant qualification of the sovereignty of states as it related to their own citizens. Now there is. In 1900, there was no consensus

about the legitimacy or acceptability of intervention in the affairs of other states when they systematically persecuted their own citizens. There is now evidence that such a consensus may be emerging. There was no international interest in the rights of women or children and how these were affected by conflict. Now there is. There was no question that the recruitment of children to fight in wars was acceptable. Now it is not. There was little significant effort to limit weapons that were particularly destructive of civilian life. Now there is. There was no significant consideration of issues other than military matters as significant aspects of security. Now there is. We may be a long way from utopia, but we are also a long way away from the unchallenged dominance of the state as the principal referent of security.[56]

11. Human Development

From Separate Actions to an Integrated Approach

- Defining the Concept
- Basic Needs: The Precursor
- Significance of Human Development for the UN System
- Missed Opportunities and Critiques
- Conclusion

Human development is one of the more innovative and comprehensive of recent UN ideas. The vision of putting "people at the centre of development" has long been a theme of the world organization, but one whose priority and practical importance has waxed and waned.[1] The Preamble of the Charter referred to the dignity and worth of the human person, equal rights of men and women, and the need to promote social progress and better standards of living in larger freedom. Human goals were embodied in the articles of association of several of the UN's specialized agencies. In 1945, the FAO began to pursue the vision of ending hunger in every country. In 1948, UNESCO recommended that primary education be made free and compulsory throughout the world. That same year, the WHO was established to address the health needs of the world's people; its charter defines health as "a state of complete physical, mental and social well-being and not merely the absence of disease or infirmity." The ILO, established in 1919 as part of the League of Nations and then made part of the UN system in 1946, saw its primary focus as improving the conditions and social well-being of workers worldwide.

These bold intentions were always present in the UN system but gained traction only in fits and starts. The First Development Decade in 1961 was one such attempt to improve traction and action. The foreword to the Proposals for Action for that decade stated that "development concerns not only man's material needs but also the improvement of the social conditions of his life and his broad aspirations. Development is not just economic growth, it is growth plus change."[2] Notwithstanding these brave words, the UN failed to develop an integrated intellectual framework for catalyzing a new system-wide approach to economic and social development.

The first time that an operational and intellectually coherent vision of a people-focused development strategy emerged was in the 1970s, when the ILO's World Employment Programme developed a strategy for meeting basic needs. This strategy was formulated after a series of interagency missions had comprehensively analyzed problems of employment, poverty, and inequality in a dozen or more countries and made proposals for national and international action to deal with them. Comprehensive employment strategy missions visited seven countries, while regional employment teams mounted missions and undertook analyses of the situation in other countries.

Based on the work of the missions and its own research program, the ILO prepared a synthesis that became *Employment, Growth and Basic Needs: A One World Problem,* the publication for the 1976 World Employment Conference.[3] After that conference, the strategy surged to global attention. Meeting basic needs or basic human needs became the dominant development priority, capturing the attention of donors and winning the support of World Bank president Robert McNamara and others in positions of international leadership.

In spite of this early and rapid rise to prominence, the basic needs strategy was killed off within five years. Its demise in the early 1980s was the result of a return to economic orthodoxy that was driven by the rise of Thatcherism and Reaganism in the developed countries, the onset of world recession, and banking policies designed to ensure that developing countries repaid their debts. Structural adjustment dominated economic policymaking in Latin America and Africa during the 1980s and much of the 1990s. Structural adjustment priorities became a condition for receiving support from the Bretton Woods institutions but were also reinforced by donors who coordinated their own support around these policies.

In 1990, partly in response to this inhospitable environment, the UNDP launched the first annual Human Development Report, which promoted a comprehensive vision and an alternative to neoliberal analysis and policy. The reports of the series brought the concept of human development to worldwide attention and gave it economic breadth and philosophical depth. They also attracted exceptional media attention in both developed and developing countries. In addition to presenting a new paradigm for economic and social development, successive reports expounded the approach in relation to key areas: inequality, public finance, participation, gender, economic growth, consumption, globalization, technology, culture, human rights, and international reform and cooperation.

Within a year or two, many individual countries began producing their own human development reports, applying the paradigm to their own national problems and policies. At the time of writing in mid-2008, more than 600 such national Human Development Reports have been produced in 140 countries and on a wide variety of themes. In addition, a number of regional Human

Development Reports were prepared and issued, most notably four outspoken reports for the Arab region and a series of annual regional reports for South Asia prepared by the Mahbub ul Haq Human Development Centre in Islamabad. Numerous books and articles about human development have also appeared and the *Journal of Human Development* has been published quarterly since 2000. An International Association for Human Development and Capabilities now has a membership approaching a thousand or so members in seventy countries that explores and debates the issues and undertakes research. This itinerary, with people at the center, is the story line of this chapter.

Defining the Concept

When the first Human Development Report was on the drawing board, it was far from clear what such a document would involve, although Mahbub ul Haq, its creator and first director, obviously had ideas.[4] A team of creative and free-thinking analysts was assembled that included both UN staff-members and outside experts, with Amartya Sen as the leading adviser (see box 11.1). A key point that encouraged creativity was the adoption of the principle that such major reports should be issued under the authority of their authors, seeking

Box 11.1. Mahbub ul Haq and Amartya Sen: UN Intellectual Innovators

The *Human Development Report* was essentially the creation of two distinguished economists—Mahbub ul Haq and Amartya Sen. Both were from South Asia and were close friends from their days in the 1950s as undergraduates studying economics in Cambridge University. Many people subsequently contributed to the reports and to developing the concepts and ideas of human development, but these two were the undoubted intellectual parents.

After completing his studies, Mahbub ul Haq took the policy-oriented route, becoming chief economist of the Pakistan government and then, during the 1970s, serving as director of the Policy Planning and Review Department of the World Bank and as a highly influential adviser to World Bank president Robert McNamara. After 1981, Haq returned to his own country to various ministerial positions, including minister of finance, planning, and commerce. In 1989, William Draper, the administrator of the UNDP, invited him to set up a Human Development Office within the organization and to lead a team to produce, in 1990, the first Human Development Report. As architect of the first report and its main author, Haq oversaw subsequent reports, which set out the basics of human development and its links with finance, inequality, human security, gender, and the global economy. In 1995, he returned to Pakistan to establish the Mahbub ul Haq Human Development Centre. In addition to his roles as government chief economist, adviser to an international banking institution, government minister, and senior author of six Human Development Reports, Haq found time to write several books before his untimely death in 1998, most

approval neither from the sponsoring institution nor its board; this principle
was pioneered by the UN's Economic Commission for Europe and the ILO's
World Employment Programme.

Human development was formally defined in the first report as "a process of
enlarging people's choices. The most critical of these wide-ranging choices are to
live a long and healthy life, to be educated and to have access to resources needed
for a decent standard of living. Additional choices include political freedom,
guaranteed human rights and personal self-respect."[5] In later reports and in
work outside the UN, especially in universities, ideas composing the core of the
concept have been refined and elaborated. For example, human development as
a paradigm now emphasizes broadening choices and strengthening capabilities,
based on conceptual and analytical work by Amartya Sen and Martha Nussbaum, among many others. Sen emphasizes a link between choices, capabilities,
and "functionings"—the latter being a subtle concept that combines the choices
and capabilities "to be and to do whatever a person has reason to value."[6]

In explaining capabilities, Sen has stressed the contrast between the great
things that human beings can achieve with the limited lives most women and
men end up having. This tension is a starting point for the human development approach, which, he underlines, "draws on the magnificence of human

notably *The Poverty Curtain: Choices for the Third World* (1976) and *Reflections on Human Development* (1995).

In contrast, Amartya Sen became a full-time academic. He held chairs in economics and philosophy in the Universities of Delhi, Cambridge, and Harvard and for shorter periods as a visitor in other universities. In 1998, Sen won the Nobel Prize in Economic Sciences; he was credited by the Royal Swedish Academy with "having restored an ethical dimension to the discussion of vital economic problems."[1] Sen's work followed in the tradition of classical writings on development, where, as he pointed out, it was always assumed that economic development was to be a benign process, in the interest of people. The view that one must ignore any kind of social sympathies for the underdog did not become the dominant thought until the beginning of modern development economics in the 1950s.[2] Sen's publications are too numerous to mention but include several that have made a major impact on development thinking—*Poverty and Famines* (1981, written for the ILO), *Inequality Re-examined* (1992), and *Development as Freedom* (1999) as well as his essays in *The Argumentative Indian* (2005).

The concept of human development is a striking example of the strength and potential for impact of ideas led by pioneering intellectuals when mutually reinforcing support comes together from all three United Nations.

1. Press release by the Royal Swedish Academy of Sciences, 14 October 1998.
2. Amartya Sen, "Development Thinking at the Beginning of the XXI Century," in *Economic and Social Development into the XXI Century*, ed. Louis Emmerij (Baltimore: Johns Hopkins University Press, 1997), 531–551.

potentiality amidst the widespread experience of narrowly circumscribed lives. Lack of schooling, meager health care, inadequate economic opportunities, violation of political liberties, denial of civil rights, and other hostile winds can totally frustrate human beings despite their potential to 'ascend on the wings.'"[7]

The Human Development Reports thus draw an important contrast between economic prosperity and human development—between economic achievements measured by GNP per capita and human achievements measured by a range of human indicators. Although there is weak correlation between the two, the data shows that many developing countries do poorly on many social and human rights indicators in spite of growth. The obverse is true as well; with clear priorities, countries can make significant progress in human development even with slow economic growth, at least for a decade or so. Yet the pursuit of growth is typically taken as the central goal of economic policymaking. In contrast, the human development approach concentrates on people-focused objectives and emphasizes that economic and political actions should be treated as means to these human ends, not as ends in themselves.

To draw attention to these ends, the *Human Development Report* now uses four key indicators:[8]

• HDI, the Human Development Index: a summary of human development in a country that measures the average achievements of people along three dimensions: living a long and healthy life, as measured by life expectancy at birth; being knowledgeable, as measured by a combination of the adult literacy rate and the combined enrollment ratio in primary, secondary, and tertiary education; and having access to a decent standard of living, as measured by an index of income per capita (GDP measured in purchasing power parity in US$ to achieve international comparability).

• GDI, the Gender-Related Development Index: an indicator that adjusts the average HDI achievement to reflect the inequalities between men and women along the three basic dimensions.

• GEM, the Gender Empowerment Measure: an indicator that focuses on the opportunities open to women. It measures inequality of opportunities in three areas: political participation and decision making; economic participation and decision making; and power over economic resources.

• HPI, the Human Poverty Index: an index that measures deprivations along the basic dimensions of human development. It combines the proportion of people in a country expected to die at a relatively early age (40 years in developing countries, 60 years in developed countries); illiteracy; and poor access to the overall economic provisioning needed for a decent standard of living.

Human development indices were one of the innovations of the reports; they deliberately shifted attention from an exclusive preoccupation with economic indicators like GNP per capita to human indicators and attracted attention to the broader messages. Though aspects of these indicators can be criticized—as can all composite indicators—the justification presented by Mahbub ul Haq is worth quoting. "We need a measure of the same level of vulgarity as GNP," he said, "just one number—but a measure that is not as blind to social aspects of human lives as GNP is."[9]

The UNDP's administrative and financial support proved critical for the rapidity with which human development ideas were promoted and caught on worldwide. This made possible a widespread program of advocacy and outreach. If the ideas of human development had been developed and promoted only in a university or research institute, the results would most probably never have been the same. The UN gave them legitimacy and the media gave them attention. UNDP offices in about 100 countries ensured that there was an annual launch in each country of a version in the major working language, often by a minister of government and frequently with headlines and front-page news coverage.

Basic Needs: The Precursor

The ILO's pioneering work on basic needs in the 1970s helped lay the foundation for the human development approach two decades later. Both were—and still are—broad-ranging and comprehensive strategies for economic and social development that provide a framework for analysis and guidelines for policy. In some respects, the basic needs approach has the edge in being more easily understandable and readily operational and the human development approach has the edge in having greater breadth of applications and more robust philosophical foundations.

As a dynamic strategy for development, the basic needs approach prioritized ensuring that the poorest group of each country should achieve a minimum standard of living within a defined time horizon—originally the end of the twentieth century, which was about twenty-five years. This required a country to give attention to two elements of basic needs: ensuring the provision of certain minimum requirements of a family for private consumption (adequate food, shelter, and clothing) and ensuring that essential services were provided by and for the community at large (safe drinking water, sanitation, public transport, health, and education).

Neither of these two components of the basic needs approach necessarily implied a need for top-down planning. Strategy was sketched in the context

of three types of economies—developing countries, Soviet-bloc socialist countries, and industrialized market-economy countries. For developing and industrialized countries, family consumption needs were to be met by employment policies that ensured that each person available for and willing to work should have an adequately remunerated job and thus have sufficient income to purchase basic consumer goods. Access to essential services was to be pursued by a range of approaches, with policies by the government and local communities to ensure that all were covered. A related point of policy that is often neglected in simpler presentations of the basic needs approach was the need for popular participation in decision making that affects the lives and livelihoods of people and their communities. Moreover, the approach was placed "within a broader framework, namely the fulfillment of basic human rights, which are not only ends in themselves but also contribute to the attainment of other goals."[10] Meeting basic needs was presented as universal, applicable to countries in all parts of the world, a rare and new feature for the time and one repeated in the human development approach.

The World Employment Programme stressed that the basic needs strategy had to be backed up by international policies that covered elements of international trade, development assistance, and other issues of special concern to the ILO. These issues and polices included assistance with trade adjustment, migration policies for both sending and receiving countries, technological choice and innovation for developing countries, and policies to regulate the activities of multinational enterprises.

The World Employment Conference in 1976 considered the basic needs strategy and agreed to many actions for follow-up by individual countries as well as by the international community of states. In spite of some bitter ideological differences, a remarkable and unusually broad consensus developed for implementation of the strategy. After the election of President Jimmy Carter, the U.S. Agency for International Development also began to promulgate the basic human needs approach.

A critical point for follow-up was that World Employment Conference formally asked the ILO to provide support to developing countries that asked for technical help in preparing basic needs strategies for their own countries. It was also asked to help assemble statistics on the existing situation with respect to basic needs and develop strategies for meeting basic needs goals within an agreed-upon timetable. This multidisciplinary support was to be provided in cooperation with other parts of the UN system. However, the ILO, unlike the UNDP fifteen years later, did not have the financial resources to implement projects in developing countries. This lack of follow-up at the local and national levels was a crucial weakness in an otherwise pathbreaking initiative.

For five years, it seemed that some of these bold initiatives would be undertaken. Many donors individually and in OECD forums expressed support for basic needs priorities—so much so that some developing countries began to be suspicious of their intentions. Robert McNamara, the president of the World Bank, encouraged by Mahbub ul Haq, who at that time was his senior adviser, and some other senior staff expressed interest and support. Yet before serious programs could get under way, the international mood became very negative. Margaret Thatcher was elected prime minister in the United Kingdom, and soon after, Ronald Reagan was elected president in the United States. Both brought a sharp swing toward monetarist and more traditional economic policies with too little social conscience and too much ideological opposition to state help. Moreover, the economic climate was deteriorating as a result of the second round of increases in oil prices in 1979. An economic slowdown became a recession. The earlier support (at times even euphoria) for basic needs went into reverse and became a single-minded focus on economic policies of stabilization and adjustment.

The result is that mainstream development thinking and policy shifted to an unwavering focus on economic growth, justified by the belief that economics and GNP indicators were and ought to be at the core of development. Much of this still continues. Many still argue that economic growth will bring the other things necessary for people to live the good life. The appeal of "trickle-down"—like neoclassical economics—is not just the analytical strength of the economic theory, which was developed in some of the best universities of the world, but also the way that its priorities match the economic and political interests and economic ideology of the major powers and more developed countries.

During the 1970s, the World Bank recognized the need for a broader economic approach. But as with basic needs in 1976, these acknowledgments were usually short lived and mainstream economic thought quickly returned to neoclassical orthodoxy. During the 1980s and 1990s, the focus of mainstream economic ideology was reinforced by the conditionalities that international financial institutions attached to loans. Structural adjustment imperatives were force-fed to developing countries that needed financial assistance from the IMF and the World Bank and were thus adopted by the majority of countries in Africa and Latin America. The results were devastating, especially for the majority of the least-developed countries. In the last few years, economic research has made clear that the cost of these policies was very high in terms of their negative effects on economic growth and their draconian cuts in resources for education, health, and other social services.[11]

Significance of Human Development for the UN System

The most important contribution of the human development approach for the UN as a whole is that it brought together and integrated the four fundamental ideas on which the UN had been founded: peace and negotiation in place of war and conflict; sovereign independence; economic and social development to achieve rising living standards; and human rights for all. Each of these was central to the Charter, yet during the world organization's first four decades, each largely became a separate pursuit both operationally and conceptually. Issues of peace and conflict resolution were left to the Security Council, the Secretary-General, and specialized parts of the UN Secretariat such as the Department of Political Affairs. Sovereign independence and early moves toward decolonization were overseen by the Trusteeship Council and supported by UN operational organizations such the Expanded Programme of Technical Assistance. Economic and social development were entrusted to DESA, the Department of Economic and Social Affairs, the EPTA and the Special Fund (precursors to the UNDP), and the UN funds and specialized agencies. Human rights were largely relegated to the Commission on Human Rights and its once-a-year session in Geneva.

One of the original aspects of human development is that it showed how the four fundamental ideas were integral parts of a more holistic approach to development, a comprehensive perspective that combines human rights, economic and social advance, self-determination, peace and human security, and participation and empowerment. The Human Development Reports analyzed these links and interconnections. This holistic approach to human development underlined why and how the four had to be pursued together. This was an important intellectual leap forward, though, as we see below, it was not always followed by implementation.

Sovereign independence might seem to be something of an exception to the way that the four ideas fit the concept of human development. The concept of human development has always emphasized the need for international action to support national strategies to further the goals of human development, a point that has attracted increasing attention in the era of globalization. But it is the concept of the responsibility to protect (see chapter 10) that has qualified the limits of sovereign independence by defining the obligation of national governments to ensure the protection and human rights of their citizens.

The human development approach is still far from accepted throughout the UN system, some of which treats human development as a little more than the ongoing theme of the UNDP's report. Even within the UNDP, human development was initially treasured as much for the publicity that the report launches

gathered each year as for the content of those reports. Gradually, however, the messages of the reports have gained influence within the UNDP, reinforced by the involvement of field offices in the 140 countries where national Human Development Reports have been prepared.

Missed Opportunities and Critiques

If we move from ideas to implementation, human development as an integrating frame for UN operations and for the role of UN resident coordinators at the country level still exists more as a hope and a vision than as a reality. Too often, UN agencies fail to see its relevance as an analytical frame of human-centered development within which their own operations could be set. UNDAF, the UN Development Assistance Framework, is still the formal frame within which country-level activities of various UN agencies are to be coordinated. This is useful for coordinating the various components of UN programs—for instance, in relation to the MDGs—but not for showing how they related to a coherent strategy for human development. The missed opportunities are all the greater when the UN fails to show how the objectives and programs of peace, economic and social development, and human rights go well beyond the narrower economic philosophies and more limited objectives of the Bretton Woods institutions.

Part of the missed opportunities can be laid at the door of misunderstandings. Human development is still too often seen as little more than sectoral concerns with education, health, and nutrition—what the World Bank means when it uses the term. The infinitely broader and richer meanings of human development as developed by Sen and Haq and presented in the annual Human Development Reports are missing.

More serious is the failure to develop a clear, comprehensive, and positive macroeconomic strategy within which the goals of human development can be pursued. True, priorities for finance, consumption, distribution, economic growth, and other aspects of national and international macrodevelopment policy have often been analyzed. But this ensemble still falls short of a coherent presentation of a comprehensive economic and social strategy. In comparison, the basic needs approach not only had a twenty-five-year strategy but one in which the objectives of ensuring the fulfillment of basic needs in each country was both easy to understand and convincing for those concerned with ending poverty.

In this respect, the Millennium Development Goals are a mixed blessing. The consensus established in the 1970s for meeting basic needs transmogrified, after two or three decades of structural adjustment, into a consensus for meeting the MDGs by 2015. In most respects these goals were a UN creation that

grew out of the long experience of the world organization in proposing goals and using them as guidelines for their own operations. But in one key respect the MDGs missed a major element, that of macroeconomic strategy. This was left to the Bretton Woods institutions, with the IMF in particular having a critical behind-the-scenes role.

The result is that the macroeconomic strategy largely continues along conventional neoliberal economic lines in which the concept of redistribution with growth is largely absent. Even policies for accelerating economic growth are missing from the economic orthodoxy of the Washington consensus. Accelerated economic growth *with redistribution* was an integral element of the macroeconomic strategy of meeting basic needs in the 1970s. Although redistribution and the need to tackle inequality has been a constant theme of human development, the specifics of a redistributive growth strategy have not been spelled out with equal clarity. The macroeconomic field has been left, politically and intellectually, to the Bretton Woods institutions.

The question should be asked why the human development approach—in spite of huge media and public attention—has not succeeded in generating large-scale attention among social scientists, national and international civil servants, and politicians. Why are the First UN and the Second UN not more involved? And why are more members of the Third UN not on the barricades to press for the implementation of this ideal?

The approach has received strong support from many NGOs and social scientists outside the economic profession, but support does not go beyond this group. There are several possible explanations. Many take human development and the successive reports as goals because too little attention is given to the micro- and macroeconomic and social frameworks that come with the goals. Even though these linkages have been set out in a succession of Human Development Reports, the public attention given to the goals and indicators too readily dominates the message.[12]

With the basic needs approach, the specific target of meeting the basic needs of the poorest 20 percent of the population was much clearer, as was the macroeconomic framework required for combining economic growth and changes in income distribution. This was followed by a determination of sector-specific policies and international trade requirements.

Sen and Nussbaum's capabilities approach to human well-being concentrated on what human beings can be and do instead of on what they possess. Moving the discussion away from the neoclassical economic focus on utility and toward capabilities allows one to distinguish means (for instance, money) from ends (for example, well-being or freedom). This has led to the thesis that it is wrong to focus on maximizing economic growth without paying direct

attention to the transformation of growth and wealth into the expansion of choices for better living conditions.

Neoliberal economists have argued, however, that criticism of orthodox economics by those adopting a human development position has gone too far. One of their key points is that estimates of national income have not been used as the only measure of aggregate social welfare since the 1950s or 1960s. National income and GNP, they claimed, were never the primary (let alone the sole) measures of development in the minds of economists or policymakers. Such critics as T. N. Srinivasan and V. V. Bhanoji Rao greeted the human development approach as old wine in a new bottle; they claimed that before development was supplanted by economic growth in the 1960s, a comprehensive view of human well-being was actually part of traditional economics.[13] Such critiques, which were actively presented in the early days of the Human Development Reports, have tended to fade away. Whether this was because of the growing academic interest and the sophistication of the human development debate on its own terms or because of a widening gap between those who were persuaded and those who stuck rigidly to neoliberal economic analysis is less clear.

Conclusion

The strength of the human development approach is that it focuses on fundamentals and explores issues that are often neglected by proponents of neoliberalism, such as non-economic issues, concerns that reach beyond the market such as intra-household income distribution and gender inequalities, the well-being of the aged, and the socialization of young children. All these are important for strengthening human values and capabilities. But they do not fit easily or reasonably in the neoliberal framework, which focuses on maximization of returns and market efficiency. This is not to deny that neoclassical and neoliberal approaches have strong theoretical foundations that are sufficient for a wide range of economic and financial issues, some of which have been used to establish empirical conclusions of considerable generality.[14]

In addition to human development's core focus on broadening choices and strengthening human capabilities, clear differences appear between it and neoliberalism. The human development approach emphasizes three areas of concern. First, a broad group of government and nongovernment actors should be brought into policy and decision making. In government, policymaking cannot be left to economic and financial decision makers alone. Other ministries or departments, particularly those concerned with nutrition, health, and education need to be a full part of the process. Outside the government, local communities need to be brought in to ensure a human focus and to give community

members a clear understanding of the options and what is needed to ensure that human opportunities are kept open and used.

Second, monitoring is also different. In place of the sharp focus on economic and financial indicators as a means to human ends, human development devises a wider range of human and social indicators that are given primary place as ends in themselves. In this, human development shares some elements with basic needs approaches of the 1970s. Thus special importance is given to human indicators that enable one to track the human situation and to respond to urgent human needs: life expectancy, nutritional status, and ultimately well-being and happiness. The challenge of human development is to avoid deterioration and to ensure that progress is maintained toward the mid-term and longer-term goals of poverty reduction, well-being, and human development.

Third, there are differences in the two approaches that reflect different attitudes toward international policy. The urgency of the need for human development requires a stronger international approach and often more rapid and more flexible financial support to provide access to markets. The human development approach also requires support for peace operations. Its values and principles include the fulfillment of human rights, justice, and human solidarity, not just the goal of economic efficiency.

Such human development alternatives are not unrealistic, but many observers dismiss them as such. Examples can be found of virtually every element of the human development approach being implemented somewhere in recent years at a reasonable cost and often with considerable success. Human development is closely aligned with the human rights commitments that most governments, including practically all of the industrialized countries, have adopted. Indeed, human rights include specific commitments by the wealthier countries to do all within their power to help poorer countries carry out their own commitments.

However, it is true that human development as a paradigm has yet to be fully grasped, even within the United Nations. Human development not only matches the values and needs of the world organization at present but it also provides a framework that is well adapted for the future. The twenty-first century is already presenting new challenges—global warming and other environmental challenges to sustainable development, the need to diminish extremes of inequality in the world, the need for participation and inclusive democracy in more and more countries. There is also the need to shift from military to human security. Human development provides a frame within which such issues can be explored and their implications analyzed, within countries and internationally.

In brief, the human development framework has potential. However, it should be translated into a macro-framework that marks its differences with other economic and social approaches in a straightforward and clear manner.

PART 3
A Future for the UN and the Planet

Our visionary perspective is the true realism and that is what we must pursue.

—Barbara Ward, 1980

12. A Balance Sheet

- Overview of the Impact of UN Ideas
- Counterfactual #1: The World without the UN and Its Ideas
- Counterfactual #2: A More Creative UN?
- Conclusion

Part 3 of this book endeavors to make good on our promise at the outset of the United Nations Intellectual History Project to do a "future-oriented history." Before attempting what some historians might consider an oxymoron, we draw up a balance sheet of the impact and contemporary relevance of the big ideas that we have elaborated in the preceding nine chapters. This chapter presents our best effort to pull together our collective views and generalize about Part 2 with a balance sheet.

As indicated, we struggled mightily with which big ideas should be the subject of commissioned volumes. Even more subjective judgments arise here as we attempt to synthesize our considered judgments about what worked well and what did not. We begin with our audacious (perhaps foolhardy) overview before exploring two counterfactuals about the world organization's past and future intellectual output.

Overview of the Impact of UN Ideas

We asked ourselves four questions about ideas that arose from and within the UN, are being promoted by it, and sometimes are being implemented by one or more of its funds and agencies: What difference have these nine UN ideas made in practice? Where, more broadly, would the world be without the UN and its ideas in the economic and social arena and in certain aspects of peace and security? Could the UN have done better with follow-up or with the ideas themselves? Might it have done worse—and where and why?

We have asked these questions of all nine topics covered in the previous part of this book in order to determine the extent to which UN ideas have had

a significant influence. We have teased out the pioneering roles of the United Nations in broadening the perspective of economic and social development, from early concerns with human rights and gender to priorities and perspectives of national and international development to the management of global resources and the need to develop sustainable strategies that combine environment with development. We have also noted more recently the UN's calls for action that combines continuing development with preserving the world's ecosystems from the consequences of greenhouse gases, global warming, and climate chaos. Moreover, our analysis has taken us beyond the economic, the social, and the environmental because we have become persuaded that development, human rights, and human security should be viewed holistically.

The UN has often pioneered ideas in these areas, as shown in our overview and in Part 2 of this book as well as in the individual volumes of the project. Admittedly, our broad concept of the UN enlarges what we count as the world organization's contributions. But that is the reality of the contemporary international system, what we have referred to as fledgling global governance. Many key ideas are those that were often initially formulated or articulated by distinguished experts as members of UN panels or as work commissioned at the request of UN staff or (less often) by governments—that is, by the Third, the Second, or the First UN. Examples are the ideas about a global economic order that initially came out of the three early committees that reported between 1949 and 1951 or (more recently) the ideas about climate change that the Intergovernmental Panel on Climate Change presented. Sometimes the ideas are those of UN staff. An example here is Hans Singer's work on the terms of trade or work by UNCTAD staff on debt problems. In other cases, the UN's contributions have not so much provided the initial spark of creativity as they have worked on particular aspects of a problem—as with the ILO missions on employment problems in the early 1970s, UNCTAD's work on the trade challenges the least-developed countries faced, or the FAO's activities on food problems since the 1970s.

Many times and on many occasions UN contributions have been multiplied by using the world body's unequaled capacity for disseminating and promoting ideas. The UNDP's annual Human Development Report and UNICEF's reports on *The State of the World's Children* achieved part of their global visibility and impact by being disseminated widely, each in about 100,000 copies in English, French, and Spanish and often in other languages as well. As mentioned earlier, there were usually media launches of these publications in the 100 or so countries in which the UNDP and UNICEF have field offices. Other than a few blockbusters by such writers as Joseph Stiglitz, Jeffrey Sachs, or Paul Collier, few academic publications have achieved such outreach. This global dissemination was increasingly reinforced by UNDP support for national and regional reports

that applied the human development methodology to problems and situations at country level.

Our contributors often found it difficult to summarize these impacts in individual books, and they undoubtedly will judge us foolhardy for attempting a synthesis in a single table, as we do in table 12.1. At the same time, many of them urged us in passionate terms to personalize our conclusions more. And so here we begin with the essential point, our considered judgment after nearly ten years' review of the record that the international organization has made substantial progress in many important areas and in spite of the distance that remains. Our approach is unashamedly optimistic, in that we choose to emphasize that the UN's glass of intellectual contributions is 10 percent full rather than 90 percent empty, just as we seek ways to pour a bit more liquid into that receptacle.

After a decade engaged in this project, we feel compelled, however imperfect our depiction, to present our collective judgment and a broad summary in table 12.1. On the vertical axis are the ideas identified under each of the nine chapter headings in Part 2 and across the horizontal axis the dimensions of influence and clout originally identified in chapter 2. We repeat them here: the international consensus and legitimacy acquired by each idea, the professional endorsement and interest generated, the support received from civil society, and the financial backing obtained, and we add a fifth dimension, namely the main places within the UN system where the idea and intellectual contribution has been embedded and continues to be pursued.

So we urge readers to take a deep breath and plunge into table 12.1. At least our critics will know where they disagree with our assessments and why, and those who urged us to take this step will either admire our courage or ask us to retire.

The impact of each UN idea has varied considerably by issue area and over time but has also been affected by particular events and origins. Earlier we cited the clear example of the presence since 1994 of a UN high commissioner for human rights. An evaluation of human rights in 1993, prior to the Vienna conference, would have lamented that such an obvious proposal had not seen the light of day since it was put before governments in 1947.

Some further explanatory comments about table 12.1 are in order. The strongest points of international consensus—at least in rhetoric—are those in the areas of human rights, social development, women's rights, and empowerment. Here the United Nations has clearly had a major influence in presenting these ideas and promoting a positive international climate of opinion, although the UN's influence has often been considerably less in implementation and practice. These are also areas where there has been considerable interest and support

Table 12.1. An Overview by Category of the Impact of Selected UN Ideas, 1945–2008

Main Categories of Ideas/Indicators of Clout	International Consensus and Legitimacy	Professional Interest and Endorsement
Human Rights for All: From Aspiration to Implementation	Universal in principle but limited and highly variable in implementation	Widespread
Gender: From Eliminating Discrimination to Promoting Women's Rights and Empowerment	Growing since 1975 but limited and highly variable in practice	Increasing since the 1970s although unevenly and still often controversial
Development Goals: From National and Regional Policies to the MDGs	Considerable within geographic regions themselves but usually weaker beyond regions	Strong among development specialists; much less enthusiasm among mainstream economists
Fairer International Economic Relations: From Aid and Mutual Interests to Global Solidarity	Controversial and mostly rhetorical	Considerable, although mainly outside mainstream economics
Development Strategies: From National Planning to Governing the Market	Planning an important influence in the UN's early years, whereas markets dominated after 1980	Planning a heavy influence in the early years of the UN but became controversial and weakened over time
Social Development: From Sectoral to Integrated Perspectives	Early strong and widespread consensus on education, health, and nutrition but often disagreement about population and reproductive health policies	Strong though support usually restricted within disciplinary boundaries
Environmental Sustainability: From Environment and Development to Preserving the Planet	Increasing decade by decade since the 1970s with global warming producing new urgency	Scientists always ahead of governments; consensus among scientists growing steadily
Peace and Security: From Preventing State Conflict to Protecting Individuals	Preventive diplomacy and conflict resolution strong from early UN years, with new initiatives after end of Cold War. Post–Cold War era saw more action and R2P proposals, though many developing countries remain skeptical and fearful about intervention and even prevention	Considerable over the UN's life; focused on disarmament, preventive diplomacy, conflict resolution, and increasing operations after Cold War with skepticism strong among so-called realists
Human Development: From Separate Actions to an Integrated Approach	Strong in rhetoric, applications growing, and considerable support from developing countries for national Human Development Reports but practice varies greatly by country and potential is yet to be realized	Increasing gradually since publication of HDRs and national HDRs but remains controversial among neoclassical economists

from professionals and from civil society and to which growing resources have been allocated. However, the lack of financial support in relation to the size of the tasks usually means that clout has been limited, even with strong rhetorical support from both governments and other donors.

In our view, the balance sheet is increasingly positive in the area of the environment and climate change. Here there is no doubt that since the 1970s, international thinking about the environment has changed, beginning with the UN's early influence in putting environment *and* development on the international

Civil Society Interest and Engagement	Financial Backing from Donors	Main UN Institutions Involved
Widespread	Limited and restricted to certain areas	OHCHR, ICC, HRC, but others through mainstreaming
Widespread and increasing, though always much stronger among women and gender-sensitive groups	Increasing after 1975, although support is concentrated among certain donors and governments	CSW, UNIFEM, but also mainstreamed
Increasing over time, though often focused on specific blockbuster reports	Usually limited to a geographic region	DESA, UNCTAD, ILO, ECE, ECLAC, ESCAP, ECA, ESCWA, World Bank
Strong support for ideals; mobilization for such specifics as aid, debt relief, fairer trade, etc.	Little; aid is mostly given on political grounds and is offset by inequalities in trade	UNCTAD, UNCTC (until fused into UNCTAD)
Highly variable	Considerable support for planning until the 1980s, when donor support shifted to structural adjustment and Bretton Woods strategies	DESA, UNDP, somewhat by other special funds
Very strong	Considerable although support fluctuates with donor fashions	UNFPA, UNICEF, WHO, FAO, UNESCO, ILO
Increasing steadily since the 1970s; current mobilization of civil society is strong	Still much less than current consensus would suggest	UNEP, WMO, HABITAT (UN Human Settlements Program), but also increasingly mainstreamed in 1990s
Continuous support from peace groups and strong support from NGOs depending on issues and time period	Increasing steadily in operational terms	Mainly Office of the Secretary-General, Department of Peacekeeping Operations, Department of Political Affairs, Office for the Coordination of Humanitarian Affairs
Strong and growing, especially as an alternative to the Washington consensus. Considerable support for national Human Development Reports	Strong support from certain governments and from certain donors	UNDP and increasingly in country offices

agenda and in giving the topic sustained and growing attention over the years. The Earth Summit in 1992 passed Agenda 21, which included the Framework Convention on Climate Change and led to the Kyoto Protocol, the Convention on Biological Diversity, and a Statement of Principles for the Sustainable Management of Forests. It also agreed that a Commission on Sustainable Development would monitor follow-up and planned two further governmental meetings to do this, the 1997 General Assembly's Special Session and the 2002 World Summit on Sustainable Development in Johannesburg. As the effects of climate

change become more visible, it is too easy to focus on this as the main and perhaps the only item on the global environmental agenda. In fact, as chapter 9 made clear, climate change is only the most evident of a range of highly important issues, most of which have been gathering increasing support from governments and gradually (too gradually, it is true) making an impact.

The balance sheet of influence and impact is different with humanitarian affairs and human security. There are signs of increasing support for the notion that United Nations should have a leading and active role, notwithstanding the tendency for the major powers to go ahead in certain areas with or without Security Council approval. But it is also true—as with some of today's major conflicts such as the ones in Afghanistan and Iraq and even more so with some less visible conflicts—that UN action and support is seen as necessary to gain international legitimacy. The UN has launched over sixty peacekeeping missions since 1948, and as we write, twenty on the ground are supported by the Department of Peacekeeping Operations. Over 100,000 UN personnel are now engaged in these operations, including over 80,000 military troops, police, and military observers; 26,000 civilian personnel; and 2,000 volunteers.

Failures and stalemates hit the headlines—Bosnia, Rwanda, Darfur, Myanmar, and Zimbabwe jump immediately to mind. But many other peace operations have had important (albeit only partial) successes as conflict prevention, peacemaking, and peacebuilding. For example, UN operations have for decades helped keep the lids on the cauldrons boiling in Cyprus, the Golan Heights, and Kashmir. Other positive outcomes must be counted. From the independence of Namibia to calming Cold War flashpoints in Central America and Asia, results have been facilitated by a UN presence. In short, a broad range of conflicts has been defused, and a number of actual or potential armed conflicts have been defused.

The economic arena is where the UN has appeared more marginal in recent decades, has had less visibility, has almost always had less clout, and accordingly has had less impact and implementation. This was not because of lack of ideas—the ideas have been numerous and often valuable—but rather because many of the ideas ran counter to current orthodoxies and the economic interests of the richer and more powerful countries. That is especially true after 1980 and reflects the way that the major economic powers have used their clout and influence to maintain the structure and regulations of the international system in a form that they consider best meets their own interests. Real power and influence has thus been concentrated within the Bretton Woods institutions, where developed countries have the dominant share of votes, and in the WTO, where in different ways developed countries can maintain the major influence. In addition, free trade, global markets that are open to flows of investment into

developing countries and often free movements of financial capital have been presented as in the interest of all countries, rich and poor, developing or developed. The international system was moved to support such policies, encouraged by a coalition of industrial countries and supported by a vocal majority of Anglo-Saxon economists. Nonetheless, the UN was able to contribute to setting goals for economic and social development, as shown in chapter 5.

At the time of completing this study in early 2009, major questions were being raised about the neoliberal approaches that had been followed internationally over the preceding decades. The damage and destruction wrought by unregulated financial markets in the second half of 2008 made clear the limits of free market ideology. The speed with which financial problems spread throughout the global economy reinforced these doubts. Beginning with the United States and Europe, financial and economic instabilities set back economic growth everywhere, even in those countries with records of strong performance and regulation. Economic growth rates plummeted and future projections downgraded. Even after the injection of literally billions of dollars, euros, and pounds sterling into apparently well-established and long-standing western financial institutions—amounting to several trillion dollars—a number of these institutions collapsed. Recession had entered western economies and was increasingly predicted in some other parts of the world.

With prospects for 2010 and well beyond in jeopardy, full-blooded free-market orthodoxy with a minimum of regulatory control has fallen out of favor, at least until another bubble of speculation dims memories. The public and politicians in many countries demand stronger regulation and more government overview and control.

In principle, these developments should increase interest in and respect for the UN's work on international economic matters. Whether the UN's contributions are accorded enhanced recognition depends on several factors:

- the policies and attitudes of China, India, and other emerging powers
- the extent of concern shown for poorer and weaker countries, especially the least developed, and
- whether reform of the voting structures and practices of the Bretton Woods institutions (and the UN) gives increasing weight to these countries and their issues
- the extent to which the major economic powers recognize the UN's value in giving legitimacy and support for broader global approaches

International economic solidarity and, after 1980, national development strategy and economic policy have been approached largely on neoliberal economic lines. The dominant policies of the Bretton Woods institutions have moved to

center stage in economic policy and the world organization has increasingly been on the sidelines. Yet UN institutions have continued to champion many of the goals and issues that richer countries have long ignored: special support for the poorest and least-developed countries, action to narrow global inequalities, and accelerated action to raise levels of education, health, social protection, and human development in poorer countries. The fact that growth in most poorer countries so badly lagged, that global gaps widened, and that levels of education, health, and social protection fell over the 1980s and 1990s reflects failures to support agreed-upon measures much more than errors or weaknesses in the UN's formulation and promotion of such objectives.

In recent years, such widening gaps have been partially disguised by the dramatic successes of China and India and to a lesser extent of a handful of rapidly growing East Asian economies. But these, as we have pointed out, have mostly been following strategies considerably at variance with the dogma of the Bretton Woods institutions and the Washington consensus. And with the crisis, even developed countries have seen the weakness of neo-liberal orthodoxy.

Counterfactual #1: The World without the UN and Its Ideas

Another way of considering the impact of UN ideas is to imagine where the world might be without a world organization or with one set up to act solely as a forum with no capacity for generating ideas of its own. This would be a markedly different UN, with a minimum of staff, presumably of ex-diplomats or facilitators who are expert in bringing groups with differences together and helping them resolve these differences but who have few ideas of their own. It would be a strange form of an international body, although not totally different from the type that extreme critics of the current world organization put forward. Such a stripped-down UN would be more limited even than the League of Nations. It had staff members in a number of specialist areas, including some who did pioneering work on nutrition and food security as well as on economics. The non-economic work is often hailed as some of the best things that the League achieved. Yet the organization was weak in more political areas.

In this world of the counterfactual, what might have happened to the ideas that the UN in its existing form has helped bring to fruition? We suspect that in the economic arena, the need for rules and regulations to facilitate international trade and other economic transactions of the global market would have generated a more limited range of institutions that would be not so different from the OECD, the European Union, and other regional economic organizations. Even to write this suggests that in the economic arena, if the world organization did not exist, it would have had to have been invented, if not in

1945 then in about 1960, with the ending of colonies, or in the 1970s, with the floating of the dollar and the surge of oil prices. A series of ad hoc meetings to cope with wide-ranging issues of such vital economic importance to the wealthier countries would rapidly be seen to be inadequate and something on a more permanent basis would have been created. Cynics might comment that this would not be much different from GATT or the present WTO, which indeed have commanded the respect and support of developed countries. And probably the ideas that would emerge from such a system might not be so different from those of the WTO.

The WTO at present employs over 600 staff, about the size the League of Nations. Most of the staff are economists and lawyers, many of who are engaged in producing research and statistical reports in areas that the UN over a much broader field is also engaged in. But there is a difference: the UN tries to produce policy ideas to face new situations. This is much less the case with the WTO, which takes the rules of the game as fixed and tries to interpret and enforce them. Solely facilitating negotiations rather than contributing substantively—including questioning the fairness of the rules of the game, who sits at the gaming table, and whether the table is level—is hardly a viable or acceptable scope of action for an international institution that is universal.

But beyond the economic imperatives required for facilitating international trade and global markets, some of what the UN does in other areas would also be required and thus need to be re-created. We illustrate this point with two examples, namely the UN's work in the area of international public goods and its work in human rights and humanitarian concerns.

Providing public goods in the form of rule setting and regulation would be needed in areas of health, food, agriculture, weather and meteorology, civil aviation, and maritime law. Economists describe meeting these needs as the provision of international public goods because they are needed by individual countries and their populations and for the efficient functioning of the global system. At the same time, they are beyond the capacity of the global market to offer, because individual countries lack the incentive and the capacity to provide them on the scale required. This is in part because of the "free rider" problem—all will benefit from the provision and none can be excluded from benefiting, even those that refuse to pay.

To ensure such public goods, many specialist organizations would need to have been invented if they did not already exist as part of the UN system. Indeed, many such specialist institutions were created long before the current generation of postwar organizations. Examples include the Pan American Sanitary Bureau, which was founded in 1902. This was transformed into the Latin American arm of the World Health Organization in 1948, renamed PAHO, the

Pan American Health Organization. Other international organizations include the Universal Postal Union and the International Telecommunication Union, whose origins lie in the mid-nineteenth century.

It is when we come to human rights that what might be lost in a world without the UN becomes more evident. It is not even clear which human rights and humanitarian concerns would be present in a world without the United Nations. Even a world focused solely on economic efficiency and free markets would be under public pressure to invent an organization to advocate for some rights. The UN, however, embraces a panoply of human rights not for reasons of economic efficiency or political necessity but as a reflection of the vision and humanity of its early founders. And today the issue of human rights reflects the continuing concerns of many governments and the continuing pressures of many citizens and NGOs—the Third UN. The founders of the UN came to these concerns by reacting against the evils of World War II. These origins are brilliantly reflected in the Preamble of the Charter and the Universal Declaration of Human Rights.

Such vision and idealism is also reflected in the mandates and work of the UN funds and specialized agencies—for instance, UNICEF and UNIFEM, the UNDP and the WFP, as well as UNESCO, the WHO, the FAO, and the ILO. They are also at the core of the work of the offices of the UN High Commissioner for Refugees and the UN High Commissioner for Human Rights as well as the work of activists dealing with the rights of minorities and indigenous peoples as well as the prevention of torture and genocide. These important and highly visible efforts are in the forefront of the world organization's work. But because their mandates put human values ahead of economic concerns and market efficiency, they often clash with the dominant interests of governments and market priorities and they often call for more political and financial support than governments are prepared to provide.

Hence, one undoubtedly can imagine a world without a body to address such concerns, but it would be a much poorer world and, at its core, much less human and humane than the one to which the present world organization aspires and at its best contributes to and achieves.

Counterfactual #2: A More Creative UN?

The present UN often fails and often achieves far less than its mandate and the vision of its founders. Part of the reason is inefficiency and weak institutions and staff that do less they might as well as governments that provide less financial support than required. But these are not the only causes. Often part of the reason for the UN's failure to fulfill its mandates or achieve its goals is that

the mandates and goals are too visionary or at least go far beyond where most governments are prepared to go.

Recalling how lofty the vision and ideals of the United Nations are is no defense for its inefficiencies or weaknesses. Nor is it a reason for suggesting that the world organization could not have done better in formulating ideas or in ensuring follow-up. Most of the volumes in our series have identified areas and ways in which the UN could indeed have done much better. Our oral history interviews of nearly eighty distinguished individuals have identified many specific ways in which such improvements could be made. Here we summarize five of the most important. Contemplating what the world organization would be like with the five changes in place involves significant imagination and certainly runs counter to contemporary practice. But it identifies directions in which the UN should go.

First, we could have a more efficient and effective United Nations if there were less interference from governments in the process of recruitment and promotion, including to the most senior positions. Dag Hammarskjöld long ago spelled out the principles for a truly dedicated and international public service. Today, it would help if greater use were made of objective and up-to-date techniques for attracting, selecting, appointing, and promoting the best and the brightest to the UN from the widest and most diverse possible pool of candidates.

Second, more creative work could have been done on issues of political economy in areas where the international system is failing to explore the reasons for failure and to explore which coalitions of interest could help solve the problems. Economic weaknesses created by how the global system limits opportunities for the least-developed countries is one such critical area; inadequate progress toward the goals of sustainable development and environmental protection is another; biases in aid is a third. This is linked to a fourth area for change: the lack of coherence in the global trade system and the failure of the developed countries to practice their public commitments to a free and open international economic system. Lack of incentives for disarmament measures for development is a fifth. There are others that lack popularity and traction, but this is one reason for UN supporters to encourage creative thinking for the longer run. Even if the ideas in such areas have little chance to be implemented in the short run, this is no reason to give up the good fight for more solidarity and a better and less conflict-ridden world.

Third, more sustained attention could have been given to the steps required to achieve a more egalitarian international system and to the pursuit of national policies that combine redistribution with growth. While it may sound hopelessly naïve even to utter the acronym "NIEO," nonetheless the sentiments that

motivate a new approach to the world economic order and a better distribution of global wealth and the benefits of growth can hardly be ignored in a world with glaring and growing gaps of power as well as income.

Fourth, far more work could have been done on the conditions needed to create stability in weak and failing states. This is emerging as a crucial issue, especially in Africa. Even in the unlikely event that international inequities are significantly reduced, far stronger efforts are needed to address inequalities within countries. The effort to pull together UN inputs in the Peacebuilding Commission is an encouraging sign that preventing a return to war has emerged as a priority, but here too glaring inequalities within fragile states contribute to instability.

Fifth, and finally, better promotion of UN ideas would have helped in all of the areas of work. The world organization should have ensured far greater outreach for the part of its work where it has originality and comparative advantage—work outside the box of neoclassical economic orthodoxy. This would have included the encouragement of multidisciplinary work in areas—and we cannot repeat this enough—where economic issues interact with human rights, human security, and human development. The UN could have engaged in debate, publicly and privately, about the weaknesses of Bretton Woods dogma and the Washington consensus. Even those staunch critics of the world organization now recognize that some of the UN's past work often led to crucial new insights into the weaknesses of conventional approaches, especially in the ways that they have an impact on poorer and least-developed countries.

All these are areas in which the United Nations could have been better and done more. There is still time.

Conclusion

The UN's intellectual work could have been smothered by caution, it could have been controlled by Secretaries-General who allowed little scope for creativity within the Secretariat and lacked any vision, and it could have been totally dominated by dogma. This could have happened so early in the world organization's life that many nonstate actors could have become disillusioned and discouraged about the UN's potential. Fortunately, this was not the case.

Instead, throughout its life, the UN has managed to attract the participation and commitment of many with outstanding intellectual or leadership capabilities to work for the Second UN and engage actively with relevant parts of the First and Third UNs. The Charter, the Universal Declaration of Human Rights, and the continuing attractiveness of humanitarian values and missions in many parts of the UN system remain central to the UN's work. At each stage of its life,

individuals and some governments have argued passionately for maintaining this vision and for applying its values to the contemporary international system. The UN could have gone the way of the League of Nations. It did not. Many members of the First, Second, and Third United Nations should be praised for ensuring the continued existence and relevance of the world organization.

The UN's achievements have also helped. Our balance sheet shows that throughout its six and a half decades, the world organization has played a pioneering role in the world of ideas. Many of the core ideas have achieved remarkably quick impact, but even those that have been rejected, sidelined, or adopted only rhetorically after long periods of time have eventually emerged—in short, they have often been ahead of the curve. Although many ideas were politically unacceptable to many countries at first, they often later became part of mainstream international discourse—these include everything from climate change to gender equality, from special measures for least-developed countries to putting people at the center of development, from human security to removing the license to kill from the attributes of sovereign states.

The UN's effectiveness can never be judged within only a short-term horizon. The past record provides a base on which future improvements should be built. It is to them that we now turn.

13. Challenges Ahead

- **Ten Global Challenges**
- **An Intellectual and Action Agenda for the UN**

As we write this chapter in late 2008, the world is in the midst of a financial and economic crisis perhaps as grave as any since the 1930s. Perhaps as much as any recent event, the global financial and economic meltdown made even clearer what many less serious previous ones had not, namely the risks, problems, and enormous costs of a global economy without adequate international institutions, democratic decision-making, and powers to bring order and ensure compliance. Most countries, especially the major powers, clearly are not yet ready to accept the need for serious international measures and the inroads that they would make on their own sovereignty. However, the logic of global interdependence and an ever-growing number of crises would seem to place this necessity more squarely on the international agenda.

In spite of the seriousness of this crisis and the clear evidence of its international dimensions, most of the initial search for remedial action consisted of western political leaders conferring among themselves. Through most of 2008, the focus was on western action to tackle the western dimensions of the crisis. Nor did western leaders give much attention to the impact on poor people and poor countries. Consultation with countries beyond the West was limited and was little reported in the media. International consultations largely avoided the Bretton Woods institutions and the United Nations.

Such an approach demonstrated only too clearly the limited perspectives within the dominant economic and financial community today. But as the crisis spread, it was becoming clear that these were inadequate for solving the global problems and that major reforms of international approaches and institutions were needed. Many commentators and political leaders around the world made this point. Governments of developed countries, though still mostly relying on national actions, have broadened international consultations beyond the G-8 to embrace the G-20, the twenty largest economies of the world. But by early 2009, the president of the UN General Assembly was organizing a truly global

summit on the economic crisis to be preceded by a working group of distinguished international economists.

The findings of our history have already identified key issues that need to be brought into the solutions for the current crisis and into reforms of existing international mechanisms to prevent a recurrence. These include stronger international regulation of financial and economic operations, mechanisms to avoid extremes of instability transmitted in the operations of the global financial and economic system, measures to help maintain medium- and long-term sustainability, and measures to protect the poorest countries and poorest people. In short, stability, sustainability, and equity need to be built into more robust global institutions. An essential step is the reform of representation within international organizations to give more weight to emerging economies and to poorer and weaker countries.

The proposals presented to the Bretton Woods conference in 1944 were bold and intellectually brilliant, drawing on the best minds of the times and going far beyond the conventional analysis and wisdom of that day or today. They were driven by the fears of repeating the 1930s, the confident hopes of building a new postwar world, and the fact that serious discussion could be limited to the three powers that mattered—the United States, the Soviet Union, and the United Kingdom. Today, the world is much more complicated, and the challenge is even greater. Incorporating mechanisms to respond to the major challenges ahead over the medium to longer run is another challenge. These also are not easy to forecast, as we can see by looking back ten years to 1999, when the UN Intellectual History Project was started.

When we launched the UN Intellectual History Project in 1999, Russia was in the most difficult of economic, social, and political situations. Ten years later it not only is back on its feet but is playing an assertive role on the international stage. In 1999, China and India were already doing reasonably well, but no comparison can be made with how they roared ahead subsequently. In 1999, although global warming was being discussed by experts or environmentalists, the threat was seen mainly in ambivalent and critical terms. A decade later there are very few doubters left, though there is still much debate about what needs to be done. In 1999, the United States was at the end of one of the longest economic booms in history, but in the years before 2008 disaster struck and a worldwide financial crisis ensued. In 1999, Africa and Latin America were in the middle of a long and sluggish economic growth period with occasional years of negative figures and the Asian miracle countries were only just recovering from financial crisis, but in the years before 2008 many have experienced five to eight years of much higher economic growth. In 1999, prices for commodities and raw material were low, but subsequently these same items sold at record highs, before falling again in 2008 and 2009. In 1999, no one ever thought that the United

States would come under attack on its own territory and would wage wars in Islamic countries, but a decade later the country is in the sixth year of war in Iraq and its eighth in Afghanistan after 9/11. What a difference a decade can make!

We therefore are uneasy about forecasting the global challenges ahead of us—in 2019, they may indeed look very different from what we imagine today. However, we hazard our own considered judgment about the priority challenges that attract (or should attract) attention from all who share wider concerns in the world. First, we present ten major challenges for the next decade and beyond. While the timing and level of urgency of these challenges may be disputed, it is impossible to deny any of them a place on a list of priorities. Next we organize them in five mega-areas in order to package them in a more focused future intellectual agenda for the world organization. Four of these areas are elaborated in this chapter and the fifth, strengthening global governance, in the concluding chapter. *Caveat lector:* This and the next chapter are more a passionate essay by seasoned observers than a detached set of social scientific conclusions.

Ten Global Challenges

We see ten top issues for the UN in the next decade.

- Tackling global warming and climate change
- Strengthening global governance in a multipolar world
- Supporting fragile states
- Balancing regionalism with globalization
- Moderating inequalities in global development
- Responding to population growth and international migration
- Bridging international divides of culture and identities
- Shifting the focus of security from states to individuals
- Incorporating culture and human rights into development
- Improving the quality of education worldwide

All will need to be combined with actions to stimulate and sustain recovery from the global economic crisis.

Tackling global warming and climate change is the first challenge. The Intergovernmental Panel on Climate Change has done a remarkable job since 1988 and completed four major reports to persuade politicians and the world at large that the present cycle of climate change is extremely serious and human-made in a way that renders it very different from past climate variations. This is an illustration of the United Nations at its best, drawing on the scientific community

to put governments on notice that urgent action is required. While a handful of countries in the northern hemisphere may benefit from global warming, the vast majority of poor countries located in the tropics will not, and poor people everywhere will face yet another threat to their livelihoods and survival. A related and pressing issue is food security, a topic that came rushing to the top of the agenda in 2008 as commodity prices and transport costs skyrocketed. Climate change could, in fact, further worsen the food situation for many of the globe's poorest in parts of Africa and Asia that will no longer be as productive.

Strengthening global governance in a multipolar world is the second challenge. Incorporating the new economic and political giants into the international system is not just a challenge but also an opportunity. After almost two decades, the days of the unipolar world are coming to an end, less because the United States is declining than because other countries are growing in economic and political strength.[1] This is the case of the European Union, Russia, Japan, China, and India, followed by Brazil, South Africa, and Nigeria further down the line and most probably others.[2] A multipolar world may be more balanced and stable than one in which a single country can determine policies for all. This must, however, be a conscious objective of agreement. Balance-of-power competition in the nineteenth and twentieth centuries shows that a multipolar world will not automatically be more peaceful.

Supporting fragile states is the third challenge, encompassing international responses to the thirty to fifty countries (depending on who does the counting) that are unable to guarantee stability and basic services to their populations.[3] In the early 1990s, the number of intrastate wars increased dramatically. These "new wars" are characterized by situations where battleground states have minimal capacity and their monopoly on violence is contested by internal armed opposition movements that pay no attention to internationally recognized borders.[4] Many have central governments whose sole existence rests on little more than membership in the UN and control of the capital or the main export industries. Although these states claim to be part of the Westphalian order, they bear virtually no resemblance to their more cohesive counterparts.[5] They do not exercise authoritative control over populations and resources, let alone provide education, health, and other basic services for their citizens. At a territorial level, these states suffer from an "unbundling" of powers, a negation of their exclusive authority as states.[6] While the use of the word "weak" to describe such states illustrates various types of vulnerability and a range of capacities, the use of the word "failed" implies that the illnesses in central authority are so grave as to be politically fatal. However, not all weak states fail (e.g., Mali), and some weak states that collapse can make a comeback (e.g., Lebanon).[7]

Balancing regionalism with globalization is the fourth challenge. Although globalization is here to stay, the question is in what form and with what content.

Globalization today is driven by the private sector with few holds barred. Held in check or at least slowed by national government policy for the UN's first four decades, the private sector now operates with increasing autonomy at the global level. In contrast, regionalism is a public sector–driven phenomenon in which the private sector plays an important role but is controlled regarding many issues by the regional equivalent of the state. This is illustrated by the European Union and its debate with Microsoft in 1993–2007, among others. More global governance is needed to counterbalance the effects of globalization, just as regionalism has, or is getting, more power to regulate what needs to be regulated. Balancing regionalism with globalization also means finding appropriate mixtures of private and public sectors within a vast variety of economic and cultural contexts.

Moderating inequalities in global development is the fifth challenge. In spite of recent positive trends in economic growth in many countries, including in some of the least developed, global gaps have widened and hundreds of millions of people continue to live without hope and without a future. The results of such massive gaps and inequalities between and within countries are the ingredients of a dangerous cocktail, stirring frustration, sometimes encouraging protest and violence, and creating situations where terrorism is often viewed with sympathy. Reducing inequalities between and within countries as part of development, therefore, is both morally compelling and a key element of sensible strategies to address root causes of terrorism and international migration. Reducing inequality would help solve two problems simultaneously.

Responding to population growth and international migration is the sixth challenge—and it is a double-barreled one. World population is projected to increase by another 2 to 3 billion over the next fifty years. This may not create a Malthusian dearth of food, but it will put new and enormous pressures on the earth's ecosystems. Many of the additional 3 billion people will be living in developing countries affected by global warming. More serious, the world's fast-growing middle class already aspires to the consumption patterns of developed countries, which, if present trends continue, will themselves be rising. Population pressures will also increase current problems such as unemployment (even for the highly educated), especially for youth. The challenge of migration will illustrate the "pull" of economic opportunity in better-off countries combined with the "push" of the lack of economic opportunities in the sending countries, often compounded by violent armed conflict. The industrialized countries are already developing a fortress mentality. They are building walls on the southern border with Mexico and patrolling the Caribbean, Mediterranean, and Adriatic Seas. They are singling out individuals at airports with the "wrong" passports and expelling immigrants who often have spent a considerable time in the

country. In a world where capital is free to move, labor is stopped at many corners, except for some of the highly educated. Urgent action is needed to channel policies into more humane and economically attractive directions. And the better mobilization of remittances—which now dwarf in volume both foreign direct investment and official development assistance—is a key consideration for cash-strapped governments. Moreover, continued migration to and within developing countries to gigantic cities without adequate infrastructure makes internal migration ever more problematic. A different kind of fortress mentality may arise to prohibit migration to these megacities.

Bridging international divides of culture and identities—perceived and real—is the seventh challenge. Divisions between the global West and the Islamic world are currently the most visible, but there are many others, often involving clashes of competing radical ideologies. While some argue that the divides are a transitory phenomenon caused by the fallout from the war on terrorism, it appears to us urgent to get a better grasp of the underlying issues to prevent the divides from becoming entrenched.[8]

Shifting the focus of security from states to individuals is the eighth challenge. The responsibility to protect is an emerging norm that attracts more and more attention. Sovereignty no longer includes the license to kill. The state no longer is able to do whatever it likes with the individuals within its borders. A global protection force to protect endangered individuals within countries would be a step in the right direction. At the same time, whatever the lens (the state or people's security), many traditional "hard" security problems such as the proliferation of WMDs (including biological, chemical, and nuclear weapons) have been exacerbated by technological and communications breakthroughs. Finally, approaches to disarmament need to go back on the UN agenda, especially in the context of rapidly increasing military expenditures in many countries. These issues are more and more pressing, whether one focuses on more traditional approaches to international security or on human security.

Incorporating concern for culture and human rights into development leads to the ninth challenge. Culture has been a great absentee in the development debate until recently. There is both need and opportunity for the UN to better understand the links—cultural and others—between human security, human rights, democracy, and development. UN involvements at the country and regional level can do much to provide richer and more sensitive perspectives of national and regional problems and a better understanding of ways forward. This is especially true for new issues such as national policies designed to respond to global warming, energy-saving strategies, rights-based policies, and education for global understanding and tolerance. These issues and the interrelationships among them are more subtle and complex than is often realized.

Improving the quality of education worldwide is the final challenge. Many might say that this is already one of the MDGs, and we indeed identify further action toward these goals as a major global objective. But we underline the quality of education at all levels, which recent analyses suggest is emerging as priority concern in many countries. The full contribution of education for parents as well as children that will build greater tolerance and global understanding and support progress in countries in general cannot be realized without paying more attention to the content and quality of the education in question. Yet in scores of countries, teachers are underpaid, buildings are collapsing, and children are in the fields instead of classrooms. Education has been often been turned over to the private sector in places where most families do not possess the resources for books, let alone for tuition. What future does this leave for tomorrow's generations? Somewhat analogous reasoning can be applied to the health care situation around the world. These problems are implicit in the analyses of most books in the series, but they were not topics on our radar screens in 1999.

An Intellectual and Action Agenda for the UN

These ten global challenges can be translated into five broad themes for the intellectual and action agenda on which the UN system should work in the years to come. These are:

- Promoting global human solidarity
- Enhancing opportunities for people throughout the world
- Preventing conflict, building peace, and fostering human security
- Sustaining the planet's ecosystem
- Strengthening global governance

The first four appear in this chapter, but the book's entire final chapter draws conclusions for strengthening global governance, noting especially the part the UN's intellectual work can play in our fifth mega-area.[9]

The order of the items is less important than the content. Some might put sustaining the world's ecosystem first on the grounds that without progress in this area, there may be no planet on which other human activities can take place. The UN Charter puts first the conditions for peace and avoiding war. The truth is that all five mega-areas are essential. We have put strengthening global human solidarity first because it often motivates people and governments to see the importance of situations beyond their borders and to support broader global action—to satisfy both their consciences and their calculations of self-interest.

The five intellectual agenda items are multidisciplinary and interrelated. Moving to sustainable development and sustainable ecosystems should be

combined with accelerating economic growth in the poorest and least-developed countries and thus change the global structure of growth. Nothing captures better the urgency and difficulties of human survival with dignity than moving ahead to protect the world's ecosystems. We build toward this topic at the end of this chapter. Before elaborating the issues, however, we would make three more general comments.

First, researchers will need to maintain the difficult and always tenuous balance between vision and realism. In the early days of the UN, and despite difficulties, the founding governments—that is, the First UN—hammered out the Charter, the Universal Declaration of Human Rights, and a vision for a planet less prone to violence and destruction. They were motivated by their reaction to the horrors and destruction of World War II but also by a determination not to repeat the economic difficulties that had led to the Great Depression of the 1930s. While the UN was not originally conceived of as a world government, nonetheless it also was not the creation of pie-in-the-sky idealists. As one historian notes, "Its wartime architects bequeathed us this system as a realist necessity vital in times of trial, not as a liberal accessory to be discarded when the going gets rough."[10]

At its best, the First UN has maintained this vision, sometimes updating and adding to it. But through most of the UN's history, it has been staff members and nonstate actors—the Second and Third United Nations—who have kept the flame alive and found practical ways to carry forward the original vision, pushing at the limits and mobilizing the pressures and support that have led governments to act. UN staff members have often been the dreamers and idealists who were in a position to draft resolutions or develop programs in ways that have made a difference. And the Third UN has played critical roles at critical junctures, pressing for action and demonstrating support and thereby changing what governments judge to be in their interests.

Second, interactions among the three UNs will continue to be important and often of growing significance. The comparative advantage of each varies issue by issue and over time. Indeed, a hybrid pattern of conflict and cooperation among all three is the norm. Reaching a better understanding of the relative power and influence of each—as well as of the vast differences among the various actors within each of the three United Nations—is a crucial research task. Scientists, for instance, have taken the lead through the IPCC to formulate the risks and consequences of global warming and climate change, working on the panel set up by the WMO and UNEP. Other global problems will require similar partnerships of government experts and independent scientists, supported by committed NGOs.

Indeed, much of what we have learned over the years points to the critical need for such independent and decentralized initiatives. Other agencies of

Box 13.1. Vision and the Challenges Ahead

Those who have contributed most to the UN over the years have been people of commitment and vision, driven by ideals and with a sense of progress for the future. Some quotable examples follow.

Dag Hammarskjöld (1954):

The United Nations was not set up to bring mankind to heaven but to save it from hell.[1]

Barbara Ward (1957):

This is the first time in the history of man that the working out of a relationship between the great civilizations of the Orient and ourselves is a matter of urgency. ... In the last four or five hundred years, the Western world has been the aggressive, outgoing, and indeed, disturbing force for all other civilizations and ways of life. ... So if we are to find ways and means of living peacefully, East and West, in our narrow world together, it is essential for us to have an idea of how we, the Westerners, have been behaving recently, how our history looks to others, and the kind of contacts with other peoples we have enjoyed or imposed or suffered in the past.[2]

Arnold Toynbee:

"Our age is the first generation since the dawn of history in which mankind dared to believe it practical to make the benefits of civilization available to the whole of the human race."[3]

Gareth Evans (1995):

The UN was founded on a mixture of idealism and pragmatism. Both were essential to build a new world fifty years ago, and over the past fifty years, that idealism has not disappeared. It was an important force in bringing about the end of the Cold War, and more than anything else, it was idealism that lay behind the process of decolonisation which shifted the tectonic plates of history.

To some, idealism will always be the enemy of practicality. But to others, it will always involve more than anything else, the courage to take advantage of new opportunities, ensuring that at least some of today's ideal will become tomorrow's reality. Perhaps now, fifty years, beyond San Francisco, we need to renew that idealism and walk down some of the uncharted paths that idealists have always been prepared to tread.[4]

Jim Grant (1991):

Crafting a new world order begins with simple visions. ... We seek a world which places the individual human being at the centre of society and at the centre of the responsibilities of states. We seek a world in which each human being is assured of his or her essential needs for nutrition, health and shelter, a world in which the role of the state is to foster and protect, and not abridge or neglect, the rights and dignity of each person.

We seek a world in which the human community has found a sustainable balance of its needs with the carrying capacity of the earth. And we seek a world in which the nations have found a different way of inter-relating than marching across borders, carpet bombing [civilians], duelling missiles in the sky and starving civilians, the great majority of whom are children and women.[5]

Mahbub ul Haq (1995):

We are at an exciting juncture in our human journey. . . . The traditional North-South divide is giving way to a more mature partnership. In this milieu, we can sing of the dawning of a new human age, guided by a new vision of human progress. At the least, such a human vision should be our guiding star—and our sincere endeavour. For human destiny is a choice, not a chance.[6]

Brian Urquhart (2000):

There is always a challenge ahead, an historic opportunity to be grasped. . . . The UN has taken the lead in many of the great historic issues of our time, and its record is far more impressive than is generally appreciated. With the surging phenomenon of globalisation and the shrinking of the powers of the nation state, it should take the lead again.[7]

Jeffrey D. Sachs (2008):

The paradox of unified global economy and divided global society poses the single greatest threat to the planet because it makes impossible the cooperation needed to address the remaining challenges.[8]

1. UN document SG/382, 13 May 1954. Quoted in Brian Urquhart, "The United Nations at Fifty," Address to the New York Museum of Art International Council, 24 October 1995, available online at http://globetrotter.berkeley.edu/UN/Urquhart/urqspeech5.html (accessed 5 October 2008).

2. Barbara Ward, *The Interplay of East and West: Points of Conflict and Cooperation* (1957; repr., New York: Norton, 1962), 11–13.

3. Quoted in *Our Creative Diversity: Report of the World Commission on Culture and Development* (Paris: UNESCO, 1996), 16.

4. Gareth Evans, "The UN at Fifty: Looking Back and Looking Forward," statement to the Fiftieth General Assembly of the United Nations by Senator Gareth Evans, Foreign Minister of Australia, New York, 2 October 1995, 9, available online at http://www.crisisgroup.org/library/documents/speeches_ge/foreign_minister/1995/021095_un50_looking_back_forward.pdf (accessed 26 July 2008).

5. James P. Grant, address to 1991 International Development Conference, Washington D.C., January 1991, quoted in Sheila Barry Tacon, "Jim Grant--In His Own Words," in *Jim Grant: UNICEF Visionary*, ed. Richard Jolly (Florence: UNICEF, 2001), 163–164.

6. Mahbub ul Haq, *Reflections on Human Development* (New York: Oxford University Press, 1995), 204.

7. Brian Urquhart, "Between Sovereignty and Globalisation—Where Does the United Nations Fit In?" *Development Dialogue* (2000): 1–2, available online at: http://www.dhf.uu.se/pdffiler/DD2000/DD2000_1-2_01.pdf (accessed 6 April 2009).

8. Jeffrey D. Sachs, *Common Wealth: Economics for a Crowded Planet* (New York: Penguin, 2008), 7.

the UN system could undoubtedly establish IPCC-like research structures in other areas of inquiry. Such temporary coalitions will not operate alone or only through formal channels. The media will play a crucial role in mobilizing concern and communicating ideas and findings to the general public. Structures of global governance need strengthening in many ways, but in the meantime—a period that may extend for many years—less formal ways of mobilizing national action in support of global goals are likely to be central.

Third, many necessary actions involve what economists call global public goods that are "non-rival" and "non-excludable," meaning that such goods or services have the quality that the use of the good or service by any one user does not limit its use by another.[11] Hence, all countries and people can benefit from global public goods whether or not they pay for them or contribute to their creation at the same time that the enjoyment by those countries and people who provide them is in no way diminished. Global systems of weather forecasting or health monitoring are examples. The creation of a more sustainable global ecosystem is another. For global governance, the fact that those who do not pay can benefit creates the classic free-rider problem, reducing the incentives to create and maintain all the global public goods that are needed. This calls for nonmarket systems for funding such goods and services. How to raise the required revenue for global public goods in ways that are financially adequate and seen to be equitable is a vital research and political challenge.

For UN member states, generating the required revenues to create global public goods should be done with international agreement. The challenge will be how to do this in ways that states see as equitable in relation to use and ability to contribute. Issues are also raised about representation in revenue management. All of these are functions that are part of the global governance of public goods and will grow in significance in a world of increasing globalization.

We now turn to our five priority issues for the UN's future intellectual and (we hope) action agenda.

Promoting Global Human Solidarity

We begin with an essential foundation, global human solidarity, which is both a means and an end toward improved international order. We see two crucial ways to promote it: narrowing economic inequality and bridging cultural divides.

NARROWING ECONOMIC GAPS

In spite of considerable economic advance and progress in poverty reduction in China, India, and a number of other developing countries, especially in Asia,

the global gaps between the richest and poorest countries of the world have widened enormously over the UN's history. If global human solidarity is to have any meaning, an international effort to narrow these gaps should be much higher on the global agenda.

Over the decades since the UN's establishment, most least-developed countries have continued to fall behind. Since the 1970s, the relative and absolute gaps between per capita income in the fifty least-developed countries and the average income in OECD countries have widened ever further. Only during the last seven years has there been any serious catch-up, largely the result of rising prices of oil and commodities. Global recession has already brought down these prices, and considerable uncertainty exists about the longer-term prospects for economic progress in the least-developed countries (even then only about half of these countries benefited from the price increases).[12]

As several volumes of the United Nations Intellectual History Project series make clear, during the first three decades of the UN's existence, considerable attention was paid to these gaps, on occasion even by the wealthiest delegations.[13] But since the 1980s, the issue of international income distribution has largely disappeared from the global agenda. Several important analyses have been published, but reactions to them and debate about their policy recommendations have been largely confined to academic circles. Even within the United Nations, little note has been taken except in rhetorical statements, as in the Millennium Declaration, which stated that "extreme poverty is an affront to our common humanity" and that "the persistence of income inequality is also troubling." This was an important recognition but not very specific in its recommendations for policy or action.[14]

Global income distribution and widening gaps between the poorest and the richest countries should be reinstated at the top of the international agenda for the next few decades, or at least until the lagging countries establish sustained economic growth and development. Action toward the Millennium Development Goals will help lay the human foundations for such economic advance in the poorest countries, but by itself this will not be enough. Indeed, with increasing numbers of those who complete an education, frustrations will rise unless increasing employment opportunities are linked to economic expansion. Expanding economies are also required if the poorest countries are to achieve other advances in fulfilling human rights, in participating more fully in global governance, in protecting their environments, and in sustainable patterns of development.

Making economic recovery sustainable in the least-developed countries will require major changes in the nature and levels of international support and objectives. At the beginning of the 1980s, two agendas were presented. At the Conference on the Least Developed Countries (1981) and after, the UN argued

for a broad range of actions and other support, emphasizing a range of national and international objectives, in particular higher aid targets. In contrast, the Bretton Woods institutions emphasized structural adjustment policies characterized by loans and grants that were linked to country performance; this became the dominant economic strategy. As several of our volumes make clear, the long-term results of the Bretton Woods strategy proved disastrous in terms of reestablishing economic growth throughout the 1980s and 1990s. Or, as one recent review of the evidence concluded, "Careful analysis of the results since the 1980s has given rise to the newly emerging consensus . . . that [the] IMF programmes hurt economic growth."[15]

Are there alternatives? For us, this is an unnecessary rhetorical question. Obviously there are alternatives. One example is the ongoing policy that the European Union has implemented over the last three or four decades that provides support to its own poorest regions. Finance for this support has amounted to about 0.7 percent of total European GDP, more or less the equivalent of the 0.7 percent international target for aid from developed and developing countries the UN first put forward over four decades ago. In the case of Europe, the resources have been channeled mostly for infrastructural and social advance and largely in support of programs drawn up locally within agreed-upon guidelines and implemented with none of the harsh externally imposed conditionality of the Bretton Woods institutions.

A second example is the Marshall Plan of 1948–1952. Programs were drawn up by the *receiving* countries and overseen by the Organisation for European Economic Co-operation, later the OECD. The $13 billion invested following the announcement of the plan by Secretary of State George Marshall in June 1947 was a conscious decision by the United States that its own interests would be served by helping a war-ravaged continent. Least-developed countries should be the subject of similar reasoning from a far larger number of wealthy countries.

Of course, a sense of shared political objectives and levels of trust and cooperation were easier to establish in both these cases. But they are precisely the elements that should be brought into international action to encourage and support sustainable advance in the least-developed countries. The principles already used in other cases need to be built upon—and they can be. At various times, appeals within the UN have been made to recapture the spirit of the Marshall Plan. But words have so far been louder than action. Much hard evidence should be brought forward by the UN—as the IPCC did for climate change—to demonstrate the disastrous consequences of continued unequal development for such issues as migration, terrorism, and the economic fate of hundreds of millions of people.

BRIDGING CULTURAL DIVIDES

A difficult and controversial area of building human solidarity relates to bridging the many divides in the world's cultures. In recent years, this topic has moved from the margins of political concern to the center, especially in relation to differences in religious traditions. Some suggest that the world faces a "clash of civilizations," a conflict based not on economic or ideological differences but on cultural and religious ones.[16] Others emphasize the diversity of identities and cultures that characterize people everywhere and its actual and potential value.[17] Focusing on religion—and race, nationality, or any other identity—to the exclusion of other identities overstates one characteristic and can lead to a dangerous misunderstanding of cultural differences, especially when introduced or played upon in the presence of conflict or against a background of wide economic and social differences. The risks of playing on such limited perceptions underline the importance of the UN's long-standing emphases on values of understanding and tolerance.

Understanding and tolerance definitely have a more positive potential when the emphasis is switched to enriching cultural diversity within all countries. Development over the last half-century has focused more on economic enrichment—increasing consumption and affluence—and has generally emphasized cultural enrichment. In *UN Voices*, Mexican anthropologist Lourdes Arizpe provides insight on the momentous challenges ahead in the cultural relationships between the West and the rest of the world:

> The first challenge of the United Nations is to create a scheme for the co-existence of cultures that are no longer juxtaposed as a mosaic of cultures but as currents in a single river . . . to create spaces, identify the people who would be able to develop these concepts and perspectives, and put them in positions where they can lead this world debate on how different cultures and religions can coexist.[18]

Expanding Opportunities for People throughout the World

This challenge is not new, though whole new dimensions, especially advances in the media and modern communications, have raised awareness and expectations of better opportunities to new levels in the world today. From its very beginning, the United Nations recognized that its work and purposes must relate to the fundamentals of human existence and society. The Preamble of the Charter refers to reaffirming "faith in fundamental human rights, in the dignity and worth of the human person and in the equal rights of men and

women and of nations large and small." The idealism of this vision will be even more important in the years ahead, especially in three areas: fulfilling human rights, respecting MDG commitments, and improving the quality of education, health, and other basic services.

ADVANCING HUMAN RIGHTS

For all countries, pressing ahead with human rights is fundamental, requiring international support as well as monitoring and criticism. Here the UN built a broad foundation, beginning with the Universal Declaration of Human Rights and elaborating rights further in subsequent conventions in many areas and for many groups. Numerous human rights treaties have been articulated within the UN system. But as the UNIHP volume by Roger Normand and Sarah Zaidi makes clear, the challenge remains implementation.[19] Although the creation of the Office of the High Commissioner for Human Rights was a long-awaited accomplishment, national and international mechanisms for ensuring implementation of their rights are still weak, as are requisite increases in UN budgetary allocations to support action.

The Convention on the Elimination of All Forms of Discrimination against Women is another key area; much real progress has been made but much more remains to be done everywhere. Focusing on women's rights will also help build human solidarity on a global scale more generally. Women are often highly conscious of what they share with women across the globe and are more ready than men are to work to strengthen the links. If women are given opportunities to take leading roles in building solidarity, there will be much faster progress and it will be all the easier to convince children of the value of broader global values.

IMPLEMENTING MDG COMMITMENTS

The Millennium Declaration and the accompanying Millennium Development Goals have strong support from all three UNs and are formal commitments made by the First UN of member states. Action toward attaining these goals should be at the top of the agenda for practical work to build human solidarity, all the more so as part of recovery and resturcturing from the global crisis. Achieving these goals would bring a dramatic reduction in the number of people living in extreme poverty and hunger and in the number of children who do not attend school. It would also move toward equality of girls and boys in school enrollments, reductions of child mortality and levels of malnutrition, and the provision of and access to water, sanitation, and hygiene—all critical and basic elements of well-being. Although it is inconceivable that all the goals will be fully achieved by 2015, this in no way implies failure in the effort. Most

countries have already accelerated their efforts to move toward the targets. The critical part of the challenge is to continue striving until the goals are achieved in every country. Even this, however, is only a beginning. The goal for reducing poverty and hunger, for example, is only for a halving of the proportion of people suffering such deficiencies by 2015. International support will need to be sustained over much of the twenty-first century.

Yet there are reasons for qualified optimism. Progress has been made, albeit unevenly. Asia leads the statistical decline in global poverty, although largely because of dramatic reductions in the number of people living in poverty in China and considerable reductions in India as well. These two nations account for some 2.4 billion people—close to 40 percent of the world's population, and half of the Third World's population—and progress in these two giants is essential and contributes to a diminishment of unequal global development. But there are other examples, Korea, Malaysia, Mauritius, Tunisia, Barbados, and Costa Rica among them. These and some other developing countries have demonstrated enormous progress toward meeting these objectives over the last two or three decades. Our argument is certainly not that the situation in these countries is satisfactory in every respect, but they demonstrate that broad progress is possible. Despair is unjustifiable.

There are other positive examples, sometimes also dramatic. The prevalence of polio has been reduced by 99 percent to the point where in 2006 there were only about 1,200 cases worldwide, compared with some 350,000 in the 1980s. The fight against malaria has taken off. Although long delayed, there has been important progress in treating HIV/AIDS in some areas, even if deaths and new infections continue to increase. This is true also of new cases of tuberculosis. Targets for access to safe drinking water are in sight, but coverage remains partial in both urban and rural areas.

However, these cannot hide ugly realities elsewhere or the dramatic setbacks resulting from the global economic and financial crisis. Estimates show increases in the proportions of hungry people everywhere. Dramatic earlier increases in food, fertilizer, and transport costs led to violence in many parts of the world. The decrease in raw commodity prices in 2008–2009 will not necessarily mean more food on the table because of lost revenues and jobs resulting from a downturn in virtually every economy in the world.

Four vital points about future challenges can be derived from this quick overview—two positive and two negative. The level of international commitment to poverty reduction and monitoring of progress worldwide exceeds anything ever before attempted, let alone achieved. Although the process is far from perfect, an international basis for future monitoring has been established. Although it is very uneven, progress in many areas of action in many countries has been impressive, as the above trends suggest.

But two important negatives should also be underlined. The variation in achievements illustrates weaknesses in the ways the goals have been formulated and are being promoted and pursued, supported by donors, and monitored. These issues need to be corrected. In addition, there are serious problem areas. Progress in the least-developed countries, including most countries of Sub-Saharan Africa, is so weak that few if any of the goals are likely to be achieved by 2015 or even in the foreseeable future, in spite of national and international commitments, including commitments of additional financial resources. This was true even before the global economic crisis. Now there is a need for more fundamental rethinking the nature of outside economic support for that continent and the role that Africa plays in the global economy. A better mixture of aid, investment, and special trade measures is in order.

Between 2002 and 2008, economic growth in half the countries of Africa picked up—between 3 and 5 percent per capita per annum—as a result of increasing prices for many raw materials and basic commodities. If global recovery takes place with attention to the poorest countries, we could be as surprised in 2019 as we were in 2008 when we compared the world situation with that of 1999. Nonetheless, positive growth is hardly guaranteed, so international solidarity is essential. Moreover, often only the elite or better-off people within these countries benefited in the early 2000s. There is a need therefore to move toward a better structure of production and distribution *within* these countries that will help sustain higher incomes and reduce levels of poverty.

As mentioned earlier, there has been an unprecedented increase in the number and proportion of persons who are literate in developing countries. In the 1950s, it was about a third; today it is well over three-quarters. The number of people educated to primary, secondary, and higher levels has increased by multiples. Various UN organizations have played a significant and sometimes essential role in these advances. This has been done typically by setting regional and international goals and guidelines, mobilizing action, and providing technical, financial, and other forms of practical support for translating the goals and guidelines into national action, especially in poorer countries. However, the quality of education and of health care has recently suffered in almost all countries or at least is under serious pressure, partially as a result of structural adjustment and partially as a result of misplaced priorities.

As was made clear in a number of UNIHP volumes, including this one, progress has been made over the UN's lifetime toward meeting objectives in education and health, nutrition and population, safe motherhood, and reproductive health. In all these areas, great advances have been made in all parts of the world and in most countries.[20] The UN has both encouraged and supported these achievements while always emphasizing the distance still to travel.

IMPROVING THE QUALITY OF EDUCATION, HEALTH, AND OTHER BASIC SERVICES

Here we emphasize the importance of future UN work on education and health in particular. Such vital elements for the future of a country and its population as education and health have often fallen short of expectations. Certainly there has been progress in expanding primary school enrollments; universal primary school enrollment is in sight in many regions but certainly not in all countries. For instance, many countries in Sub-Saharan Africa seriously lag behind. Moreover, enrollment figures often disguise deeper problems—early dropouts, poor-quality education, and gender inequality in access to education.

There is little doubt that the quality of education has received a blow in most countries, and not just in the developing world. Quantity has often come at the expense of quality. Now that the quantitative targets are in sight, the emphasis must shift toward enhancing the quality, which is not just a problem related to teachers' salaries. It is indeed remarkable that crucially important jobs for the future of a country and its people—like teaching and nursing—are badly remunerated in most cases. However, the quality of education also depends on making use of modern technology: the Internet, TV, and distance learning are but a few of such new ways of learning. UNESCO should become more central in helping countries adopt them. A competent teacher in a given subject can give a lecture by video that can be seen worldwide on the Internet with local teachers commenting before and afterward.

The UN should initiate a global initiative to include an international component in the school curricula at all levels. A globalized world requires that countries slowly adjust their national educational systems to help students gain some global perspective and improve cultural and religious understanding. Familiarity with emerging technologies is also important. Students need to leave school equipped to understand the global political, economic, and technological developments that will affect their lives.

Advances in health care were achieved during the 1970s and 1980s. The most important change came with the adoption of the Primary Health Care initiative in 1978, a joint initiative of the WHO and UNICEF that drew on the thinking and experience of both organizations. From the beginning, it required multisectoral action, community involvement, and appropriate technologies. This was a fundamentally new approach whose goal was ensuring access to health care for all.[21] The underlying principles included universal access to care and coverage on the basis of need, commitment to health equity as part of development-oriented social justice, community participation in defining and implementing health agendas, and intersectoral approaches to health.

However, the advances in health care achieved in the 1970s and 1980s in many countries are now lagging, while maternal mortality rates remain high, indicating that very little progress has been made in reducing the vulnerabilities of women in childbirth. Much has been achieved over the last six and a half decades in many domains, but obviously much remains to be done. In his recent book *Common Wealth,* Jeffrey Sachs stresses the success achieved by the Global Fund to Fight AIDS, Tuberculosis, and Malaria.[22] New developments in using mass information to promote health present major opportunities to address global health issues. Research is another need. The UN—in cooperation with the Bill and Melinda Gates Foundation—should gather leading biomedical research scientists, government officials, and private sector representatives to learn how best to focus health research for the benefit of humanity. This is another example of how the three United Nations can work together along the lines pioneered by the IPCC.

Preventing Conflict, Building Peace, and Human Security

In the area of international peace and security, the early UN vision was focused on abolishing war—replacing the use of force with commitments to abide by the rules of the Charter, in which negotiation and the rule of law replaced the law of the jungle. Individual countries were allowed to take action in self-defense.

Major limitations in the implementation of this vision of global governance followed; the UN was constrained by national interests and the divisions of the Cold War. Nonetheless, various initiatives within the UN were taken to give substance to other parts of this vision of global governance: preventive diplomacy; and arms control and disarmament measures that sought to channel resources to economic development. These proposals occurred at intervals over each of the decades from the 1950s, but it was not until the late 1980s, with the end of the Cold War, that substantial reductions in military expenditures took place. We earlier mentioned that no specific reallocations of resources to development appear to have followed. Nonetheless, an element of peace dividend was realized during the 1990s in the form of military spending cutbacks in the United States and elsewhere that led to reductions in national deficit and interest rates, which in turn led to expansion of economic growth within the United States and elsewhere.

This then is the third priority item for the future UN intellectual agenda. Bertrand Ramcharan has set out much of the agenda in his volume for the project, *Preventive Diplomacy.* He documented the substantive advances in the UN's practice of preventive diplomacy. His priorities for future action by Secretaries-General build upon past successes and lessons: spearheading the preventive

diplomacy of the United Nations, taking the lead in developing a global watch over issues that affect the future and welfare of the planet; encouraging the preventive diplomacy role of sister institutions, which means continued and energized support for international, regional, and subregional arrangements to prevent conflicts and atrocities; taking the lead in implementing a diplomacy of democracy and human rights at the country level; engaging in a diplomacy of protection, particularly with respect to groups at risk; and taking the lead in striving for an ethical world order—a world of conscience and of values.[23]

There are important areas of overlap between this theme and others. Recent research has shown that conflict is often made more likely by extremes of inequality within countries—although usually extremes of horizontal inequalities rather than vertical ones. In other words, the causes are usually inequalities *between* regions or ethnic groups within countries rather than inequalities *within* these groups.[24] Perceived extremes of economic or political injustice also stir deep resentments that can surge into armed conflict or support for violence. National or international policies that prevent these extremes are also a form of conflict prevention that deserves enhanced attention and action. Our understanding of exactly how these operate is weak and deserves more attention.

The Secretary-General's High-level Panel on Threats, Challenges and Change identified six areas of insecurity that should be reduced for a more secure world: economic and social threats, including poverty, infectious disease, and environmental degradation; interstate conflict; internal conflict, including civil war, genocide, and other large-scale atrocities; nuclear, radiological, chemical, and biological weapons; terrorism; and transnational organized crime.[25]

The NPT—the Non-Proliferation Treaty to control the spread of nuclear weapons—is another crucial initiative. The degree of support that it receives from countries with nuclear weapons and countries without them has fluctuated wildly. We seem to be entering a phase when some nuclear powers may be inclined to give stronger support to the NPT and to press other countries to do so even as still other countries scramble to become nuclear and thereby threaten the entire NPT regime.[26]

Disarmament should also be higher on the UN's agenda. After the end of the Cold War, world military expenditures fell by about a quarter from 1987 to 1996. This represented a major saving of resources and led to a period of unprecedented economic advance in the United States with favorable effects on growth in other parts of the world, including many developing countries. In contrast, in the following decade, military spending rose in many countries, in China and India as well as developed countries. The United States now accounts for about half of world military expenditures. The total costs to the United States of the war in Iraq are unofficially estimated to amount to some

$3 trillion without counting the human and economic costs in Iraq or other countries.[27] And whatever the real origins of the war and the hopes and intentions of the United States and its supporters at the beginning, most commentators now agree that the effects have been disastrous for international relations. Although the Security Council never approved the war, the UN should now use the rethinking of this decision along with future actions to provide new energy for efforts to resolve conflicts through negotiation, peacebuilding, and peacekeeping.

Sustaining the Planet's Ecosystem

What if astronomers were to identify a very large meteor on track to crash into the earth on a particular date within the next seven years? What if the consequences were shown to be equivalent of the asteroid or meteor that hit the planet 60 million years ago and is often thought to have led to the extinction of the dinosaurs?

One immediate effect—apart from asking which dinosaurs are likely to be hit this time—would be a concentration of the world's scientific and political minds, asking what could be done to avoid this looming catastrophe. The concentration would be all the more focused if prevention was possible only if certain costly actions were undertaken on every continent. Can one doubt that within months a plan would be prepared, agreement reached, and action begun and that international finance would be mobilized to support countries too poor to finance their part of the action? Free-riding and nay-saying would be irrelevant issues. Dilly-dallying to await the most recalcitrant partners would be as well. Immediate decisions and swift actions would be essential.

Global warming and climate chaos raise some of the same issues but to date have not generated anything like the same urgency. Every country will be affected. The need for action is urgent. Every country should do something, even the poorest and least able. Scientists should advise and politicians should decide. At a minimum, three forms of action are required in the years ahead: a multilateral framework for avoiding dangerous climate change under the post-2012 Kyoto framework; an agenda for mitigation that involves policies for sustainable carbon budgeting and related actions; and the development of a wide-ranging international agenda for adaptation, with support for poorer countries and links with broader issues such as poverty reduction. These are on the agenda of the UN Climate Change Conference in Copenhagen at the end of 2009.

These actions in broad terms are part of a growing international consensus, although most specific actions remain to be agreed to, especially related to cost sharing. The fact that the United Nations has been central to placing this issue

on the global agenda and providing a forum to cajole states is significant, both for the content of its appeal and for the legitimacy of its voice. The worldwide cost of mitigating global climate change is estimated to be on the order of 1 percent of GDP, not a small sum but a good deal less than most countries spend on their militaries.[28] The cost of adaptation is harder to estimate because of uncertainty about the precise impact of climate change and its multiple effects. However, as the Stern Review comments, "Adaptation to mute the impact of climate change will be essential in the poorer parts of the world" and should be integrated into development policy and planning at every level.[29]

The human impacts across the globe have been summarized in stark simplicity in the *Human Development Report 2007/2008: Fighting Climate Change:*

> While the world's poor walk the Earth with a light carbon footprint they are bearing the brunt of unsustainable management of our ecological interdependence. In rich countries, coping with climate change to date has largely been a matter of adjusting thermostats, dealing with longer, hotter summers and observing seasonal shifts. By contrast, when global warming changes weather patterns in the Horn of Africa, it means that crops fail and people go hungry, or that women and young girls spend more hours collecting water.[30]

The report concludes, "If the world acts now, it will be possible—just possible—to keep the twenty-first century's global temperatures within a 2° threshold above pre-industrial levels. Achieving this future will require a high level of leadership and unparalleled international cooperation."[31]

This finding may need some elaboration. The scientists active in the IPCC have calculated the rise in global temperature if carbon dioxide emissions double from the level before industrialization of 280 parts per million to 560 per million. This is the level we can expect in the year 2090 if action is not taken imminently. The IPCC calculation tells us that if a doubling of carbon dioxide emissions does occur, the average increase in the temperature of the world's climate will be between 2 and 4.5 degrees Centigrade, almost certainly reaching 3 degrees Centigrade (5.4 degrees Fahrenheit). However, the timeline is even shorter than this because of the tremendous rate of industrialization in China and India. If these two continue along the present path, we may reach the doubling of carbon dioxide emissions by 2050, with serious consequences for people worldwide, especially for poor people in areas threatened by rising sea levels. The impact of such a change would cause setbacks in water security, food production, and human health.

Global warming and climate change are now inching toward the top of the agenda of most (if not all) countries. This is in no small measure due to the

diligent work of the UN's IPCC, an excellent example of close cooperation between the Second and Third UNs that has forced action by the First UN, particularly action by many of its most recalcitrant member states. But the most difficult part remains—agreeing on specific action by each country within a given time frame. Additional research will be necessary to answer legitimate questions posed by governments and others. Hence, this issue should remain very high on the UN's intellectual agenda.

The refusal of the United States to ratify the Kyoto Protocol is seen by many, including many U.S. citizens, as irresponsible. But there is hope given that the political atmosphere has changed dramatically with the election of Barack Obama in November 2008. Among his first public announcements was that the United States would take a strong leadership role on climate change, which bodes well for the 2009 Copenhagen conference. The United States must be on board in a post-Kyoto agreement for China and India and other developing countries to become active participants.

A word of caution is in order. Although considerable attention is now being given to the "new" problems of climate change and global warming, the "old" environmental problems—some of which have direct links with the so-called new problems—are still with us and often are getting worse. This is the case with acid rain, air pollution, overpopulation, rainforest destruction, and desertification. Many are interrelated, and all need much more action than they have received so far in all but a small minority of countries. Action on this front is related to our first item on the UN's intellectual agenda, the issue of human solidarity.

14. Strengthening Global Governance

At the beginning of the last chapter, we gave examples of how dramatically things can change in a mere ten-year period, for better and for worse. In today's world, even the credit crunch of 2007 took only a few months to engulf almost the whole world in financial and economic crisis. The planet's economic, social, and political situations have changed dramatically over the six and a half decades of the UN's existence, in many ways beyond recognition. And while the formal decision-making structures of the United Nations have hardly changed during this period, other less formal procedures and rules are starkly different from those in place in 1945. The need to strengthen the formal and the informal ways that the world attempts to identify, understand, and solve global problems is the challenge of strengthening global governance.

Global Governance

The system of global governance has advanced and evolved considerably over the life of the UN, but in different ways, at different speeds, and with great contrasts between the four main areas of its concern and oversight: economic stability, international security, development, and human rights. The advances and setbacks, successes and failures, together with its present limitations and future challenges have been set out by Thomas G. Weiss and Ramesh Thakur in *The UN and Global Governance: An Unfinished Journey.*[1]

For those who are not specialists in international relations, it may be useful to indicate why the term "global governance" has come into use instead of

"global government." Global government would imply an international system with at least some of the capacities and powers of national governments—notably powers to control or repel threats, raise revenues, allocate expenditures, redistribute incomes, and enforce compliance as well as ensure the rights of citizens. While some distinguished commentators have declared the need for the UN system to have some of these powers—for instance, Nobel prizewinner Jan Tinbergen and former head of the World Bank Robert McNamara—clearly no such powers of government have been accorded to any international institution at present. Moreover, ideas for global government remain highly contested and are very far from being accepted politically, even as a distant objective.

For these reasons, most students of international relations prefer the term "global governance," which came into widespread use in the 1990s. Global governance implies systems with imperfections and major limitations—in a phrase, international cooperation without world government—with states pursuing their own national or regional interests and with only limited and often ineffective measures to require compliance with internationally agreed-upon rules, regulations, and decisions. Although some observers still believe that a vision of global government remains the long-run answer in an ever-more-globalizing world, realists of international relations argue that this pursuit is misleading. They see a struggle to create a world government as a vastly exaggerated and idealistic vision of what will be possible or desirable over the next few decades and, worse, a chimera that seriously distorts the elements of stronger global governance to which we can and should strive during the nearer future. In addition, some critics are philosophically opposed to a global leviathan.

This said, structures of global governance do exist and have been anything but static. International rules, regulations, institutions, and expectations have advanced and evolved considerably over the decades of the UN's existence, often increasing in strength, sometimes remaining stagnant, but rarely moving backward. Even critics would agree that in a number of technical areas—such as agreed-upon rules and regulations for shipping and international air flights, the standardization of weather systems, and the mapping of epidemiological trends—global governance has demonstrated its value. Indeed, in some areas like telecommunications and postal services, the arrangements date back to the nineteenth century, when necessities for technical coordination became obvious and institutions like the International Telegraph Union and the Universal Postal Union were established, respectively in 1865 and 1874.[2] By 1914, over thirty such institutions had been created and by the end of the twentieth century hundreds more, some of which are listed in box 14.1.

Nevertheless, as Weiss and Thakur identify and analyze in their book, today's system of global governance, even with its intentional limitations, remains

Box 14.1. Advances in Global Economic Institutions for Governance

In a dramatic change from idealistic visions of the past, creating a world government is no longer the goal of most contemporary proponents of global governance.[1] Beginning with Dante's *Monarchia* at the beginning of the fourteenth century, there is a long tradition of criticizing the existing state system (which at that time existed only in Europe) and advocating replacing it with a universal government.[2] The idealist tradition includes Hugo Grotius, the Dutch jurist whose *On the Laws of War and Peace* (1625) usually qualifies him as the "father" of international law; Emeric Cruce, the French monk who died in the same year as the Peace of Westphalia and who had dreamed of a world court, a place for nations to meet and work out disputes and disarmament; and of course Immanuel Kant, whose *Perpetual Peace* (1795) envisioned a confederation of democratic and pacific states.

A fitting image for this older view of world government can be seen in the tapestries in the Palais des Nations in Geneva—the headquarters of the League of Nations and now the UN's European Office. They "picture the process of humanity combining into ever larger and more stable units for the purpose of governance—first the family, then the tribe, then the city-state, and then the nation—a process which presumably would eventually culminate in the entire world being combined in one political unit."[3]

Today politicians, political scientists, journalists, and other commentators talk of governance—international efforts and institutions to bring global or regional order to government and nongovernment interactions without establishing a single or comprehensive global authority—"governance where there is no government," as international affairs scholar James N. Rosenau put it.

Even by these more modest standards of governance, considerable progress has been made since 1945, of which the UN itself is a major example. In fact, much more progress has taken place in the economic and social arena than in the political. The creation of the Bretton Woods institutions were the first, with the visionary aim of avoiding the problems of the Great Depression, removing the deflationary tendencies within the global economy, and making it possible for countries to pursue full employment policies. As part of this agenda, the intention was also to create a third institution, the International Trade Organization (ITO), and the ITO founding conference was held in Havana in 1948. But the U.S. Senate failed to ratify the agreement, so the organization was stillborn. Some distinguished economists like Hans Singer believed that John Maynard Keynes, the greatest architect of the postwar economic system, might have opposed the creation of the other parts of this three-legged stool of global governance without this third leg. Instead, GATT was established, which lasted until 1995, when the WTO was created with a wider scope and more capacity to enforce compliance.

Many other more specialized institutions of global economic and social governance have been established over the years. The ILO has been in existence since 1919. Since 1945 many other major institutions have been created under the UN: the FAO in 1945; UNESCO

in 1946; the WHO in 1948. On the economic side, a range of other smaller institutions were founded: the International Finance Corporation in 1956; the International Development Association in 1960; the WFP in 1961; UNCTAD in 1964; UNIDO in 1966; UNEP in 1972; the World Intellectual Property Organization in 1967; the WTO in 1995; and UN Office on Drugs and Crime in 1997.

This international institutional landscape is considerably more developed than even some of the UN's founders imagined. But the lack of authority still leaves open the question of whether governance is sufficient to deal with the global problems of an ever-more-globalizing world.

1. For an exception, see James A. Yunker, *Rethinking World Government: A New Approach* (Lanham, Md.: University Press of America, 2005).

2. Craig N. Murphy, *International Organization and Industrial Change: Global Governance since 1850* (Cambridge: Polity Press, 1994), 1.

3. Harold K. Jacobson, *Networks of Interdependence: International Organizations and the Global Political System,* 2nd ed. (New York: Alfred A. Knopf, 1984), 84.

seriously inadequate—that is, unfit for its tasks—because of five gaps that undercut the effectiveness of international action in the contemporary world. These gaps relate to knowledge, norms, policies, institutions, and compliance. To these must be added the lack of coherence of policy and action between the different areas and institutions of governance and often a serious deficiency of the resources needed to fulfill their appointed tasks. According to Weiss and Thakur, an analysis of gaps helps illustrate where work (intellectual work as well as policy developments) is needed to lay the groundwork for better implementation and compliance—the areas of failure most evident in an international system lacking an overarching authority.

Formal mechanisms of global government are not inherently impossible or unworkable but are consciously resisted by national governments that wish to maintain power in their own hands. For example, sovereign governments, especially those from developed countries, have fought hard and consistently to avoid moves toward mechanisms that would give revenue-raising powers to global institutions. Examples include resistance to proposals for charging rents for the use of under-seabed resources that are in the global domain, levying a Tobin tax on short-term international financial flows (which would help curb global speculation), or charging more than a minimum for registering patents internationally through WIPO, the World Intellectual Property Organization. All these could be justified by principles for making the global economic system work more effectively, yet all have been strongly resisted.

Governments fight to maintain their major influence over or control of institutions that do have economic power by dominating their voting systems and by appointing their senior executives (as in the Bretton Woods institutions or the WTO) or through diplomatic dominance and maneuvering. Coordination of economic policies and positions among industrialized countries is usually pursued in smaller institutional structures such as the OECD or the European Union or in less institutionalized settings such as the G-7/8. Such cooperation is hardly surprising. What is more surprising is that in spite of the existence of the Non-Aligned Movement and the Group of 77, developing countries have not yet formulated a coherent strategy to establish a measure of countervailing power to offset decades of developed-country dominance.

Various actions to strengthen governance on a global basis in the economic and social arena have been taken over the last fifty years, especially during the recent decades of globalization. The driving principles for this, however, have been defined by free-market ideology and neoclassical economics, justified on the grounds that free-market principles will extend economic efficiency throughout the global market. This may have happened in many situations, but at considerable cost. Lacking mechanisms to ensure competition, free markets have often extended monopolistic influences in ways that have had negative consequences for citizens. With global governance lacking mechanisms of enforcement, many of the rich countries have continued with subsidies and other forms of protection in agriculture and other sectors, not only failing to practice what they preach but also wasting billions of dollars and bringing harm to millions of people, especially in the developing world. Lacking mechanisms to control or offset widening inequalities, global gaps between the richest and the poorest countries have increased to historically unprecedented levels. And lacking mechanisms to maintain or restore economic and financial stability, the global system has been plunged into recession.

At the time of writing, most countries in North America and Europe are deep into recession through the international transmission of instabilities arising from failures that started in the financial and housing markets. As their crisis has spread, most other regions of the world have suffered—at enormous costs. Toward the end of 2008, it was reported that the banks alone had lost $2.8 trillion worldwide. The total global losses, including production and income foregone through recession will be much larger. Among many earlier examples, we already mentioned the economic losses on the order of $2 trillion arising from the 1997 Asian financial crisis. Stronger mechanisms of global economic oversight and regulation could have avoided many of these problems and the enormous costs associated with the failures.

These, however, are only the short-term challenges for global governance. Support for actions for economic recovery must be combined with measures to tackle the challenges of sustaining the planetary ecosystem and meeting other

longer-term global challenges. These will require more robust mechanisms than those needed to deal with immediate problems.

In the two preceding chapters, we have referred to the key question of global public goods because many individual countries have little or no incentive to support and comply with what is needed for more effective action on a global scale. The market provides insufficient incentives—and sometimes no incentives at all or even negative ones—because most of the benefits of global public goods will accrue to other countries. The same is true of political cycles; all or most of the long-term benefits of action will occur during the period when some later administration or political leader is in office. Adequate action in these situations can expected only if a stronger system of global governance exists to move toward global plans of action—that is, mechanisms and incentives to encourage compliance as well as penalties and other sanctions when countries fail to act or consciously violate agreed-upon provisions.

Which institutions and groups need to be involved in strengthening global governance in relation to these challenges? For debate and decision making, governments—the First United Nations—must be involved, along with international bodies such as the regional commissions and the OECD. Regional bodies have the weakness that they are not global, while the United Nations is too large as a forum for moving to tough positions.

Given these difficulties, there is a strong case for relying on smaller bodies, at least for the stage of brokering the framework of a global agreement. Expanding the G-8 to the G-20, including China, India, Brazil, and South Africa—that is, to include a better balance of all the larger North and South economies—would be one approach, although some way of incorporating representation for smaller countries is also needed. Another would be to create ad hoc bodies, bringing in representatives of the countries most concerned with the issue at hand. A third would be to establish a new principal organ of the United Nations, an Economic and Social Security Council, as has often been proposed. Other variations are possible. We are inclined to suggest an expanded G-8, increased to perhaps twenty to twenty-five members, assembled to respond to the most urgent of the challenges we have identified. This procedure is not ideal or even adequate for the longer run. We propose it as a workable step forward. Indeed, when agreement on these global matters is achieved, proposals should be put to the wider UN in order to increase the agreement's legitimacy and (if possible) reach a near-consensus.

Ways must be found to incorporate the private sector, transnational corporations, and employers' associations into new arrangements. They have regained much freedom of maneuver in recent years. Will these groups have the wisdom to limit their appetites and show discipline and self-control? Encouraging these qualities was the rationale for the Global Compact.[3] But as many commentators

have already said, more effective arrangements are needed for the longer run.

Ways also should be found also to reach out to civil society—NGOs, churches, trade unions, employers' associations, and so on. We have already noted the effectiveness of this Third UN when it meets in a variety of UN settings, where it acts forcefully in such fields as population, gender, and the environment. How can one bring these groups more formally into global governance?

Already NGOs and individuals are coming together at the annual World Social Forum, which is held in places such as Porto Alegre and Mumbai, to discuss the impact of globalization. The more extreme of those are known as "anti-globalizers." These groups and individuals attempt to move global policies in a more just and equitable direction. Obviously, they do not constitute a true countervailing power to the private sector, the main driving force behind globalization, but it is a beginning.

As we first argued in *Ahead of the Curve,* most of the time important decisions are taken only after a disaster has occurred or at best after a disaster has become clearly visible on the horizon. Examples are the creation of the League of Nations after World War I, the creation of the United Nations and the Marshall Plan after World War II, and the Delta Plan after the 1953 flooding that caused several thousands deaths in the Netherlands.[4]

The economic and financial crisis of 2008 and beyond has already underlined the limits of global laissez-faire and swung back public opinion and global policymakers toward stronger regulation. This crisis provides an opportunity to explore broader and longer-term mechanisms to strengthen global economic governance. Can systems be devised to incorporate concerns for stability, equity, and sustainability in addition to concerns for economic efficiency?

Another disaster on the horizon today is climate change. A reaction designed to do something effective that has been long in the making seems on the verge of taking place.[5] This has been stimulated by the work of the Intergovernmental Panel on Climate Change, composed of hundreds of scientists. Over time, its reports have become more precise and its recommended actions have been ever more urgent in tone and the panel has adopted them with more and more consensus. Public awareness has also been reinforced by a succession of very hot summers and other climate aberrations, images that chronicle the melting of glaciers and other ice formations, and weather-related disasters such as hurricanes. All this has put increasing pressure on politicians to act.

The challenge now is for the larger countries to act and thereby give a lead to others. At the UN Climate Change Conference in Bali, Secretary-General Ban Ki-moon pleaded with delegates to "deliver to the people of the world a successful outcome." The conference's dramatic eleventh hour included tears from the head of the UN Climate Change Secretariat and Papua New Guinea's

outspoken challenge to the United States: "If you're not willing to lead, get out of the way."[6] These are examples of the tactics that we think are needed to mobilize the global actions required on a number of fronts.

Enhancing UN Decision Making

For all its weaknesses and failures, the United Nations—including its specialized agencies, its development funds, and other organizations—remains the only international organization with virtually universal membership and the accompanying widespread international legitimacy. Over the last two decades, the UN has convened eight summits that have attracted heads of state or government on various topics: children in 1990, the environment and development in 1992, social development in 1995 and 2002, food security in 1996 and 2008, the Millennium Declaration and the Millennium Development Goals in 2000, and on the UN's sixtieth anniversary in 2005. Often over three-quarters of the world's countries, including all the major powers, attended these gatherings of presidents, prime ministers, and princes. Compared to earlier attempts to mobilize attention and support for the international system before 1945, including the League of Nations, efforts during the UN era stand in remarkable contrast.

Although abandoning a utopian vision of world government may be necessary, one must beware of throwing out the baby with the bathwater. At a minimum, a vision of priority actions to strengthen global governance is needed. Without such a vision we risk working only within the contours of the current inadequate international system, including an enfeebled United Nations. By not imagining a fundamentally stronger system, we make continuation of the current lackluster approach inevitable.[7] More serious still, we risk failing to take action on problems and challenges for which the very survival of humanity and the planet as we know it are at stake. Clear decisions are needed as well as stronger mechanisms to press for compliance.

Today's challenges require greater efficiency in international institutions, more effective rules and regulations, and a more democratic system of representation. An almost unending series of reforms to these ends have been tried more or less since the UN's creation, but there is a wide gap between recognizing the need for reform and formulating proposals and getting agreement to adopt and implement them. The lack of action to alter the composition and working methods of the Security Council and create an Economic and Environmental Security Council are just two examples of collective foot-dragging.

We thus end this volume with a number of pragmatic recommendations to deal with the challenges we have identified. All require action, none of which

can wait for a totally reformed UN system. We identify ways forward (not perfection) in global governance, ways that international action to tackle key problems could, we believe, be mobilized.

Our pragmatic proposals for strengthening global governance apply the positive lessons from the breakthrough work of the IPCC. Standing on the shoulders of this experience, we recommend four objectives:

- Broadening the core principles of global governance to include stability, social justice, and sustainability in addition to economic efficiency
- Strengthening the intellectual contributions of the UN and recognizing them to be central to all its work
- Mobilizing the potential of all three UNs to generate support and action
- Improving outreach through all the media to help mobilize such action

Bringing Social Justice into Global Governance

Broadening the core principles of global governance to include social justice and sustainability is vitally necessary for a more balanced approach to globalization. Most economic actions over the last two or three decades have been directed toward extending free markets and promoting economic efficiency. Judged by these objectives, they have achieved considerable success. However, though promoting democracy, human rights, and social justice has been part of the global rhetoric, initiatives with legal force have mostly focused on economic principles. Economic considerations based on free-market principles without legally enforceable limitations, as generally exist in national (but not international) legislation, almost always trump social and human considerations.

Today's challenges in the realm of strengthening global governance, however, go far beyond economic efficiency. Though stability was one of the key objectives when the Bretton Wood institutions were founded, it was increasingly downplayed and virtually abandoned with the collapse of the Bretton Woods agreement in 1971. Today only a few parts of the international system formally recognize elements of social justice or sustainability, and then only partially and inconsistently. Mostly these are parts of the UN and certain NGOs. In spite of the development objectives of the WTO's Doha Round, which began in 2002, for instance, little progress on development issues has been made in trade negotiations as they crawl along. In spite of outrage at the high prices multinational pharmaceutical corporations were charging for anti-retrovirals against HIV/AIDS in developing countries, it took several years and continual international struggle to get lower prices accepted by allowing the sale of generic pharmaceuticals manufactured in one developing country for export to another. Yet the

action required only the application of clauses that already existed in relevant WTO agreements. The difficulties of getting principles of social justice applied in international trade are obvious. Justice normally is an afterthought, not a principle. For this reason, international rules and regulations that incorporate principles of justice and international concern should be developed.

Progress toward the four agenda items mentioned in the previous chapter requires action in many other areas as well as broader principles of international economic relations. Consistency itself is not easily achieved, let alone political support for applying principles of social justice. But social and economic challenges are as serious a threat as climate change.

We repeat that the economic and social situation in many counties is such that it breeds not so much terrorism itself as passive sympathy for it. It also makes ever greater numbers of people flee their countries at the risk of their lives by crossing the Mediterranean, the Adriatic, and the Caribbean. In the developed countries, new Berlin Walls are being erected, not to prevent people from leaving their countries of origin but to prevent them from entering the country of their choice. The pull of economic opportunity and the push of wars remain dominant factors in international migration.

We have mentioned in previous chapters the plight of millions of young people in Africa, the Middle East, Latin America, and Asia who see their job prospects diminished and who undergo the humiliation of rounds and rounds of refusals in the hunt for employment. We are moving into a world in which large numbers of people with little purchasing power are seen as superfluous, unimportant for the economic growth of the rest. When that point is reached, outbursts of serious social unrest are near. These can take many forms—like the sympathy for terrorist attacks or the notion that dying while committing a terrorist act is a source of pride. It is our hope that well before this point of no return is reached, governments will take many of the broader actions required, both nationally and internationally.

New international initiatives are needed in many ways to mobilize support for government actions along these lines. Already the MDGs provide an important example. The MDG goals, however, are partial and limited. In the longer run, much more will be required.

We see a longer-term need, under a UN umbrella, for launching some form of Global Social Justice Program to support broader development in poorer countries or regions. Such a global program could take several forms, such as the creation of regional or global contracts between wealthier and poorer countries. For example, in order to reduce economic migrants seeking employment illegally in industrialized countries, the latter would benefit from investing in sending countries to provide incentives for prospective migrants to remain

at home. We have a preference in the longer run for what we propose to call "Global Development Contracts" (GDCs) that would be negotiated and concluded by a future Economic and Environmental Security Council. More akin to the Security Council than to ECOSOC, this new institution would have an essential role to play in moving toward social justice as a worldwide objective. Poverty and gross inequalities anywhere are a threat to prosperity everywhere. All countries of the planet are therefore linked. A GDC would have a global and a national dimension and result in the implementation of a better and more equitable distribution of the benefits of growth at both the international and national levels. One cannot and should not exist without the other. The failed rhetorical experiments of the 1960s and 1970s would thus become reality.[8]

The advantages of such country-by-country development contracts over current international procedures would be the following:

• They would operate within an international frame of objectives and principles but be constructed and agreed to between the international community and individual countries, though possibly with regional groups playing a facilitating role.

• They would implement a development strategy that fully embodies the priorities of each developing country. The trade-off between the short and the long run, the acceptable changes in income distribution, and the minimum satisfaction of basic needs should be based on a consensus that would be internal to a particular developing country or region.

• They would build on a longer-term perspective that recognizes that development is a matter of decades and that many of the specifics of the required policies cannot be determined in advance.

• They would insist on development that requires not only stabilization and adjustment but also an explicit strategy in which private and public institutions can participate. The structural characteristics, institutions, and traditions of a developing country or region would play a significant role in determining the nature of the strategy to be employed and the mechanisms to implement it.

• They would require reciprocity in the sense of a guarantee in terms of international trade, access to markets, international investment, credits, and aid over an extended period.

Again, we are seeking to implement earlier rhetorical agreements tailored to individual countries. If there is to be more social justice, less terrorism, and less despair, the key is to create such components of global governance to make the globalizing world somewhat more civilized. Jan Tinbergen was consistent and persistent in calling for this and in identifying which major components of national governments were needed internationally: measures of taxation

and redistribution, controls to ensure global competition, and support for the weakest and poorest and those hit by human-made and natural disasters.[9] All of these would help increase the benefits of globalization over a broader spectrum while curbing its excesses.

One could also supplement these country-by-country contracts by initiatives focused on priority global problems. Economist Jean-François Rischard, the World Bank's vice-president for Europe from 1998 to 2005, argues in his book *High Noon: 20 Global Problems, 20 Years to Solve Them* for treating every global problem in a specific and different manner and if necessary by different decision-making bodies and constellations.[10] He advocates an issue-by-issue approach and setting up a network that combines representatives from government, civil society, and business for each issue. These "global issues networks" could come under the umbrella of United Nations or other international or regional organizations—indeed, modeled on the IPCC.

Another approach would be the creation of global funds, as already exists with the Global Fund to Fight AIDS, Tuberculosis, and Malaria. In *Common Wealth*, Jeffrey Sachs suggests additional global funds to meet the challenges of mitigating the impact of global warming on the environment, curbing population growth, meeting the need in developing countries for greater infrastructure, creating greater access to and improvements in the quality of education, building more community development, and creating a green revolution in Africa.[11] Others might be identified, but these would already be an impressive contribution.

Strengthening the UN's Intellectual Work

Our history has shown that at its best, the UN's intellectual work over past decades has made important and world-changing contributions. This reality should be better recognized by governments and the other two parts of the UN and should lead to more support for this side of the world organization's work. We hope our project will provide some raw material for such lobbyists.

But the UN's intellectual work should also be strengthened by sharpening its focus, strengthening its quality, ensuring its intellectual independence, and disseminating its findings more widely in order to influence policy and have impact. The highest priorities for such intellectual work lie in increasing attention to the five issues identified in the preceding chapter: promoting solidarity on a global scale, including narrowing global gaps and bridging cultural divides; enhancing human opportunities, including promoting human rights and implementing the MDGs; advancing the perennial quest for peace; tackling global warming and sustaining the world's ecosystem; and making progress

toward stronger and more effective global governance. These priorities on the intellectual agenda will go far toward strengthening global governance and responding to the ten global challenges we identified in chapter 13.

Each of the five items involves a complex research program that covers many cross-cutting issues. Mitigating or reversing global warming involves a wide range of ecological, economic, political, and social issues. Projections must be made about how these will affect people and countries in all regions of the world, and the actions required to alleviate and mitigate the consequences of global warming. And this is not the only environmental issue that threatens sustainability. Others, such as pollution of the renewable resources of water, soil, and air and the protection and renewal of the world's forests, require far more attention.

Strengthening solidarity on a global scale raises issues that have long been on the agenda but have too often been neglected in practice. But today, it is clearer than ever that these issues have practical consequences. Here the UN agendas for research require great sensitivity to the varying perspectives, values, and perceptions of people in different regions of the world. It is not surprising that a world organization with 192 member states has difficulties establishing priorities. With the changing balance in the world's economies, there is a great need for many changes in our approaches to understanding and culture. Although universities and research institutes worldwide have an important part to play in this, the UN's role in nurturing research and providing a forum for international interaction and debate remains critical. A reconfigured and motivated United Nations University could and should play a bigger role in shaping the world organization's research agenda.

Narrowing global gaps and reducing the extremes between the economic and social situation within different countries is a further step toward strengthening global solidarity where more focused UN research is required. As mentioned, this topic was highly important in the early years of the world organization, though as we have also emphasized the focus on decreasing the chasm in the distribution of the world's wealth faded during the 1970s and after. The topic should be brought back to the top of the agenda of research and action. The European Union's experience with policies that provide support for its poorer regions over the last three decades provides something of a model of how action taken to narrow gaps can be promoted within a broadly free-market model and with enlightened self-interest very much in the forefront of justifications. We expect ongoing experiences in China and India and other Asian countries to also provide relevant models. The UN needs to study these and tease out the international lessons.

The need to enhance opportunities for people—especially in the areas of

education and health—is becoming more urgent. Now that the MDGs have set a quantitative target for access to education, the question of education quality looms large. Similarly, the problems of providing access to health care are being compounded by rapid increases in costs. Preventive care is key, but prices are crucial. Several foundations are helping here, and similar support from other members of the Third UN is crucially important.

The quest for peace has generated much useful research since the end of the Cold War and is under way in institutions such as UNRISD and the World Institute for Development Economics and Research (WIDER) at the United Nations University and in universities and research institutes worldwide. Some of this research is multidisciplinary and probes the links between development patterns, domestic inequalities, and the likelihood of armed conflict. More sophisticated and imaginative research is required, including more careful documentation and analysis of situations where the UN has been involved in peacekeeping, peacebuilding, and peacemaking. Establishing the comparative advantage of various actors is essential, including that of the UN itself. More traditional areas of research also need attention, including the cost of war, the benefits of disarmament, and the cost of alternatives to conflict resolution and peacebuilding.

Our discussion of global governance demonstrates how much remains to be done—and how much can be done—in this most important and urgent domain. To carry out this agenda effectively and to make an impact, the United Nations should strengthen its mechanisms to ensure creative thinking and careful professional analysis. Proposals for UN reform have totally neglected the intellectual and analytical dimension of the UN's work, and specific measures are required to strengthen its capacity for research and analysis for the future.

The United Nations Intellectual History Project has identified a number of priorities for improving the world organization's research, analytical, and policy work:

• The UN should do more to foster an environment that encourages creative thinking, penetrating analysis, and policy-focused research of a high intellectual and critical quality. This has implications for recruitment and promotion. It is essential to hire high-quality staff; the UN's ability to hire such individuals will depend on more professional procedures in recruitment, appointment, promotion, and organization of responsibilities.

• Whenever the UN pursues a bold and forward-looking intellectual agenda, it faces the problem of not being able to please all member states. Often messages have been watered down to satisfy the lowest common denominator among

governments. The UN needs to seek more intellectual autonomy for its research and related publications. Gunnar Myrdal, the ECE's first executive secretary, said that the proudest achievement of his ten years at the helm of that regional UN body was the intellectual autonomy he negotiated for producing the annual economic overview. Some of the UN's best work has taken place when leaders have been liberated from the need to check documents with boards or donors before publication.

• There are various ways intellectual islands can be created to provide researchers with access to policymakers and protection from excessive control. Today, this may well require special "safety zones" within organizations—such as UNRISD, WIDER, and the UNDP's offices of human development and development studies. In such zones, serious work can go on in an environment free from the pressures of daily urgent matters and where controversy can be identified and analyzed rather than suppressed.

• The UN should seek alliances with many centers of expertise—in academia, think tanks, government policy units, and corporate research centers. Just as the UN is a world center for tying countries together, so it must also be a place to network outstanding thinking. That calls for very high levels of intellectual leadership.

• Governments need to provide more financial resources for UN research, analysis, and policy exploration as a high priority. The terms on which such finance is provided is crucial, not only to ensure availability but also to ensure sustained commitments without strings. Encouraging free thinking and the exploration of ideas and approaches is vital.

• The UN's intellectual agenda should be designed for impact. It should address international problems of real significance in ways that go to the heart of solutions.[12] Basic research is best done in universities, but many elements of applied research can and should be done by the Second UN.

• Strengthening the means to disseminate new ideas, analyses, and proposals is equally important. The UN's publicizing of high-visibility reports has sometimes been very impressive. At the same time, too many high-quality analyses languish on bookshelves or in filing cabinets. Discussion should take place not only in intergovernmental settings but also in capitals with governments and among such diverse constituencies as NGOs, businesses, the media, and members of civil society.

• An important institutional challenge is rethinking and improving professional relations between the United Nations and the Bretton Woods institutions in order to encourage better exchanges of ideas and experiences and a less skewed allocation of international resources. Since 1980, the donor community has channeled increasing funds to and through the Bretton Woods institutions and has

increasingly followed their lead in terms of policy and action, both internationally and at the country level. This emphasis on international financial institutions has often led to neglect of UN organizations and their ideas, policies, and approaches. Our assessment shows the many ways that UN contributions have been neglected in key areas where the policies of the Bretton Woods institutions were too narrow and misguided or were wrong. In addition, the UN has provided important economic ideas in areas where the Bretton Woods institutions were not active. The need now is to achieve a better balance between the World Bank, the IMF, and the UN in contributing to policy leadership.

Narrowing the Gaps between Rhetoric and Reality: Mobilizing the Three UNs

"Rhetoric" in the United Nations is often a dirty world that is used to dismiss the endless speeches of government representatives as no more than theater designed mainly for consumption by other members of the diplomatic corps and for media at home rather than for any practical impact or hopes of implementation. Resolutions at the end of debates and calls for action in reports of UN organizations and funds are often treated in the same way.

Though some rhetoric may often be no more than hot air, there are many valuable forms of UN rhetoric, especially those when representatives of the world's majority are calling for action and arrangements to deal with longstanding injustices and inequalities and other problems. Opposition to such calls often takes the form of a visceral dismissal of what is termed "mere rhetoric" when in fact many such proposals are thoughtful efforts to tackle serious problems that merit serious debate.

Our history has identified many examples when such rhetoric subsequently led to action: for a special fund to provide concessional finance for poor countries in the 1950s; for faster economic growth in the 1960s; for redistribution with growth and combining environmental and development in the 1970s; for debt relief and new forms of adjustment in the 1980s; and for strengthening the UN's institutions for human rights in the 1990s.

Our historical assessment has demonstrated that visionary rhetoric often breaks new ground and then becomes the new middle ground. Often rhetorical calls are fully in line with the UN Charter or with human rights standards but are unacceptable to one or more of the major powers or to a regional or ideological group. Such calls may not be politically popular enough to gather support, but it is hardly fair to treat them all as no more than empty words.

The dramatic change in attitudes toward global warming over the last two decades, especially over the last five years, illustrates why tenacity and vision are

required. The machinery of the World Meteorological Organization and UNEP was first used to create and thus to give legitimacy to the IPCC. Then this panel, consisting of scientists who represented governments and interacted with UN professionals and scientists and other experts around the world, gave authority to a range of findings about global warming, drawing on the First, Second, and Third UNs. Only recently have the messages begun to gain traction.

The international media has played a vital part by bringing issues to wider publics and often by generating a groundswell of support for action by raising questions about the validity of justifications of and rationalizations for delay. The process of increasing attention for climate change has been far from a straightforward advance along a smooth road. Continual monitoring has been an important part of advances, as has a succession of well-promoted reports that have pointed to a worsening situation and the shortage of effective action. One can confidently expect that the next stage of interactions among international professionals, activists, and the media will produce the result that some countries will successfully take effective action. This evidence will then be used to shame other countries into more serious commitments.

This approach can be applied to the other high-priority areas of global governance. Some of this potential is already visible in the support for actions that will lead to realizing the MDGs. Parts of all three UNs have been involved in the mobilization of support, though inevitably with great variations of commitment and action at different times and places. Here also the media has played a crucial part, often helped by celebrities and other media-savvy personalities.

However, experience with the MDGs makes clear some of the risks and challenges in mobilizing widespread support for global change. Mobilization of public opinion almost always involves simplification of the objectives, the means, and the political processes required for moving toward agreed-upon goals. Industrialized countries and the media almost inevitably overplay the provision of aid as the key condition for success and invariably overplay political weakness and corruption in developing countries as the main reasons for failure. Sensationalism, nationalist perspectives, and other imbalances in the media reinforce these misrepresentations.

Earlier we mentioned that optimism is a prerequisite for such international action. Few can remain immune to the depressing gaps between rhetoric and reality. We take heart from the insight of our colleague Lourdes Arizpe:

> Someone once said that the United Nations is a dream managed by bureaucrats. I would correct that by saying that it has become a bureaucracy managed by dreamers. Certainly you have to be a dreamer to work in the United Nations with conviction. It is only if you have this sense of mission that you

can withstand the constant battering by governments who are afraid that the United Nations will become a world government. . . . So in the end, someone who works in the United Nations has to be a magician of ideas, because working for the United Nations is like working for a government in which all the political parties are in power at the same time. You have to be a magician of ideas in order to try and find that particular idea around which you can build the greatest consensus.[13]

All three United Nations—or at least important players in each—need to contribute in several ways. First, all three UNs can recognize the roles played by the others and reach out where appropriate to encourage and help the others play their roles more effectively. The First and the Second UNs, in particular, can provide information about proposed action and progress, which often can help the Third UN mobilize support.

Next, the Second UN can make much better use of the Third UN, as has been the case with the IPCC. It is crucial to draw on analysts and intellectuals in developing and developed countries who have first-hand knowledge of how international policy is having an impact on the ground.

Third, the Second UN should maintain a clear focus on the vision of the Charter and careful analysis of key global problems and potential solutions. The dangers of self-censorship, of restricting analysis to the accepted and acceptable, of holding back conclusions are always present. There is no place for political correctness in the arena of ideas.

Fourth, however, it is important to recognize that close collaboration between the three UNs is often neither possible nor even desirable. Part of the obligations of members of the Second UN—which are specified in their oath of office—is to remain true to Charter principles, which require that they remain autonomous from governments or any other external authority. Part of the strength of NGOs is putting pressure on governments and secretariats to act, and often this involves speaking out publicly and embarrassing officials in the process. But other parts of the Third UN, especially knowledgeable academics and other experts, can be drawn upon more often to provide creative thinking and new ideas.

Fifth, all three UNs should explore ways to combine international ideas and ideals with political and economic interests of governments. This skill has been part of the experience of many of the leading UN figures we interviewed. Jan Pronk spoke of the importance of ideas but also of the need to take account of the power and economic realities of the day, to make a combination between what is feasible and what needs to be done. He quoted his mentor, Jan Tinbergen: "I want to change the reality, but my time horizon is the next five years.

I won't set targets for twenty years from now. They would be just theoretical aims, and I wouldn't know how to accomplish them."[14]

Ultimately the United Nations will succeed or fail on the strength of its willingness to generate ideas about and lead in the implementation of the original vision of peace, agreement through negotiations, human rights, and human welfare. This vision must never be lost.

Conclusion

As we come to the end of this project, we feel compelled to return to our starting point—the UNs intellectual contributions since 1945. We summarize them here:

- Ideas embodied in analysis, policies, and action have often been among the UN's most important achievements.
- Intellectual contributions, embodied in the UN's leadership and operations in the economic and social arena, have had more impact and success than is often acknowledged or realized, including setting paths that others have followed.
- Ideas and innovations in the arena of preventive diplomacy and peacekeeping have also had an important impact in theory and in practice.
- Since the end of the Cold War, the UN's work and leadership in the arenas of peace, sovereignty, development, and human rights have increasingly been brought together and become more integrated intellectually, especially within the concepts of human security and human development.
- The urgent and inescapable international challenges of the future underline the importance of UN reform and the importance of strengthening the institution's capacities for the twenty-first century.

When it was awarding the 2001 Nobel Prize for Peace to the United Nations and its Secretary-General, the Nobel Committee stated why ideas and people and the UN as an institution with both types of resources matter: "Today the Organization is at the forefront of efforts to achieve peace and security in the world, and of the international mobilization aimed at meeting the world's economic, social and environmental challenges. . . . The only negotiable route to global peace and cooperation goes by way of the United Nations."[15]

We rest our case.

Notes

Introduction

1. Edward Mason and Robert Asher, *The World Bank since Bretton Woods* (Washington, D.C.: Brookings Institution, 1973); and Devesh Kapur, John P. Lewis, and Richard Webb, *The World Bank: Its First Half Century*, vol. 1, *History* (Washington, D.C.: Brookings Institution, 1997) and vol. 2, *Perspectives*, especially Nicholas Stern with Francisco Ferreira, "The World Bank as 'Intellectual Actor,'" 523–609. For the IMF, see Margaret Garritsen de Vries, *The International Monetary Fund, 1945–1965: Twenty Years of International Monetary Cooperation* (Washington, D.C.: IMF, 1969); Margaret Garritsen de Vries, *The International Monetary Fund, 1966–1971: The System Under Stress* (Washington, D.C.: IMF, 1976); Margaret Garritsen de Vries, *The International Monetary Fund, 1972–1978: Cooperation on Trial* (Washington, D.C.: IMF, 1985); and James M. Boughton, *Silent Revolution: The International Monetary Fund, 1979–1989* (Washington, D.C.: IMF, 2001). See also Norman K. Humphreys, ed., *Historical Dictionary of the IMF* (Washington, D.C.: IMF, 2000).

2. UNIHP, *The Complete Oral History Transcripts from UN Voices*, CD-ROM (New York: UNIHP, 2007).

3. Thomas G. Weiss and Sam Daws, eds., *The Oxford Handbook on the United Nations* (Oxford: Oxford University Press, 2007).

4. Stefan Zweig, *The World of Yesterday* (Lincoln: University of Nebraska Press, 1964); and Stefan Zweig, *Tagebucher* (Frankfurt: S. Fischer Verlag, 1984).

5. An important exception are some of the biographical accounts of life in the UN. See Brian Urquhart, *Hammarskjöld* (New York: W. W. Norton & Company, 1994); Brian Urquhart, *Ralph Bunche: An American Odyssey* (New York: W. W. Norton & Company, 1998); Brian Urquhart, *A Life in Peace and War* (New York: Harper and Row, 1987); Margaret Joan Anstee, *Never Learn to Type: A Woman at the United Nations* (Chichester, West Sussex: John Wiley and Sons, 2003); and Boutros Boutros-Ghali, *Unvanquished: A U.S.-U.N. Saga* (New York: Random House, 1999). The human perspective of a wider range of UN staff members is provided in Wilfred Grey, *UN Jigsaw* (New York: Vantage Press, 2000).

6. For more details, see the UNIHP Web site at www.unhistory.org.

7. Richard Jolly, Louis Emmerij, and Thomas G. Weiss, *The Power of UN Ideas: Lessons from the First Sixty Years* (New York: UNIHP, 2005), also available in Spanish.

8. Since UNIHP started, some histories have been published, including D. John

Shaw, *The UN World Food Programme and the Development of Food Aid* (Houndmills, Basingstoke, UK: Palgrave Macmillan, 2001); and Craig N. Murphy, *The United Nations Development Programme: A Better Way?* (Cambridge: Cambridge University Press, 2006). Histories are also under way at such institutions as the ILO, UNESCO, and the WHO. Details of these and other related publications are found on the UNIHP Web site. Interested readers may also wish to consult the close to fifty titles in the Global Institutions Series, edited by Thomas G. Weiss and Rorden Wilkinson and published by Routledge.

1. Overview

The full source for the epigraph for Part 1 is Winston Churchill, "The Soviet Danger: The Iron Curtain," Fulton, Missouri, 5 March 1946, quoted in David Cannadine, ed., *Blood Toil, Tears and Sweat: The Speeches of Winston Churchill* (Boston: Houghton Mifflin, 1989), 298.

1. See, for example, Charles Kindelberger, *The World in Depression 1929–39,* 2nd ed. (Berkeley: University of California Press, 1986); and Robert Gilpin, *War and Change in World Politics* (Princeton, N.J.: Princeton University Press, 1981).

2. "Truman's Inaugural Address, January 20, 1949," available at http://www.truman-library.org/whistlestop/50yr_archive/inagural20jan1949.htm.

3. United Nations, *National and International Measures for Full Employment* (New York: United Nations, 1949); United Nations, *Measures for the Economic Development of Under-Developed Countries* (New York: United Nations, 1951); and United Nations, *Measures for International Economic Stability* (New York: United Nations, 1951).

4. Hans Singer, "The Distribution of Gains between Investing and Borrowing Countries," *American Economic Review* 40, no. 2 (1950): 473–485. A description of how Singer later updated his thinking to include technology in this key area of his work is found in D. John Shaw, *Sir Hans Singer: The Life and Work of a Development Economist* (New York: Palgrave Macmillan, 2002), 49–71.

5. Transcript of oral history interview with Hans W. Singer, in *The Complete Oral History Transcripts from UN Voices,* CD-ROM (New York: UNIHP, 2007), 30.

6. League of Nations, Economic, Financial, and Transit Dept., *Industrialization and Foreign Trade* (New York: League of Nations), 154–167, 116–121.

7. United Nations, *Post-War Price Relations in Trade between Under-Developed and Industrialized Countries* (Lake Success, N.Y.: United Nations, 1949).

8. Raúl Prebisch, *The Economic Development of Latin America and Its Principal Problems* (New York: United Nations, 1950).

9. ILO, *Employment, Growth, and Basic Needs: A One-World Problem* (Geneva: ILO, 1976).

10. ILO, *Employment, Incomes, and Equity: A Strategy for Increasing Productive Employment in Kenya* (Geneva: ILO, 1972). See especially chapter 13 and technical paper 22.

11. For a recent overview article with special reference to Latin America, see Victor

Tokman, "The Informal Economy, Insecurity, and Social Cohesion in Latin America," *International Labour Review* 146, nos. 1–2 (2007): 81–107.

12. For a summary of research on the effects of IMF programs during the period 1973–1994, see James Raymond Vreeland, *The International Monetary Fund: Politics of Conditional Lending* (London: Routledge, 2007). For an IMF rebuttal, see Graham Hacche, "A Non-Definitive Guide to the IMF: A Review Article," *World Economics* 8, no. 2 (2007): 97–118.

13. See John Williamson, *Latin-American Adjustment: How Much Has Happened?* (Washington, D.C.: Institute of International Economics, 1990); and John Williamson, "The Washington Consensus Revisited," in *Economic and Social Development into the XXI Century*, ed. Louis Emmerij (Baltimore: Johns Hopkins University Press, 1997), 48–61.

14. UNICEF, *Adjustment with a Human Face* (Oxford: Clarendon Press, 1987).

15. Boutros Boutros-Ghali, *An Agenda for Peace* (New York: United Nations, 1992).

16. Robert Jenkins, *Peacebuilding and the Peacebuilding Commission* (London: Routledge, forthcoming).

17. Thomas G. Weiss and Anthony Jennings, *More for the Least? Prospects for Poorest Countries in the Eighties* (Lexington, Mass.: Lexington Books, 1983).

18. UNCTAD, *Trade and Development Report* (Geneva: UNCTAD, 1987).

19. "Shattered balance sheets" is the language of Nigel Lawson, UK chancellor of the exchequer, quoted in John Toye and Richard Toye, *The UN and Global Political Economy: Trade, Finance, and Development* (Bloomington: Indiana University Press, 2004), 260. Toye and Toye argue that "the paramount concern of the West was preserving the solvency of the commercial banks that had loaned so carelessly" (260).

20. Paul Collier, *The Bottom Billion: Why the Poorest Countries Are Failing and What Can Be Done about It* (Oxford: Oxford University Press, 2007).

21. *Delivering as One: The Report of the Secretary-General's High-level Panel* (New York: UN, 2006).

22. Thomas G. Weiss, Tatiana Carayannis, Louis Emmerij, and Richard Jolly, *UN Voices: The Struggle for Development and Social Justice* (Bloomington: Indiana University Press, 2005), 407.

2. The Three UNs and Their Impact

1. Louis Emmerij, Richard Jolly, and Thomas G. Weiss, *Ahead of the Curve? UN Ideas and Global Challenges* (Bloomington: Indiana University Press, 2001), 205.

2. Inis L. Claude, Jr., *Swords into Plowshares: The Problems and Prospects of International Organization* (New York: Random House, 1956); and Inis L. Claude, Jr., "Peace and Security: Prospective Roles for the Two United Nations," *Global Governance* 2, no. 3 (1996): 289–298.

3. Thomas G. Weiss, Tatiana Carayannis, and Richard Jolly, "The Third United Nations," *Global Governance* 15, no. 1 (2009), 123–142.

4. John Maynard Keynes, *The General Theory of Employment, Interest, and Money* (New York: Harcourt Brace Jovanovich, 1964), viii.

5. Commission on International Development, *Partners in Development* (New York: Praeger, 1969); Independent Commission on International Development Issues, *North-South: A Programme for Survival* (London: Pan Books, 1980); W. Brandt, *Common Crisis—North-South—Co-operation for World Recovery* (Cambridge, Mass.: MIT Press, 1983); Independent Commission on Disarmament and Security Issues, *Common Security: A Blueprint for Survival* (New York: Simon & Schuster, 1982); World Commission on Environment and Development, *Our Common Future* (Oxford: Oxford University Press, 1987); Independent Commission on International Humanitarian Issues, *Winning the Human Race?* (London: Zed Books, 1988); South Commission, *The Challenge to the South* (Oxford: Oxford University Press, 1990); Commission on Global Governance, *Our Global Neighbourhood* (Oxford: Oxford University Press, 1995); Independent Commission on Intervention and State Sovereignty, *The Responsibility to Protect* (Ottawa: ICISS, 2001); Commission on Human Security, *Human Security Now* (New York: Commission on Human Security, 2003). See also High-level Panel on Threats, Challenges and Change, *A More Secure World: Our Shared Responsibility* (New York: UN, 2004); and Kofi Annan, *In Larger Freedom: Towards Development, Security and Human Rights for All* (New York: UN, 2005).

6. We are grateful to Margaret Joan Anstee for suggesting this alliteration.

7. Weiss, Carayannis, and Jolly, "The Third United Nations."

8. Thant Myint-U and Amy Scott, *The UN Secretariat: A Brief History (1945–2006)* (New York: International Peace Academy, 2007), 126–128.

9. For a discussion, see Morten Bøås and Desmond McNeill, *Global Institutions and Development: Framing the World?* (London: Routledge, 2004).

10. Judith Goldstein and Robert O. Keohane, eds., *Ideas and Foreign Policy* (Ithaca, N.Y.: Cornell University Press, 1993); Kathryn Sikkink, *Ideas and Institutions: Developmentalism in Argentina and Brazil* (Ithaca, N.Y.: Cornell University Press, 1991).

11. Peter M. Haas, "Introduction: Epistemic Communities and International Policy Coordination," *International Organization* 46, no. 1 (1992): 1–36; Peter M. Haas, Robert O. Keohane, and Marc A. Levy, eds., *Institutions for the Earth: Sources of Effective International Environmental Protection* (Cambridge, Mass.: MIT Press, 1992); Peter A. Hall, ed., *The Political Power of Economic Ideas: Keynesianism across Nations* (Princeton, N.J.: Princeton University Press, 1989); Ernst B. Haas, *When Knowledge Is Power: Three Models of Change in International Organizations* (Los Angeles: University of California Press, 1994); Peter M. Haas and Ernst B. Haas, "Learning to Learn: Improving International Governance," *Global Governance* 1, no. 3 (1995): 55–284; and Kathryn Sikkink, *Activists beyond Borders: Advocacy Networks in International Politics* (Ithaca, N.Y.: Cornell University Press, 1998).

12. Thomas S. Kuhn, *The Structure of Scientific Revolutions,* 2nd ed. (Chicago: University of Chicago Press, 1970).

13. Alexander Wendt, *Social Theory of International Politics* (Cambridge: Cambridge University Press, 1999); John G. Ruggie, *Constructing the World Polity* (New York: Routledge, 1998).

14. See Robert W. Cox, ed., *The New Realism: Perspectives on Multilateralism and World*

Order (New York: St. Martin's, 1997); Robert W. Cox with Timothy J. Sinclair, *Approaches to World Order* (Cambridge: Cambridge University Press, 1996); Quentin Hoare and Geoffrey N. Smith, eds., *Selections from the Prison Notebooks of Antonio Gramsci*, trans. Quentin Hoare and Geoffrey N. Smith (London: Lawrence and Wishart, 1971).

15. Ngaire Woods, "Economic Ideas and International Relations: Beyond Rational Neglect," *International Studies Quarterly* 39 (1995): 164.

16. Emmerij, Jolly, and Weiss, *Ahead of the Curve?* 8–10.

17. Quentin E. Skinner, "Meaning and Understanding in the History of Ideas," *History and Theory* 8 (1969): 42.

18. Woods, "Economic Ideas and International Relations," 168.

19. Frederick Cooper and Randall Packard, "Introduction," in *International Development and the Social Sciences: Essays on the History and Politics of Knowledge*, ed. Frederick Cooper and Randall Packard (Berkeley: University of California Press, 1997), 17.

20. See Ramesh Thakur, ed., *What Is Equitable Geographic Representation in the Twenty-First Century?* (Tokyo: UN University, 1999).

21. Arthur O. Lovejoy, *The Great Chain of Being* (New York: Torchbook, 1960).

22. See Albert Yee, "The Causal Effects of Ideas on Policies," *International Organization* 50, no. 1 (1996): 69–108.

23. Quoted in Mahbub ul Haq, *Reflections on Human Development* (New York: Oxford University Press, 1995), 204.

24. Michael Ward, *Quantifying the World: UN Contributions to Statistics* (Bloomington: Indiana University Press, 2004), 2.

25. By the year 2000, 138 countries had brought infant mortality to below 120 per thousand and 124 countries had raised life expectancy to sixty years or more, two of the goals set in 1980. A full assessment of the achievements in relation to the fifty goals are found in "The Record of Performance," chapter 10 of *UN Contributions to Development Thinking and Practice*, by Richard Jolly, Louis Emmerij, Dharam Ghai, and Frédéric Lapeyre (Bloomington: Indiana University Press, 2004).

26. Morten Bøas and Desmond McNeill, "Introduction: Power and Ideas in Multilateral Institutions: Towards an Interpretive Framework," in *Global Institutions and Development: Framing the World?* ed. Morten Bøas and Desmond McNeill (London: Routledge, 2003), 1–12.

27. Desmond McNeill, "The Power of Moral Authority in International Development Agencies: With Special Reference to the World Bank and UNDP," paper presented at a workshop at the Institute of Social Studies, The Hague, 16 October 2007.

28. Thomas G. Weiss, Tatiana Carayannis, Louis Emmerij, and Richard Jolly, *UN Voices: The Struggle for Development and Social Justice* (Bloomington: Indiana University Press, 2005), 420.

29. Stephen D. Krasner, "Introduction," in *International Regimes*, ed. Stephen D. Krasner (Ithaca, N.Y.: Cornell University Press, 1983), 1.

30. The Soviet member who was invited to attend the first meeting of the Nuclear Commission, the forerunner to the Statistical Commission, turned up almost a week late, close to the end of the meeting. Ward, *Quantifying the World*, 38.

31. For a trenchant analysis, see Robert Wade, "Japan, the World Bank and the Art of Paradigm Maintenance: The East Asian Miracle in Political Perspective," *New Left Review* I/217 (1996). For a critique from a former insider, see Joseph Stiglitz, *Globalization and Its Discontents* (New York: Norton, 2003).

32. In the late 1950s, Barbara Ward identified five world-changing ideas: nationalism, industrialism, colonialism, communism, and internationalism. See Ward, *Five Ideas That Changed the World* (New York: W. W. Norton & Company, 1959).

3. Human Rights for All

The full source for the epigraph for Part 2 is Howard Zinn, *You Can't Be Neutral on a Moving Train: A Personal History of Our Times* (Boston: Beacon Press, 1995), 208.

1. Bertrand G. Ramcharan, "Norms and Machinery," in *The Oxford Handbook on the United Nations,* ed. Thomas G. Weiss and Sam Daws (Oxford: Oxford University Press, 2007), 441.

2. Roger Normand and Sarah Zaidi, *Human Rights at the UN: The Political History of Universal Justice* (Bloomington: Indiana University Press, 2008). Normand and Zaidi point out that it was the ILO that made the first institutional attempt to provide a holistic vision of human rights, including the protection of both civil and political rights and economic and social rights. This attempt is embedded in the Philadelphia Declaration, adopted in May 1944 at the 26th Annual Conference of the ILO.

3. Ibid., 8 and xiii.

4. Ibid., 2.

5. Thomas G. Weiss, Tatiana Carayannis, Louis Emmerij, and Richard Jolly, *UN Voices: The Struggle for Development and Social Justice* (Bloomington: Indiana University Press, 2005), 408.

6. Normand and Zaidi, *Human Rights at the UN,* Churchill quoted on 83, Roosevelt quoted on 88, and Dumbarton Oaks Charter quoted on 113.

7. Ibid., 33, 117–117.

8. See Stephen C. Schlesinger, *Act of Creation: The Founding of the United Nations. A Story of Superpowers, Secret Agents, Wartime Allies and Enemies and Their Quest for a Peaceful World* (Boulder, Colo.: Westview Press, 2003), 122.

9. Quoted in William Korey, *NGOs and the Universal Declaration of Human Rights: "A Curious Grapevine"* (New York: St. Martin's Press, 1998), 9.

10. Normand and Zaidi, *Human Rights at the UN,* 200–201.

11. Weiss, Carayannis, Emmerij, and Jolly, *UN Voices,* 409.

12. Ramcharan, "Norms and Machinery," 439.

13. Charlotte Bunch, "Women and Gender," in *The Oxford Handbook on the United Nations,* ed. Thomas G. Weiss and Sam Daws (Oxford: Oxford University Press, 2007), 499.

14. Devaki Jain, *Women, Development, and the UN: A Sixty-Year Quest for Equality and Justice* (Bloomington: Indiana University Press, 2006).

15. Normand and Zaidi, *Human Rights at the UN,* 301–302 and 309.

16. Ibid., 303.

17. Philip Alston, "Making Space for New Human Rights: The Case of the Right to Development," *Harvard Human Rights Yearbook* 1 (1988): 21

18. Susan Marks, "Nightmare and Noble Dream: The World Conference on Human Rights," *Cambridge Law Journal* (1994): 54–62.

19. Cassin's proposal had been for someone—he suggested the title of "attorney-general"—who could support an aggrieved individual against a respondent state. Normand and Zaidi, *Human Rights at the UN*, 174.

20. This account draws heavily on Andrew Clapham, "Creating the High Commissioner for Human Rights: The Outside Story," *European Journal of International Law* 5 (1994): 556–568.

21. Sean MacBride, "The Promises of the Human Rights Year," *Journal of the International Commission of Jurists* 9 (1968): i–ii.

22. "High Commissioner for the Promotion and Protection of All Human Rights," General Assembly resolution 48/141, 20 December 1993.

23. Philip Alston, "The UN's Human Rights Record: From San Francisco to Vienna and Beyond," *Human Rights Quarterly* 16, no. 2 (1994): 375–390.

24. Ramcharan, "Norms and Machinery," 451.

25. High-level Panel on Threats, Challenges and Change, *A More Secure World: Our Shared Responsibility* (New York: United Nations, 2004), 89.

26. Kofi Annan, *In Larger Freedom: Towards Development, Security and Human Rights for All* (New York: UN, 2005), 65.

27. *2005 World Summit Outcome*, General Assembly document A/60/L.1, 15 September 2005, paragraph 160.

28. Yvonne Terlinghen, "The Human Rights Council: A New Era in UN Human Rights Work?" *Ethics & International Affairs* 21, no. 2 (2007): 167–178.

29. Nico Schrijver, "The UN Human Rights Council: A New 'Society of the Committed' or Just Old Wine in New Bottles?" *Leiden Journal of International Law* 20, no. 4 (2007): 809.

30. Ramcharan, "Norms and Machinery," 451.

31. Human Rights Watch, "UN: Rights Council Ends First Year with Much to Do," *Human Rights News*, 19 June 2007, available at http://www.hrw.org/english/docs/2007/06/18/global16208.htm (accessed 30 September 2008).

32. Quoted in James Traub, *The Best Intentions: Kofi Annan and the UN in the Era of American World Power* (New York: Farrar, Straus and Giroux, 2006), 227.

33. *2005 World Summit Outcome*, paragraph 124.

34. Office of the High Commissioner for Human Rights, "Funding and Budget," available online at http://www.ohchr.org/EN/AboutUs/Pages/FundingBudget.aspx (accessed 30 September 2008).

35. International Commission on Intervention and State Sovereignty, *The Responsibility to Protect* (Ottawa: ICISS, 2001).

36. Kofi A. Annan, *The Question of Intervention: Statements by the Secretary-General* (New York: UN, 1999), 7.

37. See Program in Law and Public Affairs, *The Princeton Principles on Universal Jurisdiction* (Princeton, N.J.: Princeton University, 2001); Council on Foreign Relations,

Toward an International Criminal Court? (New York: Council on Foreign Relations, 1999); and Steven R. Ratner and James L. Bischoff, eds., *International War Crimes Trials: Making a Difference?* (Austin: University of Texas Law School, 2004).

38. Richard Goldstone, "International Criminal Court and Ad Hoc Tribunals," in *The Oxford Handbook on the United Nations,* ed. Thomas G. Weiss and Sam Daws (Oxford: Oxford University Press, 2007), 463–478. See also Richard Goldstone and Adam Smith, *International Judicial Institutions: The Architecture of International Justice at Home and Abroad* (London: Routledge, 2008).

39. Fanny Benedetti and John L. Washburn, "Drafting the International Criminal Court Treaty," *Global Governance* 5, no. 1 (1999): 1–38.

40. Teresa Whitfield, *Friends Indeed? The United Nations, Groups of Friends, and the Resolution of Conflict* (Washington, D.C.: US Institute of Peace, 2007), 9 and 2.

4. Gender

1. Devaki Jain, *Women, Development, and the UN: A Sixty-Year Quest for Equality and Justice* (Bloomington: Indiana University Press, 2005), 12.

2. Ibid., 79.

3. Ibid., 1–2, 4.

4. Quoted in ibid., 17.

5. Ibid., 17–18.

6. Ibid., 31.

7. Ibid., 46.

8. Ibid., 47.

9. Peg Snyder quoted in Thomas G. Weiss, Tatiana Carayannis, Louis Emmerij, and Richard Jolly, *UN Voices: The Struggle for Development and Social Justice* (Bloomington: Indiana University Press, 2005), 104–105.

10. Margaret Snyder, *African Women and Development: A History* (Atlantic Highlands, N.J.: Zed Books, 1995).

11. Jain, *Women, Development, and the UN,* 99.

12. René Maheu quoted in ibid., 64.

13. Esther Boserup, *Women's Role in Economic Development* (New York: St. Martin's Press, 1970).

14. Jain, *Women, Development, and the UN,* 52.

15. Ibid., 52–53, quote on 52.

16. Irene Tinker quoted in ibid., 35.

17. Ibid., 43, 45.

18. Ibid., 71.

19. Ibid., 94.

20. Ibid., 80.

21. Ibid., 86.

22. Lourdes Arizpe quoted in Weiss, Carayannis, Emmerij, and Jolly, *UN Voices,* 412–413.

23. Noeleen Heyzer quoted in ibid., 415.

24. Jain, *Women, Development, and the UN*, 100.

25. The ECA never abandoned the Lagos Plan of Action and in 1989 drew on it to provide a comprehensive and credible alternative to structural adjustment programs. The African Alternative Framework called for "adjustment with transformation," which argued for a reduction in Africa's reliance on external trade and financing, promotion of food self-sufficiency, and greater popular participation in economic decision making.

26. Jain, *Women, Development, and the UN*, 104.

27. United Nations, *World's Women 1970–1990: Trends and Statistics* (New York: UN, 1991), 95ff. For a full description of this report, see Michael Ward, *Quantifying the World: UN Contributions to Statistics* (Bloomington: Indiana University Press, 2004), 173–187. Joann Vanek of the UN Statistical Office played a leading role in UNSO's work on women and gender.

28. Nilüfer Cagatay, Caren Grown, and Aide Santiago quoted in Jain, *Women, Development, and the UN*, 118.

29. Peg Snyder quoted in ibid., 119.

30. Ibid., 96–97.

31. Amartya Sen and Caren Grown quoted in ibid., 80.

32. Ibid., 134.

33. Ibid., 135.

34. Cecile Jackson quoted in ibid., 108.

35. UNDP, *Human Development Report 1995: Gender and Human Development* (New York: Oxford University Press, 1995), 97–98.

36. Ibid., 5–6.

37. Jain, *Women, Development, and the UN*, 145.

38. Ibid., 41.

39. Noeleen Heyzer quoted in Weiss, Carayannis, Emmerij, and Jolly, *UN Voices*, 416.

40. Jain, *Women, Development, and the UN*, 148.

41. Ibid., 158–159.

42. Ibid., 165.

43. Ibid.

44. Ibid.

45. Ibid., 166.

46. Ibid.

47. Ibid., 167.

48. Lourdes Arizpe quoted in ibid.

49. Ibid., 168.

50. Ibid. See Kum-Kum Bhavnani, John Foran, and Priya Kurian, eds., *Feminist Futures: Re-Imagining Women, Culture and Development* (London: Zed Books, 2003).

51. Ibid.

5. Development Goals

1. W. Arthur Lewis, *The Theory of Economic Growth* (London: Allen and Unwin, 1955).

2. Roy F. Harrod and Evsey D. Domar independently developed a model of economic growth in 1948 that later came to be known as the Harrod-Domar model. The model, which relates savings, investments, and economic growth, builds upon Keynes's theory and theorizes about the conditions under which growth is possible at a steady and sustained rate.

3. Arturo Escobar, *Encountering Development: The Making and Unmaking of the Third World* (Princeton, N.J.: Princeton University Press, 1995).

4. For an overview of those doctrines, see Richard Jolly, Louis Emmerij, Dharam Ghai, and Frédéric Lapeyre, *UN Contributions to Development Thinking and Practice* (Bloomington: Indiana University Press, 2004), 49–73.

5. Raúl Prebisch, *The Economic Development of Latin America and Its Principal Problems* (New York: United Nations, 1950).

6. Fernando Henrique Cardoso and Enzo Faletto, *Dependency and Development in Latin America* (Berkeley: University of California Press, 1979).

7. H. W. Arndt, *Economic Development: The History of an Idea* (Chicago: University of Chicago Press, 1987).

8. See Jolly, Emmerij, Ghai, and Lapeyre, *UN Contributions,* in particular chapter 10.

9. Ibid., 247–275.

10. See Dani Rodrik, *One Economics, Many Recipes: Globalization, Institutions and Economic Growth* (Princeton, N.J.: Princeton University Press, 2007).

11. UNRISD, *The Quest for a Unified Approach to Development* (Geneva: United Nations, 1980).

12. Albert H. Maslow, "A Theory of Human Motivation," *Psychological Review* 50, no. 3 (1942): 370–396.

13. For more about the Bariloche Project, see Amilcan O. Herrera, *Catastrophe O Nueva Sociedad: Modelo Mundial Latinoamericano* (Buenos Aires, 1976).

14. For more on the basic needs approach, see two other books in the UNIHP series: Louis Emmerij, Richard Jolly, and Thomas G. Weiss, *Ahead of the Curve? UN Ideas and Global Challenges* (Bloomington: Indiana University Press, 2001), 60–79; and Jolly, Emmerij, Ghai, and Lapeyre, *UN Contributions,* 112–121.

15. On the ILO and Kenya, see ILO, *Employment, Incomes, and Equality: A Strategy for Increasing Productive Employment in Kenya* (Geneva: ILO, 1972). On the work of the World Bank, see Hollis Chenery et al., *Redistribution with Growth: Policies to Improve Income Distribution in Developing Countries in the Context of Economic Growth* (London: Oxford University Press, 1974). The latter was a joint study by the Development Research Center of the World Bank and the Institute of Development Studies at the University of Sussex and was originally suggested by Dudley Seers, based on his ILO experience.

16. UNESCO, *Our Creative Diversity* (Paris: UNESCO, 1995), 15.

17. Eisuke Sakakibara, "Globalization amid Diversity," in *Economic and Social Development into the XXI Century,* ed. Louis Emmerij (Baltimore: Johns Hopkins University Press, 1997), 41–47.

18. See Mark Weisbrot, Robert Naiman, and Joyce Kim, *The Emperor Has No Growth:*

Declining Economic Growth Rates in the Era of Globalization (Washington, D.C.: Center for Economic and Policy Research, 2001).

19. Weiss, Carayannis, Emmerij, and Jolly, *UN Voices,* 272.

20. Council of Europe, *In from the Margins* (Strasbourg: Council of Europe, 1996), 9.

21. Nancy Birdsall, "Lessons from Japan," in *Economic and Social Development into the XXI Century,* ed. Louis Emmerij (Baltimore: Johns Hopkins University Press, 1997), 394–399.

22. This section is based on Yves Berthelot, ed., *Unity and Diversity in Development Ideas: Perspectives from the UN Regional Commissions* (Bloomington: Indiana University Press, 2004).

23. The debate took place in Bangkok in February 2000 between Secretary-General Rubens Ricupero of UNCTAD and Executive Secretaries K. Y. Amoako, ECA; Yves Berthelot, ECE; Jose Antonio Ocampo, ECLAC; Adrianus Moy, ESCAP; and Hazem El Beblawi, ESCWA.

24. Henry Kissinger, "Globalization and the World Order," lecture delivered at Trinity College, Dublin, 12 October 1999, quoted in ECE, *Globalization: A European Perspective* (Geneva: United Nations, 2000).

25. Weiss, Carayannis, Emmerij, and Jolly, *UN Voices,* 283.

26. ECLAC, *Open Regionalism in Latin America and the Caribbean: Economic Integration as a Contribution to Changing Production Patterns with Social Equity* (New York: United Nations, 1994).

27. Robert Devlin, "A Latin American Trade and Integration Story: Where We Were, Where We Are, and Where We Must Go," a preliminary Inter-American Development Bank paper, 2005.

28. For more on this, see Gert Rosenthal, "ECLAC: A Commitment to a Latin American Way toward Development," in Berthelot, *Unity and Diversity in Development Ideas,* 168–232.

29. Karl W. Deutsch, *Nationalism and Its Alternatives* (New York: Knopf, 1969), 93.

6. Fairer International Economic Relations

1. United Nations, *National and International Measures for Full Employment* (New York: UN, 1949); United Nations, *Measures for the Economic Development of Under-developed Countries* (New York: UN, 1951); and United Nations, *Measures for International Economic Stability* (New York: UN, 1951).

2. John Toye and Richard Toye, *The UN and Global Political Economy: Trade, Finance, and Development* (Bloomington: Indiana University Press, 2004), 97–102.

3. Independent Commission on International Development, *North-South: A Programme for Survival* (London: Pan Books, 1980).

4. Mark Weisbrot, "Latin America: The End of an Era," *International Journal of Health Services* 36, no. 4 (2006): 3.

5. Mark Weisbrot, Robert Naiman, and Joyce Kim, *The Emperor Has No Growth: Declining Economic Growth Rates in the Era of Globalization* (Washington, D.C.: Center for Economic and Policy Research, 2001).

6. Olav Stokke, *The UN and International Development: From Aid to Cooperation* (Bloomington: Indiana University Press, 2009).

7. "Truman's Inaugural Address, January 20, 1949," available at http://www.truman-library.org/whistlestop/50yr_archive/inagural20jan1949.htm.

8. Sixten Heppling, *UNDP: From Agency Shares to Country Programmes, 1949–1975* (Stockholm: Ministry of Foreign Affairs, 1995), 23ff.

9. "Speech of 25 September 1961," reproduced in *Public Papers of the President of the United States, J. F. Kennedy, 20 January to 31 December 1961* (Washington, D.C.: U.S. Government Printing Office, 1962), 623.

10. W. W. Rostow, *The Stages of Economic Growth: A Non-Communist Manifest* (Cambridge: Cambridge University Press, 1961).

11. Colin Legum, ed., *The First United Nations Development Decade and Its Lessons for the 1970s* (New York: Praeger, 1970).

12. Commission on International Development, *Partners in Development* (New York: Praeger, 1969).

13. Louis Emmerij, Richard Jolly, and Thomas G. Weiss, *Ahead of the Curve? UN Ideas and Global Challenges* (Bloomington: Indiana University Press, 2001), 80–119. See also Robert L. Rothstein, *Global Beginning: UNCTAD and the New International Economic Order* (Princeton, N.J.: Princeton University Press, 1979); Mahfuzur Rahman, *World Economic Issues at the United Nations: Half a Century of Debate* (Boston: Kluwer Academic Publishers, 2002); Thomas G. Weiss, Tatiana Carayannis, Louis Emmerij, and Richard Jolly, *UN Voices: The Struggle for Development and Social Justice* (Bloomington: Indiana University Press, 2005), 225–233; and Richard Jolly, Louis Emmerij, Dharam Ghai, and Frédéric Lapeyre, *UN Contributions to Development Thinking and Practice* (Bloomington: Indiana University Press, 2004), 111–137.

14. James Raymond Vreeland, *The International Monetary Fund: Politics of Conditional Lending* (London: Routledge, 2007), 58.

15. Nigel Lawson, *The Memoirs of a Tory Radical* (London: Bantam Press, 1992), 520.

16. Louis Emmerij, "Aid as a Flight Forward," *Development and Change* 33, no. 2 (2002): 247–259.

17. "United Nations Millennium Declaration," General Assembly resolution 55/2, 8 September 2000.

18. MDG Gap Task Force, *Delivering on the Global Partnership for Addressing the Millennium Development Goals* (New York: UN, 2008), vii–viii.

19. Toye and Toye, *The UN and Global Political Economy*, 276–298.

20. For more details on this important issue, see Martin Khor, "The WTO Doha Negotiations and Impasse: A Development Perspective," November 2006, available at the Third World Network Web site at http://www.twnside.org.sg/pos.htm (accessed 12 November 2008).

21. Toye and Toye, *The UN and Global Political Economy*, 258–275.

22. United States Department of the Treasury, Alexander Hamilton, *Report on Manufactures* (1791; repr., Washington, D.C.: Government Printing Office, 1913).

23. Ha-Joon Chang, *Kicking Away the Ladder: Development Strategy in Historical Perspective* (London: Anthem Press, 2002).

24. Friedrich List, *The National System of Political Economy,* translated by Sampson S. Lloyd (1841; London: Longmans Green, 1885).

25. Dieter Senghaas, *Von Europa Lernen: Entwicklungsgeschichtliche Betrachtungen* (Frankfurt: Suhrkamp Verlag, 1982).

26. Transcript of Gamani Corea oral history interview in UNIHP, *The Complete Oral History Transcripts from UN Voices,* CD-ROM (New York: Ralph Bunche Institute, 2007), 31.

27. Tagi Sagafi-nejad in collaboration with John Dunning, *The UN and Transnational Corporations: From Code of Conduct to Global Compact* (Bloomington: Indiana University Press, 2008).

28. Thomas G. Weiss, Tatiana Carayannis, Louis Emmerij, and Richard Jolly, *UN Voices: The Struggle for Development and Social Justice* (Bloomington: Indiana University Press, 2005), 235.

29. *Tripartite Declaration of Principles concerning Multinational Enterprises and Social Policy,* 4th ed. (Geneva: ILO, 2006).

30. Ibid., 236–237.

31. Nayan Chanda, "Runaway Globalization without Governance," *Global Governance* 14, no. 2 (2008): 119. See also Nayan Chanda, *Bound Together: How Traders, Preachers, Adventurers and Warriors Shaped Globalization* (New Haven, Conn.: Yale University Press, 2007).

32. Jan Aart Scholte, *Globalization: A Critical Introduction,* 2nd ed. (Houndmills, Basingstoke, UK: Macmillan, 2005), xiv.

33. The Millennium Development Goals report states that "worldwide the number of people in developing countries living on less that $1 a day fell to 980 million in 2004, down from 1.25 billion in 1990." However, in most of the regions of the world outside Eastern Asia and Southeast Asia, the number of poor people has been increasing. UN Development Programme, *The Millennium Development Goals* (New York: UN, 2007), 6.

34. Sidney Dell, "The Origins of UNCTAD," in *UNCTAD and the North-South Dialogue,* ed. Michael Zammit Cutajar (New York: Pergamon Press, 1985), 19.

35. Jan Tinberger, Anthony J. Dolman, and Jan van Ettinger, eds., *Reshaping the International Order: A Report to the Club of Rome* (London: Hutchinson, 1977), a report for which Professor Tinbergen was the coordinator, was a comprehensive survey of global needs and the institutional changes necessary to meet those needs. The publication is a good example of intellectual contributions by members of the Second and Third UNs. Many of its contributors, then mostly Third UN members, later became Second UN staff members, three as heads of UN agencies.

36. Robert McNamara, "The Two Great Challenges of Our Time," in *A Society for International Development: Prospectus 1984,* ed. Ann Matis (Chapel Hill, N.C.: Duke Press Policy Studies, 1983), 42–50. This essay is derived from McNamara's Barbara Ward lecture at the 1982 Society of International Development conference in Baltimore.

37. The G-20 is a forum that promotes dialogue between advanced and developing countries on issues regarding economic growth and the financial system.

38. Weiss, Carayannis, Emmerij, and Jolly, *UN Voices,* 416.

7. Development Strategies

1. Thomas G. Weiss, Tatiana Carayannis, Louis Emmerij, and Richard Jolly, *UN Voices: The Struggle for Development and Social Justice* (Bloomington: Indiana University Press, 2005), 192.

2. Richard Jolly, Louis Emmerij, Dharam Ghai, and Frédéric Lapeyre, *UN Contributions to Development Thinking and Practice* (Bloomington: Indiana University Press, 2004), 91–94.

3. Jan Tinbergen, *The Design of Development* (Baltimore: Johns Hopkins University Press, 1958).

4. Wolfgang Stolper published a book by that title after his experience of working with the Nigerian government to devise a five-year plan without a statistical base. Wolfgang F. Stolper, *Planning without Facts: Lessons in Resource Allocation from Nigeria's Development* (Cambridge, Mass.: Harvard University Press, 1966).

5. Michael Ward, *Quantifying the World: UN Ideas and Statistics* (Bloomington: Indiana University Press, 2004), 2.

6. Ibid., 4.

7. Ibid.

8. Strictly speaking, the first meeting of the Nuclear Commission, which was comprised of transitory members, was in May 1946. The commission set up the Statistical Commission proper and then recommended that a Central Statistical Unit of the UN secretariat be established.

9. United Nations Statistical Office, *A System of National Accounts and Supporting Tables* (New York: UN, 1953).

10. See Ward, *Quantifying the World*, 49; and Devaki Jain, *Women, Development, and the UN: The Sixty-Year Quest for Development and Justice* (Bloomington: Indiana University Press, 2005), 30–32.

11. D. V. McGranahan and UNRISD, *Contents and Measurement of Socio-economic Development* (New York: UNRISD and Praeger, 1972).

12. World Fertility Survey, *World Fertility Survey: Major Findings and Implications* (London: World Fertility Survey, 1984). This survey was begun in 1972 and completed in 1984. It compiled information on forty-two developing and twenty developed countries.

13. United Nations, *The World's Women, 1997–1990: Trends and Statistics, 1991* (New York: UN, 1991).

14. United Nations, *The World's Women, 1995: Trends and Statistics* (New York: UN, 1995).

15. UNDP, *Human Development Report 1995* (New York: Oxford University Press, 1995), 6.

16. Donella H. Meadows et al., *The Limits to Growth: A Report for the Club of Rome's Project on the Predicament of Mankind* (London: Pan, 1972).

17. For the year 2000, this simple exercise yields a larger estimate than the true (unknown) figure. This is because most countries count immigrants better than they

monitor those who leave the country. At the world level, these international migrant flows should cancel out in reality.

18. Richard Jolly, Louis Emmerij, Dharam Ghai, and Fredérich Lapeyre, *UN Contributions to Development Thinking and Practice* (Bloomington: Indiana University Press, 2004), 91–94.

19. United Nations, *World Economic Survey,* Part I, *Trade and Development Trends: Needs and Policies* (New York: UN, 1963).

20. United Nations, *Studies in Long-Term Economic Projections for the World Economy: Aggregate Models* (New York: UN, 1964).

21. See Yves Berthelot, ed., *Unity and Diversity in Development Ideas: Perspectives from the UN Regional Commissions* (Bloomington: Indiana University Press, 2004).

22. Michal Kalecki, *Essays on Developing Countries* (New York: Harvester Press, 1976), 32. Kalecki was, of course, referring to the distinction between indicative and Soviet-type planning.

23. Ian M. D. Little, Tibor Scitovsky, and Maurice F. G. Scott, *Industry and Trade in Some Developing Countries* (London: Oxford University Press, 1970).

24. Ian M. D. Little and James A. Mirrlees, *Manual of Industrial Project Analysis* (Paris: OECD Development Center, 1968). See also I. M. D. Little and James A. Mirrlees, *Project Appraisal and Planning for Developing Countries* (London: Heinemann, 1974).

25. Amartya Sen, Stephen Marglin, and Partha Dasgupta, *Guidelines for Project Evaluation* (New York: United Nations/UNIDO, 1972).

26. Dani Rodrik, *One Economics, Many Recipes* (Princeton, N.J.: Princeton University Press, 2007). See also his *The Global Governance of Trade: As If Development Really Mattered,* the published version of a paper prepared for the UNDP (New York: UNDP, 2001).

27. S. Lall, "Conflicts of Concepts: Welfare Economics and Developing Countries," *World Development* 4, no. 3 (1976): 181–195.

28. Frances Stewart, "The Fragile Foundations of the Neoclassical Approach to Development," *Journal of Development Studies* 21, no. 2 (1985): 282–292.

29. Robert Wade, *Governing the Market: Economic Theory and the Role of Government in East Asian Industrialization* (Princeton, N.J.: Princeton University Press, 1990).

30. Weiss, Carayannis, Emmerij, and Jolly, *UN Voices,* 191. See pages 289–294 for further discussion of the UN's role in measuring development.

31. Marshall Goldman, "Planning," in *The Elgar Companion to Development Studies,* ed., David Alexander Clark (Cheltenham, UK: Edward Elgar Publishing Ltd., 2006), 435–436.

8. Social Development

1. Louis Emmerij, Richard Jolly, and Thomas G. Weiss, *Ahead of the Curve? UN Ideas and Global Challenges* (Bloomington: Indiana University Press, 2001), 60–79, 120–145; and Richard Jolly, Louis Emmerij, Dharam Ghai, and Frédéric Lapeyre, *UN Contributions to Development Thinking and Practice* (Bloomington: Indiana University Press, 2004), 186–244.

2. WHO, *The World Health Report 1998: Life in the 21st Century: A Vision for All* (Geneva: WHO, 1998), 19.

3. The Convention on the Elimination of All Forms of Discrimination against Women, adopted by the General Assembly on 18 December 1979, available at http://www.un.org/womenwatch/daw/cedaw (accessed 14 November 2008); "Convention on the Rights of the Child," General Assembly resolution 44/25, 20 November 1989, available at http://www.unhchr.ch/html/menu3/b/k2crc.htm (accessed 14 November 2008).

4. Measuring quality is fraught with methodological difficulties in health and education. The WHO, UNESCO, and the OECD have a research project under way in these areas.

5. United Nations, *Development in an Ageing World: World Economic and Social Survey 2007* (New York: UN, 2007), 17.

6. For a recent review of compelling reasons to slow population growth as much as possible, see Jeffrey D. Sachs, *Common Wealth: Economics for a Crowded Planet* (New York: Penguin Press, 2008), 159–182.

7. Department of Economic and Social Affairs, Population Division, *The World of Six Billion* (New York: UN, 1999).

8. Efforts to raise population issues in the League of Nations also aroused intense controversy, especially the efforts of Margaret Sanger, the pioneering birth control advocate, who had argued for a world conference to discuss population problems and recommend solutions. Attempts to treat population growth as a serious problem failed. When attention shifted to two closely related issues—birth control and international migration—controversy boiled over. In many countries in the 1920s and 1930s, the dissemination of information about contraception or abortion was suppressed under the laws relating to obscenity. See Jolly, Emmerij, Ghai, and Lapeyre, *UN Contributions*, 189–190.

9. United Nations, *Report of the United Nations World Population Conference, 1974* (New York: UN, 1975), 11. See also Jolly, Emmerij, Ghai, and Lapeyre, *UN Contributions*, 192.

10. United Nations, *Review and Appraisal of the World Population Plan of Action: 1984 Report* (New York: UN, 1984), 184.

11. The world's lowest fertility rates are now found in eighteen developed and former communist countries: Japan, Italy, Greece, Slovenia, the Czech Republic, Hungary, Poland, Lithuania, Slovakia, Croatia, Bulgaria, Romania, Bosnia and Herzegovina, Russia, Belarus, Ukraine, Armenia, and Moldova all have fertility rates of 1.2 or 1.3 births per woman. In developing countries, the lowest fertility rates are Hong Kong (0.9), Korea (1.2), Singapore (1.4), Barbados (1.5), Cuba (1.6), Trinidad and Tobago (1.6), China (1.7), and Thailand (1.9).

12. United Nations, *Development in an Ageing World*, v–xx.

13. League of Nations, *The Relation of Nutrition to Health, Agriculture and Economic Policy*, Final Report of the Mixed Committee of the League of Nations (Geneva: League of Nations, 1937).

14. Quoted in J. M. Cohen and M. J. Cohen, *The Penguin Dictionary of Twentieth-Century Quotations* (London: Penguin Books, 1993), 214.

15. World Food Summit Plan of Action, World Food Summit, Rome, 13–17 November 1996, paragraph 1, available at www.fao.org/docrep/003/w3613e/w3613e00.HTM (accessed 24 July 2008).

16. UN Standing Committee on Nutrition, *Fifth Report on the World Nutrition Situation* (Geneva: SCN, 2005), iii.

17. The Standing Committee on Nutrition has published many state-of-the-art reviews of research findings and periodic assessments of the world nutritional situation. It also publishes a biannual newsletter.

18. D. John Shaw, *World Food Security: A History since 1945* (Houndmills, Basingstoke, UK: Palgrave Macmillan, 2007), 389–390.

19. UN Standing Committee on Nutrition, *Fifth World Report on the World Nutrition Situation* (Geneva: SCN, 2005), Appendix 4, Table 1, 71.

20. WHO, *The World Health Report 1998: Life in the Twenty-First Century: A Vision for All* (Geneva: WHO, 1998), 45 and 95.

21. See Carter Center, "Guinea Worm Eradication Program," available at http://www.cartercenter.org/health/guinea_worm/index.html (accessed 13 November 2008).

22. WHO, *The World Health Report 1998*, 23.

23. Ibid., 144.

24. Declaration of Alma-Ata, International Conference on Primary Health Care, Alma-Ata, USSR, 6–12 September 1978, available at http://www.who.int/hpr/NPH/docs/declaration_almaata.pdf (accessed 14 November 2008).

25. See WHO and UNICEF, *Primary Health Care: Report of the International Conference on Primary Health Care, Alma Ata, USSR, 6–12 September 1978* (Geneva: WHO/UNICEF, 1978); and WHO, *The World Health Report 1998*, 139–163.

26. Devesh Kapur, Richard P. Webb, and John P. Lewis, eds., *The World Bank: Its First Half Century*, vol. 1, *History* (Washington, D.C.: Brookings Institution, 1997), 265.

27. Ibid., 326–327.

28. Mark W. Zacher and Tania J. Keefe, *The Politics of Global Health Governance: United by Contagion* (New York: Palgrave Macmillan, 2008).

29. UNESCO, *Basic Facts and Figures: International Statistics Relating to Education, Culture, and Mass Communications 1958* (Paris: UNESCO, 1959), 11.

30. Increases calculated from UNESCO, *Basic Facts and Figures: International Statistics Relating to Education, Culture, and Mass Communications 1961* (Paris: UNESCO, 1962), 21; and UNESCO, *Strong Foundations: Education and Early Childhood* (Paris: UNESCO, 2006), Statistical Annex Table 5, 268–269.

31. United Nations, *The Millennium Development Goals Report 2007* (New York: UN, 2007), 10–11.

32. Kapur, Lewis, and Webb, *The World Bank: Its First Half Century*, 1:259–260.

33. Ibid., 260.

34. UNESCO, *A Brief Bibliography of the Economics of Education*, EDAD/22, Paris, 19 August 1963, available at http://unesdoc.unesco.org/images/0014/001446/144697eb.pdf (accessed 1 October 2008).

35. Jan Tinbergen and H. C. Bos, *Econometric Models of Education: Some Applications* (Paris: OECD, 1965).

36. Richard Jolly, "Jim Grant: The Man Behind the Vision," in *Jim Grant—UNICEF Visionary*, ed. Richard Jolly (Rome: UNICEF Innocenti Research Centre, 2001), 45–66.

37. National Committees are autonomous NGOs that have a formal relationship with UNICEF. In 2008, there were thirty-six National Committees in industrialized countries.

9. Environmental Sustainability

1. Nico Schrijver, *Development without Destruction: The UN and Global Resource Management* (Bloomington: Indiana University Press, forthcoming).

2. World Commission on Environment and Development, *Our Common Future* (Oxford: Oxford University Press, 1987).

3. United Nations, *Problems of the Human Environment: Report of the Secretary-General* (New York: United Nations, 1969), 4.

4. Donella H. Meadows et al., *The Limits to Growth: A Report for the Club of Rome's Project on the Predicament of Mankind* (London: Pan, 1972).

5. Thomas G. Weiss, Tatiana Carayannis, Louis Emmerij, and Richard Jolly, *UN Voices: The Challenge of Development and Social Justice* (Bloomington: Indiana University Press, 2005), 219.

6. World Commission on Environment and Growth, *Our Common Future*, 8.

7. "United Nations Conference on Environment and Development," General Assembly resolution 44/228, 22 December 1989.

8. Mustafa K. Tolba, *Global Environmental Diplomacy: Negotiating Environmental Agreements for the World 1973–92* (Cambridge, Mass.: MIT Press, 1998).

9. Louis Emmerij, Richard Jolly, and Thomas G. Weiss, *Ahead of the Curve? UN Ideas and Global Challenges* (Bloomington: Indiana University Press, 2001), chapter 4.

10. R. R. K. Pachauri, "Climate Change Is Unequivocal," in *Climate Action*, ed. David Simpson (New York: Sustainable Development International and UNEP, 2007), 7. Pachauri is the chairman of the IPCC and shared the 2007 Nobel Prize for Peace with Al Gore. See also Sir Nicolas Stern, "The Cost of Climate Action," 26 November 2007, available at http://www.climateactionprogramme.org/features/article/the_cost_of_climate_action (accessed 25 July 2008).

11. Bjorn Lomborg, *The Skeptical Environmentalist: Measuring the Real State of the World* (Cambridge: Cambridge University Press, 2001).

12. IPCC, *Climate Change 2007: Synthesis Report* (Geneva: IPCC, 2007), available at http://www.ipcc.ch/pdf/assessment-report/ar4/syr/ar4_syr.pdf (accessed 13 November 2008).

13. Nicolas Stern, *The Economics of Climate Change: The Stern Review* (Cambridge: Cambridge University Press, 2006).

14. Ibid., 29.

15. UNDP, *Human Development Report 2007/2008: Fighting Climate Change: Human Solidarity in a Divided World* (Houndmills, Basingstoke, UK: Palgrave Macmillan, 2007), 294–297.

16. Stern does not discount the benefits to future generations. In *A Question of Balance: Weighing the Options on Global Warming Policies* (New Haven, Conn.: Yale

University Press, 2008), William Nordhaus takes a different view that discounts the benefits of the future and produces a very different ranking of costs and desirable actions.

17. Ibid., 16.

18. See John Browne and Nick Butler, "We Need an International Carbon Fund," *Financial Times,* 16 May 2007.

19. The aggregate concentration of carbon in the atmosphere is about 380 parts per million, having risen by 1.9 parts per million per annum during the past ten years. Scientific judgment puts the "safe" level between 400 and 550 parts per million; the consensus is toward the lower end of the range.

20. George Monbiot, "We've Been Suckered Again by the US: So Far the Bali Deal Is Worse than Kyoto," *Guardian Unlimited,* 17 December 2007; Ben Cubby, "Answer to Hot Air Was in Fact a Chilling Blunder," *The Sydney Morning Herald,* 18 December 2007.

21. John Vidal, "US Pours Cold Water on Bali Optimism," *Guardian Unlimited,* 17 December 2007.

22. Juliette Jowit, Caroline Davies, and David Adam, "Late-Night Drama Pushes US into Climate Deal," *The Observer,* 16 December 2007.

23. John Bartlett and Justin Kaplan, *Bartlett's Familiar Quotations,* 16th ed. (Boston: Little Brown, 1992), 572.

24. Weiss, Carayannis, Emmerij, and Jolly, *UN Voices,* 424.

25. Ibid., 417.

26. Nico Schijver, "Natural Resource Management and Sustainable Development," in *The Oxford Handbook on the United Nations,* ed. Thomas G. Weiss and Sam Daws (Oxford: Oxford University Press, 2007), 606.

27. Ibid., 608.

28. Barbara Ward, *Progress for a Small Planet* (London: Earthscan Publications, 1988), 253–254, 265.

10. Peace and Security

1. Although there are many more academic treatments, Wikipedia (2008) summarizes estimates of total casualities at 50 to 72 million, the higher estimate using post–Cold War Russian data. This latest estimate of 72 million includes 25 million military and 47 million civilian deaths.

2. Eric Hobsbawm, *The Age of Extremes: A History of the World, 1914–1991* (New York: Pantheon, 1994), 43.

3. Robert J. Rummel, *Death by Government* (New Brunswick, N.J.: Transaction Publishers, 1994), chapter 1.

4. See Hugo Slim, *Killing Civilians: Method, Madness, and Morality in War* (New York: Columbia University Press, 2008).

5. Thomas G. Weiss, Tatiana Carayannis, Louis Emmerij, and Richard Jolly, *UN Voices: The Struggle for Development and Social Justice* (Bloomington: Indiana University Press, 2005), 410.

6. Paul Kennedy, *The Parliament of Man: The Past, Present, and Future of the United Nations* (New York: Random House, 2006), 77.

7. This is a theme in Brian Urquhart, *Hammarskjöld* (New York: Knopf, 1972).

8. Human Security Report Project, *Human Security Report 2005* (Oxford: Oxford University Press, 2005); and Human Security Report Project, *Human Security Brief 2006* (Oxford: Oxford University Press, 2006); Human Security Report Project, *Human Security Brief 2007* (Vancouver: Simon Fraser University, 2008).

9. Bertrand G. Ramcharan, *Preventive Diplomacy at the UN* (Bloomington: Indiana University Press, 2008), 2.

10. Javier Pérez de Cuéllar, *Perspectives for the 1990s* (New York: United Nations, 1987); and Boutros Boutros-Ghali, *An Agenda for Peace: Preventive Diplomacy, Peace-making, and Peace-keeping* (New York: United Nations, 1992).

11. Kofi A. Annan, *Facing the Humanitarian Challenge: Towards a Culture of Prevention* (New York: United Nations, 1999).

12. Carnegie Commission on Preventing Deadly Conflict, *Preventing Deadly Conflict* (New York: Carnegie Commission, 1997).

13. Ramcharan, *Preventive Diplomacy at the UN,* 214–215.

14. See M. J. Peterson, "General Assembly Majorities on the Preferred Nuclear Order," in *The United Nations and the Nuclear Order,* ed. Jane Boulden, Ramesh Thakur, and Thomas G. Weiss (Tokyo: United Nations University Press, forthcoming); and Thomas G. Weiss and Ramesh Thakur, *Global Governance and the UN: An Unfinished Journey* (Bloomington: Indiana University Press, forthcoming).

15. See Devesh Kapur, John P. Lewis, and Richard Webb, *The World Bank: Its First Half Century,* vol. 1, *History* (Washington, D.C.: Brookings, 1997), 533.

16. United Nations, *The United Nations Development Decade: Proposals for Action* (New York: UN, 1962), 12–13 and 24–25.

17. Joseph Stiglitz and Linda Bilmes, *The Three Trillion Dollar War: The True Cost of the Iraq Conflict* (New York: Norton, 2008).

18. SIPRI (Stockholm International Peace Research Institute), "Recent Trends in Military Expenditure," 2008, available at www.sipri.org (accessed 1 October 2008), also available in SIPRI, *Yearbook 2008: Armaments, Disarmament and International Security* (Oxford: Oxford University Press, 2008), chapter 5.

19. The Thorsson Report, as quoted in Richard Jolly, Mac Graham, and Chris Smith, *Disarmament and World Development* (Oxford: Pergamon Press, 1986), 235.

20. In his interview with UNIHP, Lawrence Klein discusses disarmament and development and the use of the LINK model for analyzing the relationships between the two. Transcript of Lawrence Klein oral history interview in UNIHP, *The Complete Oral History Transcript from UN Voices,* CD-ROM (New York: Ralph Bunche Institute, 2007), 20–24. See also Joseph E. Stiglitz, *The Roaring Nineties* (New York: Norton, 2003). Project LINK is an international research activity that integrates national econometric models into a global econometric model; for more, see UN Development and Policy Analysis Division, "Project LINK," available at http://www.un.org/esa/policy/link (accessed 13 November 2008).

21. SIPRI, *SIPRI Yearbook 2006* (Stockholm: Swedish International Peace Research Institute, 2006), chapter 8.

22. This summary is based on Thomas G. Weiss, David P. Forsythe, Roger A. Coate,

and Kelly-Kate Pease, *The United Nations and Changing World Politics,* 5th ed. (Boulder, Colo.: Westview, 2007), chapter 1.

23. Max Harrelson, *Fires All around the Horizon: The UN's Uphill Battle to Preserve the Peace* (New York: Praeger, 1989), 89.

24. Boutros Boutros-Ghali, *An Agenda for Peace* (New York: United Nations, 1992), 28.

25. Other definitions can be found in United Nations, *The Blue Helmets: A Review of United Nations Peace-Keeping* (New York: United Nations, Department of Public Information, 1990), 4; Alan James, *Peacekeeping in International Politics* (London: Macmillan, 1990), 1; and Boutros-Ghali, *Agenda,* 11.

26. Marrack Goulding, "The Changing Role of the United Nations in Conflict Resolution and Peace-Keeping," speech given at the Singapore Institute of Policy Studies, 13 March 1991, 9. See also Marrack Goulding, "The Evolution of Peacekeeping," *International Affairs* 69, no.3 (1993): 451–464. See also Marrack Goulding, *Peacemonger* (London: John Murray, 2002). For an early historical overview, see Alan James *Peacekeeping in International Politics* (London: Macmillan, 1990); and Paul Diehl, *International Peacekeeping* (Cambridge: Polity Press, 2008).

27. For a discussion of UN and non-UN operations in a comparative military perspective in this period, see John Mackinlay, *The Peacekeepers* (London: Unwin Hyman, 1989). See also Augustus Richard Norton and Thomas G. Weiss, *UN Peacekeepers: Soldiers with a Difference* (New York: Foreign Policy Association, 1990); William J. Durch, ed., *The Evolution of UN Peacekeeping* (New York: St. Martin's Press, 1993); and Paul Diehl, *International Peacekeeping* (Baltimore: Johns Hopkins University Press, 1993).

28. For a discussion of this period, see S. Neil MacFarlane, *Superpower Rivalry and Third World Radicalism* (Baltimore: Johns Hopkins University Press, 1985); Elizabeth Valkenier, *The Soviet Union and the Third World* (New York: Praeger, 1985); and Jerry Hough, *The Struggle for the Third World* (Washington, D.C.: Brookings Institution, 1986).

29. Center for International Cooperation, *Global Peace Operations 2008* (Boulder, Colo.: Lynne Rienner, 2008).

30. Panel on United Nations Peace Operations, *Report of the Panel on United Nations Peace Operations,* General Assembly document A/55305 and Security Council document S/2000/809, 21 August 2000.

31. This story is told in Thomas G. Weiss, *Humanitarian Intervention: Ideas in Action* (Cambridge: Polity, 2007).

32. International Commission on Intervention and State Sovereignty, *The Responsibility to Protect* (Ottawa: International Development Research Centre, 2001).

33. See, for example, Donald Rothchild, Frances M. Deng, I. William Zartman, Sadikiel Kimaro, and Terrence Lyons, *Sovereignty as Responsibility: Conflict Management in Africa* (Washington, D.C.: Brookings, 1996); Kofi A. Annan, *"We the Peoples": The United Nations in the 21st Century* (New York: UN, 2000); and Kofi A. Annan, *The Question of Intervention: Statements by the Secretary-General* (New York: UN, 1999).

34. Weiss, Carayannis, Emmerij, and Jolly, *UN Voices,* 378.

35. *2005 World Summit Outcome,* UN document A/60/L.1, 15 September 2005, paragraphs 138–139.

36. Alan J. Kuperman, "Mitigating the Moral Hazard of Humanitarian Intervention: Lessons from Economics," *Global Governance* 14, no. 2 (2008): 219–240.

37. For the difficulties encountered on the ground, see Samantha Power, *Chasing the Flame: Sergio Vieira de Mello and the Fight to Save the World* (New York: Penguin Press, 2008), particularly chapters 9–16.

38. S. Neil MacFarlane and Yuen Foong Khong, *Human Security and the UN: A Critical History* (Bloomington: Indiana University Press, 2006).

39. UNDP, *Human Development Report 1994: New Dimensions of Human Security* (New York: Oxford University Press, 1994), 22–24.

40. Ibid., 23.

41. For details of this story, see Richard Ponzio, "The Advent of the *Human Development Report*," in *Pioneering the Human Development Revolution: An Intellectual Biography of Mahbub ul Haq*, ed. Khadija Haq and Richard Ponzio (New Dehli: Oxford University Press, 2008), 88–111.

42. See Adam Roberts and Richard Guelff, eds., *Documents and Laws of War*, 3rd ed. (Oxford: Oxford University Press, 2000); and Michael Byers, *Law War: Understanding International Law and Armed Conflict* (New York: Grove Press, 2005).

43. Department of Foreign Affairs and International Trade (Canada), "Human Security: Safety for People in a Changing World," April 1999, available at http://www.summit-americas.org/Canada/HumanSecurity-english.htm (accessed 13 November 2008).

44. *Report of the Secretary General to the Security Council on the Protection of Civilians in Armed Conflict*, Security Council document S/1999/957, 8 September 1999.

45. Thomas G. Weiss, Tatiana Carayannis, Louis Emmerij, and Richard Jolly, *UN Voices: The Struggle for Development and Social Justice* (Bloomington: Indiana University Press, 2005), 302.

46. *Prevention of Armed Conflict: Report of the Secretary General*, General Assembly document A/55/985 and Security Council document S/2001/574, 7 June 2001.

47. Commission on Human Security, *Human Security Now* (New York: United Nations, 2003); High-level Panel on Threats, Challenges and Change, *A More Secure World: Our Shared Responsibility* (New York: United Nations, 2004).

48. International Commission on International Development Issues, *North-South: A Programme for Survival* (London: Pan Books, 1980).

49. Eveline Herfkens, "Foreword," in Juan Somavía, *People's Security: Globalising Social Progress* (Geneva: ILO, 1999), viii.

50. World Bank and Human Security Project, *Mini Atlas of Human Security* (Brighton, UK: Myriad Editions, 2008), 1.

51. Weiss, Carayannis, Emmerij, and Jolly, *UN Voices*, 299.

52. Andrew Mack, "Human Security in the New Millennium," *Work in Progress: A Review of Research of the United Nations University* 16, no. 3 (2002): 4.

53. High-level Panel on Threats, Challenges and Change, *A More Secure World*, viii.

54. See David Rieff, *A Bed for the Night: Humanitarianism in Crisis* (New York: Vintage, 2002); Fiona Terry, *Condemned to Repeat: The Paradox of Humanitarian Action* (Ithaca, N.Y.: Cornell University Press, 2002); and Rama Mani, "The Root Causes of

Terrorism and Conflict Prevention," in *Terrorism and the UN,* ed Jane Boulden and Thomas G. Weiss (Bloomington: Indiana University Press, 2004).

55. UNDP, *Human Development Report 1994,* 59.

56. MacFarlane and Khong, *Human Security and the UN,* 269–270.

11. Human Development

1. UN *Report of the World Summit of Social Development,* A/Conf. 166/9, 19 April 1995, 125.

2. United Nations, *United Nations Development Decade: Proposals for Action* (New York: UN, 1962), 5.

3. ILO, *Employment, Growth, and Basic Needs: A One-World Problem* (Geneva: ILO, 1976).

4. See Khadija Haq and Richard Ponzio, eds., *Pioneering the Human Development Revolution: An Intellectual Biography of Mahbub ul Haq* (New Delhi: Oxford University Press, forthcoming).

5. UNDP, *Human Development Report 1990: Concept and Measurement of Human Development* (Oxford: Oxford University Press, 1990), 1.

6. Amartya Sen, *Poverty and Famines: An Essay on Entitlement and Deprivation* (Oxford: Oxford University Press, 1982); Amartya Sen, *Inequality Re-examined* (Oxford: Oxford University Press, 1992); Amartya Sen, *Development as Freedom* (New York: Knopf, 1999); and Amartya Sen, *The Argumentative Indian: Writings on Indian Culture, History, and Identity* (New York: Farrar, Straus, Giroux, 2005).

7. Amartya Sen, "Foreword," in *Readings in Human Development: Concepts, Measures and Policies for a Development Paradigm,* ed. Sakiko Fukuda-Parr and A. K. Shiva Kumar (Oxford: Oxford University Press, 2003), vii.

8. Fuller details can be found at the back of all Human Development Reports. Note that the components of the indices have been changed over time to take account of the availability and reliability of data and improvements in methodology.

9. UNDP, *Human Development Report 1999: Globalization with a Human Face* (New York: Oxford University Press, 1999), 23. This quotation is cited by Amartya Sen, who made the additional comment that "Mahbub got this exactly right."

10. ILO, *Employment, Growth, and Basic Needs: A One-World Problem* (Geneva: ILO, 1976), 7.

11. A recent summary of the research showing the anti-growth effects of structural adjustment policies and the Washington consensus can be found in James Raymond Vreeland, *The International Monetary Fund: Politics of Conditional Lending* (London: Routledge, 2007), 73–94. A quasi-official IMF review of this evidence appears in Graham Hacche, "A Non-Definitive Guide to the IMF," *World Economics* 8, no. 2 (2007): 97–118.

12. The Human Development Report was subjected to an early critique by T. N. Srinivasan ("Human Development: A New Paradigm or Reinvention of the Wheel?" *American Economic Review* 84, no. 2 [1994]: 238–243) and to later criticism by David

Henderson ("False Perspective: The UNDP View of the World," *World Economics* 1, no.1 [2000]: 1–19). A rebuttal was published in Richard Jolly, "False Attack: Misrepresenting the Human Development Report and Misunderstanding the Need for Rethinking Global Governance," *World Economics* 1, no. 3 (2000): 1–15.

13. Srinivasan, "Human Development: A New Paradigm or Reinvention of the Wheel?"; V. V. Bhanoji Rao, "Human Development Report 1990: Review and Assessment," *World Development* 19, no. 10 (1991): 1451–1460.

14. Based on Richard Jolly, "Human Development and Neo-Liberalism: Paradigms Compared," in *Readings in Human Development: Concepts, Measures and Policies for a Development Paradigm,* ed. Sakiko Fukuda Parr and A. K. Shiva Kumar (Oxford: Oxford University Press, 2003), 82–92.

12. A Balance Sheet

The full source for the epigraph for Part 3 is Barbara Ward, "Where There Is No Vision, the People Perish," *International Development Review* 4 (1980), reprinted in *Development* 40, no. 1 (1997): 84–87, quote at 87.

13. Challenges Ahead

1. See Charles Krauthammer, "The Unipolar Moment," *Foreign Affairs* 70, no. 1 (1990/1991): 23–33; and Charles Krauthammer, "The Unipolar Moment Revisited," *National Interest* 70 (Winter 2002/2003): 5–17.

2. Fareed Zakharia, *The Post-American World* (New York: Norton, 2008).

3. The discussion draws on Peter J. Hoffman and Thomas G. Weiss, *Sword & Salve: Confronting New Wars and Humanitarian Crises* (Lanham, Md.: Rowman & Littlefield, 2005), chapter 3; Gerald B. Helman and Steven R. Rather, "Saving Failed States," *Foreign Policy* 89 (Winter 1992–1993): 3–20.

4. Mary Kaldor, *New and Old Wars: Organized Violence in a Global Era* (Cambridge: Polity Press, 1999).

5. See Bertrand Badie, *The Imported State: The Westernization of the Political Order* (Stanford, Calif.: Stanford University Press, 2000).

6. John Gerard Ruggie, "Territoriality and Beyond: Problematizing Modernity in International Relations," *International Organization* 47 (Winter 1993): 165.

7. Robert I. Rotberg, "Failed States in a World of Terror," *Foreign Affairs* 81, no. 4 (2002): 127–140. For a fuller discussion of Africa's problems, see Martin Meredith, *The State of Africa: A History of Fifty Years of Independence* (London: Free Press, 2005).

8. See "Developmental and Cultural Nationalisms," ed. Radhika Desai, special issue, *Third World Quarterly* 29, no. 3 (2008).

9. We acknowledge assistance in this endeavor from an inquiry held among members of the World Academy of Art and Science, especially the assistance of Bob Berg.

10. Dan Plesch, "How the United Nations Beat Hitler and Prepared the Peace," *Global Society* 22, no. 1 (2008): 137.

11. Inge Kaul, Isabelle Grunberg, and Marc A. Stern, eds., *Global Public Goods:*

International Cooperation in the 21st Century (Oxford: Oxford University Press, 1999) has brought together some important papers on these issues. See also Inge Kaul, Pedro Conceicao, Katell Le Goulven, and Ronald U. Mendoza, eds., *Global Public Goods: Managing Globalization* (Oxford: Oxford University Press, 2003).

12. On the recent positive trend (since 2002), see United Nations, *World Economic Situation and Prospects 2008* (New York: UN, 2008). Table 1.1 shows that the fifty least-developed countries have experienced an average annual growth rate of between 6.3 and 8.4 percent over the last seven years, compared to a growth rate of between 1.3 and 3 percent among developed countries.

13. See, for example, Richard Jolly, Louis Emmerij, Dharam Ghai, and Frédéric Lapeyre, *UN Contributions to Development Thinking and Practice* (Bloomington: Indiana University Press, 2004), 56–61. See also Gunnar Myrdal, "The Widening Income Gap," originally published for the Society for International Development in *International Development Review* (September 1963): 3–6, and reprinted in *Development* 40, no. 1 (1997): 25–30.

14. Kofi Annan, "*We the Peoples*": *The Role of the United Nations in the 21st Century* (New York: United Nations, 2000), 19.

15. James Raymond Vreeland, *The International Monetary Fund: Politics of Conditional Lending* (London: Routledge, 2007), 90.

16. Samuel P. Huntington, *The Clash of Civilizations and the Remaking of the World Order* (New York: Simon and Schuster, 1996).

17. Amartya Sen, *The Argumentative Indian: Writings on Indian History, Culture, and Identity* (London: Allen Lane/Penguin, 2005) discusses the diversity of identities in the Indian context.

18. Thomas G. Weiss, Tatiana Carayannis, Louis Emmerij, and Richard Jolly, *UN Voices: The Struggle for Development and Social Justice* (Bloomington: Indiana University Press, 2005), 433.

19. Roger Normand and Sarah Zaidi, *Human Rights at the UN: The Political History of Universal Justice* (Bloomington: Indiana University Press, 2008), chapters 9 and 10.

20. For a summary of these achievements, see "Building the Human Foundations," in Richard Jolly, Louis Emmerij, Dharam Ghai, and Frédéric Lapeyre, *UN Contributions to Development Thinking and Practice* (Bloomington: Indiana University Press, 2004), 186–219.

21. See WHO, *The World Health Report* (Geneva: WHO, 1998), chapter 5.

22. Jeffrey Sachs, *Common Wealth: Economics for a Crowded Planet* (New York: Penguin Press, 2008), 297–300.

23. Bertrand G. Ramcharan, *Preventive Diplomacy and the UN* (Bloomington: Indiana University Press, 2008), 209–215.

24. Frances Stewart and the Centre for Research on Inequality, Human Security and Ethnicity have published a number of reports documenting the effects of horizontal inequalities and what can be done about them. See www.crise.ox.ac.uk.

25. High-level Panel on Threats, Challenge and Change, *A More Secure World: Our Shared Responsibility* (New York: United Nations, 2004).

26. See Jane Boulden, Ramesh Thakur, and Thomas G. Weiss, eds., *The UN and Nuclear Orders* (Tokyo: UN University Press, forthcoming).

27. Joseph Stiglitz and Linda J. Bilmes, *The Three Trillion Dollar War: The True Cost of the Iraq Conflict* (New York: Norton, 2008).

28. The Stern Review estimated that the costs of action—defined as "reducing greenhouse gas emissions to avoid the worst impacts of climate change"—can be limited to around 1 percent of global GDP each year; see Nicholas Stern, *The Economics of Climate Change: The Stern Review* (Cambridge: Cambridge University Press, 2007), xv. See also UNDP, *Human Development Report 2007/2008: Fighting Climate Change* (Houndmills, Basingstoke, UK: Palgrave Macmillan, 2007), table 19, pages 294–297, which shows that over three-quarters of the 145 countries that have collected data spend more than 1 percent of GDP on military spending.

29. Nicholas Stern, *The Economics of Climate Change,* 486.

30. UNDP, *Human Development Report 2007/2008,* 3.

31. Ibid.

14. Strengthening Global Governance

1. Ramesh Thakur and Thomas G. Weiss, *The UN and Global Governance: An Unfinished Journey* (Bloomington: Indiana University Press, forthcoming 2009).

2. Craig N. Murphy, *International Organization and Industrial Change: Global Governance since 1850* (Cambridge: Polity Press, 1994), 47–48, identifies thirty-three international organizations that existed in 1914–1915 that had a mandate concerning fostering industry, five for managing potential social conflict, four for strengthening states and the state system, and nine for strengthening society in such areas as human rights, relief and welfare, health, and education.

3. On the Global Compact, see Tagi Sagafi-nejad in collaboration with John Dunning, *The UN and Transnational Corporations: From Code of Conduct to Global Compact* (Bloomington: Indiana University Press, 2008).

4. The Holland Ring, "1953: Flood Disaster. The Dutch Struggle against the Waters," available at http://www.thehollandring.com/1953-ramp.shtml.

5. See Nico Schrijver, *Development without Destruction: The UN and Global Resource Management* (Bloomington: Indiana University Press, forthcoming).

6. Juliette Jowit, Caroline Davies, and David Adam, "Late-Night Drama Pushes US into Climate Deal," *The Observer,* 16 December 2007.

7. For an effort to move in this direction, see Thomas G. Weiss, *What's Wrong with the UN and How to Fix It* (Cambridge: Polity Press, 2009).

8. An early advocate of development contracts was Thorvald Stoltenberg, who was successively minister of development, of defense, and of foreign affairs in Norway. See his "Towards a World Development Strategy," in *One World or Several?* ed. Louis Emmerij (Paris: OECD, 1989), 241–242.

9. Jan Tinbergen, Anthony J. Dolman, and Jan van Ettinger, *Reshaping the International Order* (New York: Dutton, 1976).

10. Jean-François Rischard, *High Noon: 20 Global Problems, 20 Years to Solve Them* (New York: Basic Books, 2002).

11. Jeffrey Sachs, *Common Wealth: Economics for a Crowded Planet* (New York: Penguin, 2008), 300–302.

12. The UN University was set up in 1973 to do precisely that. Unfortunately, it has largely failed to take charge of setting the intellectual agenda or influencing the quality and the types of research undertaken by the UN. However, on occasion it has pursued an independent path and could be turned into an important asset.

13. Thomas G. Weiss, Tatiana Carayannis, Louis Emmerij, and Richard Jolly, *UN Voices: The Struggle for Development and Social Justice* (Bloomington: Indiana University Press, 2005), 342–343.

14. Ibid., 409.

15. United Nations, "The Nobel Peace Prize 2001," *UN Chronicle* 38, no. 4 (2001–2002): 4.

Index

About the Authors

RICHARD JOLLY is co-director of the UN Intellectual History Project and Honorary Professor and Research Associate of the Institute of Development Studies at the University of Sussex, where he was director from 1972 to 1981. He worked for the UN as an Assistant Secretary-General for almost twenty years; from 1982 to 1995 he was Deputy Executive Director for Programmes for UNICEF and from 1996 to 2000 he was Senior Adviser to UNDP's Administrator and principal coordinator of the widely acclaimed Human Development Report. Jolly has been a trustee of OXFAM, chairman of the United Nations Association-UK, and a council member of the Overseas Development Institute. In 2001 he was knighted by the queen of England for his contributions to international development. He has worked as an economist in some dozen countries and written or edited some twenty books and more than 100 articles with a special focus on adjustment with a human face, disarmament and development, human development, global and national inequality, and strategies of redistribution with growth.

LOUIS EMMERIJ is Senior Research Fellow at The CUNY Graduate Center, where he is co-director of the United Nations Intellectual History Project. Until 1999 he was Special Adviser to the President of the Inter-American Development Bank. Before that he served as President of the OECD Development Centre, Rector of the Institute for Social Studies in The Hague, and Director of the ILO's World Employment Programme. Among his recent books are *Economic and Social Development into the 21st Century*, editor; *Limits to Competition*, co-author; *Nord-Sud: La Grenade Dégoupillée*; *Financial Flows to Latin America*, co-editor; *Science, Technology and Science Education in the Development of the South*; *One World or Several?*, editor; and *Development Policies and the Crisis of the 1980s*.

THOMAS G. WEISS is Presidential Professor of Political Science at The CUNY Graduate Center and Director of the Ralph Bunche Institute for International Studies, where he is co-director of the United Nations Intellectual History Project. He is President of the International Studies Association (2009–2010) and Chair of the Academic Council on the UN System (2006–2009). He has served as editor of *Global Governance,* Research Director of the International Commission on Intervention and State Sovereignty, Research Professor at Brown University's Watson Institute for International Studies, Executive Director of the Academic Council on the UN System and of the International Peace Academy, a member of the UN secretariat, and a consultant to several public and private agencies. He has written or edited some thirty-five books and 150 articles and book chapters about multilateral approaches to international peace and security, humanitarian action, and sustainable development. His latest book is *What's Wrong with the United Nations and How to Fix It.*

LOUIS EMMERIJ, RICHARD JOLLY, and THOMAS G. WEISS are co-authors of *Ahead of the Curve? UN Ideas and Global Challenges* (Indiana University Press, 2001) and, with Tatiana Carayannis, authors of *UN Voices: The Struggle for Development and Social Justice* (Indiana University Press, 2005). Both are volumes in the United Nations Intellectual History Project Series.

About the United Nations
Intellectual History Project

Ideas and concepts are a driving force in human progress, and they are arguably the most important contribution of the United Nations. Yet there has been little historical study of the origins and evolution of the history of economic and social ideas cultivated within the world organization and of their impact on wider thinking and international action. The United Nations Intellectual History Project is filling this knowledge gap about the UN by tracing the origin and analyzing the evolution of key ideas and concepts about international economic and social development that were born or nurtured under UN auspices. UNIHP began operations in mid-1999 when the secretariat, the hub of a worldwide network of specialists on the UN, was established at the Ralph Bunche Institute for International Studies of The CUNY Graduate Center.

UNIHP has two main components, oral history interviews and a series of books on specific topics. The seventy-nine in-depth oral history interviews with leading contributors to crucial ideas and concepts within the UN system provide the raw material for this volume and other volumes. In addition, complete and indexed transcripts are available to researchers and the general public in an electronic book format on CD-Rom distributed by the secretariat.

The project has commissioned fifteen studies about the major economic and social ideas or concepts that are central to UN activity, which are being published by Indiana University Press.

• *Ahead of the Curve? UN Ideas and Global Challenges,* by Louis Emmerij, Richard Jolly, and Thomas G. Weiss (2001)

• *Unity and Diversity in Development Ideas: Perspectives from the UN Regional Commissions,* edited by Yves Berthelot with contributions from Adebayo Adedeji, Yves Berthelot, Leelananda de Silva, Paul Rayment, Gert Rosenthal, and Blandine Destremeau (2003)

• *Quantifying the World: UN Contributions to Statistics,* by Michael Ward (2004)

• *UN Contributions to Development Thinking and Practice,* by Richard Jolly, Louis Emmerij, Dharam Ghai, and Frédéric Lapeyre (2004)

- *The UN and Global Political Economy: Trade, Finance, and Development,* by John Toye and Richard Toye (2004)
- *UN Voices: The Struggle for Development and Social Justice,* by Thomas G. Weiss, Tatiana Carayannis, Louis Emmerij, and Richard Jolly (2005)
- *Women, Development, and the United Nations: A Sixty-Year Quest for Equality and Justice,* by Devaki Jain (2005)
- *Human Security and the UN: A Critical History,* by S. Neil MacFarlane and Yuen Foong Khong (2006)
- *Preventive Diplomacy at the UN,* by Bertrand G. Ramcharan (2007)
- *Human Rights at the UN: The Political History of Universal Justice,* Roger Normand and Sarah Zaidi (2008)
- *The UN and Transnational Corporations: From Code of Conduct to Global Compact,,* by Tagi Sagafi-nejad in collaboration with John Dunning (2008)
- *The UN and Development: From Aid to Cooperation,* by Olav Stokke (2009)
- *UN Ideas That Changed the World,* by Richard Jolly, Louis Emmerij, and Thomas G. Weiss (2009)

Forthcoming Titles:

- *Global Governance and the UN: An Unfinished Journey,* by Thomas G. Weiss and Ramesh Thakur
- *Development without Destruction: The UN and Global Resource Management,* by Nico Schrijver

The project also collaborated on *The Oxford Handbook on the United Nations,* edited by Thomas G. Weiss and Sam Daws, published by Oxford University Press in 2007.

For further information, the interested reader should contact:
UN Intellectual History Project
The CUNY Graduate Center
365 Fifth Avenue, Suite 5203
New York, New York 10016-4309
212-817-1920 Tel
212-817-1565 Fax
UNHistory@gc.cuny.edu
www.unhistory.org

CPSIA information can be obtained
at www.ICGtesting.com
Printed in the USA
LVOW12s1107090717
540729LV00005B/676/P